This book series addresses the urgent need to advance knowledge in the fields of cybercrime and cybersecurity. Because the exponential expansion of computer technologies and use of the Internet have greatly increased the access by criminals to people, institutions, and businesses around the globe, the series will be international in scope. It provides a home for cutting-edge long-form research. Further, the series seeks to spur conversation about how traditional criminological theories apply to the online environment. The series welcomes contributions from early career researchers as well as established scholars on a range of topics in the cybercrime and cybersecurity fields.

More information about this series at
http://www.palgrave.com/gp/series/14637

Palgrave Studies in Cybercrime and Cybersecurity

Series Editors
Marie-Helen Maras
Department of Security, Fire
and Emergency Management
John Jay College of Criminal Justice
New York, NY, USA

Thomas J. Holt
Michigan State University
East Lansing, MI, USA

Karen Lumsden · Emily Harmer
Editors

Online Othering

Exploring Digital Violence and Discrimination on the Web

Editors
Karen Lumsden
Independent Researcher
Leicester, UK

Emily Harmer
Department of Communication and Media
University of Liverpool
Liverpool, UK

Palgrave Studies in Cybercrime and Cybersecurity
ISBN 978-3-030-12632-2   ISBN 978-3-030-12633-9   (eBook)
https://doi.org/10.1007/978-3-030-12633-9

Library of Congress Control Number: 2019930706

© The Editor(s) (if applicable) and The Author(s) 2019
This work is subject to copyright. All rights are solely and exclusively licensed by the Publisher, whether the whole or part of the material is concerned, specifically the rights of translation, reprinting, reuse of illustrations, recitation, broadcasting, reproduction on microfilms or in any other physical way, and transmission or information storage and retrieval, electronic adaptation, computer software, or by similar or dissimilar methodology now known or hereafter developed.
The use of general descriptive names, registered names, trademarks, service marks, etc. in this publication does not imply, even in the absence of a specific statement, that such names are exempt from the relevant protective laws and regulations and therefore free for general use.
The publisher, the authors and the editors are safe to assume that the advice and information in this book are believed to be true and accurate at the date of publication. Neither the publisher nor the authors or the editors give a warranty, express or implied, with respect to the material contained herein or for any errors or omissions that may have been made. The publisher remains neutral with regard to jurisdictional claims in published maps and institutional affiliations.

This Palgrave Macmillan imprint is published by the registered company Springer Nature Switzerland AG
The registered company address is: Gewerbestrasse 11, 6330 Cham, Switzerland

Acknowledgements

This edited collection started out life as an idea over lunch which we then developed into a one-day symposium on 'Online Othering' at Loughborough University's Centre for Research in Communication and Culture (CRCC). We invited a group of academics from different disciplines as well as practitioners from the police and voluntary/charitable organisations who all recognised the challenges posed by diverse forms of online discrimination and who were willing to explore the latest research and responses to these issues. We would therefore like to thank Professor John Downey, Director of Loughborough University's CRCC, for agreeing to fund the original event and the speakers and participants who attended on the day for reaffirming our suspicions that an interdisciplinary response to these issues would be welcomed. We would also like to thank all of the authors, some of whom were not present at the original one-day symposium, for contributing their innovative and timely work to this volume.

Contents

1   Online Othering: An Introduction   1
Emily Harmer and Karen Lumsden

Part I   Online Culture Wars: The Rise of the Alt-Right, Trumpism and White Masculinities
Emily Harmer and Karen Lumsden

2   Online Hate: From the Far-Right to the 'Alt-Right' and from the Margins to the Mainstream   39
Aaron Winter

3   Cucks, Fags and Useful Idiots: The Othering of Dissenting White Masculinities Online   65
Alex Green

4   '"I Want to Kill You in Front of Your Children" Is Not a Threat. It's an Expression of a Desire': Discourses of Online Abuse, Trolling and Violence on r/MensRights   91
Karen Lumsden

Part II	Experiences of Online Abuse: Gendered Othering, Sexism and Misogyny	
	Emily Harmer and Karen Lumsden	
5	Online/Offline Continuities: Exploring Misogyny and Hate in Online Abuse of Feminists *Ruth Lewis, Mike Rowe and Clare Wiper*	121
6	'The Price of Admission': On Notions of Risk and Responsibility in Women's Sexting Practices *Rikke Amundsen*	145
7	'There's a Bit of Banter': How Male Teenagers 'Do Boy' on Social Networking Sites *John Whittle, Dave Elder-Vass and Karen Lumsden*	165
8	Othering Political Women: Online Misogyny, Racism and Ableism Towards Women in Public Life *Rosalynd Southern and Emily Harmer*	187
Part III	Online Exclusion: Boundaries, Spaces and Intersectionality	
	Karen Lumsden and Emily Harmer	
9	The 'Online Othering' of Transgender People in Relation to 'Gender Neutral Toilets' *Ben Colliver, Adrian Coyle and Marisa Silvestri*	215
10	Young Men with Physical Disabilities Struggle for Digital Sex(uality) *Herminder Kaur*	239
11	Rural Racism in the Digital Age *Nathan Kerrigan*	259

Part IV	Responding to, Regulating and Policing Online Hate	
	Karen Lumsden and Emily Harmer	
12	'When I Saw Women Being Attacked … It Made Me Want to Stand Up and Fight': Reporting, Responding to, and Resisting Online Misogyny	287
	Jo Smith	
13	Disability Hate Speech: Interrogating the Online/Offline Distinction	309
	Philippa Hall	
14	Challenges in Policing Cyberstalking: A Critique of the Stalking Risk Profile in the Context of Online Relationships	331
	Brianna O'Shea, Roberta Julian, Jeremy Prichard and Sally Kelty	
15	'Why Don't You Block Them?' Police Officers' Constructions of the Ideal Victim When Responding to Reports of Interpersonal Cybercrime	355
	Alex Black, Karen Lumsden and Lee Hadlington	
16	Conclusion: Researching 'Online Othering'—Future Agendas and Lines of Inquiry	379
	Emily Harmer and Karen Lumsden	
Index		**397**

Notes on Contributors

Rikke Amundsen is a doctoral candidate in Sociology at the University of Cambridge, UK. Her current research explores adult women's accounts and experiences of 'sexting' as a form of mediated intimacy. More specifically, Rikke examines how notions of mediated intimacy are articulated in and through adult women's sexting practices and focuses on the role that women's individual thoughts, feelings and experiences play as private sexual images acquire meaning throughout the communicative process. Rikke's research is also published in journals like *Feminist Media Studies*.

Alex Black is a Lecturer in Criminology in the Department of Law and Criminology at Sheffield Hallam University, UK. She has a Ph.D. in Sociology from the University of York. Alex is a criminologist with an interest in policing and the management of public space. Her recent work has focused on migrants' experiences of hate crime in the wake of the Brexit vote, frontline responses to domestic violence, access to police services for groups with disabilities and police understandings of cybercrime. She is a member of the British Society of Criminology and Associate Fellow of the Higher Education Academy.

Ben Colliver is a Lecturer in Criminology at Birmingham City University, UK. His research interests include hate crime, queer studies, gender and sexuality studies. His current project focuses on 'everyday' and 'mundane' incidents of discrimination and hate crime targeting transgender and non-binary communities, with a specific interest in online interactions. This research project aims to highlight the lived reality of experiences of low-level incidents of hate crime and to challenge current hate crime hierarchies.

Adrian Coyle is Professor of Psychology at Kingston University, London. He is a Social Psychologist, and his research and publications have principally addressed psychological issues in identity, sexualities, religion and society, and loss and bereavement. He was co-editor of the award-winning book, *Lesbian & Gay Psychology: New Perspectives* (with Celia Kitzinger: BPS Blackwell, 2002), and *Analysing Qualitative Data in Psychology* (with Evanthia Lyons: SAGE, 2007, 2016).

Dave Elder-Vass is a Reader in Sociology at Loughborough University, UK. His recent book *Profit and Gift in the Digital Economy* (Cambridge University Press, 2016) develops a theory of appropriative practices in the digital economy and their implications for social theory and politics. He has also published extensively on social ontology and social theory from a critical realist perspective, including *The Causal Power of Social Structures* (Cambridge University Press, 2010) and *The Reality of Social Construction* (Cambridge University Press, 2012).

Alex Green is an EPSRC-funded research student at the Web Science Institute, University of Southampton. His Ph.D. focuses on the construction and mediation of extreme-right discourses in online spaces. He was previously Operation Manager for Culture and Society at the Wellcome Trust where he led digital humanities initiatives, coordinated digitisation programmes and curated the exhibition *Here Comes Good Health!* an exploration of early health promotion technology in interwar London.

Lee Hadlington is an Associate Professor in Cyberpsychology at De Montfort University, UK. His current research focus centres on exploring how human factors can serve to influence individual cybersecurity posture both in and outside the organisation context. He has worked alongside a variety of organisations, including law enforcement, military and business examining topics such as insider threat, automated cyber defence and the gamification of cybersecurity. He completed his Ph.D. at the University of Wolverhampton in 2006 in an area related to applied cognitive psychology and human factors.

Philippa Hall is an independent writer and researcher in the UK whose interests include social policy, legal reform, political economy and education policy. Several of these research themes have been examined within the context of the history, politics and implementation of neoliberal policy. She has written a range of magazine articles, book chapters, journal articles and book reviews. Her current research is on EU law, hate speech and media culture.

Emily Harmer is a Lecturer in Media in the Department of Communication and Media at the University of Liverpool. Her research interests centre on the relationship between gender, media and politics and the extent to which these have changed over time. Emily has co-convened the UK Political Studies Association's Media and Politics Specialist Group since 2013 and also works as the Assistant Editor for the *European Journal of Communication*.

Roberta Julian is a Professor in Sociology and Foundation Director of the Tasmanian Institute of Law Enforcement Studies (TILES) in the College of Arts, Law and Education at the University of Tasmania, Australia. She has over 30 years of academic experience in teaching and research on social justice issues with a focus on migrant and refugee settlement, policing and criminology (including projects on youth justice, family violence and forensic science). Roberta is a member of the Board of Studies of the Australian Institute of Police Management (AIPM) and a past president of The Australian Sociological Association (TASA).

Herminder Kaur is a Lecturer in Digital Sociology in the Department of Criminology and Sociology at Middlesex University, London, UK. Herminder was previously at Loughborough University completing her doctoral study funded via a Loughborough University Doctoral College studentship. Her research uses and develops ethnographic and visual methods to study young people with physical disabilities use of digital media. There are four key themes in her research: rhythms and movements of Internet use, online relationships, stigma and exclusion, Internet regulation by teachers and parents and the enactment of disability.

Sally Kelty is an applied psychologist and criminologist specialising in forensic/criminal and management psychology in the Centre for Applied Psychology, University of Canberra, Australia. She has expertise in project and program development, evaluation and research within the criminal justice, health and disability sectors. She has worked in criminal justice agencies, within policing agencies, university research centres and as a practitioner within private industry and government. Sally currently works as Senior Lecturer at the University of Canberra and is part of the centre for Applied Psychology where she teaches applied forensic psychology and research supervision from honours to Ph.D.

Nathan Aaron Kerrigan is Lecturer in Criminology in the School of Social Science at Birmingham City University, UK. With a Ph.D. Sociology, his research interests include rurality and the English countryside. Nathan explores the ways 'host' English rural communities enact informal social control to militate the impact of globalised social problems through protecting, maintaining and controlling the boundaries around what it means to be 'rural' and the exclusionary consequences this process has on specific groups living in rural areas. He has published a monograph, book chapters, journal articles, and a Department for Environment Food and Rural Affairs evidence summary.

Ruth Lewis is Associate Professor in the Department of Social Sciences at Northumbria University, UK. Her research focuses on gender-based violence (GBV). Recent work examines online abuse and GBV in universities (e.g. *Gender-Based Violence in University Communities: Policies, Prevention and Educational Initiatives* (2018) edited with Sundari Anitha and a special issue of *Violence Against Women* (2019) edited with Susan Marine). Earlier research with Rebecca Dobash, Russell Dobash and Kate Cavanagh examined legal responses to domestic violence, including perpetrator programmes, and an examination of homicide. She has been involved in feminist activism and networks of various kinds, in and beyond universities.

Karen Lumsden is a sociologist, qualitative researcher, trainer, author and consultant. She is the author of over 40 publications including the books: *Reflexivity: Theory Method and Practice*, *Reflexivity in Criminological Research*, and *Boy Racer Culture: Youth, Masculinity and Deviance*. She has a Ph.D. in Sociology from the University of Aberdeen and has held academic positions at Loughborough University, the University of Aberdeen, the University of Abertay Dundee and the University of Leicester. Her research interests and work focus on policing, victims, online abuse, critiques of the neoliberal academy, and qualitative methods including reflexivity, ethnography and narrative inquiry.

Brianna O'Shea is a Teaching Fellow in Police Studies at the University of Tasmania, Australia. Brianna was awarded an Australian Postgraduate Award for her Ph.D. titled 'The Investigation and Prosecution of Cyberstalking in Australia'. She has a Bachelor of Behavioural Science majoring in Psychology, Criminology and Behavioural Neuroscience and a Bachelor of Arts with First Class Honours in Criminology from the University of Tasmania. Brianna is a member of the Australian and New Zealand Society of Criminology and presented her work at the International Conference on Cybercrime and Computer Forensics.

Jeremy Prichard is an Associate Professor of Criminal Law at the Law School, University of Tasmania, Australia. He conceptualised and coordinates an interdisciplinary unit for police officers and undergraduates titled Sex Crimes and Criminals. As well as completing a contract report on child pornography for the Royal Commission into Institutional Responses to Child Sexual Abuse, Jeremy has published analyses of online sexual exploitation in journals of law, IT and criminology. He is the lead CI of a large grant on preventing cyber-sexual crime. He is a member of the Tasmanian Law Reform Institute.

Michael Rowe is Professor of Criminology in the Department of Social Sciences at Northumbria University. He has an international reputation for research and publications in the field of policing in broad terms but paying particular attention to policing, race and racism, police culture and the policing of domestic violence. He has completed a series of studies exploring the motivation and engagement of offenders in desistance programmes. He has published seven books on policing, crime, race and related issues; is (co)author of more than 30 articles in scholarly journals; and is Editor of the *International Journal of Police Science and Management*.

Marisa Silvestri is Reader in Criminology at the University of Kent. Her work lies at the intersections of gender, crime and criminal justice. She has a long-standing record of research and has published extensively in the field, including *Gender and Crime: A Human Rights Approach* (with Chris Crowther-Dowey: SAGE, 2008, 2016). She is an executive committee member of the British Society of Criminology and is also Chair of its Women, Crime and Criminal Justice Network.

Jo Smith is a Teaching Fellow in the Department of Criminology at the University of Leicester, UK, and is completing her Ph.D. at the University of Surrey. Her research explores the experiences of feminist women who have been the victims of online gendered hate. Drawing on a decade of work as a solicitor specialising in criminal law and her work as a legal advisor for Rights of Women, other research interests include violence against women and girls, women's experiences of the criminal justice system, gender and hate crime, and street harassment.

Rosalynd Southern is Lecturer in Political Communication at the University of Liverpool. Her research focuses on online political communication, particularly during election campaigns in the UK. She has a Ph.D. in Social Statistics from the Cathie Marsh Institute at the University of Manchester. Her post-doctoral work built a longitudinal picture of online campaigning in the UK. She has worked on the 2015 British Election Study on the iBES project, which assessed voters' use of social media during the election campaign. In addition to this, she has conducted work on female politicians and their use of, and treatment via, various media.

John Whittle is a Senior Research Strategist for Further (UK) and its sister company Versiti (UK). His role is to provide digital research expertise, deliver rigorous social and market research and teach best practice across the industry. John has worked with clients such as Channel 4, Unicef, RNIB, Guide Dogs, Barclays and EY. Much of his recent work has been focused on highlighting diversity and researching minority or 'hard to reach' groups in order to address contemporary power and resource imbalances. His passions include CrossFit, video games and all dogs everywhere.

Aaron Winter is Senior Lecturer in Criminology at the University of East London, UK. His research is on the far right with a focus on racism, mainstreaming and violence. He is co-editor of *Discourses and Practices of Terrorism* (Routledge, 2010), *Reflexivity in Criminological Research* (Palgrave, 2014) and *Historical Perspectives on Organised Crime and Terrorism* (Routledge, 2018). His work has been published in *Ethnic and Racial Studies*, *Sociological Research Online* and *Women and Performance*. He is on the Editorial Board of *Identities: Global Studies in Culture and Power* and is co-editor of the Manchester University Press series, *Racism, Resistance and Social Change*.

Clare Wiper is a Research Associate at Northumbria University, UK. Her research has focused on feminist anti-violence activism in austerity Britain, the changing structural landscape of violence against women under neoliberalism and the online/offline continuum of misogynistic violence and hate speech against women. Clare is active in her local and regional communities around issues related to gender inequality, gender violence and social justice.

List of Tables

Table 8.1	List of MPs selected plus their intersecting characteristics and party	195
Table 15.1	Focus group break down according to operational background	364

1

Online Othering: An Introduction

Emily Harmer and Karen Lumsden

Introduction

In this introductory chapter, we set the scene for the edited collection by first outlining the social, political and cultural contexts which shape and seep into online communications including 'Trumpism' in the USA, 'Brexit' in the UK, and the rise of the 'Alt-Right'. We then review studies of discrimination, harassment and hate on the Web including examples of flaming, trolling, misogyny, racism and Islamophobia, and the ways in which political organisations, activists and feminists have resisted these toxic online behaviours and discourses.

E. Harmer
Department of Communication and Media,
University of Liverpool, Liverpool, UK

K. Lumsden (✉)
Leicester, UK

We develop and outline our concept of 'online othering', situating our discussion within an overview of sociological literature and social theories on 'othering', 'The Other' and 'stereotyping'. We argue that the concept of 'online othering' encapsulates the myriad power contestations and abusive behaviours which are manifested on/through online spaces (including, e.g., as racism, Islamophobia, sexism, misogyny, homophobia, ableism) and which are resisted and challenged by various social actors and groups. The concept of 'online othering' is a means of analysing and making sense of the myriad behaviours, conversations and discourses which seek to (re)draw boundaries in, around, and between virtual spaces, and which shape the rules and norms concerning which individuals and groups are endowed with status and legitimated to participate in these spaces, and those who are not. We then outline the synopsis of the edited volume, its contribution and aims, and the focus of each part and its respective chapters.

Online Participation, Inequalities and the Political Economy of the Internet

The Internet plays a vital role in many aspects of our social, political and cultural lives, and in the early days of its expansion there was much enthusiasm for its potentially transformative role in providing a space for individuals to construct their identities, communicate with others and share ideas and concerns (Turkle 1995; Papacharissi 2002). Early proponents of these arguments were hopeful that the Internet could operate as a virtual extension of the public sphere to deliberate on political and social issues. Much more than this, it was celebrated as a potential space where one's identity or background could be circumvented and made irrelevant (van Zoonen 2002). In her essay, *The Virtual Sphere*, Zizi Papacharissi (2002) sought to question the ability of the Internet to promote rational public debate and enhance social life or whether its revolutionary potential would become absorbed by commercial culture. If we take into account the feminist critique of the concept of a universal public sphere, advanced by scholars like

Nancy Fraser (1990), it now seems obvious that the virtual sphere is not a neutral space and that it reflects the inequalities that are experienced in the offline world. Fraser's argument that discursive interaction within the public sphere is governed by protocols of style and decorum that are in themselves markers of status which therefore act as 'informal impediments' to equal participation, is important to consider when discussing the extent to which online participation can be thought of as inclusive (Fraser 1990: 63).

Inclusive participation can also be disrupted by the political economy of the Internet (Fuchs 2017). Political economy approaches to the analysis of communication industries focus on the relationship between the economic structure and the dynamics of media corporations (McQuail 2010). Fuch (2009) suggests that the Internet's economic model is built on the commodification of its users whereby free to access platforms essentially deliver users up as targets for advertisers. In relation to social media, he argues that there are huge asymmetries in the visibility of different content providers and he suggests that this limits the ability for social media sites to enable participation. For example, his analysis of the most viewed videos on YouTube indicates that transnational media corporations control what he refers to as the attention economy, whereby the majority of these videos are corporate music videos, meaning that the most viewed content comes from providers who already have other means of distributing their content, while smaller providers are squeezed out. He also argues that the digital affordances of platforms impact the quality of participation, for instance microblogging sites such as Twitter, where the number of characters in tweets is limited, can lead to simplistic and superficial engagement. It is therefore clear that corporations dominate social media, and the Internet's status as a capitalist enterprise means that these platforms exist to accumulate profits rather than to enable equal participation. Despite the potential for digital technology to democratise the communication process, it is clear that pre-existing social, political and economic inequalities have intelligible impacts on the ability of people to participate in online cultures, and the manner in which that participation is realised.

Discrimination, Harassment and Hate Online

It is perhaps unsurprising then that an unintended consequence of digital technology has been the extent to which some individuals and groups have used the freedom to participate online to engage in hateful or discriminatory communicative practices in these loosely regulated spaces, often hiding behind the cloak of anonymity (Papacharissi 2004). One of the earliest examples is #Gamergate, where online users systematically harassed women game developers, journalists and critics in a form of backlash against women's use of technology and participation in public life (Massanari 2017). Women in the public eye have found themselves subjected to hate crime on Twitter (Citron 2016) in the form of online harassment, sexism and trolling. Moreover, the aftermath of the Brexit vote in the UK saw a rise in reports of hate speech including racism, Islamophobia and anti-Semitism, in both online and offline contexts (Devine 2018; Komaromi and Singh 2016; Awan 2016). These instances also highlight the intersectional nature of online hate as studies indicate that the majority of victims of online Islamophobia tend to be female (Feldman and Littler 2014). The reasons given for this include women being more likely to report online abuse and also in offline cases the greater visibility related to items of clothing (such as the hijab) (Gerard and Whitfield 2016). The evolution of the Internet demonstrates that the affordances of digital media technologies often serve to replicate and perpetuate the social inequalities that people already experience. This is underscored by the work of Safiya Umoja Noble (2018) which shows how existing prejudices about social differences are built into the very architecture of the Internet at source, which ultimately serves to reflect and perpetuate existing inequalities. Her study of the Google search engine reveals that the algorithms used by the company are based upon and perpetuate harmful racist and misogynistic stereotypes. Similarly, scholars have demonstrated that the nature of programming languages used to write digital code can be used to express misogyny (Easter 2018). Moreover, Massanari (2017) argues that the design, culture and policies of platforms such as Reddit encourage certain toxic behaviours which can suppress equal participation.

The Internet has also been implicated in othering and discrimination in people's everyday domestic lives. Concerns have been expressed over its use in crimes such as identity theft, fraud, buying illicit substances or weapons, stalking and technology-facilitated domestic abuse (Powell and Henry 2016; Dragiewicz et al. 2018). *The New York Times* reported in 2018 that smart home technology and connected home devices which monitor and regulate thermostats, locks and lights are being used as 'digital tools of domestic abuse', and a means for harassment, monitoring, revenge and control (Bowles 2018). Moreover, various smartphone apps can also be used by perpetrators to stalk and coerce in intimate partner violence. Chatterjee et al. (2018) found that over 200 apps and services offer 'would-be stalkers' a variety of capabilities, including basic location tracking to harvesting texts and secretly recording video. In the design of these technologies, it is rarely considered how they could be used to control, coerce and/or stalk, by individuals who have sinister or harmful motives. Digital media have also enabled incidents of cyberbullying and harassment, 'revenge porn' or image-based sexual abuse (McGlynn et al. 2017; Smith, this volume) whereby personal images are shared online without the person's consent, and 'Deepfake' pornography where digital images are manipulated to include the faces of people who are not in the original image.

Social scientists have also explored the social media phenomenon referred to as 'trolling' (Phillips 2015; Binns 2012; Jane 2014a, b; Herring 1999, 2003; Hardaker 2010; Hardaker and McGlashan 2016; Marwick and Ellison 2012; Lumsden and Morgan 2017). Trolling can be likened to a form of cyberbullying and involves the sending or submission of provocative emails, social media posts or 'tweets' (Twitter messages), with the intention of inciting an angry or upsetting response from its intended target or victim. In contrast to visibility, anonymity has been deemed important for making trolling possible in a variety of online spaces (Hardaker 2010; Hardaker and McGlashan 2016; Hutchens et al. 2015) and this form of online bullying is often committed incognito. Trolling attempts to hijack and disrupt normative interactions and communication practices and also to 'oust' the victim from participation in public forums of debate.

Trolling developed from early Internet users' 'flaming' of online forms and bulletin boards (Donarth 1999; Kiesler et al. 1985; Lea et al. 1992; Lee 2005; O'Sullivan and Flanagin 2003; Hmielowski et al. 2014). The term is now used to refer to abuse or harassment of individuals or groups on social media sites, online comments pages, blogs and social networking. For Herring et al. (2002: 372): 'Trolling … differs from flaming in that the goal of flame bait is to incite any and all readers, whereas the goal of a stereotypical troll is to draw in particularly naive or vulnerable readers'. In her study of self-identifying 'subcultural trolls' in the USA, Phillips highlights trolling's relationship to the wider media cultural landscape. For instance, trolls can engage in 'media fuckery', which is the 'ability to turn the media against itself' (2015: 2). This is accomplished by amplifying or inventing a sensational news story, i.e. 'fake news'. In this sense:

> Trolls … fit very comfortably within the contemporary, hypernetworked digital media landscape. Not only do they put Internet technologies to expert and highly creative use, their behaviours are often in direct (if surprising) alignment with social media marketers and other corporate interests … In short, rather than functioning as a counterpoint to 'correct' online behavior, trolls are in many ways the grimacing poster child for the socially networked world. (Phillips 2015: 8)

Prominent forms of abuse targeted at women online which are often part of trolling behaviour/s include rape threats and death threats. 'Rape culture' can be seen to have re-emerged within popular discourses over the past five years and is 'a socio-cultural context in which an aggressive male sexuality is eroticized and seen as a "healthy", "normal", and "desired" part of sexual relations' (Keller et al. 2016: 5; Herman 1978). Jane (2014a: 535) notes that this discourse has become normalised to the extent that 'threatening rape has become the modus operandi for those wishing to critique female commentators'. Mantilla (2015) identifies 'gendertrolling' as distinct from forms of trolling which more generally attempt to disrupt or hijack online interactions. 'Gendertrolls' have a different motivation and 'gendertrolling is exponentially more vicious, virulent, aggressive, threatening, pervasive, and enduring than generic trolling … gendertrolls take their cause seriously, so they are therefore able to rally others who share in their convictions … [and] are devoted to targeting the designated person' (Mantilla 2015: 11). New forms of media can also exacerbate issues surrounding sexual violence by creating digital spaces wherein the perpetration and legitimisation of sexual violence takes on new qualities (Dodge 2015). Moreover, online abuse both redeploys existing manifestations of rape culture and intensifies them due to the speed at which images and written communications can be shared online (Shariff and DeMartini 2015).

As Lumsden and Morgan (2017) note, trolling can cross the boundary from an exchange of teasing remarks or humour, to sustained abuse by one or more individuals, and which can be viewed as a form of gendered and/or 'symbolic violence' or a 'silencing strategy'. Advice to victims on how to respond to trolling includes such statements as: 'do not feed the troll' (Binns 2012) and 'ignore the troll'. The implication implicit in this advice for dealing with trolls is that victims should be silenced. This is particularly problem in relation to women, who have become particularly susceptible to online gendered and symbolic violence by cyber-trolls and who are being advised, implicitly or explicitly, to 'put up and shut up', reminiscent of advice given concerning how best to respond to gendered violence and sexism in the past (Lumsden and Morgan 2017).

The term trolling is also problematic in that it is now widely utilised by the media and others to also describe the posting of offensive messages per se by an individual in addition to the more proactive, deliberate and organised hate campaigns engaged in by groups of individuals, in a pre-meditated manner. As Hardaker argues trolling has become a 'catch-all term for any number of negatively marked online behaviours' (2010: 224) which is why there is a need to reconceptualise how we understand abusive and hateful behaviours online, as we do in this edited collection via the concept of 'online othering' (which will be outlined in more detail below). As well as being used to describe the above, trolling is drawn on to describe individual messages posted online which are deemed by the recipient and/or audience to be defamatory or abusive. Hence, with these instances of trolling, the question of intent is important in the creation of the communication, as is the interpretation of the message by the recipient and wider audience—as 'in the eyes of the beholder'. These above analyses of online abuse also highlight the tension between 'libertarian and communitarian values, in that harassment often arises in spaces known for their freedom, lack of censure, and experimental nature' (Herring et al. 2002: 374; Herring 1999). For these reasons, trolling as a catch-all term is problematic in that it does not acknowledge the implications and impact of online abuse and toxic interactions on individuals and groups in the way that our concept of 'online othering' permits.

A Threat to Democracy? The Rise of the Alt-Right and Trumpism

The contemporary political landscape also gives us pause for thought. In contrast to the early optimism about the use of digital technologies for the advancement of democracy, recent events have instead seen some disturbing trends which, rather than enhancing democratic deliberation, have in fact come to threaten democracy itself. The rise of neo-fascist politics in online spaces characterised as the so-called Alt-Right has been the focus of much attention (Hawley 2017; see also Winter, this volume), in addition to the rise in various forms of hate speech such as misogyny, racism and Islamophobia (Citron 2016; Awan 2016). The 'Alt-Right' is a political movement which came to prominence in the wake of the 2016 US Presidential Election. According to Squirrell (2017a), anecdotal evidence largely suggests that the movement incorporates individuals from the 'manosphere', anti-progressives from the #GamerGate movement, 4chan trolls, far-right conservatives, racists and conspiracy theorists. There have also been concerns about the ways in which social media in particular have endangered the political process itself, including the rise of 'Trumpism' online (Bessire and Bond 2017; Squirrell 2017b). Rumours abound about the alleged interference in the US presidential election and the EU referendum in the UK by foreign powers, and the potential impact of so-called fake news coming from Russian and Eastern European Troll farms, which platforms like Facebook and Twitter have struggled to challenge.

We have already seen that the economic imperatives and design of most mainstream Internet platforms have implications for the reproduction of existing social inequalities, but this is further exacerbated by the reticence on the part of these platforms to regulate themselves in any way, citing concerns about the chilling effect on freedom of speech and expression which are therefore easily exploited by those who wish to continue using cyberspace as a vehicle for engaging in online othering and discrimination. Police and criminal justice agencies report difficulties in keeping up with the rise in the numbers of reports of online crime and abuse, while there are currently ineffective means of legislating against and/or investigating and prosecuting cases (Bishop 2013). Social media corporations, such as Twitter, have been called to task for their slow responses to dealing with online abuse. In 2015, the Chief Executive Officer of Twitter, Dick Costolo, was quoted as stating in a leaked memo: 'We lose core user after core user by not addressing simple trolling issues that they face everyday … I'm frankly ashamed of how poorly we've dealt with this issue during my tenure as CEO. It's absurd' (Griffin 2015).

Facebook, for example, has been criticised for failing to ban groups engaging in the sharing of sexual images of children (Crawford 2017). Twitter proved to be reluctant to moderate content at all, only adding an 'in-tweet' reporting function for inappropriate or hateful content in 2013 after pressure from users who had experienced harassment and threats of violence. Platforms have also been accused of discrimination. YouTube faced a backlash from some of its LGBTQ content creators for allegedly filtering out videos about same-sex marriage and trans issues (Cuthbertson 2018). Twitter has also been urged by disability charities to do more to help disabled users report hate speech against them on the site, with claims that it remains too difficult to report disability-related abuse. According to Muscular Dystrophy UK, the lack of a clear option to label abusive tweets based on disability is preventing more reporting of such hate speech (ITV News 2018). In addition to demonstrating an unwillingness to moderate content, there have been a number of incidents which show the complexities of moderating platforms with a global reach. For example, Facebook has faced intense criticism for failing to curb anti-Rohingya propaganda in Burma at a time where state-sponsored violence has already been used to devastating effect against this minority Muslim community. Facebook has blamed a lack of moderators with the right language skills for its difficulties (see Rajagopalan et al. 2018). It is clear that the scale of the problem facing these technology corporations is proving impossible to respond to and regulate effectively. There have been some positive moves though. As discussed previously, Twitter introduced a report function and Facebook have made some efforts to moderate hate speech and hate groups but there is clearly a long way to go.

Political Organisation, Activism and Resistance to 'Online Othering'

Despite the seemingly overwhelming examples where online sites and technologies reinforce and perpetuate social inequalities and contribute to the further exclusion of already marginalised groups and individuals, it is important to remember that the advent of such digital technologies offer significant opportunities for resistance and political organisation in order to counter some of the unfortunate consequences of online othering. Feminist groups have demonstrated a sustained commitment to organising online despite its many challenges (see, e.g., Keller et al. 2016; Williams 2015). There has been a proliferation of activism, online blogs, groups and press reports, which highlight the trolling and abuse experienced by women online. As Korn and Kneese (2015: 208) note, feminist scholars have demonstrated the ways in which 'online interactions over particular social media platforms coincide with existing inequalities and hierarchies situated in specific communities' and also the ways in which feminists, as counter-publics, can garner support and attention via social media. Specific blogs and platforms have also been created in order to share experiences and raise awareness of feminist causes such as the Everyday Sexism Project, founded in the UK but which now has sites in many different languages which allow women to share experiences of sexism or harassment online (Bates 2014). The proliferation of social media hashtags designed to challenge social and political inequalities is another example. The #MeToo movement calling out sexual misconduct in media industries, and the #Blacklivesmatter matter movement began as online campaigns (Tynes et al. 2016) demonstrating the potential for digital technologies to be used to effectively challenge the status quo.

Keller et al. (2016) focus on the ways in which girls and women use digital media platforms to challenge the rape culture, sexism and misogyny they experience in everyday life. A special issue of *Feminist Media Studies* (2015) also highlights the use of feminist hashtags to expose the transnational pervasiveness of gendered violence, to create a space for women to share their experiences and therefore to challenge commonsense understandings of abuse and promote solidarity (Berridge and Portwood-Stacer 2015). Examples include black feminists' use of social media to fill the gap in national media coverage of black women's issues, including how race and gender 'affect the wage gap to the disproportionate amount of violence committed against black transgender women' (Williams 2015: 343). Khoja-Moolji (2015) highlights the use of 'hashtagging' as a form of activism which is encouraged by campaigns for girls' empowerment, while Eagle (2015) focuses on their use as part of a campaign to improve women's use of transport and public space, without the fear of sexual harassment. In addition, research by Parker and Song (2006) on young South Asian and Chinese communities in Britain's use of websites demonstrates that Internet discussion forums can act as witnesses to social inequalities and through sharing experiences of racism and marginalisation, an oppositional social perspective may also develop. They demonstrate how the campaigns stimulated by users of these websites challenged mainstream institutions and began to alter the terms of engagement between the ethnic groups and wider society.

However, Berridge and Portwood-Stacer (2015: 341) highlight the dangers that feminists can encounter in relation to threats of gendered violence that occur within online spaces. For women accessing the public space of the Internet, it is a double-edged sword in that it promotes freedom of expression and provides a space for feminist activism, while it also presents the risk of a backlash from potential trolls, as a means of curtailing women's appropriation of, and participation in, online spaces. As Keller et al. (2016: 5) note, 'anyone who challenges popular misogyny puts themselves at risk of becoming the subject of sexist attacks and abuse'.

Many of the above studies focus more specifically on the experiences of feminist scholars and feminist activists already in the public eye (and with an online presence). In addition to this work, we also need increased social scientific analysis of the everyday experiences of women (and men) utilising various forms of online and digital communications, which this edited collection addresses. For example, in a study by Sills et al. in which they interviewed young people about their exposure and responses to 'rape culture' on social media, their participants conveyed a sense of 'living within a matrix of sexism: that is, an environment in which sexism, misogyny, and elements of rape culture merge as a normalized backdrop to everyday life' (2016: 6). These behaviours then are becoming normalised on and offline, and for these young people, 'victim-shaming' and 'slut-shaming' were viewed as commonplace and every day.

In the context of this rapidly changing and politically contested social media landscape, this edited collection explores the othering and discrimination propagated and encountered by individuals online and in social media contexts and cultures. It problematises and analyses the dichotomy presented between real and virtual worlds (and spaces) by exploring the motivations behind certain offending and othering behaviours, and the impact this has on the targets of online abuse and hate speech. This includes the extent to which 'online othering' constitutes a new phenomenon and how the motivations for committing forms of cyber-abuse, cyber-hate and othering relate to the expression of these attitudes and behaviours in the offline context. It explores the extent to which forms of information and communication technologies facilitate, exacerbate and/or promote the enactment of traditional offline offences (such as domestic abuse and stalking). Finally, the collection addresses the role of the police and other agencies in terms of their interventions, and the regulation and governance of virtual space(s).

The edited collection takes an interdisciplinary approach to these phenomena. Contributors come from a variety of disciplines including sociology, communication and media studies, psychology, criminology, political studies, information science and gender studies. Contributions address the ways in which various groups and identities are subjected to othering in online environments, and those groups and cultures doing the othering. This includes examples from a variety of online media and mediums including news websites, social media platforms (i.e. Twitter, Facebook, Instagram, YouTube.), blogs, and forums such as Reddit and 4chan. Some contributions explore othering across multiple contexts. In addition, chapters cover historical and theoretical perspectives on 'online othering' and empirical research using a variety of methods. Contributions also consider the implications for the regulation of the Internet by police and prosecutors, policy and practice. Topics covered in the book include: trolling and gendered online abuse/harassment; sexting and revenge porn; the rise of the Alt-Right and Trumpism; Men's Rights Activists; cyberstalking; online racism; transphobia; and the policing and prosecution of online hate crime.

'Online Othering', Agency and Resistance

> if there were no other, one would invent it. (Cixous and Clement 1975: 71)

In this volume, we develop and propose the concept of 'online othering' as a means of describing and making sense of the myriad behaviours, interactions and discourses which seek to (re)draw boundaries in, around, and between virtual spaces, and shape the rules and norms concerning which individuals and groups are endowed with status and legitimated to participate in these spaces, and those who are not. Furthermore, we recognise the various strategies and responses to the experiences of 'online othering' thus ensuring that the agency of 'others' and means of resisting and responding to prejudice and discrimination online (i.e. via activism) are accounted for. The concept of 'online othering' also allows us to examine the justifications and motivations of those who perpetrate or enact online discrimination, prejudice, hate and/or abuse, ultimately 'othering' those who are deemed to be 'them', 'outsiders' or members of the 'out-group'. 'Online othering' can be done remotely, 'at a distance', with little regard to the real-world consequences and harms which are experienced by those who are 'othered' in online spaces.

As noted above, thus far understandings of online hate and/or cyber-deviance have focused on specific phenomena such as 'abuse', 'harassment', 'trolling', 'hate speech' or 'hate crime'. We do not wish to minimise the real harm and implications which these phenomena and behaviours have for victims and/or survivors. However, we argue that currently these terms alone do not adequately help us to understand and conceptualise how exclusion from the Internet and its spaces operates across various groups, individuals and contexts. Many forms of abuse are not recognised as 'harmful' or are not incorporated as 'hate crime' in laws and legislation, and what is defined as hate speech (or even if it can be deemed to 'hate speech' given the online versus offline nature) also varies across countries and continents. For example, recent developments in the UK have included a proposal in 2018 to classify misogyny as a 'hate crime' and proposals to classify 'upskirting' (which involves taking a photograph under a victim's skirt) as a crime.

Moreover, despite the inclusion of the term '*online*', we, like others, believe it is important to acknowledge that these behaviours do not occur in a 'virtual vacuum'—they are part and parcel of everyday life and have real consequences in what some have chosen to call the 'real' (versus the 'virtual') world. We must throw out the well-worn dichotomies of 'online versus offline', and 'virtual world' versus 'real world', and instead acknowledge the interconnected and fluid nature of our everyday use of information and communication technologies (see also Lumsden and Morgan 2017; Papacharissi 2016).

The practices and processes through which the 'outsider' is constructed are encapsulated via the notion of 'othering'. According to Lister, othering is a 'process of differentiation and demarcation, by which the line is drawn between "us" and "them" – between the more and the less powerful – and through which social distance is established and maintained' (2004: 101). It involves constructions of the self or 'in-group', and the other or 'out-group', through identification of what the former has and what the latter lacks in relation to the former (Brons 2015: 70). It is the means of defining into existence a group perceived to be 'inferior' (Schwalbe et al. 2000: 422). Jensen (2011) traces the establishment of the concept of 'othering' through Hegel, de Beauvoir, Said, Lacan, Althusser and Spivak, to its current general usage to signify 'classed', 'raced' and 'gendered' processes through which powerful groups simultaneously claim a monopoly on crucial knowledge and technologies, use ways of actively demonstrating their power and construct/exclude less powerful others as pathological, 'dangerous' and/or morally inferior. For the psychoanalyst Jacques Lacan (1977), the discourse of the 'other' is the unconscious mind of the subject. According to Lacan, infants develop a sense of self during the 'looking-glass-phase' through differentiating their self from Others. This results in the construction of a 'self for others', always 'referential to the other' (Segal 1994: 131). Therefore, as Kitzinger and Wilkinson argue it is important that as scholars and researchers we always remember that 'we' use the 'other' to define ourselves: '"we" understand ourselves in relation to what "we" are not' (1996: 8).

The concept of 'othering' also attempts to capture the practices and processes through which the 'outsider' is produced. For Bauman, identities are set up as dichotomies:

> In dichotomies crucial for the practice and vision of social order the differentiating power hides as a rule behind one of the members of the opposition. The second member is but the other of the first, the opposite (degraded, suppressed, exiled) side of the first and its creation. Thus abnormality is the other of the norm … woman the other of man, stranger the other of the native, enemy the other of friend, 'them' the other of 'us'. (1991: 14; see also Gingrich 2004)

By defining itself against an 'other', the dominant group silences or delegitimises the 'other' (Kitzinger and Wilkinson 1996). Moreover, 'others'' representations of themselves or the dominant group are viewed as a threat by dominant groups (Sampson 1993). As Stuart Hall (1997) notes, representation through language is central to the processes by which meaning is produced, and visual representations of 'otherness' hold cultural authority. Hall's work, including his writings on race and racism, can be characterised as encompassing 'the desire to contest, to pry open, essentialized claims of national identity … to find a space for the "others" in the national imaginary' (Alexander 2009: 464; i.e. see Hall 2000). Therefore, dominant or hegemonic groups can exert control over processes of representation while representations of otherness can also be read as inverted representation of those doing the othering (i.e. see early ethnographies of non-Western cultures) (Kitzinger and Wilkinson 1996; hooks 1990).

Early work on 'othering' focused on *woman* as 'other', mainly drawing on Simone de Beauvoir's seminal work *The Second Sex*, in which she appropriates Hegel's concept of 'the Other' to demonstrate that:

> [Woman] is defined and differentiated with reference to man and not he with reference to her; she is the incidental, the inessential as opposed to the essential. He is the Subject, he is the Absolute – she is the Other. (1976 [1949]: 16)

De Beauvoir's notion of 'the Other' was heavily influenced by Hegel's dialectic of identification and distantiation in the encounter of the self with an 'other' as written in his 'Master-Slave Dialectic' (1807 B.IV.A cited in Brons 2015: 69). The concept of woman as 'Other' more often than not involves the central claim that: '… Otherness is projected onto woman by, and in the interests of, men, such that we are constructed as inferior or abnormal' (Kitzinger and Wilkinson 1996: 4). Above all, it is women's sexual bodies which are the focal point for othering, an othering which has become ever more sophisticated as a result of the masculine institution of medicine and masculine modes of knowledge (Jackson et al. 1993). Ussher argues that the oppression of 'mad women' can be seen as a form of 'misogynistic torture' whereby 'misogyny makes women mad either through naming us as "the Other", through reinforcing the phallocentric discourse, or through depriving women of power, privilege and independence' (1991: 7). However, women do not have a monopoly to 'otherness' (Kitzinger and Wilkinson 1996) as Simone de Beauvoir herself highlighted in her reference to what she termed 'other Others':

> No group ever sets itself up as the One without at once setting up the Other over against itself … [T]o the native of a country all who inhabit other countries are 'foreigners'; Jews are 'different' for the anti-Semite,

Negroes are 'inferior' for American racists, aborigines are 'natives' for colonists, proletarians are the 'lower class' for the privileged. (1976 [1949]: 52)

Black feminist scholars have recognised the intersectional aspects of 'othering' in relation to the oppression of woman of colour and non-Western people (i.e. see Hill Collins 1990; Patai 1991; Fine 1994). These works recognise that 'representations of women which "imply" a homogenous category of Otherness render invisible the different experiences of women of varied ethnic, sexual and class locations' (Kitzinger and Wilkinson 1996: 5). Patricia Hill Collins (1990) discusses what she calls 'marginal outsiders' and the notion of 'othering' is incorporated as part of her 'matrix of domination', a paradigm which explains the overall organisation of power within society and which has a particular arrangement of intersecting systems of oppression. The systems come together in a manner which is historically and socially specific. They are also organised via four interrelated domains of power: structural, disciplinary, hegemonic and interpersonal. Patricia Hill Collins (1991 [1986]) outlines a black feminist standpoint and draws attention to women's marginal status which she refers to as an 'outsider within status'. For Collins, intersectionality is key as diversity of experiences will be reflected in and shaped by other aspects of identity including class, religion, age and sexuality (see also Crenshaw 1989). Therefore, acknowledging that intersectionality is part of 'othering' further permits us to account for how social categories are positioned in such a way as to distinguish 'insiders from outsiders' (Hill Collins 1998: 69).

Othering is also evident in the construction and representation of discourses of the oppressed, which act to justify the oppressor, as noted in Edward Said's (1978) anthropological critique of orientalism. Said's work is concerned with the scholarly disciplines and ideological and imaginative representations by which the West has constructed and come to know the non-Western world as 'Other'. According to Said, Europe constructed a discourse of 'Otherness' in order to come to terms with colonies in the Orient. This involved the recreation of their history of people 'outside of it', justifying colonial rule and explaining the fall of Oriental cultures. For example, in relation to India, Said notes that: 'The bulk of colonial writing in India focused on demonstrating the peculiarities of Hindu civilisation, and the barbaric practices pertaining to women' (1978: 34). The representation of these civilisations as 'Other' thus operates to reinforce the power and superiority of those with control over processes of representation (Kitzinger and Wilkinson 1996). Thus, in addition to gender, 'othering' has also been used to theorise race, ethnicity and colonialism (Kitzinger and Wilkinson 1996).

Stereotypes are one aspect of 'othering'. Michael Pickering (2001) argues that stereotypes are a system of categorisation which installs order. They represent cultural processes, practices and understandings which create meaning. Stereotypes are endowed with ideological views and values and 'create a sense of order through the negation of broader or expansive understandings, foreclosing many of the issues relating to the difference and diversity of a subject matter before these same issues can be subsequently put forward, made known or engaged with' (Allen 2010: 143). Stereotypes construct 'difference as deviant for the sake of normative gain' (Pickering 2001: 7) and operate by creating boundaries and fixing meaning as to what is positive or negative, normal or deviant/alien/'Other'. Pickering (2001) claims that a historical understanding of stereotypes can assist in making evident how stereotypes often draw on long-standing images of particular groups which have remained largely dormant. For Pickering (2001: 48):

> Stereotyping is ... a way of warding off any threat or disruption to 'us' as the 'same together' through the generation of the essentialized Otherness ... It is a collective process of judgement which feeds upon and re-enforces powerful social myths.

Therefore, stereotypical traits are used to reinforce the notion of otherness. Stereotyping involves a heightened focus on the other (as 'different') and a disavowal or distancing of those who are 'Othered' (see also Hall 1997). For Essed (1991), othering also involves people opting out of seeing or responding to discrimination such as racism.

The concept of 'othering' is not without its critics. For example, it has been criticised for denying agency to those who are 'othered' (Bhatt 2006). Jensen (2011) argues that the binary nature of 'othering' sets up a frame of reference which fails to see the in-between, the 'thirdspace'

(Soja 1996), and which, in the context of the differentiation referred to earlier in relation to people, temporalities, geographical locations and social spaces, denies active agency to a supposedly unified 'voiceless subaltern' (Jensen 2011: 101). In the *Location of Culture*, Bhabha's (1994; see also Soja 1996) theory of cultural difference provides us with the conceptual vocabulary of 'hybridity' and the 'third space'. He develops Turner's concept of liminality to propose the concept of third space as a position from which new identities and potentialities emerge. 'Third space' is critical of essentialist positions of identity and of 'originary culture' (Bhabha 1994). Third space contains new possibilities. It is a space in which cultural meaning and representation have no 'primordial unity or fixity' (Bhabha 1994).

Other writers have, with explicit reference to Spivak's (1985) use of Jacques Lacan, spoken of othering as 'psychoanalytical fatalism in critical disguise' (Gingrich 2004: 11). Spivak (1985) coined the theoretical concept of othering in her essay on 'The Rani or Sirmur' in which she discusses three dimensions of othering in archival material of British colonial power in India. These three dimensions include: the operation of power in terms of producing the other as subordinate; constructing the other as pathological and morally inferior; and the implication that knowledge and technology are the property of a 'powerful, empirical self, not the colonial other' (Jensen 2011: 65). Spivak's notion of othering has much in common with the concept of intersectionality (Crenshaw 1991) and 'interlocking systems of oppression' (Hill Collins 1989) discussed above, since it is multidimensional and deals with several forms of social differentiation (Jensen 2011). Therefore, in Spivak's work:

> … othering concerns the consequences of racism, sexism, class (or a combination hereof) in terms of symbolic degradation as well as the processes of identity formation related to this degradation. (Jensen 2011: 65)

Jensen (2011) addresses objections to the concept of othering by building on McLaren's (1994) notion of 'oppositional agency'. From McLaren's perspective, the conservative/liberal stress on sameness and the left-liberal emphasis on difference form a false opposition.

Sameness and difference should not be seen as essentialist categories: rather, 'difference is always a product of history, culture, power, and ideology. Differences occur between and among groups and must be understood in terms of the specificity of their production' (McLaren 1994: 126). In his study of young ethnic minority men in Denmark, Jensen restores agency to the othered through strategies such as: 'capitalization' (appropriating elements of othering discourses in an attempt to imbue the category with symbolic value) and 'refusal' (articulating distance from the category by 'talking back' to the othering gaze). Jensen's interviewees attempted to carve out a third space which was 'not defined by firstness and otherness, but transcends the dichotomy: simply as a normal human being—not Danish, but also not different from the Danish' (2011: 74).

People have resisted or challenged 'online othering' through various strategies such as: the reporting of abuse; campaigning for more effective reporting systems on social media platforms; campaigning against online hate and sexual harassment; feminist activism; social media hashtags designed to challenge social and political inequalities. Prominent examples of effective hashtags include the #MeToo movement calling out sexual misconduct in media industries and the #Blacklivesmatter matter movement. Various Internet sites have also been set up which focus on advice to resist and challenge online hate and trolls. Internet users have also publicly called out the abusive behaviour/s of Internet trolls or attempted to open up dialogue with them. For example, the Cambridge classicist scholar Professor Mary Beard adopted the strategy of publicly 'naming and shaming' her trolls (Ellis-Petersen 2014). Other popular anecdotal advice on how to effectively respond to trolls has included the now well-known adage: 'do not feed the troll'. However, as discussed above, writers have noted how this strategy can further silence the voices of particular individuals/groups in online spaces (Lumsden and Morgan 2017).

By introducing the concept of 'online othering', examples of which are provided and analysed in this edited volume, we aim to also address the above criticisms of 'othering'. Our concept of 'online othering' can be summarised as:

- Providing readers with a conceptual tool through which to analyse and make sense of the myriad toxic and harmful behaviours which are being created through, or perpetuated by, information and communication technologies including the spaces of the Internet, social media platforms, smartphone apps and other interconnected technologies such as smart home technologies (i.e. 'the internet of things').
- Moving beyond the inflexible and often politically loaded ways of categorising examples of harmful behaviours online referred to in varying contexts as 'abuse', 'harassment', 'hate', 'hate speech', 'hate crime' and/or 'trolling'.
- Acknowledging the seriousness of certain aspects of 'online othering' and its repercussions. Online abusive communications and behaviours may not always be taken seriously by social media corporations and/or the authorities, but the effects are nonetheless real in terms of the everyday impact on those individuals who are on the receiving end. As Billig (2002) writes in relation to prejudice, not all prejudice and stereotyping are equivalent, and the same can be said, for instances, of 'online othering'. He argues that:

> Even if it is conceded that prejudice is inevitable and that human thinking about social groups involves some or other form of stereotyping, then this does not mean that all prejudices and all stereotyping are equivalent. Indeed, the term 'prejudice' may be too anodyne to cover all forms of intergroup stereotyping. Stereotypes, even if they are broadly 'negative', can be distinguished in terms of their intensity and ideological importance. (Billig 2002: 177)

- Addressing the role of power and privilege at various levels including in the design of information-communication technologies (largely by those in privileged positions [read: white, middle-class men]), and without consideration of unanticipated (potentially harmful) consequences and the ways in which technologies can be used for purposes not initially considered or planned in their design (i.e. the use of smartphone apps for stalking and coercion).
- Acknowledging how 'online othering' entails intersectionality with social characteristics and locations such as class, gender, age, race,

ethnicity, religion, nationality, disability and sexuality thus conceptualising across/between/betwixt these, in varying contexts on and offline.
- Incorporating responses to 'online othering' which recognise its oppositional nature and acknowledge the agency of the othered and how resistance to othering can empower and challenge. Thus, we draw on the concepts of 'thirdspace' and 'liminality' to recognise that the Internet, social media and how individuals use these also result in the emergence of new identities and potentialities. We move beyond essentialist positions of identity and of 'originary culture' (Bhabha 1994).
- Challenging the outdated *offline (real) versus online (virtual) dichotomy*. Despite our use of the term '*online*', we, like others, believe it is important to acknowledge that these behaviours do not occur in a 'virtual vacuum'—they are part and parcel of everyday life and have real consequences in what some have chosen to call the 'real' (versus the 'virtual') world. We must discard the well-worn dichotomies of 'online versus offline', and 'virtual world' versus 'real world', and instead acknowledge the interconnected and fluid nature of our use of ICTs.
- Acknowledging that when 'interrupting' otherness as scholars and/or researchers, we must think about our own and others' 'otherness' without viewing these as essential, fixed attributes. Drawing on the work of Linda Alcoff (1991) who highlights 'the problem of speaking for others', we acknowledge that we must also enquire as to why *we* have an impulse to speak for others. If we decide to proceed, we must make explicit how our autobiographies impact on what we say, be open to criticism, and must also acknowledge the effects of speaking on the wider social, cultural, political, discursive and material context(s). This entails a reflexive sensibility which is mindful of those individuals or groups whom we seek to 'speak for' or 'speak of' (see also Lumsden 2019).

Synopsis of Book and Overview of Chapters

The overall aim of *Online Othering* is to contribute to and advance social scientific understandings of the 'othering', discrimination and abuse which occurs in/on/via online spaces, the role of information and communication technologies (and particularly digital and social media) in making possible, facilitating and/or exacerbating 'online othering'. The edited collection explores both experiences of online victimisation and othering, and the activist response to online abuse. It further aims to explore the related policing and regulation of online and social media spaces. We explore these themes through the presentation of diverse case studies from both academics and practitioners. Moreover, the relationships between various macro factors and sociopolitical institutions and experiences of hate or othering online are explored.

The book is organised into four parts which reflect the overall aims of this edited collection: to understand 'online othering' within the wider social, political, cultural and historical context; to explore the perpetrators of online hate and abuse; to provide an insight into individual and group experiences of 'online othering' including intersections of othering via, for example, gender, race, ethnicity, sex and sexuality, and disability; to analyse how groups resist 'online othering'; and how the authorities respond to and regulate online abuse and hate. Part I brings together three chapters tackling the rise of political extremism online in the guise of the Alt-Right and Men's Rights Activists. The contributions in this part focus in particular on how these groups make use of the digital environment to recruit followers and perpetuate online hatred. This part is also concerned by the ways in which political extremism is gendered, and therefore, the chapters also address the ways in which masculinity is policed within extremist contexts online in such a way that it allows misogyny, racism and other forms of prejudice to flourish. Aaron Winter examines the history of the American far-right's use of the Internet by analysing how this history developed in response to political changes and emerging technologies; how the adoption of digital technologies changed the status of such movements and their brand of hate and analyses the relationship between their online activity and traditional forms of communication. Alex Green follows by offering an account of the ways in which far-right online communities uphold and police themselves by actively othering dissenters through intersectional categories of gender, racial and sexual deviance. Green argues that straight white men are placed as intellectually, morally and racially superior and analyses a particular case of when these discourses become unstable when 'insiders' express political opposition. This is seen through strategies of policing that wield homophobia and hegemonic masculinity against dissidents. The final chapter in this part by Karen Lumsden focuses on Men's Rights Activists' (MRA) discussions of trolling and gendered violence on Reddit. Her analysis shows that this group routinely engage in the online othering of 'outsiders', including denigrating and abusing feminists and so-called social-justice warriors. Lumsden shows how MRAs deny that women and feminists are victims of online violence and instead suggest that it is largely men who are victimised in online spaces.

Part II foregrounds the extent to which online othering often has a gendered dimension. This part includes accounts of the lived experiences of those who have been subjected to othering in online contexts and their perceptions of online abuse. Ruth Lewis, Mike Rowe and Claire Wiper discuss experiences of online abuse among women who are engaged in feminist politics. They use debates about violence against women and girls (VAWG) and hate crime to consider the continuities and breaks between online and offline victimisation, arguing that online abuse should be considered to be a form of VAWG and a hate crime but that describing online abuse as a form of hate obscures the complex emotional context when perpetrators are known to the victims, and because 'hate crime' has not reflected the intersectional nature of some offences which target victims' identities. Rikke Amundsen's contribution explores how women make sense of the risk of having their private sexual images (PSIs) shared without their consent. Her analysis focuses on the way that postfeminist ideas about individualism, free choice and female empowerment influence women's accounts of this particular sexting-related risk. Her findings suggest placing emphasis on making the right choices in terms of whom to trust effectively renders women primarily responsible for their own risk mitigation; therefore, victims of such non-consensual sharing receive little empathy. John Whittle, Dave Elder-Vass and Karen Lumsden draw on semi-structured interviews and focus groups with boys and girls aged 11–16 years old to explore how 'banter' is a common form of social interaction within male peer groups interacting online and how this can represent a means of othering, and of performing and constructing hegemonic masculinity. The final chapter in this part by Rosalynd Southern and Emily Harmer draws on an inductive thematic analysis of 12,436 tweets to examine the extent to which abusive and more everyday forms of sexism, misogyny, ableism and racism pervade Twitter interactions between politicians and citizens. Their analysis identified four themes: gendered and racist abuse; silencing and dismissal; questioning intelligence and position; and 'benevolent' othering.

Part III includes three chapters which aim to highlight less mainstream experiences of othering than those which have previously been discussed in the literature or, indeed in the book itself. These contributions highlight the importance of taking an intersectional approach to online othering. Ben Colliver, Adrian Coyle and Marisa Silvestri provide a critical analysis of some ways in which transgender people are 'othered' online and details attempts to resist or challenge such othering. They analyse 1756 online comments made in response to ten YouTube videos concerning 'gender neutral toilets' and develop three recurring themes: 'Gender neutral toilets as sites of sexual danger'; 'Claiming victimhood: Gender neutral toilets as undermining the rights of cisgender people'; and 'The delegitimisation and othering of transgender people'. Herminder Kaur uses ethnography to explore the way that young people with physical disabilities make use of digital technology to explore their sexual identity and highlights the extent to which their access is policed by parental interventions which inadvertently other them by denying their sexuality. The final chapter in this part, by Nathan Kerrigan, explores the ways residents of a rural community in the south of England use the Internet to construct an online rural space through giving meaning to the forum as 'rural', and the extent to which this excludes and 'others' those with perceived differences, leading to targeted hate and victimisation for those individuals online.

Part IV, the final part of the book, focuses on the questions of how we should respond to, regulate, and police online spaces. Digital media corporations have typically been slow to act and respond to user concern regarding toxic online cultures, hate speech and abuse, while police agencies are faced with an ever-changing socio-technical landscape in terms of emerging social media technologies and apps, and therefore struggle to detect and prosecute those responsible. This part also demonstrates that digital technology can be used to resist and challenge online othering. Jo Smith highlights how women have responded to instances of online misogyny, including reporting these and/or resisting them via fight responses and 'digilante' actions. She further highlights that policing and regulating online misogyny is further complicated by the nature of online space, calls to respect freedom of speech, limited legislative provisions, and ambiguity over whether these behaviours are indeed 'criminal'. Phillipa Hall's chapter analyses the online othering of disabled people via hate speech on social media platforms. Hall argues that social and legal initiatives to confront online disability hate speech must address and contend with Internet companies' business imperatives. She also argues that the tendency to conceptualise online and offline as distinct spaces further legitimises calls for the continued deregulation of online space/s in relation to disability hate speech. Brianna O'Shea, Roberta Julian, Jeremy Prichard and Sally Kelty draw on findings from interviews with police investigators and prosecutors on the challenges for policing cyberstalking to examine how it is investigated by the police in Australia. They argue that for police investigators and prosecutors to be proactive in the policing of cyberstalking, risk assessments must constantly adapt to changing technologies and their implications for interpersonal relationships. The final chapter of this volume by Alex Black, Karen Lumsden and Lee Hadlington discusses police officer and civilian staff views of reports of interpersonal cybercrime in England. The authors demonstrate how police officers' notions about the 'ideal victim' of online crime frames their response to public reports of online harassment and cybercrime. The police response results in victim-blaming of online users who are viewed as making themselves vulnerable to cybercrime and hate via their occupation of, and refusal to withdraw from, particular virtual spaces.

References

Alcoff, L. (1991, Winter). The problem of speaking for others. *Cultural Critique, 20*, 5–32.
Alexander, C. (2009). Stuart Hall and 'race'. *Cultural Studies, 23*(4), 457–482.
Allen, C. (2010). *Islamophobia*. Farnham: Ashgate.

Awan, I. (Ed.). (2016). *Islamophobia in Cyberspace*. London: Routledge.
Bates, L. (2014). *Everyday Sexism*. London, UK: Simon & Schuster.
Bauman, Z. (1991). *Modernity and Ambivalence*. Cambridge: Polity Press.
Berridge, S., & Portwood-Stacer, L. (2015). Introduction: Feminism, hashtags and violence against women and girls. *Feminist Media Studies, 15*(2), 341.
Bessire, L., & Bond, D. (2017). The rise of Trumpism. *Hot Spots, Cultural Anthropology*. https://culanth.org/fieldsights/1030-the-rise-of-trumpism. Accessed October 13, 2018.
Bhabha, H. K. (1994). *The Location of Culture*. New York: Routledge.
Bhatt, C. (2006). The fetish of the margins: Religious absolutism, anti-racism and postcolonial silence. *New Formations, 59*, 95–115.
Billig, M. (2002). Henri Tajfel's 'cognitive aspects of prejudice' and the psychology of bigotry. *British Journal of Social Psychology, 41*, 171–188.
Binns, A. (2012). Don't feed the trolls! *Journalism Practice, 6*(4), 547–562.
Bishop, J. (2013). The art of trolling law enforcement: A review and model for implementing 'flame trolling' legislation enacted in Great Britain (1981–2012). *International Review of Law, Computers and Technology, 27*(3), 301–318.
Bowles, N. (2018). Thermostats, locks and lights: Digital tools of domestic abuse. *The New York Times*. https://www.nytimes.com/2018/06/23/technology/smart-home-devices-domestic-abuse.html. Accessed October 13, 2018.
Brons, L. (2015). Othering, an analysis. *Transcience, 6*(1), 69–90.
Chatterjee, R., Doerfler, P., Orgad, H., Havron, S., Palmer, J., Freed, D., et al. (2018). The spyware used in intimate partner violence. *2018 IEEE Symposium on Security and Privacy (SP)*. https://ieeexplore.ieee.org/abstract/document/8418618. Accessed October 13, 2018.
Citron, D. K. (2016). *Hate Crimes in Cyberspace*. Cambridge, MA: Harvard University Press.
Cixous, H., & Clement, C. (1975). *The Newly Born Woman*. Minneapolis: University of Minnesota Press.
Crawford, A. (2017). Facebook failed to remove sexualised images of children. *BBC News*. https://www.bbc.co.uk/news/technology-39187929. Accessed October 20, 2018.
Crenshaw, K. (1989). Demarginalizing the intersection of race and sex: A black feminist critique of antidiscrimination doctrine, feminist theory and antiracist politics. *University of Chicago Legal Forum, 1*(8), 139–167.
Crenshaw, K. (1991). Mapping the margins: Intersectionality, identity politics, and violence against women of color. *Stanford Law Review, 43*(6), 1241–1299.

Cuthbertson, A. (2018). Pride month 2018: YouTube runs 'anti-LGBT ads' while demonetising transgender videos. *The Independent*. https://www.independent.co.uk/life-style/gadgets-and-tech/news/pride-month-2018-youtube-anti-lgbt-ads-demonetising-transgender-gay-videos-a8386181.html. Accessed October 20, 2018.

De Beauvoir, S. (1976 [1949]). *The Second Sex*. Paris: Gallimard.

Devine, D. (2018). Hate crime did spike after the referendum—Even allowing for other factors. *Brexit, LSE*. http://blogs.lse.ac.uk/brexit/2018/03/19/hate-crime-did-spike-after-the-referendum-even-allowing-for-other-factors/. Accessed October 13, 2018.

Dodge, A. (2015). Digitizing rape culture: Online sexual violence and the power of the digital photograph. *Crime, Media, Culture, 12*(1), 65–82.

Donarth, J. S. (1999). Identity and deception in the virtual. In M. A. Smith & P. Kollock (Eds.), *Communities in Cyberspace* (pp. 29–59). London: Routledge.

Dragiewicz, M., Burgess, J., Matamoras-Fernandez, A., Salter, M. Suzor, N. P., Woodlock, D., et al. (2018). Technology facilitated coercive control: Domestic violence and the competing roles of digital media platforms. *Feminist Media Studies*, ifirst. https://doi.org/10.1080/14680777.2018.1447341.

Eagle, R. B. (2015). Loitering, lingering, hashtagging: Women reclaiming public space via #BoardtheBus, #StopStreetHarrassment, and the #EverydaySexism Project. *Feminist Media Studies, 15*(2), 350–353.

Easter, B. (2018). 'Feminist_Brevity_in_light_of_masculine_long-windedness:' Code, space, and online misogyny. *Feminist Media Studies, 18*(4), 675–685.

Ellis-Petersen, H. (2014). Mary reveals she befriended Twitter trolls following online abuse. *The Guardian*. https://www.theguardian.com/books/2014/aug/27/mary-beard-befriends-twitter-trolls-online-abuse. Accessed October 24, 2018.

Essed, P. (1991). *Understanding Everyday Racism*. London: Sage.

Feldman, M., & Littler, M. (2014). *Tell MAMA reporting 2013/14 anti-Muslim overview, analysis and 'cumulative extremism'*. Centre for Fascist, Anti-Fascist and Post-Fascist Studies, Teesside University, UK. http://tellmamauk.org/wp-content/uploads/2014/07/finalreport.pdf. Accessed March 11, 2016.

Fine, M. (1994). Working the hyphens: Reinventing self and other in qualitative research. In N. K. Denzin & Y. S. Lincoln (Eds.), *Handbook of Qualitative Research*. London: Sage.

Fraser, N. (1990). Rethinking the public sphere: A contribution to the critique of actually existing democracy. *Social Text, 25–26,* 56–80.

Fuchs, C. (2009). Information and communication technologies and society: A contribution to the critique of the political economy of the internet. *European Journal of Communication, 24*(1), 69–87.

Fuchs, C. (2017). *Social Media: A Critical Introduction* (2nd ed.). London: Sage.

Gerard, J. F., & Whitfield, K. C. (2016). The experiences of victims of online Islamophobia. In I. Awan (Ed.), *Islamophobia in Cyberspace*. London: Routledge.

Gingrich, A. (2004). Conceptualizing identities. In G. Bauman & A. Gingrich (Eds.), *Grammars of Identity/Alterity—A Structural Approach*. Oxford: BergHahn.

Griffin, A. (2015). Twitter still 'sucks' at protecting users from abuse, says CEO. Independent 5th February 2015. https://www.independent.co.uk/life-style/gadgets-and-tech/news/twitter-still-sucks-at-protecting-users-from-abuse-says-ceo-10026328.html. Accessed September 2, 2018.

Hall, S. (Ed.). (1997). *Representation: Cultural Representations and Signifying Practices*. London: Sage.

Hall, S. (2000). The multicultural question. In B. Hesse (Ed.), *Un/Settled Multiculturalisms*. London: Zed Press.

Hardaker, C. (2010). Trolling in asynchronous computer mediated communication: From user discussions to academic definitions. *Journal of Politeness Research, 6,* 215–242.

Hardaker, C., & McGlashan, M. (2016). 'Real men don't hate women': Twitter rape threats and group identity. *Journal of Pragmatics, 91,* 80–93.

Hawley, G. (2017). *Making Sense of the Alt-Right*. Columbia: Columbia University Press.

Herman, D. F. (1978). The rape culture. In J. Freeman (Ed.), *Women: A Feminist Perspective* (pp. 41–63). Mountain View, CA: Mayfield.

Herring, S. C. (1999). The rhetorical dynamics of gender harassment on-line. *The Information Society, 15,* 151–167.

Herring, S. C. (2003). Computer-mediated discourse. In D. Schiffrin, D. Tannen, & H. E. Hamilton (Eds.), *The Handbook of Discourse Analysis* (pp. 612–634). Oxford: Blackwell.

Herring, S. C., Job-Sluder, K., Scheckler, R., & Barab, S. (2002). Searching for safety online: Managing 'trolling' in a feminist forum. *The Information Society, 18,* 371–384.

Hill Collins, P. (1989). The social construction of black feminist thought. *Signs, 14*(4), 745–773.

Hill Collins, P. (1990). *Black Feminist Thought: Knowledge, Consciousness, and the Politics of Empowerment.* New York: Routledge.

Hill Collins, P. (1991 [1986]). Learning from the outsider within: The sociological significance of black feminist thought. In M. M. Fonow & J. A. Cook (Eds.), *Beyond Methodology: Feminist Scholarship as Lived Experience* (pp. 35–59). Bloomington: Indiana University Press.

Hill Collins, P. (1998). It's all in the family: Intersections of gender, race and nation. *Hypatia, 13*(3), 62–82.

Hmielowski, J. D., Hutchens, M. J., & Cicchirillo, V. J. (2014). Living in an age of online incivility: Examining the conditional indirect effects of online discussion on political flaming. *Information, Communication & Society, 17*(10), 1196–1211.

hooks, b. (1990). *Yearning: Race, Gender and Cultural Politics.* Boston: South End Press.

Hutchens, M. J., Cicchirillo, V. J., & Hmielowski, J. D. (2015). How could you think that?!?!: Understanding intentions to engage in political flaming. *New Media & Society, 17*(8), 1201–1219.

ITV News. (2018). *Twitter urged to do more to tackle abuse of disabled users.* http://www.itv.com/news/2018-02-20/twitter-charity-disabled-abuse/. Accessed October 20, 2018.

Jackson, S., Prince, J., & Young, P. (1993). Science, medicine and reproductive technology: Introduction. In S. Jackson (Ed.), *Women's Studies: A Reader.* London: Harvester Wheatsheaf.

Jane, E. A. (2014a). You're a ugly, whorish, slut. *Feminist Media Studies, 14*(4), 531–546.

Jane, E. A. (2014b). 'Back to the kitchen, cunt': Speaking the unspeakable about online misogyny. *Continuum, 28*(4), 558–570.

Jensen, S. Q. (2011). Othering, identity formation and agency. *Qualitative Studies, 2*(2), 63–78.

Keller, J. M., Mendes, K. D., & Ringrose, J. (2016). Speaking 'unthinkable things': Documenting digital feminist responses to rape culture. *Journal of Gender Studies.* Pre-print version. https://lra.le.ac.uk/handle/2381/33121. Accessed March 14, 2016.

Khoja-Moolji, S. (2015). Becoming an 'intimate publics': Exploring the affective intensities of hashtag feminism. *Feminist Media Studies, 15*(2), 347–350.

Kiesler, S., Zubrow, D., & Moses, A. M. (1985). Affect in computer-mediated communication: An experiment in synchronous terminal-to-terminal discussion. *Human–Computer Interaction, 1*(1): 77–104.

Kitzinger, C., & Wilkinson, S. (1996). Theorizing representing the other. In S. Wilkinson & C. Kitzinger (Eds.), *Representing the Other* (pp. 1–32). London: Sage.

Komaromi, P., & Singh, K. (2016). *Post-referendum Racism and Xenophobia*. London: PostRefRacism.

Korn, J. U., & Kneese, T. (2015). Guest editors' introduction: Feminist approaches to social media research—History, activism, and values. *Feminist Media Studies, 15*(4), 707–710.

Lacan, J. (1977). *Ecrits: A Selection*. London: Tavistock.

Lea, M., O'Shea, T., Fung, P., & Spears, R. (1992). 'Flaming' in computer-mediated communication: Observations, explanations, implications. In M. Lea (Ed.), *Contexts of Computer-Mediated Communication* (pp. 89–112). New York: Harvester Wheatsheaf.

Lee, H. (2005). Behavioral strategies for dealing with flaming in an online forum. *The Sociology Quarterly, 46*(2), 385–403.

Lister, R. (2004). *Poverty*. Cambridge: Polity Press.

Lumsden, K. (2019). *Reflexivity: Theory, Method and Practice*. London: Routledge.

Lumsden, K., & Morgan, H. M. (2017). Media framing of trolling and online abuse: Silencing strategies, symbolic violence and victim blaming. *Feminist Media Studies, 17*(6), 926–940.

McGlynn, C., Rackley, E., & Houghton, R. (2017). Beyond 'revenge porn': The continuum of image-based sexual abuse. *Feminist Legal Studies, 25*(1), 25–46.

McLaren, P. (1994). White terror and oppositional agency. In D. T. Goldberg (Ed.), *Multiculturalism: A Critical Reader*. Oxford: Blackwell.

Mantilla, K. (2015). *Gendertrolling*. Westport, CT: Praeger.

Marwick, A., & Ellison, N. B. (2012). 'There isn't wifi in heaven': Negotiating visibility on Facebook memorial pages. *Journal of Broadcasting & Electronic Media, 56*(3), 378–400.

Massanari, A. (2017). #Gamergate and the Fappening: How Reddit's algorithm, governance, and culture support toxic technocultures. *New Media and Society, 19*(3), 329–346.

McQuail, D. (2010). *Mass Communication Theory* (6th ed.). London: Sage.

Noble, S. U. (2018). *Algorithms of Oppression: How Search Engines Reinforce Racism*. New York: New York University Press.

O'Sullivan, P. B., & Flanagin, A. J. (2003). Reconceptualizing 'flaming' and other problematic messages. *New Media & Society, 5*(69), 69–94.

Papacharissi, Z. (2002). The virtual sphere: The internet as a public sphere. *New Media and Society, 4*(1), 9–27.

Papacharissi, Z. (2004). Democracy online: Civility, politeness, and the democratic potential of online political discussion. *New Media and Society, 6*(2), 259–283.

Papacharissi, Z. (2016). The real-virtual dichotomy in online interaction: New media uses and consequences revisited. *Annals of the International Communication Association, 29*(1), 216–238.

Parker, D., & Song, M. (2006). New ethnicities online: Reflexive racialization and the internet. *Sociological Review, 54*(3), 575–594.

Patai, D. (1991). US academics and third world women: Is ethical research possible? In S. Berger Gluck & D. Patai (Eds.), *Women's Words: The Feminist Practice of Oral History*. London: Routledge.

Phillips, W. (2015). *This Is Why We Can't Have Nice Things*. Cambridge, MA: MIT Press.

Pickering, M. (2001). *Stereotyping: The Politics of Representation*. Basingstoke: Palgrave.

Powell, A., & Henry, N. (2016). Policing technology-facilitated sexual violence against adult victims: Police and service sector perspectives. *Policing & Society, 28*(3), 291–307.

Rajagopalan, M., Vo, L. T., & Soe, A. N. (2018). How facebook failed The Rohingya in Myanmar. Buzzfeed 27th August. https://www.buzzfeednews.com/article/meghara/facebook-myanmar-rohingya-genocide. Accessed September 6, 2018.

Said, E. (1978). *Orientalism*. New York: Pantheon Books.

Sampson, E. E. (1993). *Celebrating the Other: A Dialogic Account of Human Nature*. London: Harvester Wheatsheaf.

Schwalbe, M., et al. (2000). Generic processes in reproduction of inequality: An interactionist analysis. *Social Forces, 79*(2), 419–452.

Segal, L. (1994). *Straight Sex: The Politics of Pleasure*. London: Virago.

Shariff, S., & DeMartini, A. (2015). Defining the legal lines: eGirls and intimate images. In J. Baley & V. Steeves (Eds.), *eGirls, eCitizens* (pp. 281–306). Ottawa: University of Ottawa Press.

Sills, S., Pickens, C., Beach, K., Jones, L., Calder-Dawe, O., Benton-Greig, P., et al. (2016). Rape culture and social media: Young critics and a feminist counterpublic. *Feminist Media Studies*, iFirst. https://doi.org/10.1080/14680777.2015.1137962.

Soja, E. W. (1996). *Thirdspace: Journeys to Los Angeles and Other Real-and-Imagined Places*. Oxford: Blackwell.

Spivak, G. C. (1985). The Rani of Sirmur: An essay in reading the archives. *History and Theory, 24*(3), 247–272.

Squirrell, T. (2017a). New digital methods can be used to analyse linguistic terms and better understand Reddit communities. *LSE US Centre*. http://blogs.lse.ac.uk/usappblog/2017/08/02/new-digital-methods-can-be-used-to-analyse-linguistic-terms-and-better-understand-reddit-communities/. Accessed October 13, 2018.

Squirrell, T. (2017b). Linguistic data analysis of 3 billion Reddit comments shows the alt-right is getting stronger. *Quartz*. https://qz.com/1056319/what-is-the-alt-right-a-linguistic-data-analysis-of-3-billion-reddit-comments-shows-a-disparate-group-that-is-quickly-uniting/. Accessed October 13, 2018.

Turkle, S. (1995). *Life on the Screen: Identity in the Age of the Internet*. New York: Simon & Schuster.

Tynes, B. M., Schuschke, J., & Noble, S. U. (2016). Digital intersectionality theory and the #blacklivesmatter movement. In S. U. Nobe & B. M. Tynes (Eds.), *The Intersectional Internet: Race, Sex, Class, and Culture Online* (pp. 21–40). New York: Peter Lang.

Ussher, J. (1991). *Women's Madness: Misogyny or Mental Illness?*. London: Harvester Wheatsheaf.

Van Zoonen, L. (2002). Gendering the internet: Claims, controversies and cultures. *European Journal of Communication, 17*(1), 5–23.

Williams, S. (2015). Digital defense: Black feminists resist violence with hashtag activism. *Feminist Media Studies, 15*(2), 341–344.

Part I

Online Culture Wars: The Rise of the Alt-Right, Trumpism and White Masculinities

Emily Harmer and Karen Lumsden

Editors' Introduction

The contemporary political and social climate offer many opportunities for considering examples of 'online othering'. The rise of authoritarian populist leaders and technological advancements has allowed far right, and other forms of reactionary politics, to flourish in the online environment. This first part of the book seeks to offer important insights into how these political movements are essentially gendered and how this is central to the ways in which they operate; specifically, the ways in which white male identities are asserted as superior, whilst those which deviate from this norm are othered and rejected.

This topic has previously been explored in the work of Michael Kimmel (2013), which has influenced the chapters in this part of the edited collection. His book *Angry White Men* offers an analysis of white men from the USA who appear to be mourning the loss of the privileges and entitlements they feel ought to be theirs by virtue of their sex, a process which he refers to as 'aggrieved entitlement'. He argues that these 'angry white men' feel victimised by the march of social change and the progress made by women and previously underprivileged groups. This trope of male victimhood has been picked up by feminist media scholars analysing online harassment (Marwick and Caplan 2018; Garcia-Favaro and Gill 2016; Banet-Weiser and Miltner 2016). A similar phenomenon has been noted in relation to young men who have been involved in high school shootings in the USA, where marginalised white students vent their rage at being excluded from the promises of white male privilege, this time because they do not conform to the traditional demands of hegemonic masculinity (Consalvo 2003). White masculinity and manhood have always been central to conservative politics and the ideology of the far right (Katz 2013) so it should come as no surprise that these attitudes which exist in aspects of the political mainstream also seep into some online communications and online cultures including for example via the expressions of misogynistic and racist attitudes.

The contemporary political context with the election of right-wing authoritarian politicians such as Donald Trump in the USA, Matteo Salvini in Italy and Viktor Orban in Hungary has led to men's perceived entitlement becoming increasingly asserted, and overtly politicised. Trump has been accused of sexual assault himself as well as openly bragging about doing so in a videotape that emerged during his election campaign. Orban has relentlessly attacked academic freedom in Hungary, threatening to ban any form of gender or women's studies from its universities. In the digital era, the Internet has become an outlet for the expression of political rage, racism, misogyny and far-right agendas, and this part of the book seeks to throw light on this by bringing together three chapters which discuss the rise of political extremism online in the guise of the far-right, the Alt-Right and Men's Rights Activists.

The first chapter in this part, by Aaron Winter, examines the history of the American far-right's use of the Internet in the light of the recent resurgence and mainstreaming of their discourses due to the advent of social media. The purpose of the chapter is to situate this resurgence in a historical context. Winter argues that the far right was slow to harness the power of the Internet and explores how these groups responded to both political changes and emerging technologies to transform their recruitment and modes of communication. He also considers how online communication reflected and changed the status of such movements and their brand of hate, and discusses the relationship between online activity and traditional forms and methods of communication.

Alex Green's chapter also deals with the use of online platforms by the 'Alt-Right'. He interrogates the norms of these communities and seeks to understand how these are upheld and policed through the othering of dissenters and through the intersectional categories of gender, racial and sexual deviance. Green argues that the Alt-Right's usual discourse of straight white male superiority became unstable when 'insiders' expressed political opposition. The chapter focuses on a prominent case study of two white male anti-Trump protestors who were subject to an onslaught of online memes and insults and targeted for abuse both on and offline. Green finds that whiteness and heterosexual masculinity remain the fundamental moral order in the online spaces occupied by the 'Alt-Right', which is seen through strategies of policing that wield homophobia and hegemonic masculinity against dissidents, reflecting similar strategies to those used in multiple authoritarian, nationalist and conservative contexts.

The final chapter in this part by Karen Lumsden focuses on the use of Reddit by Men's Rights Activists (MRAs). Lumsden argues that this online culture perpetuates and encourages forms of 'online othering', including misogyny and violence. The chapter focuses specifically on MRA discussions about trolling and gendered violence, and their 'online othering' of outsiders, including the denigration and abuse aimed at feminists and so-called social justice warriors (SJWs). Lumsden's findings suggest that these communities routinely deny and dismiss the abuse suffered by women and feminists online. They instead choose to emphasise the victimisation of men online. Lumsden also demonstrates how MRAs on Reddit construct online violence. Her chapter examines these previously unexplored online discourses which provide valuable insights into the construction of notions of online acceptability and deviance in digital communication, the boundaries between online/offline violence, and (online) culture wars which characterise the current political climate.

References

Banet-Weiser, S., & Miltner, K. M. (2016). #MasculinitySoFragile: Culture, structure, and networked misogyny. *Feminist Media Studies, 16*(1), 171–174.

Consalvo, M. (2003). The monsters next door: Media constructions of boys and masculinity. *Feminist Media Studies, 3*(1), 27–45.

Garcia-Favaro, L., & Gill, R. (2016). 'Emasculation nation has arrived': Sexism rearticulated in online responses to Lose the Lads' Mags campaign. *Feminist Media Studies, 16*(3), 379–397.

Katz, J. (2013). *Leading Men: Presidential Campaigns and the Politics of Manhood*. Northampton, MA: Interlink Books.

Kimmel, M. (2013). *Angry White Men: American Masculinity at the End of an Era*. New York: Nation Books.

Marwick, A. E. (2018). Drinking male tears: Language, the manosphere, and networked harassment. *Feminist Media Studies, 18*(4), 543–559.

2

Online Hate: From the Far-Right to the 'Alt-Right' and from the Margins to the Mainstream

Aaron Winter

Introduction

In the late 1990s and early 2000s, there was much discussion of both the democratizing and anti-democratic implications of the Internet in the absence of clear controls or regulations and boundaries. In relation to the former thesis were progressive social movements, and in the latter, the far-right using the Internet to spread their racist hate, to network and to recruit both domestically and globally (Back et al. 1998; Daniels 2009; Neiwert 2017).

Despite early fears and claims that the Americans were at the forefront of the far-right Internet revolution (Back et al. 1998; Daniels 2009), they did not harness or exploit this new technology quickly, effectively or widely (Daniels 2009), with the exception of Don Black's Stormfront. According to Peter Sills, some of the early media coverage of the neo-Nazi BBS bulletin board network was 'exaggerated'

A. Winter (✉)
Criminology, University of East London, London, UK

(Berlet 2008). Many networks were still using printing presses and scanning and uploading material onto web pages or 'cut and paste brochures'. Where the Internet was harnessed was in countries with greater hate speech regulation, such as Europe and Canada (Back et al. 1998). In these contexts, material produced in America was reproduced on the Internet, in much the same way American-printed ephemera and recordings had previously been disseminated through the post to places where it was illegal. Since the late 2000s, there has been an increased use of the Internet by the far-right, which has led to greater attention being paid to it by the media, monitoring organizations and researchers. The latter of these groups have focused on the far-right online in relation to everything from identity and community formation (Bowman-Grieve 2009; Perry and Scrivens 2016) to monitoring, detection and countering extremism (Scrivens et al. 2017). This interest has increased in the Trump era in response to the Alt-Right and the proliferation of far-right and white identity and misogynistic movements and subcultures, as well as more general online racism and misogyny.

Such work on online extremism also relates to studies of wider everyday online racism (Daniels 2009; Sharma and Brooker 2016) and online misogyny (Garcia-Favaro and Gill 2016; Lumsden and Morgan 2017), as well as their intersection (Noble 2018), which has been on the rise and normalized under Trump. Yet, online racist extremism and wider online racism are rarely explicitly connected in work on the former, in the same way that work on the far-right/right-wing extremism and terrorism is often separated from work on mainstream, institutional, structural and everyday racism (Mondon and Winter 2017, 2018; Winter 2017, 2018; for exceptions see Daniels 2009). This chapter contributes to research on far-right extremism by focusing on online activity and adding a historical perspective. It will also contribute to contemporary research and analysis of 'online othering', particularly racism and misogyny, by connecting it to research and analysis of the far-right. It will focus not on othering itself, but the movements involved in its production, dissemination and weaponization, the processes and politics involved, and the end results. It will also examine where wider 'online othering' and the far-right intersect in terms of radicalization or 'red pilling'. In particular, the chapter will examine the history of the American far-right's use of the Internet with respect to: (1) how this history developed in response to political changes and emerging technologies; (2) how it reflected and changed the status of such movements and their brand of hate; and (3) the relationship between online activity and traditional forms and methods of communication.

A New Era and a New Technology

The story of the modern far-right which introduced the movement to and eventually operationalized the Internet began in the post-civil rights era: the late 1970s and early 1980s. After a period defending legal, institutional white supremacy, often through harassment, intimidation and violence, the Klan was faced with not only the passing of the Civil Rights Act in 1964, but investigation by the FBI's counterintelligence programme COINTELPRO and government hearings into the *Activities of the Ku Klux Klan in the United States*, which declared the organization 'un-American' (Winter 2018).

These developments pushed the once mainstream Klan into the margins and political wilderness. In response, new strategies emerged in the 1970s and 1980s, including former Grand Wizard of the Klan David Duke's attempt to 'mainstream' and run for elected office, including for president. Perhaps the most significant strategic path was taken by more radical Klansmen, Patriots, neo-Nazis and Christian Identity adherents, such as Aryan Nations, in what has been termed the 5th era. They rejected the mainstream, underwent paramilitarization and advocated armed insurgency and white separatism. Many retreated, going off-grid and online. Corresponding to their politics and conspiracy theories, they viewed the Internet as free from government and Jewish control.

> The 5th era began when former Texas Klansman and Aryan Nations ambassador and strategist Louis Beam Jr. issued his call to arms in the *Inter-Klan Newsletter & Survival Alert*: 'where ballots fail, bullets will prevail' (Ridgeway 1990: 87). It was also in this traditional printed publication, in the Spring 1984 issue, that Beam announced Aryan Nations Liberty Net, cited as the first white supremacist online system and bulletin board (Berlet 2008).

In the article 'Computers and the American Patriot', Beam wrote: 'American know-how has provided the technology which will allow those who love this country to save it from an ill-deserved fate' (Berlet 2008). In a subsequent article titled, 'Announcing Aryan Nations/Ku Klux Klan Computer Net', he announced a 'special electronic code access available only to Aryan Nations/Ku Klux Klan officers and selected individuals' (Berlet 2008). In August 1984, a flyer circulated in Canada announced remote access to material banned under Canadian law through Aryan Liberty Net.

It has also been claimed that it was George P. Dietz who launched his Info. International Network or Liberty Bell Net before Beam, earlier in 1984 (Berlet 2008). Dietz claimed it was '[t]he only computer bulletin board system and uncontrolled information medium in the United States of America dedicated to the dissemination of historical facts–not fiction!' (Berlet 2008). Dietz had been mailing printed neo-Nazi publications throughout the USA and to Europe where much of it was banned, and the BBS system was seen as a way around postal security. The early text on Dietz's BBS, run on an Apple][e., consisted of articles from his monthly *Liberty Bell* magazine, published in print form from 1973 (Berlet 2008).

The year after Beam and Dietz set their systems up, former Klansman Tom Metzger, who founded and led White Aryan Resistance (WAR), announced the WAR Computer Terminal, which ran on a Commodore 64 with a 300 bps modem in *War '85*, his printed newspaper (Berlet 2008). According to Metzger: 'Already White Aryan comrades of the North have destroyed the free speech blackout to our Canadian comrades' (Berlet 2008). He also provided a forum for racist video games such as 'Drive by 2' and 'Border Patrol' and ran listserv@resist.cpm (Daniels 2009), and established The Insurgent network, which followed the trend of devolving responsibility and authority to individual activists, much as Beam would with his Leaderless Resistance strategy (Winter 2011a). According to Metzger, the Insurgent was 'a NETWORK of highly motivated White Racists. Each person is an individual leader in his or her own right. THE INSURGENT promotes the Lone-Wolf tactical concept' (Daniels 2009: 103). Each Insurgent associate was expected to post a message online directed at 'any Aryan patriot in America' to arrange for local cable access channel broadcast of Metzger's new cable TV programme The World as We See It, later named Race and Reason (Daniels 2009: 101). He also ran call-in telephone hot lines, including the WAR Hotline with recorded messages containing racist material (Berlet 2008). This was not a technological revolution but entrepreneurship and expansion of platforms and opportunities for recruitment and exposure that also included appearances on TV talk shows, most notably *Geraldo*.

The groups that dominated the era were Aryan Nations, led by Richard Butler and including Beam as a member, and National Alliance, led by William Pierce. Despite Beam's bulletin board, Aryan Nations disseminated its message primarily through its magazine *Calling Our Nation*, *Aryan Nations Newsletter* and prison newsletter *The Way*, as well as their annual

> Aryan World Congress (Winter 2011a). It was at the 1983 Congress that The Order was formed and began its two-year wave of terror, including the murder of Jewish talk radio host Alan Berg in 1984 (Winter 2011b). The National Alliance produced the printed *National Vanguard* and Pierce wrote the books *The Turner Diaries* and *Hunter*, the former of which inspired The Order and Oklahoma City bomber Timothy McVeigh in 1995. In the 5th era, it was written material and physical meetings which played a more significant role.

The Far-Right Get a Website

The first far-right website was Stormfront, created by former Alabama Klansman Don Black in 1995. He set it up after learning IT in prison while serving time for plotting to overthrow a Caribbean island (Berlet 2008). The name Stormfront was chosen for its connotations of a political or military front, and reference to Nazi stormtroopers, the Sturmabteilung or SA, as well as an analogy to a destructive, but cleansing weather front according to the Southern Poverty Law Center (SPLC). The motto was 'White Pride Worldwide', articulating the notion of translocal or global whiteness noted by Back, Keith and Solomos (1998), Daniels (2009) and Perry and Scrivens (2016). According to Black: '[o]ur mission is to provide information not available in the controlled news media ['Jews media'] and to build a community of White activists working for the survival of our people' (Perry and Scrivens 2016).

Other far-right groups and activists were also developing websites at this time, such as Ed Fields of the National States Rights Party (NSRP) who published *Truth at Last* and Thom Robb of the Klan who published *The Torch*, as well as owning kkk.com and kkk.biz. Yet, these were one-way transfers of information where text was uploaded and viewed like traditional printed ephemera, termed 'cut and paste brochures' (Daniels 2009). Stormfront was a larger more interactive, participatory forum for white nationalists. Building on the bulletin boards for its discussion message board, Stormfront users could post, read and respond to opinions, articles, news and events, and engage with each other.

In their 2012 study of Stormfront, Caren, Jowers and Gaby noted that the white supremacist movement relies on the Internet's elimination of spatial boundaries to 'draw in otherwise isolated movement participants'. This results in what McKenna and Bargh refer to as 'demarginalization' (cited in King and Leonard 2014: 259), socially, politically and geographically, allowing for the creation of a virtual white supremacist community (De Koster and Houtman 2008; Bowman-Grieve 2009), as opposed to a traditional organization dependant on formal recruitment. In her analysis of the development and potential of Stormfront's online recruitment, Daniels (2009) differentiates between active (create content and community) and passive (read only) participants. Under active, there are: active creators, innovators, early adapters, active sustaining members, active supporting members and active oppositional members. Under passive, there are: passive supportive lurkers, passive curiosity seeking lurkers and passive oppositional lurkers. In terms of its geography, Stormfront featured in chat rooms in Australia, Belgium, Britain, Canada, France, Germany, Hungary, Italy, Netherlands, South Africa and Switzerland (Daniels 2009).

In the mid-1990s, Milton Kleim Jr., who was affiliated with National Alliance, authored the 'National Socialism Primer' and created the Usenet newsgroup, rec.music.white-power, published 'On Tactics and Strategy for USENET' on the Aryan Crusader Library Web and Aryan Network. In it, he argued:

> USENET offers enormous opportunity for the Aryan Resistance to disseminate our message to the unaware and the ignorant. It is the only relatively uncensored (so far) free-forum mass medium which we have available. (Back et al. 1998: 78)

Kleim's strategy also included a call for 'cyber guerrillas', an online version of lone wolves and Leaderless Resistance, to 'move out beyond our present domain, and take up positions on "mainstream" groups' (Back et al. 1998: 79). Kleim included a list of user groups to do this through: alt.politics.nationalism.white, alt.politics.white-power, alt.revolution.counter, alt.skinheads and alt.revisionism (Back et al. 1998).

Internet use by the far-right increased substantially in the early 2000s and the USA came to dominate the scene. In 2003, the Council of Europe noted that the majority of hate sites were American with 2500 out of 4000 being US-based (Daniels 2009). Increased far-right online activity and mobilization were partly due to advances in technology, increased use, the normalization of the Internet, new actors on the scene and new strategies. The far-right online community initiative expanded from 2002 to 2003 with Jamie Kelso joining Stormfront and the emergence of Web 2.0 technology (Daniels 2009). Kelso attempted to increase its profile and ideological range, and with Black, asserted a relatively non-sectarian stance. They invited participants to post and recruited established writers from traditional publishing, including Sam Dickson of the Council of Conservative Citizens and Willis Carto of the Holocaust-denial journal, *The Barnes Review* (Southern Poverty Law Center NDb). Duke also started participating that year, joining Thom Robb and others (Daniels 2009). Stormfront also developed a 'Ladies Forum' (Daniels 2009: 72). As Black told the Newhouse News Service: 'Anyone can work to promote our ideas without being a member of any organization. I used to be annoyed by people who didn't join my organization, but I see the advantage now' (Southern Poverty Law Center NDb).

In 2001, *USA Today* called Stormfront 'the most visited white supremacist site on the net' (Southern Poverty Law Center NDb). At the same time, other groups were starting to utilize the Internet. World Church of the Creator (WCOTC) (operating under different variations of the name), founded by Ben Klassen and later led by Matt Hale (who took over upon Klassen's death and had global aspirations and an interest in the potential of the Internet), registered numerous domains such as rahowa.com and wcotc.com (Daniels 2009). Hale established a website and a web page for children (WTOTC Kids!) although he later admitted that it was a publicity stunt to generate media attention (Anti-Defamation League 2013). They lost the website in 2002 in a copyright infringement lawsuit (Southern Poverty Law Center NDa). By 2003, Stormfront saw membership reach 11,000 and by 2008 membership included over 133,000 registered users, although only approximately 20,000 were known to be active posters (Southern Poverty Law Center NDb). The growth of Stormfront and the far-right Internet followed the wider growth and popularization of the Internet and events around which the far-right mobilized, including 9/11 and the elections of Barack Obama and Donald Trump.

Between 9/11 and a Black President

The terrorist attacks on 9/11 resulted in a boom in both Internet conspiracy theories, most notably Alex Jones' InfoWars, and, for a far-right in decline, an opportunity to get in on the action, including most notably the organization Aryan Nations. The organization had lost its dominant position following a SPLC lawsuit that resulted in them losing their compound, in addition to leadership struggles. With founder Richard Butler in ill health at the time of 9/11, a breakaway faction called Aryan Nations/Posse Comitatus led by former webmaster August Kreis attempted to grab the momentum by trying to establish an alliance with Al-Qaeda. Kreis posted: 'Why Islam Is Our Ally' and, in the lead-up to the invasion of Iraq, issued an online call for volunteers (Southern Poverty Law Center 2001). While this has been used to show that an alliance was possible or building, it came only from the far-right and nothing resulted from it (Winter 2014).

In 2008, Obama's election led to an increase in far-right activism, recruitment and online activity (Anti-Defamation League 2009; Holthouse 2009; US Department of Homeland Security 2009). According to Don Black, 2000 people joined Stormfront the day after the election, which was central to its growth during this period. David Duke referred to Obama as a 'visual aid' that helped attract interest and recruits, claiming that his website saw traffic by 'unique users' increase from 15,000 to 40,000 a day (Winter 2018). In 2010, Stormfront introduced the more traditional forums of Stormfront Radio and annual Smoky Mountain Summit near Knoxville, Tennessee, similar to what WAR and Aryan Nations did in the 1980s. By its 20th anniversary in 2015, Stormfront claimed 300,000 members (Southern Poverty Law Center NDb). In the light of increased attention and controversies,

Stormfront introduced guidelines in which members were warned not to use profanity or 'racial epithets', and not to post violent threats or describe illegal activity. Emojis of beer steins replaced swastikas (Southern Poverty Law Center NDb).

In the past number of years, we have seen a significant growth in the role of the Internet, particularly social media, in far-right politics, attributable to both new technologies and platforms and Trump, as well as the backlash that brought them together. Trump's racist, nativist, white nationalist rhetoric online and offline simultaneously attracted the far-right, many of whom, including Duke, Black and Stormfront, endorsed him (Winter 2018), and allowed for the legitimization and normalization of some of their ideas (Mondon and Winter 2018). Key to this was the emergence of a social media savvy Alt-Right, who were able to spread their ideas more diffusely and penetrate the mainstream using social media, and new platforms, in ways that traditional exclusive far-right forums could not.

Social Media Gateway

In their 2008 report *Online Terror + Hate: The First Decade*, the Simon Wiesenthal Center (SWC) analysed the use of Web 2.0 technologies by the far-right, pioneered by Stormfront, noting that it allowed for faster, as well as wider, more global, uploading, dissemination, sharing and participatory engagement with ideas and material that could help them engage with youth cultures and recruit. This was backed up by research from the International Network Against Cyberhate (INACH) (King and Leonard 2014). As Daniels (2009) and Simi and Futrell (2010) argue, Web 2.0 allows for the creation of a virtual community, but with the emergence and popularization of social media, its potential and reach extend beyond what Stormfront had developed. It allows for 'demarginalization', compensating for the lack of 'critical mass in their own locale' (Simi and Futrell 2010: 97), but unlike traditional exclusive far-right sites, social media allows the far-right to access and attract a wider, non-affiliated, white (predominantly male) population.

According to the SWC, the far-right has increased its use of and activity on social media, including Facebook, as well as Second Life, YouTube, forums and blogs. They report that in 2014–2015, there was a spike from 1500 to 11,500 in social networks, websites, forums and blogs promoting anti-Semitism, homophobia, hate music, terrorism and wider violence. While, previously, the growth area for the far-right 'white nationalists' and their online presence was traditional websites, in this period, it was almost entirely in social networking (King and Leonard 2014: 137–138). Between 2012 and 2016, according to a report by George Washington University's Program on Extremism, there was a 600% increase in followers of American white nationalist movements on Twitter alone (Reitman 2018). The SPLC noted the emergence of Facebook groups representing known hate groups: Aryan Nations, European Americans United, American Renaissance and League of the South (King and Leonard 2014). In his manifesto, Anders Breivik, who killed eight people in a bombing in Oslo and 69 people in a gun attack at a Workers' Youth League (AUF) camp on Utøya in Norway on 22 July 2011, wrote about the function and potential of Facebook:

> I spent thousands of hours doing this over a duration of more than 6 months (from 2 Facebook accounts) and I, alone, managed to send the compendium to more than 8000 dedicated nationalists this way. If only 100 of these 8000 heed the call we will be able to send the compendium to 800,000 nationalists. (King and Leonard 2014: 135–136)

The SPLC also noted the emergence of new social networking sites devoted to white supremacism and nationalism, more targeted than generic social media but more modern and youthful than Stormfront, such as Dylan Wheller's Folkscom.com, which was founded in 2005 and attracted 2000 members before closing the same year. The following year, Todd Findley founded the National Socialist Movement affiliated NewSaxon.org. There was also Nazi Space ('White Powered') and Aryan Space, which explained its rationale: 'The reason why we established Aryan Space is very simple, there are many social networks for Moslems, Blacks, Asians etc., but I was unable to find any for Aryans' (King and Leonard 2014: 156).

In addition to such technology contributing to a sense of a global white nationalist community, operating in general online spaces can invite crackdowns on the presence of hate groups and hate speech, such as Facebook bans. This, as Daniels (2009) points out, can aid the sense of community by reaffirming narratives of persecution or victimization that made people vulnerable to the far-right and which fuels their politics and recruitment. The combination of the creation of a community of white—and male—victimization and the ability to bring into it a broad base is a key to understand the success of Trump (an avid Twitter user, who has retweeted the far-right on occasion) and the growth and mainstream penetration of the far-right, most notably the Alt-Right, and its ideas.

The Alt-Right

The Alt-Right is a phenomenon that has become familiar to many in the wake of Trump's campaign and election, having put the far-right in the mainstream public consciousness and mobilized the Internet. The SPLC defines it as 'a set of far-right ideologies, groups and individuals whose core belief is that "white identity" is under attack by multicultural forces using "political correctness" and "social justice" to undermine white people and "their" civilization' (Southern Poverty Law Center NDc). It is known for its use of social media, trolling, online memes such as #whitegenocide and Pepe the Frog, the rejection of establishment conservatism, edginess, youth orientation, white identitarianism and white nationalism (Southern Poverty Law Center NDc).

The term 'Alt-Right', based on 'Alternative Right', was coined in 2008 by Richard Spencer, a Trump supporter who was an editor of *The American Conservative* and *Taki's Magazine*, executive director of Washington Summit Publishers, founder of *Radix Journal* and heads the white nationalist think tank National Policy Institute, to describe a new movement organized around white identity and Western civilization. Spencer launched the movement in 2010 with the establishment of the Alternative Right blog, where he worked to develop the movement's ideological tenets. Other high-profile proponents include Greg Johnson of the publishing house Counter-Currents, Jared Taylor of the journal *American Renaissance* and Matthew Heimbach of the neo-Nazi Traditionalist Youth Network (TYN) (Southern Poverty Law Center NDc).

Two websites and virtual communities are the preeminent propaganda machines for the Alt-Right according to the SPLC, The Daily Stormer and The Right Stuff (TRS) (Hatewatch 2018b). The Daily Stormer is a neo-Nazi and white supremacist site founded in 2013 and edited by Anglin, replacing his previous website Total Fascism, and hosted by GoDaddy. It was named after the Nazi paper, *Der Sturmer,* and is known for its memes and troll army (Hatewatch 2018a). Anglin was also claimed to have mentioned (like WCOTC before him) the targeting of children for indoctrination (Hatewatch 2018a). TRS is an online forum established by Mike 'Enoch' Peinovich. It started as a political blog in 2012 and has since transformed into one of the largest Alt-Right media platforms, hosting a message board called the 504um and dozens of podcasts (Hatewatch 2018b).

Alt-Right is a contested term for the ways it obscures its racist white nationalism, white supremacism and fascism, and makes it appear different from the traditional far-right. Yet, what is particularly significant about the Alt-Right is its ability to appear new and edgy, and appeal to youth culture and the fact that one ideology or organizational form does not prevail. According to George Hawley in *Making Sense of the Alt-Right*, in contrast to previous far-right movements, the Alt-Right exists predominantly on social media (Hawley 2017). According to Anglin who argued: '[t]he movement (AR) is, at this point, entirely leaderless. The people involved in contributing to and/or consuming the content are on different Alt-Right sites and forums, many are on Twitter, Reddit, 4chan etc.' (Hawley 2017: 70). The general population of the Alt-Right is composed of relatively anonymous youths who were exposed to the movement's ideas through online message boards and discussion threads like 4chan and 8chan's /pol/ and more mainstream Internet platforms like Reddit, Facebook, Twitter and YouTube.

While it is known for its focus on fun, irony, irreverence and edginess, for those who would not associate with Klan or NSM

(Hawley 2017), the Daily Stormer is clearly fascist. Others attempt to bring these together, as demonstrated by the TRS's Fash the Nation (a reference to Face the Nation) and Daily Shoah (a reference to The Daily Show) podcasts. Other popular 'ironic' fascist references and memes include Adolf Hitler holding a PlayStation controller and anime characters such as 'Nazi Ponies', which was a Tumblr blog, a Twitter feed and a series of YouTube videos (Reitman 2018).

According to Keegan Hankes of the SPLC: 'If you make racism or anti-Semitism funny, you can subvert the cultural taboo. Make people laugh at the Holocaust – you've opened a space in which history and fact become worthless, period' (Reitman 2018). This, and its anonymity, permits people to make unacceptable and even extreme comments, often moving from a discussion thread or Facebook group to more extreme forums and websites. This is a universe made up, as Mike Wendling argues, of racialists, intellectuals, channers, meninists, neo-Nazis, conspiracy theorists and the violent fringe (Wendling 2018), as well as Men's Rights Activists (MRAs) (see also Lumsden, this volume). The less top-down, active and uniform route into the Alt-Right and fascism is linked to 'red pilling' or being red pilled, a term derived from The Matrix where taking a red pill allows one to see reality. In this context, it refers to the liberation of men from a life of delusion, particularly feminist delusion (Ging 2017), in line with the conspiracy culture of the far-right and the Internet, where the passive lurker is welcomed at various levels and radicalization can occur as an individual becomes enculturated in an extreme, reactionary worldview (Ganesh 2018; Hawley 2017). It is about opening the 'Overton window', expanding the range of acceptable options and ideas on offer that can be seen as acceptable and be accepted (Wendling 2018: 91).

The Alt-Lite, Mainstream and 'Red Pilling'

According to research by the SPLC, the pathway to the Alt-Right is not singular. There are a range of platforms, individuals, organizations and movements, such as the so-called Alt-Lite, that populate the reactionary right-wing backlash which sees at its extreme end, the Alt-Right and fascism.

In their study of pathways to the Alt-Right, the SPLC examines how people ended up at Daily Stormer and TRS, and what 'stepping stones' and 'in-betweeners' they engaged with and were influenced by Hatewatch (2018b). In the SPLC and wider scholarly research, 4chan and 'chan culture' are identified as a significant factor in the rise of both the far-right and 'radicalization'. Nearly 23% of respondents to the SPLC study said that chan culture helped them land at TRS (Hatewatch 2018b). The main factor is the 'politically incorrect' 4chan /pol/ message board that is anonymous, traffics in humour and transgression, and operates away from mainstream scrutiny (Wendling 2018), which has nurtured the early Alt-Right and, especially, its misogyny and racism (Reitman 2018). In 'All-American Nazis', Janet Reitman notes how 4chan's 'veil of obscurity' was used to incubate white nationalism. Discussion threads on white supremacist sites 'considered how /pol/ might be used to help young people become "racially aware" in an example of red pilling' (Reitman 2018). Alongside /pol/, Reddit was another crucial space in the growth of the Alt-Right, particularly the subreddit r/The_Donald, that arose in support of Donald Trump's presidency (Hatewatch 2018b). According to the SPLC, YouTube's algorithm, which determines what will autoplay or be recommended after one video has finished, also plays a role in bringing viewers into the 'deeper depths of the alt-right' by presenting them with escalating extreme content (Hatewatch 2018b).

In many cases, particular individuals and organizations are identified, as well as their online platforms, such as the more mainstream YouTube, The Rebel Media based in Canada, and *Breitbart* which was co-founded and run by former Trump advisor Steve Bannon. TRS 504um forum posters describe their radicalization as a 'gradual process', with Alt-Lite personalities like Canadian Gavin McInnes, founder of the Proud Boys, Vice Media and *Vice Magazine*, as well as a contributor to *Taki's Magazine* and The Rebel Media, and introducing them to ideas about race, Islam, women and political correctness. Such social media figures (as well as lighter and more extreme ones) often present themselves and their ideas as a radical alternative and challenge to mainstream politically correct media and public opinion, and those who have accepted it, termed 'normies'. In this sense, they provide both rebellion and access to 'reality' for followers. One TRS 504um poster cited Stefan Molyneux, a Canadian 'Race Realist' anti-feminist YouTube vlogger and lecturer who has over 770,000 subscribers and 230 million views of his videos, as 'a great stepping stone between the Alt-Lite and the Alt-Right'. Other Alt-Lite personalities include Lauren Southern, also Canadian and a former contributor to Rebel Media. Over 12% of TRS 504um users cited former *Breitbart* tech editor, anti-feminist, Islamophobic and 'free speech' activist Milo Yiannopoulos as a factor in the escalation of their journey to the Alt-Right (Hatewatch 2018b).

Yiannopoulos was important as a central figure in the popularization of the Alt-Right, a popular representative of the Alt-Lite and a bridge between them and the mainstream. This is due to his role in Gamergate, which is alleged to have unleashed the Alt-Right, Alt-Lite and wider backlash, and where he made his name, and his position at *Breitbart*. In August 2014, a harassment campaign targeted several women in the video game industry, including developers Zoë Quinn and Brianna Wu, as well as feminist media critic Anita Sarkeesian who was, with others, critical of sexism and racism in games and gamer culture (Hawley 2017). #GamerGate hashtag users represented a backlash against such criticism and progressive politics in gamer culture. They also accused Quinn of an unethical, sexual, relationship with journalist Nathan Grayson in exchange for positive reviews. Gamergate supporters organized anonymously or pseudonymously on online platforms such as 4chan, Internet Relay Chat, Twitter and Reddit. After 4chan's founder Christopher Poole banned discussions of Gamergate from the site, the campaign's supporters migrated to the more extreme 8chan (Southern Poverty Law Center NDc). While racism is central to the Alt-Right, misogyny was always a significant factor in entry into the universe and being red pilled, which is itself an anti-feminist, MRA term (see also Lumsden, this volume). According to Debbie Ging (2017: 1): 'Since the emergence of Web 2.0 and social media, a particularly toxic brand of antifeminism has become evident across a range of online networks and platforms'. She argues that the technological affordances of social media are especially well suited to the amplification of new articulations of aggrieved manhood. It can be expressed and fed through the wide network of blogs, forums and websites termed the 'manosphere'. Red pilling allows for the movement of the aggrieved and MRAs into the world of the more extreme Incel movement and white nationalism (Ging 2017). Yiannopoulos became famous by supporting critics and white male game culture through his writing and media appearances (Hawley 2017). He was joined by Trump supporter Ricky Vaughn, a white nationalist who trolled in support of Trump during the election, and Michael Cernovich (O'Brian 2017). Yiannopoulos would later engage in other campaigns focusing on media and popular culture, most notably against the female *Ghostbusters* reboot, which included the racist trolling of Lesley Jones, leading to him and Vaughn being banned from Twitter (Hawley 2017).

Following Gamergate, Yiannopoulos appeared in the mainstream media, was appointed editor at *Breitbart* and joined a growing group of controversial(ist) liberal, libertarian and conservative online commentators and public 'intellectuals' who represent themselves as exiles from and free speech rebels against mainstream politically correct or 'PC' culture for their opposition to anti-racism, feminism, transgender rights, identity politics and the left. They include authors, YouTube vloggers and podcasters, such as Joe Rogan, Sargon of Akkad, Sam Harris, Ben Shapiro, Dave Rubin and Christina Hoff Sommers, as well as academics Bret and Eric Weinstein and Jordan Peterson, some of whom would later become known as part of the 'Intellectual Dark Web' (Weiss 2018). At the same time as occupying an increasingly mainstream position, Yiannopoulos wrote a primer on the Alt-Right, appeared with Richard Spencer, solicited advice from Daily Stormer system administrator Andrew 'Weev' Auernheimer and with *Breitbart*, promoted, provided a platform for, and mainstreamed the Alt-Right and their ideas (Bernstein 2017). This period of mainstream popularity and influence for Yiannopoulos ended in 2017 when he was revealed to have made pro-paedophilia comments, leading to *Breitbart* firing him and widespread rejection by media outlets, online platforms, fellow commentators and activists.

Online to Offline and a Crackdown

What happens online can have an impact in the offline world. Trump's election, which was also promoted by Yiannopoulos, Bannon and *Breitbart*, is one case in point, and violence is another. The Unite the

Right rally in Charlottesville on 12 August 2017 was organized by Alt-Right webmaster Jason Kessler and attended by Richard Spencer, David Duke, the Klan, League of the South, Fraternal Order of Alt-Knights, Daily Stormer clubs, Traditionalist Worker Party, Vanguard America, Identity Evropa and others, in defence of the statue of Confederate General Robert E. Lee in Emancipation Park, and as an attempt to unite and show the strength of the far-right (Winter 2017). It exposed the movement's fascism and brought them from behind computer screens onto the streets, demonstrating that online hate can coexist with old fashion tactics such as rallies and violence. The latter was demonstrated by the murder of counter-protester Heather Heyer by James A. Fields of Vanguard America and the attack on DeAndre Harris by Jacob Goodwin, affiliated with the far-right ShieldWall Network, and others.

Since the election, there has been a rise in hate crimes, racist violence and vandalism in the USA (Hatewatch 2016; Winter 2018), as well as more localized offline examples of far-right activity such as flyering and flyposting. Greg Johnson of the website Counter-Currents spoke about the benefits of gaining media coverage through flyering and flyposting as a 'valuable form of asymmetrical cultural warfare' (Schwencke 2017). It also allows the far-right to target and stoke fear in communities directly and intimately in ways that the Internet does not allow for. Since September 2016, white supremacist groups have covered university campuses with fliers 118 times, according to the Anti-Defamation League (ADL) (Schwencke 2017). In addition to flyering and flyposting, universities have also seen public speeches by Alt-Right and Alt-Lite figures such as Spencer, McInnis, Yiannopoulos and others (Hawley 2017). Universities have become significant offline spaces for such far-right and more mainstream right-wing activism because they are seen as the front line in the fight for Western civilization and free speech against the left, identity politics, political correctness, anti-racism, feminism and LGBTQ rights, and so-called social justice warriors (SJWs).

In terms of online far-right hate being linked to violence, prior to Charlottesville registered Stormfront users have been disproportionately responsible for some of the most lethal hate crimes and mass killings (Southern Poverty Law Center 2014). Between 1999 and 2014, they murdered nearly 100 people, 77 of whom were massacred by Breivik

(Southern Poverty Law Center 2014). Other examples of online-related violence include the case of Dylann Roof. On 17 June 2015, Roof launched an armed attack on black worshippers at the Emanuel African Methodist Episcopal Church in Charleston, South Carolina. As he wrote in his manifesto, the Trayvon Martin killing 'prompted me to type in the words "black on white crime" into Google, and I have never been the same since that day' (Hatewatch 2018c). His search led him to the website of the Council of Conservative Citizens which documented an alleged war against whites being waged by violent black people (Hatewatch 2018c). In another example, the neo-Nazi group Atomwaffen Division combined online activity on IronMarch.org, where they announced their formation, 4chan, Daily Stormer, Discord, Twitter and YouTube, with offline tactics, such as flyposting on university campuses, and violence (Reitman 2018). This included combat training, hate attacks and terrorist plots (Reitman 2018). On Friday 19 May 2017, member Devon Arthurs shot his roommates and fellow members Andrew Oneschuk and Jeremy Himmelman in Florida. They met online and used 4chan. In another case, Brandon Russell, also a roommate of Arthurs and active blogger, was arrested and convicted for possessing explosives in 2017–2018. The same year, member Samuel Woodward, was arrested and charged for the killing of a gay Jewish student Blaze Bernstein in California (Reitman 2018).[1]

In response to the violence at the Unite the Right rally, a number of prominent tech companies decided, under pressure, to enforce existing 'acceptable use' policies and take action against groups that participated in the rally. As the SPLC (2018) stated, it took 'blood in the streets for tech companies to take action'. Yet, they argue that still 'some of the biggest tech companies keep hate group sites up and running', noting that PayPal, Bitcoin, Stripe, Network Solutions and others continue to provide services to designated hate groups (Southern Poverty Law Center 2018).[2]

Cases where there have been crackdowns include Twitter enforcing new policies to combat hate speech, abusive behaviour and particularly violence, leading to the suspension of accounts associated with white nationalism and banning groups 'that use or promote violence against civilians to further their causes' (Neidig 2017). GoDaddy pulled Richard Spencer's 'altright' website, and he was banned from Facebook (Broderick 2018). Despite this, Facebook parsed white reactionary ideologies, banning white supremacists, but allowing white nationalists and separatists (Kozlowska 2018), ignoring how these are related as racist ideologies, and that the latter two are used as part of the spin and softer appeal of the Alt-Right. The Daily Stormer found itself in digital exile after Anglin wrote an article mocking Heather Heyer, which led GoDaddy, Google, Namecheap and Cloudflare to cancel Daily Stormer's service (Lavin 2018). In response to the social media crackdown, there was a migration of far-right groups and racist content to Google+, although a Google spokesperson asserted their dedication 'to keeping violent content and hate speech off our platforms' (Cuthbertson 2018). Fearing a crackdown, YouTube vloggers Southern, Molyneux and others moved to BitChute and cross-posted videos, while others moved to Gab (Daro and Lytvynenko 2018), set up in 2016 by Andrew Torba as a right-wing 'free speech' alternative to Twitter. Gab came under scrutiny and pressure though in October 2018 following the anti-Semitic attack at the Tree of Synagogue in Pittsburgh, Pennsylvania, which left 11 dead and others injured, by Robert Bowers, who had been active on the platform (BBC 2018).

However, the focus has primarily been on the role and responsibility of the private sector. While important, placing regulatory power in the hands of corporations is problematic. It depends on their fear of market and profit losses, leads to inconsistency and promotes unaccountability. Government action, although problematic and potentially repressive, is not forthcoming. Trump not only failed to condemn the far-right following Charlottesville, but blamed 'many sides', referring to Antifa and other counter-protestors (Winter 2017). Furthermore, Homeland Security has targeted Antifa as a threat (Pasha-Robinson 2017). Anti-fascist activists have also been opposing the far-right online. Notable examples include the anarchist, anti-fascist online community and network It's Going Down, We Hunted the Mammoth, which 'tracks and mocks the white male rage underlying the rise of Trump and Trumpism' (We Hunted The Mammoth 2018), and Whack-a-Mole, a set of data mining programs that monitor 400,000 accounts of white nationalists on Facebook and other websites and feeds into a centralized database (Clark 2018). Anti-fascist and anti-racist activists also use 'doxxing', the tactic of releasing documents and data belonging to far-right activists online, to expose them, something the Alt-Right also engages in against targets and opponents

(Hawley 2017). In addition to such online activism, there are also non-governmental organizations (NGOs) who monitor and combat the far-right online and offline, such as the ADL, SPLC, SWC, Political Research Associates (PRA) and Hope Not Hate. It is an ongoing challenge in a context where the far-right and online hate adapt to opposition and obstacles.

Conclusion

This chapter examined the history, development and contemporary manifestations of the American far-right online in relation to political and technological change, the changing status of the far-right and its brand of hate, and traditional forms and methods of communication. It sought to add a movement focused perspective to the analysis of wider 'online othering' in this collection and both online and offline othering, particularly racism and sexism, more widely, including in mainstream politics and culture, and to demonstrate the link between these.

Notes

1. The relationship between online hate and violence is not limited to the far-right. According to Müller and Schwarz (2016), Trump's anti-Muslim tweets have been a reliable predictor of the level of attacks against Muslims.
2. According to Ebner (2018), unregulated digital cryptocurrencies such as Bitcoin appeal to and have helped fund the far-right.

References

Anti-Defamation League. (2009). *Rage grows in America: Anti-government conspiracies*. http://www.adl.org/special_reports/rage-grows-in-america/default.asp. Accessed November 23, 2009.

Anti-Defamation League. (2013). *Matt Hale*. https://www.adl.org/sites/default/files/documents/assets/pdf/combating-hate/Hale-Matt-EIA.pdf. Accessed June 22, 2018.

Back, L., Keith, M., & Solomos, J. (1998). Racism on the internet: Mapping neo-fascist subcultures in cyberspace. In J. Kaplan & T. Bjorgo (Eds.), *Nation and Race: The Developing Euro-American Racist Subculture* (pp. 73–101). Boston: Northeastern University Press.
BBC. (2018, October 28). Pittsburgh shooting: What we know so far. *BBC*. https://www.bbc.co.uk/news/world-uscanada-46003665. Accessed December 20, 2018.
Berlet, C. (2008). *When hate went online.* http://www.researchforprogress.us/topic/34691/when-hate-went-online/. Accessed April 14, 2017.
Bernstein, J. (2017, October 5). Here's how Breitbart and Milo smuggled white nationalism into the mainstream. *Buzzfeed*. https://www.buzzfeed-news.com/article/josephbernstein/heres-how-breitbart-and-milo-smuggled-white-nationalism. Accessed July 20, 2018.
Bowman-Grieve, L. (2009). Exploring 'Stormfront': A virtual community of the radical right. *Studies in Conflict & Terrorism, 32*(11), 989–1007.
Broderick, R. (2018, May 3). Richard Spencer's website has been pulled offline by GoDaddy. *Buzzfeed*. https://www.buzzfeed.com/ryanhatesthis/richard-spencers-website-has-been-pulled-offline-by-godaddy?utm_term=.ftEk7w-7MNA#.hhenY2Yxq3. Accessed May 4, 2018.
Clark, D. B. (2018, January 16). Meet Antifa's secret weapon against far-right extremists. *Wired*. https://www.wired.com/story/free-speech-issue-antifa-data-mining/. Accessed June 20, 2018.
Cuthbertson, A. (2018, June 15). Nazis and other extremists appear to be migrating to Google Plus after a crackdown from other social networks. *The Independent*. https://www.independent.co.uk/life-style/gadgets-and-tech/news/nazi-google-plus-facebook-twitter-white-supremacist-extremist-groups-a8401156.html. Accessed June 20, 2018.
Daniels, J. (2009). *Cyber Racism: White Supremacy Online and the New Attack on Civil Rights*. Lanham: Rowman & Littlefield.
Daro, I. N., & Lytvynenko, J. (2018, April 18). Right-wing YouTubers think it's only a matter of time before they get kicked off the site. *Buzzfeed*. https://www.buzzfeed.com/ishmaeldaro/right-wing-youtube-alternative-platforms?utm_term=.tq5AqdqEVj#.ngj6rxr97M. Accessed June 20, 2018.
De Koster, W., & Houtman, D. (2008). 'Stormfront is like a second home to me': On virtual community formation by right-wing extremists. *Information, Communication & Society, 11*(8), 1155–1176.
Ebner, J. (2018, January 24). The currency of the far-right: Why neo-Nazis love bitcoin. *The Guardian*. https://www.theguardian.com/commentisfree/2018/jan/24/bitcoin-currency-far-right-neo-nazis-cryptocurrencies. Accessed August 18, 2018.

Ganesh, B. (2018, June 7). What the red pill means for radicals. *Fair Observer*. https://www.fairobserver.com/world-news/incels-alt-right-manosphere-extremism-radicalism-news-51421/. Accessed June 20, 2018.

Garcia-Favaro, L., & Gill, R. (2016). 'Emasculation nation has arrived': Sexism rearticulated in online responses to Lose the Lads' Mags campaign. *Feminist Media Studies, 16*(3), 379–397.

Ging, D. (2017). Alphas, betas, and incels: Theorizing the masculinities of the manosphere. *Men and Masculinities*, iFirst. https://doi.org/10.1177/1097184X17706401.

Hatewatch. (2016, December 16). Update: 1094 bias related incidents in the month following the election. *Southern Poverty Law Center*. https://www.splcenter.org/hatewatch/2016/12/16/update-1094-bias-related-incidents-month-following-election. Accessed 1 April 2017.

Hatewatch. (2018a, January 18). Andrew Anglin brags about 'indoctrinating' children into Nazi ideology. *Southern Poverty Law Center*. https://www.splcenter.org/hatewatch/2018/01/18/andrew-anglin-brags-about-indoctrinating-children-nazi-ideology. Accessed May 15, 2018.

Hatewatch. (2018b, April 19). McInnes, Molyneux, and 4chan: Investigating pathways to the alt-right. *Southern Poverty Law Center*. https://www.splcenter.org/20180419/mcinnes-molyneux-and-4chan-investigating-pathways-alt-right. Accessed April 22, 2018.

Hatewatch. (2018c, June 14). The biggest lie in the white supremacist propaganda playbook. *Southern Poverty Law Center*. https://www.splcenter.org/20180614/biggest-lie-white-supremacist-propaganda-playbook-unraveling-truth-about-'black-white-crime. Accessed June 20, 2018.

Hawley, G. (2017). *Making Sense of the Alt-Right*. New York: Columbia University Press.

Holthouse, D. (2009). The year in hate: Number of hate groups tops 900. *Intelligence Report*. Spring. https://www.splcenter.org/intel/intelreport/article.jsp?aid=1027. Accessed October 12, 2009.

King, R. C., & Leonard, D. J. (2014). *Beyond Hate: White Power and Popular Culture*. Farnham: Ashgate.

Kozlowska, H. (2018, May 26). Facebook forbids white supremacy, but allows white separatism and nationalism. *Quartz*. https://qz.com/1290044/facebook-forbids-white-supremacy-but-allows-white-separatism-and-nationalism/. Accessed May 30, 2018.

Lavin, T. (2018, January 7). The neo-Nazis of the Daily Stormer wander the digital wilderness. *New Yorker*. https://www.newyorker.com/tech/elements/the-neo-nazis-of-the-daily-stormer-wander-the-digital-wilderness. Accessed April 22, 2018.

Lumsden, K., & Morgan, H. M. (2017). Cyber-trolling as symbolic violence: Deconstructing gendered abuse online. In N. Lombard (Ed.), *The Routledge Handbook of Gender and Violence* (pp. 121–132). London: Routledge.

Mondon, A., & Winter, A. (2017). Articulations of Islamophobia: From the extreme to the mainstream? *Ethnic and Racial Studies Review, 40*(13), 2151–2179.

Mondon, A., & Winter, A. (2018, August 26). Understanding the mainstreaming of the far-right. *openDemocracy*. https://www.opendemocracy.net/can-europe-make-it/aurelien-mondon-aaron-winter/understanding-mainstreaming-of-far-right. Accessed August 26, 2018.

Müller, K., & Schwarz, C. (2016). *Making America hate again? Twitter and hate crime under Trump*. https://papers.ssrn.com/sol3/papers.cfm?abstract_id=3149103. Accessed June 20, 2018.

Neidig, H. (2017, December 18). Twitter launches hate speech crackdown. *The Hill*. http://thehill.com/policy/technology/365424-twitter-to-begin-enforcing-new-hate-speech-rules. Accessed May 10, 2018.

Neiwert, D. (2017). *Alt-America: The Rise of the Radical Right in the Age of Trump*. London: Verso.

Noble, S. U. (2018). *Algorithms of Oppression: How Search Engines Reinforce Racism*. New York: New York University Press.

O'Brian, L. (2017, May 4). Trump's most influential white nationalist troll. *HuffPost US*. https://www.huffingtonpost.co.uk/entry/trump-white-nationalist-troll-ricky-vaughn_us_5ac53167e4b09ef3b2432627. Accessed June 15, 2018.

Pasha-Robinson, L. (2017, September 4). Antifa: US security agencies label group 'domestic terrorists'. *The Independent*. https://www.independent.co.uk/news/world/americas/antifa-domestic-terrorists-us-security-agencies-homeland-security-fbi-a7927881.html. Accessed April 20, 2018.

Perry, B., & Scrivens, R. (2016). White pride worldwide: Constructing global identities online. In J. Schweppe & M. Walters (Eds.), *The Globalisation of Hate: Internationalising Hate Crime* (pp. 65–78). New York: Oxford University Press.

Reitman, J. (2018, May 2). All-American Nazis: How a senseless double murder in Florida exposed the rise of an organized fascist youth movement in the United States. *Rolling Stone*. https://www.rollingstone.com/politics/news/all-american-nazis-fascist-youth-united-states-w519651. Accessed May 30, 2018.

Ridgeway, J. (1990). *Blood in the Face: The Ku Klux Klan, Aryan Nations, Nazi Skinheads, and the Rise of the New White Culture*. New York: Thunder's Mouth Press.

Schwencke, K. (2017, March 24). A 2-for-1 for racists: Post hateful fliers, and revel in the news coverage. *ProPublica.* https://www.propublica.org/article/a-2-for-1-for-racists-post-hateful-fliers-and-revel-in-the-news-coverage. Accessed April 22, 2018.

Scrivens, R., Davies, G., & Frank, R. (2017). Searching for signs of extremism on the web: An introduction to sentiment-based identification of radical authors. *Behavioural Sciences of Terrorism and Political Aggression, 10*(1), 39–59.

Sharma, S., & Brooker, P. (2016). #Notracist: Exploring racist denial talk on Twitter. *Digital Sociologies* (pp. 463–485). Bristol: Policy Press.

Simi, P., & Futrell, R. (2010). *American Swastika: Inside the White Power Movement's Hidden Spaces of Hate.* Lanham: Rowman & Littlefield.

Southern Poverty Law Center. (2001). Reaping the whirlwind. *Intelligence Report.* http://www.splcenter.org/intelligenceproject/ip-4t3.html. Accessed December 10, 2008.

Southern Poverty Law Center. (2014, March 31). *White homicide worldwide.* https://www.splcenter.org/20140331/white-homicide-worldwide. Accessed April 22, 2018.

Southern Poverty Law Center. (2018). *How tech supports hate.* https://www.splcenter.org/hate-and-tech. Accessed June 22, 2018.

Southern Poverty Law Center. (NDa). *Matt Hale.* https://www.splcenter.org/fighting-hate/extremist-files/individual/matt-hale. Accessed May 20, 2018.

Southern Poverty Law Center. (NDb). *Stormfront.* https://www.splcenter.org/fighting-hate/extremist-files/group/stormfront. Accessed April 10, 2017.

Southern Poverty Law Center. (NDc). *Alt-Right.* https://www.splcenter.org/fighting-hate/extremist-files/ideology/alt-right. Accessed April 10, 2017.

US Department of Homeland Security. (2009). *Rightwing extremism: Current economic and political climate fueling resurgence in radicalization and recruitment.* https://www.fas.org/irp/eprint/rightwing.pdf. Accessed March 17, 2017.

We Hunted the Mammoth. (2018). www.wehuntedthemammoth.com. Accessed April 20, 2018.

Weiss, B. (2018, May 8). Meet the renegades of the intellectual dark web. *New York Times.* https://www.nytimes.com/2018/05/08/opinion/intellectual-dark-web.html. Accessed June 10, 2018.

Wendling, M. (2018). *Alt-Right: From 4chan to the White House.* London: Pluto Press.

Winter, A. (2011a). Richard Butler. In J. I. Ross (Ed.), *Religion and Violence: An Encyclopaedia of Faith and Conflict* (pp. 122–126). Armonk: M. E. Sharpe.

Winter, A. (2011b). The Order. In J. I. Ross (Ed.), *Religion and Violence: An Encyclopaedia of Faith and Conflict* (pp. 542–546). Armonk: M. E. Sharpe.

Winter, A. (2014). My enemies must be friends: The American extreme right, conspiracy theory, Islam and the Middle East. In M. Reinkowski & M. Butter (Eds.), *Conspiracy Theories in the Middle East and the United States: A Comparative Approach* (pp. 35–58). Berlin: De Gruyter.

Winter, A. (2017). Charlottesville, far-right rallies, racism and relating to power. *openDemocracy.* https://www.opendemocracy.net/aaron-winter/charlottesville-far-right-rallies-racism-and-relating-to-power. Accessed October 10, 2018.

Winter, A. (2018). The Klan *is* history: A historical perspective on the revival of the far-right in 'post-racial' America. In J. Morrison, A. Silke, J. Windle, & A. Winter (Eds.), *Historical Perspectives on Organised Crime and Terrorism* (pp. 109–132). Abingdon: Routledge.

3

Cucks, Fags and Useful Idiots: The Othering of Dissenting White Masculinities Online

Alex Green

Introduction

Internet forums have provided a fertile ground for the coalescence and growth of new manifestations of extreme-right communities, often referred to under the umbrella term 'Alt-Right'. The norms of these communities are upheld and policed through the othering of dissenters and threats through intersectional categories of gender, racial and sexual deviance. Straight white men are placed as intellectually, morally and racially superior, while others occupy a hierarchy of inferiority. However, these discourses become unstable when 'insiders' express political opposition; the privileged traitor who expresses liberal politics is a particular threat to the normative hierarchy of identities.

While these right-wing communities are engaged in racist projects, and much of their discourse is directly racist, this chapter focuses on the ways in which extreme-right communities use strategies of othering

A. Green (✉)
University of Southampton, Brighton, UK

to discipline dissenting white men and neutralise perceived threats. It focuses on a prominent case study of two anti-Trump protestors who were filmed at a 2016 rally, with video of them broadly circulated in right-wing forums, including the Donald Trump Reddit subforum and 4chan's /pol/ board. Following this, the protestors were subject to an onslaught of derogatory memes and insults; their identities were uncovered and published; and they and their families were targeted for abuse in their workplaces. 'AIDS Skrillex' and 'Carl the Cuck',[1] as they became known, have joined the canon of right-wing targets, becoming to many posters the face of social justice warriors (SJWs)[2]; featured on lists of SJWs and the subject of innumerable memes.[3] Fake Twitter and Facebook accounts have been created to mock them,[4] and you can buy t-shirts and other merchandise featuring depictions of them,[5] designed with community input.[6] In his painting *Rise of the Republic*, notorious pro-Trump artist Jon Proby places AIDS Skrillex among: 'the forces of the Global political establishment', alongside Hillary Clinton, the Pope, George Soros, Barack Obama and Mark Zuckerberg.[7]

In this chapter, I present unedited examples of the offensive insults used by online trolls. This is not for its shock value, but to accurately portray the obscenity and violence of the attacks directed at the two individuals at the centre of this case study. As Jane (2014) has argued, only by representing the unexpurgated entirety of such discourse can we adequately analyse it. I debated whether this policy should apply to the offensive names given to the two men involved in this case study, but while I intend to interrogate the speech of right-wing trolls, I do not wish to join them in applying it. This would, after all, be reifying the trolls' project to enact power over the individuals in this case by determining their identities. Nor do I wish to further expose their identities by using their real names. Instead, I will refer to them by the initials 'AS' and 'CC', removing the offensive terminology while retaining the link to their given epithets to aid the readability of this chapter. Related to this concern, there are several instances where I will not provide references to the original material as it contains personally identifying data.

Firstly, this chapter outlines the case study at its centre, compiling a timeline of activity across 4chan and Reddit to trace the evolution of AS and CC as memetic phenomena. Following this, it takes three axes of analysis: focusing on the roles of the network, the online troll, and the nature of attacks on AS and CC. Building on the work of Danielle Citron (2014), the first of these considers the transformative effects of online networks on the practice and effects of online abuse. Then, turning to the troll, it interrogates conceptions of the troll as a ludic prankster, arguing that trolling cannot be considered outside its social context and that abusive actions emerge as the product of broader networks. This leads into a consideration of how the abuse documented in this case study is shaped by political discourses, patterns of local sociality, and the ordering of online experience, arguing that rather than coherent and stable communities, the boards of Reddit and 4chan represent loose and shifting assemblages, subject to multiple pressures and contexts. Finally, it considers how attacks on AS and CC are articulated to discipline their dissent, concluding that while shifting network compositions can lead to flexible definitions of insider, outsider and stranger, discourses are uniformly structured by white nationalism and heterosexual masculinity.

The Origins of a Meme

On 11 March 2016, two young men joined their friends to protest at a campaign rally for the then-presidential candidate Donald Trump at the Peabody Opera House in St. Louis, Missouri, USA. Following heated debate between the rally attendees and protestors, the rally turned violent. Local news reported that 31 people were charged with disturbing the peace by St Louis police and one with third-degree assault (Soley-Cerro and Winter 2016). One of the protestors, an unnamed black man, was left bloodied and received medical treatment from attending paramedics. This was one of a series of Trump rallies leading up to the 2016 presidential election. CNN reported that the violence at these protests was 'unprecedented in the history of modern presidential campaigns' and the inevitable result of Trump's rhetoric when addressing supporters (Byers 2016).

Following the protest, an 18-minute video of interaction between pro- and anti-Trump protesters was posted on The Alex Jones Channel, an extreme-right YouTube channel that currently has over 2.3 million subscribers and 1.5 billion views. Alex Jones is a prominent extreme-right American radio show host and conspiracy theorist who also owns and operates the notorious website https://www.infowars.com, a highly popular extreme-right media platform which has promoted multiple conspiracy theories and fake news stories (Southern Poverty Law Center 2018). The video shows a mixed group of anti-Trump protestors debating with Owen Shroyer, a pro-Trump 26-year-old radio host from St Louis.[8] It begins with Shroyer and an older white man engaged in heated debate with a group of black protestors. After approximately three and a half minutes, AS enters the frame, answering Shroyer's monologue about the negative effects of industrial outsourcing with the observation that 'capitalism cannot exist without exploitation'. Throughout the video, Shroyer engages with multiple protestors, including black and white men and women. CC is on screen for approximately 20 seconds of the 18 minutes and AS for under three minutes. Shroyer is clearly prepared for a filmed encounter, rolling out pre-prepared lines and addressing asides directly to camera. Capitalising on the exposure he gained through the video, Shroyer was later hired as a reporter by Infowars, adopting the moniker: 'Owen Shroyer, The Cuck Destroyer' and boasting of his ability to 'face these people en masse, and … make them look like total cucks' (Shukman 2016).

The video was posted on 4chan's /pol/ board on 11 March at 19:34,[9] the evening after the protest. This first thread[10] is dominated by direct attacks on black protestors using generic racial slurs; however, some attention was paid to AS, including the first visual meme at 20:35:

Anonymous Sat 12 Mar 2016 19:45:38
\>\>67049778
\> sanders supporters.
\> any kind of threat.
I mean don't get me wrong, I'd never pick a fight with one of those faggots for fear of getting in contact with their blood and getting AIDS, but they don't strike me as particularly intimidating.

3 Cucks, Fags and Useful Idiots: The Othering of Dissenting White …

Anonymous Sat 12 Mar 2016 19:52:20
\>>67051964
He looks like Skrillex.

Anonymous Sat 12 Mar 2016 20:26:09
\>>67049778
lol @ that fucking white balding cuck faggot @ 7:30.

At 22:09 the first /pol/ thread focused on AS was posted,[11] and at 01:45 the first comment singling out CC was posted:

Anonymous Sat 12 Mar 2016 06:45:05
Quoted By: >>67091331 >>67098666 >>67100740 >>67129767 >>67089855
The souless eyes of a braindead cuck.[12]

Following initial posts of the original 18-minute video, shorter edited versions were posted on YouTube and Twitter, likely in response to complaints by users who were unwilling to watch such a long video. These focused on the interchanges between Shroyer, AS and CC, removing the majority of the black protestors except where they shared the frame with AS and CC.[13] These videos were then posted in general Donald Trump threads on /pol/, introducing AS and CC as topics for discussion.[14] In one of these threads AS is first named:

Washington State For Trump Sat 12 Mar 2016 01:58:49
Quoted By: >>67092153 >>67093261
\>>67091867
'You are fucking a white male.'
- Gay Skrillex.[15]

This epithet does not immediately stick, and AS is referred to by a range of different names across pro-Trump threads. The first usage of 'AIDS Skrillex' on 4chan is not until 14 March.[16] As videos are multiply reposted and included in broader pro-Trump threads on /pol/, AS becomes the subject of intense derogatory commentary. For example[17]:

Anonymous Sat 12 Mar 2016 07:08:05
\>\>67092677
Someone get that kid some Rogaine. What a self-loathing freak MUH WHITE PEOPLE YEA UH I KNOW IM WHITE Kill yourself, faggot.

Anonymous Sat 12 Mar 2016 07:20:46
\>\>67092677
\>WE SHOULD ALL DISCOUNT YOUR OPINIONS BECAUSE OF YOUR RACE BUT YOU'RE NOT A RACIST.
literally will never understand liberals.
just hope one day it's a /pol/ tard that falls in nuclear waste, becomes a superman, and just purges the world of its idiots, starting with this self-hating white apologist effeminate wimp faggot.

Anonymous Sat 12 Mar 2016 07:22:56
\>\>67092677
I've only used the word cuck like 4 times on here, but this man is the definition of a white guilt cuck.

On 16 March, one of the edited videos was posted on Reddit in the r/videos/ subreddit by user SherlockDoto. r/videos/ is a general forum for posting videos of interest, and unlike other subreddits, it has no expressed political alignment. The video became a popular thread, attracting over 11,000 upvotes and 6000 comments. The original posted video has now been deleted from YouTube, but the thread remains on Reddit.[18] The same day, an anonymous poster on 4chan's /pol/ board had identified Shroyer, encouraging other forum users to support Shroyer's work and claimed to be working towards discovering CC's identity.[19] Users of 4chan ultimately discovered and posted the real names, addresses, social media accounts and phone numbers of both AS and CC, along with videos of AS's band and images from both of their social media accounts. They also targeted their families, posting the names, social media accounts, and workplaces of CC's parents, along with the social media accounts of CC's sisters. Following targeted abuse across social media platforms, AS was reported to have deleted social media accounts.[20]

As the videos of AS and CC were circulated, they were met with an outpouring of what Jean Burgess (2006) has described as vernacular creativity, ranging from the simplest template generated memes to more complex video work. With relatively low effort required for their production, crude visual memes were the most common. These frequently presented grotesque caricatures of AS and CC, accompanied by insults.[21] On YouTube, multiple remix videos were posted, which took cut up footage from the original protest video, incorporate additional visual material and set the result to new soundtracks, often incorporating samples of the original audio.[22] Some of the video productions representing AS and CC have a surprising level of sophistication and must represent a significant amount of production effort. An example of this is Sexy Justice Warriors, an animated cartoon featuring offensive caricatures of AS and CC joining up with ISIS.[23]

Through numerous memes, remix videos and other derivative media, AS and CC entered the shared culture of pro-Trump and associated right-wing communities across YouTube, Reddit and 4chan. They remain familiar names today, part of the vernacular mythology of the communities on /pol/, r/mr_trump and r/The_Donald. AS and CC are often invoked as benchmarks to which new targets are compared, with users asking 'is this Aids Skrillex v2?'.[24] Within these communities, shared culture is important in maintaining community identity, but also individual status. Along with heightening inventiveness and imagination (Knuttila 2011), the ephemeral posting cultures of Reddit and 4chan allow long-resident individuals to acquire social capital and assert superiority through the accumulation and administration of community memory. This is often seen in reminiscence threads and the practice of retelling stories to newcomers.[25] In tandem with this retelling of the story of AS and CC, pursuit of the real people behind the caricatures has also continued. In May 2017, AS was 'spotted' working at a grocery store,[26] news of which quickly spread across 4chan and Reddit, prompting elaboration of the story to newcomers and a round of reposts and reminiscence. One of the tensions I have faced in writing this chapter is that it again resurrects the characters and narratives, while also providing trolls with the online commodity they most desire: attention.

Networked Effects: Performative Artefacts, Collective Coordination and Meme Magic

Having outlined the development of AS and CC as part of the memetic mythology of right-wing online communities, this section explores how the web can transform abusive behaviour through the creation and maintenance of performative artefacts, the collective coordination of abusers and the potential for offline action via 'meme magic'. Following this, the next sections will analyse the concept of the troll in relation to this case study, situating the actions of Reddit and 4chan posters in their broader contexts and interrogate the nature of the abuse levelled at AS and CC.

The actions perpetrated against AS and CC are harassment and have clear parallels to other persistent forms of abuse. In this way, it might seem that the web acts as merely another channel among many for abuse, yet prominent legal scholar Danielle Citron (2014) argues that we should understand this as a distinct form of abuse: cyberharassment. Citron points to the need to recognise the transformative nature of networked technologies in increasing the reach and effect of harassment behaviours. Citron identifies three affordances through which this occurs: the extended life of attacking media; the broader audience for harassment; and the ability to recruit and organise others in harassment campaigns. Building from this model, I extend the last of these to include the greater capability of the collective intelligence of online communities to identify targets, generate media and conduct attacks, and add the web's potential to empower abusers with greater ability to generate offline effects.

The active participation of human users in the online abuse of AS and CC has certainly passed its peak, but that does not mean its effects are lessened. Many of the YouTube videos are still accessible, the comment threads are still up on Reddit and the memes catalogued on multiple sites. This chapter attests to the wealth of content readily available. Drawing on the work of Barad and Haraway, it acknowledges a posthumanist notion of performativity, one that offers 'an accounting of "nonhuman" as well as "human" forms of agency' (Barad 2003: 810) while also problematising the discursive separation of human and non-human. Following this, we might consider that the artefacts created in the online abuse of AS and CC, the memes, the videos, the entries on Encyclopedia Dramatica[27] and the comment threads, continue to perform a form of violence against AS and CC. For example, Citron (2014) describes the lasting effects that these artefacts can have on future employment prospects when combined with corporate CV screening practice. Furthermore, they continue to shape the ongoing discourse of dissenting white masculinities, co-constituting an archetypal identity category that is used as both warning and weapon against future dissenters.

The web can intensify the impact of harassment behaviour through provision of a larger audience for victims' humiliation. Through the recruitment and mobilisation of accomplices, it can also increase the volume of attacks on individuals. This increase can be more than arithmetic, with groups able to leverage a collective intelligence forming more than the sum of their parts. In the case of AS and CC, the dispersed collective intelligence of the group led to rapid discovery of their offline identities, with one Reddit poster claiming that AS was a fellow student at their school[28] and multiple claimed doxxing successes. Further, as described in the previous section, the coordination of a community of online posters can lead to heightened creativity in the formulation of attacks through the rapid interchange and iteration of digital content, what Milner (2013) has termed 'memetic remix'.

The Wiki page of r/The_Donald describes 'meme magic' as 'when a meme "transcends the realm of cyberspace and results in real life consequences"'.[29] To some participants in right-wing online communities, this is the ultimate goal of their actions; eliciting jubilant posts of 'meme magic!'. To this end, participants make direct attempts to manifest memes offline. In a prank call to the Washington Journal call-in show on C-SPAN a caller asked about 'the abundance of references to AIDS Skrillex' in Hilary Clinton's emails.[30] In a further, characteristically 4chan, piece of trolling, a /pol/ poster started a rumour that AS had perpetrated a shooting at UCLA, thus simultaneously attempting to troll the media and fellow participants.[31] In more troubling direction AS's real name and place of work were posted on /pol/ on 13 March.[32]

This information was used to post multiple fake reviews of AS's place of work on Yelp and Google, for example:

> As I was checking out, one of the cashiers a white male with long hair mumbled 'fucking white male pig' I was shocked!! Do not stole here.[33]

These reviews have subsequently been removed, although screenshots of them still exist in archived comment threads. Following the release of information on AS and CC's families, fake reviews were also posted on the Facebook page of CC's mother's business, making reference to CC's supposed sexual deviance.

Behind the Trolling Mask

The kind of abusive online behaviour that has been meted out to AS and CC in online forums is frequently described by the catch-all term 'trolling'. In her insightful study of trolling, Whitney Phillips describes trolling as a form of play, an extreme form of sick humour that dishes out equal opportunity offence:

> Trolls derive lulz from other trolls, from trolls attempting to derive lulz from other trolls, from innocent bystanders, from media figures, from entire news organizations, from anything and everything they can get their hands on. (Phillips 2015: 28)

The term 'lulz' in trolling communities is highly flexible, referring to both the humour derived from a joke and the outrage elicited from targets. Phillips explains that lulz functions as both punishment and reward in trolling communities, operating as a 'nexus of social cohesion and social constraint' (2015: 93). From a series of interviews with self-identified trolls, and referencing Goffman's concept of 'front' (Goffman 1959), Phillips describes the 'mask of trolling' (2015: 99) as a dissociative separation of self into online and real-life personas with different social rules. This, Phillips explains, frames the actions of trolls as a form of detached play, a game recognised and joined by other trolls but often misread by outsiders. Following this logic, trolls claim that their online persona is mere performances: constructions which are separate from their character and behaviour in everyday life. However, I argue, any uncritical acceptance of this claim acts to obscure the motivations and objectives of trolls by distancing bad behaviour to the unreal plane of 'online' or a 'trolling mode'. Indeed, Phillips explains that this 'lulz fetishism' can obscure 'the social conditions and interpersonal strife' (2015: 99) that frame behaviour.

This is not to deny that the affordances of online environments have real effects in mediating social behaviour. In his study of psychology in digital environments, Suler (2004) identifies an 'online disinhibition effect', a loosening of behavioural norms due to the perceived anonymity of online spaces. However, online life is part of real life; online interactions are interweaved with offline experiences, and any boundaries between the two are at the least indistinct. Certainly, the actions taken by trolls against protestors in this case required significant action offline. Trolls are not operating in absence of context, trolling personas are not independent of their authors, and there is a continuity of intention and responsibility. Furthermore, as Phillips notes, effective trolling is premised on sophisticated understanding of, and empathy with, targets' vulnerabilities and the effects of attacks. This is an understanding and empathy that can only be drawn from a 'real-life' understanding of social realities, thus collapsing any claimed isolation of trolling performance from context. Similarly, any claim of trolling activity as mere play can be problematised when we interrogate its norms; when we ask questions like why this joke and not that joke? Could we imagine an online forum where trolling mobilises slurs that attack the white, straight, privileged and male? If trolling were merely a ludic practice seeking to elicit maximum response from its targets, then there's plenty of outrage to extract from rich white heterosexual men. Instead, trolling behaviours are near uniformly structured by North American norms of masculinity, whiteness, privilege and heteronormativity.

Angry White Men

The interaction of protestor and troll is clearly fuelled by a broader political context, motivating the original march and the subsequent attacks on participants. In his study of white men in the USA, Kimmel describes multiple aphoristic and jingoistic exchanges with the 'angry white men' that he interviews, suggesting that their trolling behaviour is direct repetition of extreme-right media discourse:

> They sit alone, listening to the radio, listening to Rush Limbaugh and Mike Savage and Sean Hannity. They meet online, in chat rooms and on websites, whether promoting antifeminist men's rights or the re-Aryanization of America. They troll cyberspace, the anti-PC police, ready to attack any blogger, columnist, or quasi liberal who dares to say something with which they disagree. (2013: 91)

Tracing causation to media discourses is attractive in offering up a clear culprit and neat story, but it also diminishes the agency and responsibility of trolls. Furthermore, as described earlier, the destructive creativity of trolling exhibited in this case goes far beyond echoing talk radio. Karen Evans has argued that rather than being novel social groupings, online communities instead closely replicate long-standing social formations, 'reflecting rather than transforming existing states of being and thinking' (Evans 2013: 87). Following this, the trolling behaviour of 4chan and Reddit communities could be considered reflective of broader, complex and long-standing political and social development, emboldened by the white nationalist and masculinist political rhetoric of Donald Trump. This encompasses socio-economic changes to the white working class, alongside a 'backlash' against feminist action and rights movements stretching back to the 1980s (Faludi 1992; Jordan 2016). In the current context of US politics, it is worth noting that multiple writers have argued that nationalist political projects are mutually constitutive of hegemonic masculinities (Anand 2007; Conway 2012; Enloe 2014; Nagel 1998).

Assemblages of Outrage

Alongside the national, political context of these attacks, it is important to consider the localised, social context. It is certainly arguable that participation in online abuse can be a form of community building,

3   Cucks, Fags and Useful Idiots: The Othering of Dissenting White …

offering solidarity and an escape from loneliness or isolation. Divorced from context, the repeated slogan of 'you're fucking a white male' in Reddit and /pol/ threads quickly loses its original meaning, becoming a base for word substitution puns. These comments from a Reddit thread give a flavour of the discourse; the thread they are excerpted from is over 1800 comments long[34]:

AcesNLaces 4 points 1 year ago
You're a white male.

[deleted] 5 points 1 year ago
YOU'RE A FUCKING WHITE MALE!!! REEEEEEEEEEEEEEEE!

beardedclamfeederDEU 5 points 1 year ago
you're fucking a white whale!

RikersaCA 4 points 1 year ago
YOU'RE A WHITE MALE.

BasketOfPepes1776 3 points 1 year ago
YOURE A WHITE MALE.

the_sky_god151776 4 points 1 year ago
You're a white male.

Bisuboy 4 points 1 year ago
YOU'RE FUCKING A WHITE MALE.

diggrecluse RUS 4 points 1 year ago
YOU'RE A FUCKING WHILE MALE. A WHITE MAN.

DontwearthatsockGA 4 points 1 year ago
You're a white mail.

kriegsonUSAF 3 points 1 year ago
Thanks e-…Eh.
"YOU'RE HUNTING A WHITE WHALE!"

VolarionneVA 3 points 1 year ago
Ok Im out of the loop on this one, who is this guy?

Alexander_RayTWN 2 points 1 year ago
You're a wight nail, sell it for 5gp.

In her study of the international 'hacktivist' group Anonymous, Gabriella Coleman describes the magnetic power of this kind of online joking to both generate cohesion among an anonymous collective, thereby forming an in-group (Coleman 2015). Here, we can glimpse the obscuring separation of Phillips' 'lulz fetishism', which divorces abusive action from abusive identity. We could also consider that this joking works to form an increasing emotional gap between trolls and their victims; shaping a community identity defined in direct relation to the other. Community, however, is a problematic term when considering the groups that post on these forums. Halford et al. (2010) offer us an alternative conception drawn from Actor-Network Theory. Adopting a term from Latour, they introduce the term immutable mobile, to describe the web as a temporarily stabilised set of sociotechnical relations that encompasses both human and technological actors. While similar in its impermanence, this introduces the idea that such 'communities' may involve both technological and human actors.

While it is easy to characterise the temporary heterogeneous assemblages of 4chan and Reddit as coherent actors, this is an assumption we cannot make easily, and such reductive analytical strategies risk obscuring both the complexity of behaviours and the role of non-human actors in producing them. This disrupts the simple category of 'trolls' and troubles description of them as having coherent motivations and operating within discrete contexts. Instead, we might consider ourselves viewing the operation and output of temporary assemblages of human and technological actors operating at multiple scales, from the local to the global. The final sections of this chapter explore further how the structuring of online experience by its technical architecture shapes behaviour and the broader commonalities in the contexts and repertoires of practice in disciplining of white masculinities.

The Ordering of Online Experience

In the introduction to *Modernity and Ambivalence*, Bauman describes a modern 'Quest for Order', a determined fight against ambiguity to fragment the world into a manageable state, a state that can be mastered and subordinated (2007: 1–17). Despite being written prior to the great growth of the web, it is perhaps this foundational premise that allows it to resonate so strongly. The web, and in particular Web 2.0 as a sociotechnical construct, is highly indebted to the drive to order which Bauman describes; its structure premised on the classifications of data types and documents. The web's origins are indebted to grand modern projects of knowledge organisation (Buckland 1992; Gillies 2000; Hapke 1998; Rayward 1994). The ongoing evolution of the next stage of the web, the semantic web, also rests on the design of detailed ontological structures, with development centred on three ordering tasks: the naming of data entities, the structuring of data and the processing of data (Halford et al. 2013). These tasks seek to separate and define entities, asserting knowledge and, by extension, ownership over them. This ordering principle is not confined to the engineering of the web, but instead extends through its architecture; from the unseen backend to the visible frontend interface. From this, the experience of the web is structured by the logic of binary classification: users like or do not like, vote up or vote down, are group members or are not, and navigate through tree structures to experience one place or another. Social platforms actively encourage users to classify not only the data flowing through them, using hashtags and photo tagging, but also themselves through group memberships and the performance of identity characteristics.

In the online abuse of AS and CC, we can discern multiple binaries that separate group insiders and outsiders. Some of these are hegemonic over others, forming a hierarchy of marginalisation: Christian > Muslim; Conservative > Democrat; White > PoC; Male > Female; Straight > Gay. This classificatory schema also acts as a moral order, casting the other as a resistance to be overcome and defining group insiders as 'carriers of moral rights' (Bauman 2007: 38). However, it is important to note that such schema is localised and extemporary, arising as previously argued from the temporary assemblage of web actors under varying contextual forces. This can result in shifting category placements and apparent contradictions as posters renegotiate positions in response to transient needs to maintain and defend classificatory schema. For example, in the same thread where AS is first described as 'gay skrillex', a self-identified gay poster receives qualified acceptance. This can result in an environment where othering is not an intrinsic principle but a functional one: attacks are targeted on dissenting action rather than identity, but discipline via identity[35]:

Anonymous Sat 12 Mar 2016 07:10:11
Quoted.
By: >>67093186 >>67093190 >>67093242 >>67093314 >>67093316 >>67093377 >>67093693 >>67093971 >>67093991 >>67094243 >>67095413
Guys, I'm a fag who's 100% for Trump.
I even turned my boyfriend into a Trump supporter, too.
Are gays who are pro-Trump welcome? I want to be part of the movement;
Anonymous Sat 12 Mar 2016 07:12:18
Quoted By: >>67093606 >>67092991
Of course you are, don't forget to vote.
Anonymous Sat 12 Mar 2016 07:12:21
Quoted By: >>67093606 >>67092991
The God Emperor[36] hasn't said anything about fags being enemies of America.
So you are clear so far.
Criminals and Muslims however are forbidden.
Blackstar Sat 12 Mar 2016 07:13:48
Quoted By: >>67093606 >>67092991
We generally don't care who or what you are so long as you're not a commie fuck and vote to MAGA.[37]

Deviants, Dupes and Degenerates

Kimmel argues that masculinity is the thread that ties together the disparate and frequently contradictory discourses of the US right. In these discourses, Kimmel identifies two gendered strategies: the repeated narratives of white men's political emasculation in right-wing media, and attacks on the 'fraudulent masculinity' of the other as both hypo- and hyper-masculine; simultaneously weakening and competing with the white American man (Kimmel 2013: 502). In parallel to Bauman, Kimmel roots this in the pseudoscientific discourses of eugenics and nineteenth-century racial science.

By opposing the racist and misogynist discourse of the extreme right, the non-conforming straight white man can no longer be seen as a friend. But he can also not be positioned as an enemy, or other, for to do so would call into question the ontology of binaries that define insiders and outsiders. Instead, following Bauman (2007), he becomes a stranger, fitting no category. By their presence, strangers disrupt the ontology of othering, troubling the borders between categories. While the presence of the enemy provides a focal point for group unification and reifies the division between insider and outsider, the stranger creates anxiety through questioning the hegemony of white masculinity. As Bauman explains, the act of defining order can make artificial structures seem natural through an illusion of symmetry: '… dichotomy is an exercise in power and at the same time its disguise' (2007: 14). At the protest, the actions of AS and CC disrupt this 'natural' disguise by aligning themselves with black protestors and against their 'natural' white allies.

AS and CC are particularly disruptive as strangers. They are straight, white men. Men who are not economically or geographically distant—they are not easily identifiable as being part of a liberal metropolitan elite—but men very much like those who are attacking them online. They speak the same language, dress the same, visit the same bars and eat the same food. They could be neighbours, they could be work colleagues. It is this closeness that both intensifies their disruptive power and drives the ferocity of the attacks against them. It is unsurprising therefore that many of the attacks on AS and CC reflect wider practices of stigmatising strangers. Shane Phelan's work on citizenship of sexual minorities argues that LGBT+ communities are strangers in the USA and that homophobic discourse aims to stigmatise and deny acknowledgement as citizens (Phelan 2001). Similarly, in his study of white resistance to apartheid in South Africa, Conway argues that the social organisation of apartheid rested on a number of binaries defining insider and outsider, essentially white insiders and black outsiders. In this context, Conway argues that white South African critics of apartheid and white male war resisters were disruptive strangers and that stigmatisation of white objectors' and peace activists sexual identities, regardless of their self-identified sexuality, was the most effective strategy to negate their political protests and reinforce the racial binaries of apartheid (Conway 2008).

The clearest example of this policing through sexual identities is in the names given to AS and CC. AIDS is a clear reference to homosexuality, and 'cuck' is derived from cuckold, the husband of an adulterous wife. Cuck is also a genre of pornography where men watch their female partners have sex with other, frequently black, men. As AS and CC were further investigated by forum members, images from social media accounts provided further fuel for attacks. An image of AS in a department store posing next to a cardboard cut-out of a character from the animated children's TV series My Little Pony led his identification as a Brony. Bronies are adult male fans of My Little Pony, and the subject of widespread ridicule in online forums, in the words of one poster: 'His family should be ashamed of his degeneracy, so low can't even be called a faggot'.[38]

In the /pol/ and Reddit comment threads described earlier in this chapter, AS is described as effeminate, weak, a faggot, a wimp and a beta male. Other personal characteristics which do not meet a dominant, normative masculinity are attacked, including his lack of muscles, his pale complexion and in particular his hair. There are multiple calls for 'someone [to] get that kid some Rogaine'.[39] Discussions of AS's hair are particularly interesting in exposing the tense relationship between users and the masculine ideals they are using to discipline AS.

As Connell (2005) has argued, while broad groups of men (and women) are engaged in the project of constructing and upholding hegemonic masculinity, very few men fully meet its narrowly defined standards. In a 4chan thread discussing AS, many commentators confess that they too have experienced hair loss.[40] They argue that hair loss is in fact due to higher levels of testosterone, and therefore a masculine characteristic, but find an alternative point of marginalisation in asserting that AS is wrong in not cutting his hair short or shaving his head. Similar negotiations of subordination can be seen around discussion of AS wearing a top with logo of the band American Nightmare, a hardcore punk band from Boston, Massachusetts. Posters express that they also like the band and search to find further points of difference between themselves and AS. In confronting a dissenting man who is uncomfortably close in appearance, tastes and background to them, the intense attacks of Reddit and /pol/ users work hard to demarcate their identities, striving to maintain the binary logic of insiders and outsiders.

An alternative strategy for neutralising AS and CC is positioning them as useful idiots or dupes. CC in particular is often labelled an idiot to excuse his behaviour, possibly because his physical appearance offers less opportunity for attack:

Anonymous Tue 21 Nov 2017 08:37:37
Feel bad for that guy. He probably didn't have a father and was the only kid raised by a single mom. Maybe in some years he will realise what an idiot he was, but by then everyone will know him as Carl the cuck and there'll be nothing he can do to undo that.[41]

SkyOwl15OR 72 points 2 years ago
I honestly love Carl the Cuck, he has brought me so much joy. I feel like he'll come around, he's just misinformed.[42]

This classification of AS and CC as idiots parallels the cultural myth of dupes who unwittingly further communist plots, a common tactic for othering protest during the Cold War (Conway 2008). In this way, the fundamental 'truth' of racialised binaries can be maintained by denying agency to white 'traitors'. It enables the positioning of dissenting white men as still essentially good, and 'one of us', but presents the excuse that their ability to make the right choice has been diminished through ignorance, trickery or coercion.

Conclusion

The case of AS and CC illustrates the unstable politics of right-wing communities where continual policing of the 'insider' is as important as the expulsion of the 'outsider'. More broadly, it shows the transformative effect the web can have on this policing. The web can amplify the actions and effects of abusive behaviour through the enduring action of performative artefacts, the recruitment and coordination of audiences and accomplices, and the increased ability it affords abusers to generate offline effects.

When examining 'online othering', we must also consider the amorphous nature of online communities. The posters attacking AS and CC are not just engaged in trolling games to derive 'lulz'; they exist within a broader political context where white nationalism has been emboldened by racist political rhetoric. This is further mediated by local social contexts for participants, including the social and economic alienation of certain groups of white men. However, these groups are loose and temporary assemblages, rather than coherent and stable communities. Finally, the transient nature of these communities can lead to multiple and shifting definitions of insider, outsider and stranger, where hierarchies of marginalisation become flexible depending on contingent political needs. For example, AS and CC can be the targets of vicious homophobic abuse, while at the same time self-identified gay subjects, such as Milo Yiannopoulos, are praised and included because they endorse and reinforce the politics of white nationalism.

Despite these shifting and flexible categories of belonging, whiteness and heterosexual masculinity remains the fundamental moral order. This is seen through strategies of policing that wield homophobia and hegemonic masculinity against 'insider' dissidents, strategies that have been used in multiple authoritarian, nationalist and conservative contexts. The strength of the vitriolic attacks against AS and CC reveals the significance of the threat dissident 'strangers' can pose to white nationalism. The actions of posters on Reddit and 4chan successfully closed the space for debate and contestation, defining the identities of AS and CC and transforming them into archetypes which are still used to discipline dissent. This raises clear questions about whether the web should be allowed to be a space of unfettered free speech, and who such free speech serves.

Notes

1. 'Cuck', in this context, derives from an abbreviation of cuckold, the husband of an adulterous wife. Cuck is also a genre of pornography where men watch their female partners have sex with other, frequently black, men. As is discussed in this chapter, Cuck has been adopted by online right-wing communities as an insult denoting weakness or emasculation.
2. A pejorative term for left-wing individuals.
3. Know Your Meme has a page devoted to AS and CC, displaying many examples of memes about them: http://knowyourmeme.com/memes/carl-the-cuck-and-aids-skrillex.
4. See https://twitter.com/cuckcarl and https://twitter.com/aidsskrillex.
5. T-shirts are available at Redbubble and Cameron Lee Worldwide: https://www.redbubble.com/shop/aids+skrillex+and+carl+the+cuck+t-shirts and https://www.cameronleeworldwide.com/products/aids-skrillex-carl-the-cuck-mens-t-shirt.
6. In this Reddit thread, the creator of a t-shirt design based on AS and CC seeks community input in developing the final artwork: https://www.reddit.com/r/The_Donald/comments/4ba28o/centipedes_i_need_help_designing_my_aids_skrillex/.
7. A low-resolution copy of the painting can be viewed here: http://jonproby.com/images/rise-republic-360.jpg. AS is depicted to the right of Mark Zuckerberg.
8. The video can be viewed on The Alex Jones Channel at the following link. Multiple derivative edits of the interchange exist, but this is the original posting: https://www.youtube.com/watch?v=YU3vcvGpALQ.
9. 4chan time is EST without daylight savings.
10. The thread is archived at: http://archive.4plebs.org/pol/thread/67049778/.

11. This thread is archived at: http://archive.4plebs.org/pol/thread/67070350/.
12. This comment is archived at: http://archive.4plebs.org/pol/thread/67089855/#67090852.
13. This is one of the earliest edits still accessible, many of the edited videos have subsequently been removed. It was posted on 12 March 2016, and then circulated on Reddit and 4chan: https://www.youtube.com/watch?v=FCjjVSmop5Q.
14. See for example: http://archive.4plebs.org/pol/thread/67090363/#67091867 and http://archive.4plebs.org/pol/thread/67092523/#q67092618.
15. This comment is archived at: http://archive.4plebs.org/pol/thread/67090363/#q67092048.
16. This comment is archived at: http://archive.4plebs.org/pol/thread/67352244/#67352698.
17. These comments are taken from the thread archived at: http://archive.4plebs.org/pol/thread/67092523/.
18. The Reddit thread can be seen here: https://www.reddit.com/r/videos/comments/4apx71/you_fucking_white_male/.
19. This 4chan post is archived here: http://archive.4plebs.org/pol/thread/67681922/#q67681922.
20. This Reddit thread claims to show AS's final tweet prior to deleting his social media accounts: https://www.reddit.com/r/The_Donald/comments/4gv3ec/aids_skrillexs_final_tweet_before_deleting.
21. AS and CC memes can be found here: https://www.funnyjunk.com/Cuck+carl+aids+skrillex/funny-pictures/5861711 and http://knowyourmeme.com/memes/carl-the-cuck-and-aids-skrillex.
22. Example remix videos can be seen at: https://www.youtube.com/watch?v=tvfhmhITkYY, https://www.youtube.com/watch?v=ErhbJgEL5jQ and https://www.youtube.com/watch?v=xFOvqrrV_2k.
23. Sexy Justice Warriors can be seen at: https://www.youtube.com/watch?v=JcUi5_eNoqk.
24. For example, see this Reddit thread from 2017: https://www.reddit.com/r/The_Donald/comments/59oac3/this_scumbag_attacked_a_homeless_trump_supporter/.
25. For examples of reminiscence about AS see: https://www.reddit.com/r/The_Donald/comments/77319u/aids_skrillex_was_one_of_the_best_moments_of_2016 and https://www.reddit.com/r/The_Donald/comments/5cveww/never_forget_aids_skrillex.
26. https://twitter.com/joshdcaplan/status/863950199181455360.

27. See https://encyclopediadramatica.rs/AIDS_Skrillex_and_Carl_the_Cuck.
28. See https://www.reddit.com/r/The_Donald/comments/4feshg/my_carl_the_cuck_aids_skrillex_tshirt_came_today/d28ed8n/.
29. The Wiki for r/The_Donald is available here: https://www.reddit.com/r/The_Donald/wiki/index.
30. See https://www.youtube.com/watch?v=BMSKx78nZyc.
31. See the archived /pol/ thread here: https://yuki.la/pol/75811397 and a related thread on r/The_Donald: https://www.reddit.com/r/The_Donald/comments/4m44uq/guys_i_think_aids_skrillex_just_shot_up_ucla/.
32. For obvious reasons, no reference to this identifying information is provided.
33. The thread this is taken from contains personal information on AS and CC and, therefore, no reference will be given.
34. This Reddit thread is available here: https://www.reddit.com/r/The_Donald/comments/5cveww/never_forget_aids_skrillex/.
35. This thread is archived at: http://archive.4plebs.org/pol/thread/67092523/.
36. 'God Emperor' is adopted in some forums as a nickname for Trump. It may be derived from the science fiction series Dune or a character in the tabletop game Warhammer 40,000.
37. MAGA is an acronym for the Trump campaign slogan 'Make America Great Again'.
38. See https://np.reddit.com/r/The_Donald/comments/4axgne/of_course/.
39. Rogaine is a brand name for Minoxidil, a hair-regrowth medication.
40. This thread is archived at: https://archive.4plebs.org/pol/thread/125653367/.
41. This comment is archived at: http://archive.4plebs.org/pol/thread/150292301/#q150303494.
42. This comment is archived at: https://www.reddit.com/r/The_Donald/comments/4feshg/my_carl_the_cuck_aids_skrillex_tshirt_came_today/d28ez16/.

References

Anand, D. (2007). Anxious sexualities: Masculinity, nationalism and violence. *British Journal of Politics and International Relations, 9,* 257–269.

Barad, K. (2003). Posthumanist performativity: Toward an understanding of how matter comes to matter. *Signs, 28,* 801–831.

Bauman, Z. (2007). *Modernity and Ambivalence*. Cambridge: Polity Press.
Buckland, M. K. (1992). Emanuel Goldberg, electronic document retrieval, and Vannevar Bush's memex. *Journal of the American Society for Information Science and Technology, 43*(4), 284–294.
Burgess, J. (2006). Hearing ordinary voices: Cultural studies, vernacular creativity and digital storytelling. *Continuum, 20*, 201–214.
Byers, D. (2016). Donald Trump rallies are turning violent. *CNN Money*. Accessed March 29, 2018. http://money.cnn.com/2016/03/10/media/donald-trump-rallies-violence/index.html.
Citron, D. K. (Ed.). (2014). *Hate Crimes in Cyberspace*. Cambridge, MA: Harvard University Press.
Coleman, G. (2015). *Hacker, Hoaxer, Whistleblower, Spy: The Many Faces of Anonymous*. London: Verso Books.
Connell, R. W. (2005). *Masculinities* (2nd ed.). Cambridge: Polity Press.
Conway, D. (2008). The masculine state in crisis: State response to war resistance in apartheid South Africa. *Men and Masculinities, 10*, 422–439.
Conway, D. (2012). *Masculinities, Militarisation and the End Conscription Campaign: War Resistance in Apartheid South Africa*. Oxford: Oxford University Press.
Enloe, C. (2014). *Bananas, Beaches and Bases: Making Feminist Sense of International Politics* (2nd ed.). Berkeley: University of California Press.
Evans, K. (2013). Re-thinking community in the digital age? In K. Orton-Johnson & N. Prior (Eds.), *Digital Sociology: Critical Perspectives* (pp. 79–94). Basingstoke: Palgrave Macmillan.
Faludi, S. (1992). *Backlash: The Undeclared War Against Women*. London: Random House.
Gillies, J. (2000). *How the Web Was Born: The Story of the World Wide Web*. Oxford: Oxford University Press.
Goffman, E. (1959). *The Presentation of Self in Everyday Life*. London: Penguin.
Halford, S., Pope, C., & Carr, L. (2010). *A manifesto for web science?* Presented at the WebSci10: Extending the Frontiers of Society On-Line, Raleigh, NC.
Halford, S., Pope, C., & Weal, M. (2013). Digital futures? Sociological challenges and opportunities in the emergent semantic web. *Sociology, 47*, 173–189.
Hapke, T. (1998). *Wilhelm Ostwald, the 'Brücke' (bridge), and connections to other bibliographic activities at the beginning of the twentieth century*. http://www.chemheritage.org/HistoricalServices/ASIS_documents/ASIS98_Hapke.pdf.

Jane, E. A. (2014). 'Back to the kitchen, cunt': Speaking the unspeakable about online misogyny. *Continuum, 28,* 558–570.

Jordan, A. (2016). Conceptualizing backlash: (UK) men's rights groups, anti-feminism, and postfeminism. *Canadian Journal of Women and Law, 28*(1). https://doi.org/10.3138/cjwl.28.1.18.

Kimmel, M. (2013). *Angry White Men: American Masculinity at the End of an Era*. New York: Avalon Publishing Group.

Knuttila, L. (2011). User unknown: 4chan, anonymity and contingency. *First Monday, 16.* http://dx.doi.org/10.5210/fm.v16i10.3665.

Milner, R. M. (2013). Hacking the social: Internet memes, identity antagonism, and the logic of lulz. *The Fibreculture Journal, 22.* http://twentytwo.fibreculturejournal.org/fcj-156-hacking-the-social-internet-memes-identity-antagonism-and-the-logic-of-lulz/.

Nagel, J. (1998). Masculinity and nationalism: Gender and sexuality in the making of nations. *Ethnic and Racial Studies, 21,* 242–269.

Phelan, S. (2001). *Sexual Strangers: Gays, Lesbians, and Dilemmas of Citizenship*. Philadelphia: Temple University Press.

Phillips, W. (2015). *This Is Why We Can't Have Nice Things: Mapping the Relationship Between Online Trolling and Mainstream Culture*. Cambridge: MIT Press.

Rayward, W. B. (1994). Visions of Xanadu: Paul Otlet (1868–1944) and hypertext. *American Journal of the American Society of Information Science and Technology, 45,* 235–250.

Shukman, H. (2016). Owen Shroyer, Cuck Destroyer interview: The golden boy of alt-right media. *Tab US*. Accessed March 30, 2018. https://thetab.com/us/2016/12/01/owen-shroyer-cuck-destroyer-56235.

Soley-Cerro, A., & Winter, K. (2016). *Violence Erupts at Donald Trump Rally in St. Louis: At Least 32 People Arrested*. Los Angeles, CA: KTLA.

Southern Poverty Law Center. (2018). *Alex Jones*. Accessed March 30, 2018. https://www.splcenter.org/fighting-hate/extremist-files/individual/alex-jones.

Suler, J. (2004). The online disinhibition effect. *Cyberpsychology & Behavior, 7,* 321–326.

4

'"I Want to Kill You in Front of Your Children" Is Not a Threat. It's an Expression of a Desire': Discourses of Online Abuse, Trolling and Violence on r/MensRights

Karen Lumsden

Introduction

Recently there have been a plethora of studies of online misogyny, e-bile (Jane 2014), trolling (Herring et al. 2002; Mantilla 2015; Phillips 2015) and online hate. This includes the abuse received by feminist activists online (Megarry 2014; Lewis et al. 2016). However, abusive online discourses and representations of online misogyny are still relatively understudied (Lumsden and Morgan 2017), as are victims' everyday experiences of online abuse, and the ways in which it is framed, defined, constructed and understood by online users—both victims and perpetrators. Moreover, to date there have been few studies of the American social news site, Reddit. The site has become embroiled in many recent controversies such as the sharing of

K. Lumsden (✉)
Leicester, UK

leaked celebrity photographs on r/TheFappening, its involvement in #GamerGate and the Pizzagate[1] conspiracy, and controversial subreddits such as pro-Donald Trump subreddit r/The_Donald and banned subreddits such as r/FatPeopleHate. Reddit has been described as a 'toxic technoculture' (Massanari 2017a; Massanari and Chess 2018) and can be viewed as part of the 'manophere' (Ging 2017; Marwick and Caplan 2018).

This chapter focuses on a community of Men's Rights Activists (MRAs) on the subreddit r/MensRights. It presents findings from a qualitative analysis of threads and comments in this subreddit and focuses on findings including: (1) the denial of women and feminists as victims of online violence; (2) the victimization of men online; and (3) constructions of online violence. The chapter adds to the growing body of literature on online misogyny and Reddit by focusing on an online culture which perpetrates and encourages forms of 'online othering', including misogyny and violence. It focuses on Men's Rights Activists' (MRA) discussions of trolling and gendered violence, and their 'online othering' of women and feminists. This includes the denigration and abuse aimed at feminists and social justice warriors (SJWs). These unexplored online discourses and interactions provide a valuable insight into the construction of notions of online acceptability and deviance vis-à-vis digital communication, the boundaries between online/offline violence and (online) culture wars.

The first section of the chapter outlines the background behind Reddit, and more specifically, the subreddit which we focus on herein—r/MensRights. It then outlines recent studies of Reddit which highlight its controversial nature, its role in the presentation of self and identity online, anonymity, and its promotion of toxic and abusive online behaviours—particularly towards women, feminists and 'social justice warriors'. The chapter then outlines the history of men's rights movements and the development of the 'manosphere'. After a discussion of methods, I present findings which centre on: denial of women and feminists as victims of online violence; the victimization of men online; and constructions of online violence.

Researching Reddit and Toxic Technocultures

The Rise of Reddit

Founded in 2005 by Steve Huffman and Alexis Ohanian,[2] Reddit describes itself as the 'front page of the internet' and aims to bridge 'communities and individuals with ideas, the latest digital trends, and breaking news' through its online bulletin board system (Reddit 2017). The American social news site includes features such as web content rating and discussions. Reddit users (referred to as 'Redditers') participate in more than 45,000 communities to find, share, rate and discuss content and opinions in real time from all over the web (Reddit Help 2017). Reddit is the fifth-largest site in the USA and is the most influential online community. As of January 2017, Reddit had 274 million unique visitors. 54% of the audience were from the USA and 64% were international. In addition, 63% of users were under 25 years old and 87% were under 35 years old (Reddit Help 2017). Research by the Pew Research Center (2013) found that young men are especially likely to visit the site with 15% of male Internet users aged 18–29 saying they used the site in 2013, in comparison with only 5% of women in the same age bracket.

Reddit consists of various communities known as 'subreddits', which focus on different topics and themes. In 2016, there were approximately 11,400 active subreddits (Digital Tracking Blog 2017). If a subreddit gains enough subscribers it can become part of the default homepage, driving additional traffic and subscribers. For instance, communities like r/atheism and r/minecraft appear regularly on the front page (Silverman 2012). Any user can create a subreddit. Members of Reddit can submit content to the site which includes posts, links, videos and images. According to Caplan and Purser (2017: 5): 'Each post to a subreddit contains multiple comment threads, with a parent comment replying directly to the poster and a child comment replying to the parent, thus creating an intricate nested system of ongoing comments'. These comments are 'up-voted' or 'down-voted' by other members.

This unique feature of Reddit displays discussions hierarchically, with more popular posts at the top of the page (Caplan and Purser 2017). Reddit users can also show appreciation for a user's comments by giving them Reddit gold, which is paid for by the giver in actual money or Bitcoin as part of an enhanced membership option (Caplan and Purser 2017). Each link and comment also displays a score which corresponds to the number of 'upvotes' and 'downvotes' an item has received and this score translates into 'karma points' for a user's account (Massanari 2017a: 331). Reddit accounts are also pseudonymous which means that elements of play are encouraged on Reddit, with administrators assuming a 'hands off' approach to moderation and content (Massanari 2017a: 331).

r/MensRights

The Men's Rights subreddit (r/MensRights) describes itself as 'a place for those who wish to discuss men's rights and the ways said rights are infringed upon'. At the time of conducting the data collection in 2016, it had approximately 118,566 readers. The front page of r/MensRights typically contains various posts tagged under 'feminism' (i.e. 'Critique these feminist arguments people!') 'discrimination' (i.e. 'Man arrested and convicted of lewd act for receiving oral sex on a train. Woman was let off with a warning'), 'legal rights' (i.e. 'Man arrested and accused of sexually assaulting his 7-year-old autistic son based on evidence provided by a psychic vision'), 'marriage/children', 'education/occupation' (i.e. 'US universities are now blatantly funding social justice and radical feminist ideology'), and 'social issues'. In its Frequently Asked Questions section, r/MensRights is defined as: '…a subreddit consisting of both men and women who believe that there is serious discrimination against men inherent in western societies…' (r/MensRights 2013).

Massanari and Chess (2018: 5) argue that because anyone can create a community on Reddit it has become a hub for the alt-right and related communities (i.e. r/KotakuInAction, r/mensrights, r/theredpill, r/The_Donald, etc.) which 'share misogynistic worldviews and believe that "political correctness" is stifling free speech'. Reddit has been a focus of controversy because of this and its 'hands off' approach to moderation.

It played a key role in #GamerGate and also in the sharing of nude celebrity photographs on the subreddit r/thefappening which were accessed via the hacking of iCloud (Topinka 2017). The majority of subreddits demonstrate that Reddit is largely anti-feminist and although there are some progressive and resistant subreddits, Massanari (2017b: 2) notes that on Reddit '…women, people of color, LGBTQIA folks, and anyone else potentially seen as harboring "social justice" tendencies serve as potential threats to be silenced, harassed, or objectified'.

Studies of Reddit

There are few studies of Reddit despite the rich data which is publicly provided via its various subreddits. Studies to date have focused on presentation of self and the construction of identity on Reddit (Shelton et al. 2015; Robards 2018; Bergstrom 2011; Van der Nagle and Frith 2015), racist nationalism (Topinka 2017), online misogyny and toxicity (Massanari 2017a; Massanari and Chess 2018), and feminist humour on progressive and resistant subreddits (Massanari 2017b). Shelton et al. (2015: 10) analyse how Reddit users refer to content in external websites and offline conversations in order to ascertain how unique features of the anonymous Reddit communities impact on self-presentation, and how shared histories diffuse into external interactions. They argue that anonymous media sites such as Reddit emphasize the use of anonymity which gives rise to 'a culture of disinhibition and open disclosure' (see also Massanari 2017a). Many of the users they interviewed made strategic decisions about what to reveal to individuals offline about Reddit, including not discussing content from Reddit in person. Van der Nagle and Frith (2015) focus on the behaviours enabled through anonymous identity construction on the subreddit r/gonewild: a subreddit in which Redditors submit nude or semi-nude photos of themselves. They argue that the richness of these communities (even if they offend sensibilities) could 'be lost in a rush to embrace the singular identities of the "real name" Internet movement' (p. 2). Robards (2018) has conducted research on the subreddit r/TotallyStraight, concluding that it serves as a space for the sharing of pornography and personal narratives about sexual identity. Finally, Bergstrom (2011) provides an example of a Reddit community member who failed to provide an authentic representation of their offline self. As a result, accusations of trolling were used to justify shutting down debates about community expectations, as well as actions that violated the Reddit terms of service.

A growing body of recent work has highlighted the toxic and offensive behaviours facilitated on/through online sites such as Reddit. Topinka (2017) discusses the racist nationalist discourse in comments and images posted on r/I'mGoingToHellForThis, a subreddit which emerged in the week following news coverage of the photograph of Alan Kurdi (a Syrian boy whose dead body was photographed on a beach in Turkey). These discourses included the 'mocking of political correctness' (p. 2) and 'resistance in the shape of racism and resurgent nationalism through the cloak of anti-politically correct humor' (p. 3). Topinka (2017: 4) argues that 'redditors use freedom of speech and humor to cloak racist and nationalist ideologies and agendas'. Massanari's (2017a: 330) ethnography of Reddit culture further highlights how its design, algorithm and platform policies support 'toxic technocultures' which incorporate problematic aspects of 'geek masculinity'.

Men's Rights Activists (MRAs) and the Manosphere

The History of Men's Rights Movements

Coston and Kimmel (2013) argue that the men's rights movement was born out of the seeds of second-wave feminism in the 1970s which prompted a crisis of masculinity as traditional gender roles and meanings were challenged (Messner 1998). 'Men's Liberation' was born in a critique of the male sex role and the argument that men were '… exiled from the home, turned into soulless robotic workers, in harness to a masculine mystique, so that their only capacity for nurturing was through their wallets' (Coston and Kimmel 2013: 369). The 'Men's Liberation' movement subsequently split into two factions—pro- and anti-feminist (Messner 2016); the latter representing a 'backlash' (Flood 1998). This split was due to what they deemed to be the cause of men's problems: '… the critique of the oppressive male sex role, and the desire to free men from it, morphed into a celebration of all things masculine, and a near-infatuation with the traditional masculine role itself' (Coston and Kimmel 2013: 372).

This anti-feminist movement is reactionary and explains its role as defending the rights of men (Halberstam 2012). It mainly consists of 'angry, straight, white men' (Coston and Kimmel 2013: 380). In his article on men's rights intellectuals and literature, Allan argues that the movement 'co-opted the language of affect, emotion, feeling, and the personal being political to meet its own ends' thus appropriating 'the language of feminist consciousness-raising' (2016: 26). Members of the movement view themselves as victims of feminism (Allan 2016). Feminism is the enemy and is a political strategy which aims to take power away from men (Coston and Kimmel 2013). However, MRAs' positions on a number of issues are contradictory. For example, in relation to women, some members are approving of the traditional 'women's role' (i.e. as wife, mother and housekeeper), while other denigrate it pointing out that women in this role are merely 'gold-diggers':

> So Men's Rights activists hate those traditional women because they enslave men, gluing them to gold-digger trophy wives, who spend, preen, and otherwise ignore their hardworking husbands. No, wait. Men's Rights activists love traditional women who won't compete outside the home for scarce jobs that should go to men anyway … (Coston and Kimmel 2013: 372)

Some members argue for the rejection of traditional (hegemonic) masculinity, while others champion it (Kimmel 2017 [2013]). As a result, the feelings of MRA communities have turned to that of rage and anger with the main aim being the (re)appropriation of power. Although they maintain most of the power in public and work life, these men feel that women have all the power. Kimmel (2017 [2013]) argues that white men's anger stems from the fusion of two sentiments: 'aggrieved entitlement' and a sense of victimization. In the 1990s, the Southern Poverty Center in the USA included MRAs in their survey of hate groups, as a result of the virulent misogynistic and hateful discourses they propagated, which included encouraging acts of violence against women and children (Coston and Kimmel 2013).

Scholars have argued that men who are part of contemporary online MRA movements are not hegemonically masculine (Banet-Weiser and Miltner 2016). According to Nagle (2016) the 'beta rebellion', which takes place on MRA sites and in some 'geeky subcultures', should be viewed as the sign of a 'new net-bred brand of misogyny'. The 'beta male' is a form of identification which includes self-mockery and belonging (Nagle 2016). This rebellion has its roots in the 'libertarian ethos' which permeated the early hacker cultures of the 1960s and 1970s, and the 'Californian rebel capitalism of the dotcom neoliberalism of the nineties.' Members of these largely all-male online cultures have been referred to as 'geeks' or 'nerds' (Banet-Weiser and Miltner 2016). Ging (2017) argues that we should describe them as 'hybrid masculinities, whose self-positioning as victims of feminism and political correctness enables them to strategically distance themselves from hegemonic masculinity, while simultaneously compounding existing hierarchies of power and inequality online'. For Bridges and Pascoe (2014: 246), hybrid masculinity 'refers to men's selective incorporation of performances and identity elements associated with marginalized and subordinated masculinities and femininities'. Nagle (2016) points out that the beta-male rebellion in these online spaces runs counter to the arguments of sociologists of masculinity such as Kimmel and Connell because it draws from a 'countercultural genealogy and identifies itself against feminism but also against social conservatism, political correctness, mainstream consumer culture, and … hegemonic masculinity…'

The Manosphere

According to Marwick and Caplan (2018: 1), the Internet has been crucial to the success of MRAs. They refer to the 'manosphere'[3] as a 'loose online network' which consists of 'a set of blogs, podcasts, and forums comprised of pickup artists, men's rights activists, anti-feminists, and fringe groups'. Ging (2017) notes that the term which has been adopted by MRAs, also features in media coverage of online misogyny and high-profile events such as mass shootings and college campus rape in the USA. The politics of the manosphere centres on the idea of the Red Pill:

> … an analogy which derives from the 1999 film *The Matrix*, in which Neo is given the choice of taking one of the two pills. Taking the blue pill means switching off and living a life of delusion; taking the red pill means becoming enlightened to life's ugly truths. The Red Pill philosophy purports to awaken men to feminism's misandry and brainwashing … (Ging 2017: 3)

Participants of the manosphere have adopted a common language and believe that 'feminist values dominate society that this fact is suppressed by feminists and "political correctness," and that men must fight back against an overreaching, misandrist culture to protect their very existence' (Marwick and Caplan 2018: 4). Using the example of #GamerGate, Marwick and Caplan highlight how many of the networked harassment techniques used were introduced by groups in the manosphere. 'Misandry', which refers to hatred of men, is used as a 'boundary object' in order to 'coordinate and convey meaning amongst ingroup and outgroup participants, depending on the source of its use' (p. 11). In addition, by: 'Setting up feminism—and feminists—as villains, and men as victims' MRAs can justify 'the networked harassment that often emerges from the manosphere' (Marwick and Caplan 2018: 5). Ging (2017) also outlines the characteristics of the manosphere and the new 'hybrid masculinities' which characterize this online space. They are preoccupied with 'operationalizing tropes of victimhood', 'beta masculinity,' and 'involuntary celibacy (incels)' (Ging 2017: 1).

The new anti-feminist politics present in these online spaces involves features such as 'transnational homogenization', 'extreme misogyny' and 'proclivity for personal attacks' (Ging 2017: 8). The discourses characterizing these cultures include the 'othering' of those outside of the culture, a rationalistic masculinity and applications of evolutionary psychology (Ging 2017: 8). Massanari and Chess (2018) have researched the construction of social justice warrior (SJW) memes on Reddit by alt-right supporters.[4] SJW is 'used as a pejorative within these communities to describe individuals who they claim are overly invested in identity politics and political correctness. The "SJW" is a humourless shrill who takes pleasure in demonstrating their superiority by policing the behavior of others' (Massanari and Chess 2018: 2). They argue that these memes are deployed by Redditors 'to emphasize opponents as having non-normative, problematic bodies, different brains (ones ruled by emotion rather than logic), and monstrous characteristics' (p. 1). They also entail dehumanization and an eliminationist and genocidal rhetoric which can be viewed as hate speech. The former entails the use of images pertaining to disease or demonic identities (i.e. 'the monstrous feminine') (Massanari and Chess 2018: 14; see also Goldhagen 2009). However, they are also keen to point out that feminists may have the necessary tools to recreate the SJW as an image of power.

Banet-Weiser and Miltner (2016: 171) use the term 'networked misogyny' to refer to this 'virulent strain of violence and hostility towards women in online environments'. This 'othering' includes a tendency to view women as sexual objects or 'unwelcome interlopers'. The 'fear of female encroachment' in online spaces extended from the early Internet forums of the 1990s and the trolling and meme cultures of the 2000s, through to recent gaming cultures (i.e. exemplified in #GamerGate), social media platforms and communities on Reddit and 4/chan). As Benet-Weiser and Miltner argue, this fear of encroachment extends to the place of women in offline technological and industrial spaces, with the accusation that women are taking men's jobs (2016: 173; Lumsden and Morgan 2017). A growing body of literature now exists which acknowledges that these types of online spaces are hostile to women and that online discourse is gendered (i.e. see Massanari 2017a). Often, the aim is to silence women or oust them from these male-dominated spaces (Lumsden and Morgan 2017). Moreover, online harassment and sexism can also be framed as acceptable by constructing it as a form of humour (Drakett et al. 2018).

This chapter adds to this body of work by analysing discourses on the subreddit r/MensRights. It provides a valuable insight into the construction of notions of online acceptability and deviance vis-à-vis digital communication, the boundaries between online/offline violence and (online) culture wars. It also highlights the rampant misogyny aimed at women and feminists online. In particular, the 'othering' of women and feminists by these MRAs is evident in and via their denial of victim status, denial of injury and appeal to higher loyalties.

Methods

The study involved a search of the r/MensRights subreddit for threads which contained the words 'troll' and/or 'trolling' in the title post or comments. From a search conducted on 5 October 2016, a total of $n=24$ threads were identified which contained one or both of these terms. This resulted in a total of $n=1931$ comments for analysis. The date of the original posts for each thread ranged from 6 June 2010 to 20 April 2016.

The research aimed to explore the discourses of trolling that emerged on r/MensRights and included five initial questions: (1) How do MRAs discuss trolling on the Reddit sub-forum? (2) How do MRAs construct digital violence or abuse against women and feminists? (3) How is feminism and online feminist activism constructed in MRA online discussions? (4) How do MRAs justify their online interactions? The study aimed to contribute to significant gaps in social scientific literature including understandings of MRAs on Reddit, and on online abuse and trolling, by investigating how individuals in an online space typically conceived of as deviant in relation to its views towards feminism and social justice, engaged in online othering, and how members constructed notions of digital violence, online abuse and trolling.

I used qualitative analysis 'to document and understand the communication of meaning, as well as to verify theoretical relationships' (Altheide 1987: 68). This is a distinctive form of analysis because of the reflexive and interactive nature of the investigator, concepts, data collection and analysis. With this interpretive approach, the idea is to allow for reflexivity, 'while being systematic and analytic, but not rigid' (Altheide 1987: 68). I allowed my initial research questions, categories and themes to guide the analysis, but others also emerged throughout the analysis. In particular, thematic analysis was utilized to analyse the r/MensRights comments which allowed for the identification of key themes and patterns emerging from the transcripts (Braun and Clarke 2006). Microsoft Excel was used to record, categorize and code each of the threads and respective comments.

As with previous studies of online spaces such as Reddit, the decision was made to view the comments posted on the r/MensRights subreddit as public comments (Kitchin 2002). I cleaned all data including removing the user name of the person posting. As Caplan and Purser point out: 'even though posts are written under anonymized screen names, the nature of Reddit and other social media sites means that a community often forms and people become "known" by screen name' (2017: 11). The study received institutional ethical approval from the university.

In the discussion below I focus on the findings relating to the second research question: (2) How do MRAs construct digital violence or abuse against women and feminists? I analyse comments from three of the threads—2, 22 and 24, which focus specifically on celebrity and United Nations attempts to classify online abuse and trolling as violence. Thread 2 followed on from a post and link to a Guardian press report claiming that the celebrity Ashley Judd intended to report Twitter users who sexually harass her to the authorities.[5] Thread 22 focuses on an Alternet report detailing how women who are outspoken on social media are subject to online abuse and threats (Diels 2013).[6] Thread 24 focuses on a Time article on a United Nations report detailing that cyber violence is the equivalent to physical violence (Alter 2015).[7] The themes discussed below focus on: (1) denial of women and feminists as victims of online violence; (2) the victimization of men online; and (3) constructions of online violence.

Findings: The Construction of Digital Violence and Abuse on r/MensRights

Denial of Women and Feminists as Victims of Online Violence

Repeatedly in each of the threads, women's status as 'legitimate' victims of online violence, abuse or trolling was questioned and denied (Sykes and Matza 1957). In the below comment which relates to women's experiences of sexual harassment online, the user mockingly refers to 'the feels' as the rationale for a woman believing an action to be sexual harassment, and thus explicitly denies them victim status. Stereotypical constructions of women as 'irrational' and 'emotional' were prominent in the comments:

> Because of the *feels*[8] man because of the feels. If it *feels* like sexual harassment, then clearly it must be even if it is nowhere near the actual definition. (Thread 2, emphasis added)

Women were constructed as having underlying motives for drawing attention to online sexual harassment and violence, or the under-representation of women in various spaces. For example, women who reported online abuse were referred to as 'damsels' who wanted to be 'protected' by men, or of trying to 'appeal to [men's] chivalry', while online comments were viewed as 'offending their sensibilities'. In relation to the article about celebrity Ashley Judd, a user wrote:

> Sounds like she making an appeal to chivalry. Damsel must be protected. Tradcons[9] and feminists can agree on one thing: Women must be protected. Generation after generation has been indoctrinated to believe such drivel. It's too bad this protection turns them into spoiled entitled, whiny hyper-sensitive children who can get away with cold blooded murder. *Ashley Judd is like…making a change or something by framing redundant run of the mill abuse as like…a woman only problem.* (Thread 2, original emphasis)

While denying the celebrity (and women who report online abuse) any form of victimhood, this MRA is also denigrating the traditional sex role of women as weak, vulnerable and sensitive. The claim that they were exaggerating online violence or abuse was coupled with frequent use of 'eliminationist' and 'genocidal rhetoric' (Goldhagen 2009; Massanari and Chess 2018). For example, the above MRA draws on 'eliminationist' language in their reference to women's calls for action to tackle sexual harassment as akin to 'cold-blooded murder'; ultimately a threat to men who are viewed as the 'true' victims of discrimination and abuse. We can also see the use of 'eliminationist' and 'genocidal rhetoric' in the below references to terrorism, torture and the holocaust:

> *Comment 1*: Next time, they'll insist it to be called 'torture'. And 'terrorism' next time. Who knows, exaggeration treadmill may reach 'holocaust' level sometime.
> *Comment 2*: At this point, it wouldn't surprise me very much. They've completely lost any sense of proportion they once might have had. (Thread 2)

Other stereotypical assertions included female celebrities being 'desperate' to have their five minutes of fame thus using accusations of online violence to do so, of women 'crying violence' or 'throwing around rape accusations':

> Oh look, yet another washed up 'celebrity' desperately trying to have her fifteen minutes of fame again. Some do it by throwing around rape accusations, others by crying about violence against women over social media. (Thread 2)

Moreover, in relation to sexual harassment in online spaces, one user commented that sexual harassment could not be experienced as such if it had been perpetrated by strangers:

> You … can't experience sexual harassment from strangers … Sexual harassment happens at work or in a place of education and is done by the institution that fails to provide equal protection or service to you based on your sex. … (Thread 2)

Women were also viewed as 'money-grabbers'. For instance, the campaign in the UK for a woman to appear on a banknote was referred to by users as an example of 'abusive shit' towards men, and of another means through which feminists were attempting to gain power without having 'earned it':

> Because you know damn well they didn't just ask for Jane Austen to get out on the bill. They brought up all sorts of lying bullshit about how 'wommin were oppressed by men' and complained about how men get too much credit and shouldn't be on all of the bills. That's fucking bullshit. You don't get ahead by tearing down other people and expect

to be respected for it … That deserves abuse. How about you EARN it instead of always demanding special treatment just because you have a vagina? … (Thread 24)

In the above excerpt, the MRA de-legitimizes women as victims of online violence or trolling. In addition to denying victim status, users also associated blame with some women who they claimed were 'asking for it' because of their feminist views about men. This reflects an attitude which is supportive of online 'rape culture' and violence or abuse towards women online. For instance, in this all-male online space 'a definitional climate' has been fostered which is 'conducive to the neutralization of negative attitudes' towards online rape and/or abuse and in which women are 'asking for it' because of their feminist views and/or calls for gender equality (Boeringer 1999: 83). 'Feminist views' were seen as threatening, abusive towards men, and a means of 'verbally attacking' MRAs, while feminism itself was viewed as a dangerous ideology:

> *'Women who say abusive shit about men get verbally attacked by men.'* Are they really fucking surprised? STOP SAYING ABUSIVE SHIT! (Thread 24, original emphasis)

Hence, the MRAs were able to both normalize and justify online abuse and attacks against feminists as they viewed this as a response to feminism as 'the enemy' (Kimmel 2017 [2013]), and as engaging in its own forms of abusive, violent and trolling behaviour(s) in online spaces.

The Victimization of Men Online

In the MRA subreddit, a message frequently repeated was that feminism erases men's victimization (Gotell and Dutton 2016). Comments centred on men as the 'real' victims of online violence and harassment as the below excerpt demonstrates:

> Why do women get special protection from online harassment? How is this sexual harassment other than a few gendered words being part of it? These were tweets in response to her posting sports opinions. Many men who

post sports opinions get harassed, abused, and trolled with much stronger language, and it also often includes gendered words … A man being called a dick is the equivalent of a woman being called a cunt … (Thread 2)

The evidence presented for online violence was also challenged or questioned by users. In addition to being questioned, online violence was also viewed as part and parcel, the 'norm', of online communications and 'part of the territory'. As Gotell and Dutton (2016) have noted in their study of MRAs, there is also a tendency to present sexual violence as 'gender-neutral':

…I see no conclusive evidence that women are the primary victims of this type of harassment. I've been advocating men's rights for years and years, and I can't count the amount of times people have attempted to bully me into silence … People have attempted to publicly humiliate me, I've received death threats, I've had people conveniently bring up my own address in private messages – but I don't complain. I know this is part of the territory … (Thread 24)

Users also questioned the evidence presented in reports and studies, claiming that more men are victims of online harassment. Here, we also see the emergence of the 'socially maladjusted male' as the 'main target' and thus victim of trolling:

…where are they taking their statistics from? Didn't the latest Pew study show men are actually more likely to be harassed online? Men are often the biggest victims of harassment and trolling I've seen, just look at most of the trolling/shaming subreddits and see who the main targets are. (Hint: It's socially maladjusted males) Why do I have the feeling they're only taking into account occurrences of a sexual nature when it comes to so-called cyber violence? … (Thread 22)

Women's claims of having experienced online violence were also viewed by some users as evidence of feminists attempting to 'reclaim' or 'take back' power, part of the wider 'feminist agenda' and conspiracy against men:

> *Comment 1*: … Feminists don't care about consistency.
> *Comment 2*: Yes, with the exception of anything that gives them more power. They're pretty consistent about that. (Thread 2)

The MRA reaction was also a backlash against the gains which women were viewed to have achieved regarding equality and power. As Sylvia Walby (1993) argues backlash is not only about resisting feminism or seeking to slow its progress; it is also a means of reaffirming the patriarchal domination of women. In the excerpt below, progress towards equality for women was viewed as having been achieved at the expense of men (Kimmel 2017 [2013]). Women are also accused of lying and being able to falsely accuse by 'crying rape' (Gottell and Dutton 2016):

> When those gains are explicitly at the expense of men, such as their ability to abandon their traditional gender role en masse, while still insisting, with threat of law, that men continue theirs? … The ability to cry rape, and have no consequences to you, but massive damage to the accused even if you are shown, often even if there is evidence that you were lying? … Hell yes those 'gains' need to be stripped away … (Thread 24)

Constructions of Online Violence: 'You Need a Good Smashing up the Arse' is Not a Threat

In addition to denying victimhood to women and feminists who reported experiences of online violence, and claiming that men were the victims, MRAs denied that online abuse was a form of 'violence' and also denied the female victim's injuries (Sykes and Matza 1957). They claimed that there was: 'No such thing as verbal violence' or 'online violence' and that: 'You can't experience violence over the internet'.

More specifically, MRAs would distinguish between the wording of a 'threat' and a 'taunt'. They normalize these forms of communication ('mean comments') as part of the everyday discourses and expectations of online spaces, the *lingua franca* of these communities (see Phillips 2015; Lumsden and Morgan 2017), as the below comment demonstrates:

… A threat is a threat. Telling someone to shut up is not a threat, nor is there any implied threat … 'This is a systemic issue, the people doing this, this is their hobby, they just move from target to target, they're like a roaming gang of some kind,' explains developer and consultant Adria Richards. That's exactly how you know these aren't actually threats, they're just mean comments. (Thread 2)

In relation to definitions of rape threats on Twitter, the same MRA goes on to explain that:

… 'You need a good smashing up the arse' is not a threat. A threat requires the expression of intent, such as 'I'm going to give you a good smashing up the arse,' though even with the latter, context will tell if it's meant to just be a nasty remark or if it's meant to convey actual intent. (Thread 2)

He then goes on to provide a dictionary definition of 'threat' to further demonstrate how 'I want to kill you …' is different from the intent ('I will kill you…'):

Merriam Webster: 'an expression of intention to inflict evil, injury, or damage' Black's Law: 'A communicated intent to inflict harm or loss on another or on another's property.' It's not my definition of threat, it's the definition of threat. So no, 'I want to kill you in front of your children' is not a threat. It's an expression of a desire, not of an intent … (Thread 2)

Online violence which was seen to include acts like trolling, was also viewed by members of the MRA subreddit as different from *offline* violence, demonstrating the problematic dichotomous framing of the online/virtual world as having no offline 'real world' consequences, while offline harassment was taken seriously. Online violence was not viewed as harmful like physical or verbal violence in the offline world and anecdotal evidence and examples are drawn on to demonstrate their points:

> *Commenter 2*: If physical attacks were equal to psychological attacks, you could even claim self-defense when attacking someone who shouts at you, since he could have driven you to suicide.
> *Commenter 1*: Good point! 'Officer, he hit me with his words and hurt my feels. An urge to kill myself flooded my mind, so in self-defense I punched him in the throat and cut out his tongue. I think he got off easy really.'
> *Commenter 3*: If words were equal to physical attack, I wouldn't have been so afraid to beat the living shit out of my bullies in high school who pushed me to the brink of suicide.
> *Commenter 4*: '911 how may I help you?' 'I'd like to report an incidence of violence! Somebody punched me at the bar…' 'I'm sorry ma'am but all resources have been diverted to catch a person that ridiculed another's ideas online so you will have to wait.' (Thread 22)

In the final sentence above, the MRA's denial of online violence can also be seen to entail an appeal to higher loyalties (Sykes and Matza 1957), in that the moral values of policing and responding to calls of violence should coalesce on taking physical violence seriously.

Conclusion

This chapter provided an analysis of MRA discussions of online violence and victimization on the r/MensRights subreddit. It focused on findings including: denial of women and feminists as victims of online violence; the victimization of men online; and constructions of online violence. It argues that these previously unexplored online discourses and interactions provide us with a valuable insight into the construction of notions of online acceptability and deviance vis-à-vis digital communication, the boundaries between online/offline violence, (online) culture wars, and the ethos and attitudes of MRAs on the 'manosphere' (Ging 2017; Marwick and Caplan 2018).

Although there has been a plethora of studies of MRA campaigns on parenting and father's rights (see Boyd 2004; Collier 2009) and domestic violence (Dragiewicz 2008; Mann 2008), there are few studies of MRAs engagement with feminists, views of feminism, and/or discussions of online violence and trolling. The findings above echo the observations of previous studies such as the work of Gotell and Dutton (2016) who analysed sexual violence on North American and Canadian anti-feminist MRA websites. They also note the rise in online 'rape culture' and the assertion made by MRAs 'that rape culture is a feminist-inspired moral panic is a predominant theme within a broader backlash to anti-rape feminism' (Gotell and Dutton 2016: 75). They draw attention to the ways in which these campaigns focus on young men as the main victims of feminism. In their analysis of MRA websites, Schmitz and Kazyak (2016) also observe how these communities promote men's entitlement to social power, which was evident in the above MRA discussions of men as the victims of online abuse, and their efforts to present sexual violence as gender-neutral (Gotell and Dutton 2016). In Schmitz and Kazyak's (2016) study of MRA websites which they classify under the theme of 'Cyber Lads', they found that users frequently degraded women, demonized feminist tenets, viewed feminism as the source of men's oppression and demeaned the feminist principle of gender equality via humour and jokes. Moreover, the above findings demonstrate that men's rights while still occupied with issues of family law and parenthood have also shifted to an intensely personal and anecdotal focus (Ging 2017). This is reflected above in users' accounts of what they deem to be their own victimization and victim status (Coston and Kimmel 2013; Kimmel 2017 [2013]).

The above discourses also entailed dehumanization and an eliminationist and genocidal rhetoric which can be viewed as hate speech (see also Massanari and Chess 2018; Goldhagen 2009). The 'othering' of women and feminists by these MRAs is evident in and via their denial of victim status, denial of injury, and appeal to higher loyalties (Sykes and Matza 1957) in terms of the correct policing and definition of 'real violence' and 'threats' as opposed to online violence and harassment, accounts of which were de-legitimized. Moreover, women's accounts of sexual harassment online were either presented as 'gender-neutral' (Gotell and Dutton 2016) and/or were dismissed via anecdotal accounts that men are the victims and feminism is the 'enemy'.

While it shines light on the discourses of MRAs in relation to online violence and feminism, the chapter also shows how more social scientific research is necessary to understand 'toxic technocultures' (Massanari 2017a) such as various subreddits, the evolution of men's rights movements and their online presence, the resurgence in misogyny and sexism online (including online harassment of women), and also the ways in which these online communities attempt to police, regulate and control groups/individuals who occupy online spaces and social media through various strategies of 'online othering'.

Notes

1. r/Pizzagate was a subreddit for people who believed that high-ranking staffers of Hillary Clinton's Presidential campaign, and possibly Clinton herself, were trafficking child sex slaves (Marantz 2018).
2. Later joined by Christopher Slowe and Aaron Swartz.
3. Ging (2017) notes that the term first appeared in 2009 on a Blogspot blog to describe an online network of men's interest communities. It was popularized by the porn marketer and author Ian Ironwood, porn marketer.
4. These far-right communities include white ethnonationalists, Islamophobes, and misogynistic men's rights activists (Massanari and Chess 2018: 1).
5. Beaumont-Thomas, B. (2016). Ashley Judd to press charges against Twitter users over sexual harassment. *The Guardian*. https://www.theguardian.com/film/2015/mar/18/ashley-judd-to-press-charges-twitter-sexual-harassment, accessed June 2018.
6. Diels, K. (2013). The shocking ways that women's free speech is under attack. *Alternet*. https://www.alternet.org/gender/womens-free-speech-under-attack, accessed June 2018.
7. Alter, C. (2015). U.N. says cyber violence is equivalent to physical violence against women. *Time*. http://time.com/4049106/un-cyber-violence-physical-violence/, accessed June 2018.

8. A term originating from youths in the late 2000s/early 2010s which means 'feelings'.
9. 'Tradcon' refers to someone of traditional conservative politics.

References

Allan, J. A. (2016). Phallic affect, or why men's rights activists have feelings. *Men and Masculinities, 19*(1), 22–41.

Altheide, D. L. (1987). Ethnographic content analysis. *Qualitative Sociology, 10*(1), 65–77.

Banet-Weiser, S., & Miltner, K. M. (2016). #MasculinitySoFragile: Culture, structure and networked misogyny. *Feminist Media Studies, 16*(1), 171–174.

Bergstrom, K. (2011). 'Don't feed the troll': Shutting down debate about community expectations on Reddit.com. *First Monday, 16*(8).

Boeringer, S. B. (1999). Associations of rape-supportive attitudes with fraternal and athletic participation. *Violence Against Women, 5*(1), 81–90.

Boyd, S. B. (2004). Demonizing mothers: Fathers' rights discourses in child custody law reform processes. *Journal for the Association of Research on Mothering, 6*(1), 52–74.

Braun, V., & Clarke, C. (2006). Using thematic analysis in psychology. *Qualitative Research in Psychology, 3*(2), 77–101.

Bridges, T., & Pascoe, C. J. (2014). Hybrid masculinities: New directions in the sociology of men and masculinities. *Sociology Compass, 8*, 246–258.

Caplan, M. A., & Purser, G. (2017). Qualitative inquiry using social media: A field-tested example. *Qualitative Social Work*, ifirst. http://journals.sagepub.com/doi/10.1177/1473325017725802.

Collier, R. (2009). Fathers' rights movement, law reform, and the new politics of fatherhood: Some reflections on the UK experience. *University of Florida Journal of Law and Public Policy, 20*, 65–111.

Coston, B. M., & Kimmel, M. (2013). White men as the new victims: Reverse discrimination cases and the men's rights movement. *Nevada Law Journal, 13*, 368–385.

Digital Tracking Blog. (2017). By the Numbers 60+ Amazing Reddit Statistics. https://expandedramblings.com/index.php/reddit-stats/. Accessed March 15, 2018.

Dragiewicz, M. (2008). Patriarchy reasserted: Fathers' rights and anti-VAWA activism. *Feminist Criminology, 3*(2), 121–144.

Drakett, J., Rickett, B., Day, K., & Milnes, K. (2018). Old jokes, new media—Online sexism and constructions of gender in internet memes. *Feminism & Psychology, 28*(1), 109–127.

Flood, M. (1998). Men's movements. *Community Quarterly, 46,* 62–71.

Ging, D. (2017). Alphas, betas, and incels: Theorizing the masculinities of the manosphere. *Men & Masculinities,* ifirst. https://doi.org/10.1177/1097184x17706401.

Goldhagen, D. J. (2009). *Worse Than War.* New York: Public Affairs Press.

Gotell, L., & Dutton, E. (2016). Sexual violence in the 'Manosphere': Antifeminist men's rights discourses on rape. *International Journal for Crime, Justice and Social Democracy, 5*(2), 65–80.

Halberstam, J. J. (2012). *Gaga Feminism.* Boston, MA: Beacon Press.

Herring, S. C., Job-Sluder, K., Scheckler, R., & Barab, S. (2002). Searching for safety online: Managing 'trolling' in a feminist forum. *The Information Society, 18,* 371–384.

Jane, E. A. (2014). You're a ugly, whorish, slut. *Feminist Media Studies, 14*(4), 531–546.

Kimmel, M. (2017 [2013]). *Angry White Men.* New York: Nation Books.

Kitchin, H. A. (2002). The tri-council on cyberspace: Insights, oversights, and extrapolations. In W. C. Van den Hoonaard (Ed.), *Walking the Tightrope.* Toronto, Canada: University of Toronto Press.

Lewis, R., Rowe, M., & Wiper, C. (2016). Online abuse of feminists as an emerging form of violence against women and girls. *British Journal of Criminology, 57*(6), 1462–1481.

Lumsden, K., & Morgan, H. M. (2017). Media framing of trolling and online abuse: Silencing strategies, symbolic violence and victim blaming. *Feminist Media Studies, 17*(6), 926–940.

Mann, R. M. (2008). Men's rights and feminist advocacy in Canadian domestic violence policy arenas. *Feminist Criminology, 3*(1), 44–75.

Mantilla, K. (2015). *Gendertrolling.* Westport, CT: Praeger.

Marantz, A. (2018, March 19). Reddit and the Struggle to Detoxify the Internet. *New Yorker.* https://www.newyorker.com/magazine/2018/03/19/reddit-and-the-struggle-to-detoxify-the-internet. Accessed June 8, 2018.

Marwick, A. E., & Caplan, R. (2018). Drinking male tears: Language, the manosphere, and networked harassment. *Feminist Media Studies,* ifirst. https://doi.org/10.1080/14680777.2018.1450568.

Massanari, A. (2017a). #Gamergate and the fappening: How Reddit's algorithm, governance, and culture support toxic technocultures. *New Media & Society, 19*(3), 329–346.

Massanari, A. (2017b). 'Come for the period comics. Stay for the cultural awareness': Reclaiming the troll identity through feminist humor on Reddit's r/TrollXChromosomes. *Feminist Media Studies*, ifirst. https://doi.org/10.1080/14680777.2017.1414863.

Massanari, A., & Chess, S. (2018). Attack of the 50 foot social justice warrior: The discursive construction of SJW memes as the monstrous feminine. *Feminist Media Studies*, ifirst. https://doi.org/10.1080/14680777.2018.1447333.

Megarry, J. (2014). Online incivility or sexual harassment? Conceptualising women's experiences in the digital age. *Women's Studies International Forum, 47,* 46–55.

Messner, M. A. (1998). The limits of 'the male sex role': An analysis of the men's liberation and men's rights movements' discourse. *Gender and Society, 12,* 255–276.

Messner, M. A. (2016). Forks in the road of men's gender politics: Men's rights vs feminist allies. *International Journal for Crime, Justice and Social Democracy, 5,* 6–20.

Nagle, A. (2016). The new man of 4/Chan. *The Baffler,* 30. http://thebaffler.com/salvos/new-man-4chan-nagle. Accessed June 6, 2016.

Phillips, W. (2015). *This Is Why We Can't Have Nice Things*. Cambridge, MA: MIT Press.

r/MensRights. (2013). Frequently asked questions. https://www.reddit.com/r/MensRights/wiki/faq. Accessed March 15, 2018.

Reddit. (2017). *About*. https://about.reddit.com. Accessed March 15, 2018.

Reddit Help. (2017). *Audience and Demographics*. https://reddit.zendesk.com/hc/en-us/articles/205183225-Audience-and-Demographics. Accessed March 15, 2018.

Robards, B. (2018). 'Totally straight': Contested sexual identities on social media site Reddit. *Sexualities, 21*(1–2), 49–67.

Schmitz, R. M., & Kazyak, E. (2016). Masculinities in cyberspace: An analysis of portrayals of manhood in men's rights activist websites. *Social Sciences, 5*(2), 1–16.

Shelton, M. L., Lo, K. M., & Nardi, B. A. (2015). Online media forums as separate social lives: A qualitative study of disclosure within and beyond Reddit. In *iConference 2015 Proceedings*.

Silverman, M. (2012). Reddit: A beginner's guide. *Mashable UK*. https://mashable.com/2012/06/06/reddit-for-beginners/#55j1Xg7ZlEq5. Accessed March 15, 2018.

Sykes, G., & Matza, D. (1957). Techniques of neutralization: A theory of delinquency. *American Sociological Review, 22*(6), 664–670.

Topinka, R. J. (2017). Politically incorrect participatory media: Racist nationalism on r/ImGoingToHellForThis. *New Media & Society*, first. http://journals.sagepub.com/doi/10.1177/1461444817712516.

Van der Nagel, E., & Frith, J. (2015, March). Anonymity, pseudonymity, and the agency of online identity: Examining the social practices of r/GoneWild. *First Monday*, 20(3–2). http://firstmonday.org/ojs/index.php/fm/article/view/5615/4346.

Walby, S. (1993). Backlash in historical context. In M. Kennedy, C. Lubelska, & V. Walsh (Eds.), *Making Connections* (pp. 79–89). Washington, DC: Taylor & Francis.

Part II

Experiences of Online Abuse: Gendered Othering, Sexism and Misogyny

Emily Harmer and Karen Lumsden

Editors' Introduction

In this part of the book, each chapter focuses on attitudes towards, and experiences of, different forms of 'online othering'. Furthermore, the contributors all emphasise the extent to which these experiences are ultimately gendered. Recent academic scholarship has made this abundantly clear (Jane 2014, 2016; Lumsden and Morgan 2017; Fox et al. 2015). Much of this research looks at the ways in which online interactions can be experienced as sexist, misogynistic and hateful. Mantilla (2015) refers to this as 'gendertrolling', which she categorises as a distinct form of online harassment. Mantilla argues that trolling in general represents an attempt to disrupt or hijack online interactions, whereas 'gendertrolls' are motivated by sexism and misogyny meaning that 'gendertrolling' is considerably more vicious, aggressive and threatening.

Crucially, the experience of being othered in the online realm is not only about gender: online harassment is very often racist in nature as well as sexist (Banet-Weiser and Miltner 2016), which is unsurprising given the extent to which the Internet is a space also demarcated by race and other forms of social inequality (Gabriel 2016). Importantly, the gendered experience of 'online othering' does not only impact on women and girls; men and boys also negotiate their gendered identity/ies online. Studies have found that digital spaces can be sites for perpetuating specific ideas about acceptable forms of masculinity and stress that the forms of gender performance afforded by many digital spaces can result in hostile environments for those who do not conform (Kendall 2000; Massanari 2017; Salter 2018; Whittle et al., this volume). Ultimately, for women and other marginalised groups, the Internet holds both challenges and opportunities. On the one hand, individuals can use it for their own freedom of expression and as a space to discuss issues pertinent to their lives; whilst on the other hand it also exposes them to those who may wish to curtail their appropriation of, and participation in, online spaces (Berridge and Portwood-Stacer 2015).

The first chapter in this part by Ruth Lewis, Mike Rowe and Claire Wiper explores the experiences of online abuse amongst women who discuss feminist politics in digital spaces. Using data from a national UK study, the chapter uses debates about Violence Against Women and Girls (VAWG) and hate crime to consider the continuities and breaks between online and offline forms of victimisation. The authors argue that online abuse should be considered to be a form of VAWG and a hate crime, although these categories are problematic because they reflect inappropriate distinctions between private and public offences. They also suggest that 'hate' is a clumsy description of the complex emotional context when perpetrators are known to the victims, and also because 'hate crime' does not reflect the intersectional nature of some offences which target victims' identities.

Rikke Amundsen's chapter explores how women make sense of the risks of having their private sexual images (PSIs) shared without their consent. Amundsen uses interview data to discuss the ways in which women's responses to the issue seem to reflect a postfeminist sensibility, marked by an emphasis on individualism, free choice and female empowerment. Amundsen finds that these women emphasise making the right choices in terms of who to trust with their PSIs, resulting in accounts where women effectively render themselves primarily responsible for their own risk mitigation. She also suggests that (would-be) victims of such non-consensual sharing receive little empathy, due to their perceived inability to protect themselves from risk by exercising their free choices in the 'correct' way.

John Whittle, Dave Elder-Vass and Karen Lumsden's chapter discusses teenage boys' use of 'banter' on social networking sites such as Facebook. They present data collected via semi-structured interviews and focus groups with boys and girls aged 11–16. They examine the role of 'banter' in male teenagers' social media interactions. 'Banter' is characterised by the use of confrontational exchanges to explore social boundaries and values amongst friends, and is strongly involved in male bonding rituals. It is also employed as a means of negotiating status and of in-group inclusion and out-group exclusion. They also argue that 'banter' is a means of othering and of performing and constructing hegemonic masculinity. Their analysis focuses on: how male teenagers learn to 'banter'; the relationship between 'banter' and bullying; and how 'banter' overflows into distinct but related othering practices.

The final chapter in this part focuses on the forms of othering experienced by elected politicians in the UK. Rosalynd Southern and Emily Harmer employ an inductive thematic analysis of 12,436 tweets to examine the extent to which abusive and more everyday forms of sexism, misogyny and racism pervade Twitter interactions between politicians and citizens. Their analysis identifies four themes: gendered and racist abuse; silencing and dismissal; questioning intelligence and position; and 'benevolent' othering. They argue that since communicating with constituents is an essential part of any political representatives' role, it can be difficult to avoid receiving abuse online. It is therefore essential to ensure that being subjected to 'online othering' in the everyday working environment of women of colour does not become a way of excluding this historically under-represented group from formal political affairs.

References

Banet-Weiser, S., & Miltner, K. M. (2016). #MasculinitySoFragile: Culture, structure, and networked misogyny. *Feminist Media Studies, 16*(1), 171–174.

Berridge, S., & Portwood-Stacer, L. (2015). Introduction: Feminism, hashtags and violence against women and girls. *Feminist Media Studies, 15*(2), 341.

Fox, J., Cruz, C., & Lee, J. Y. (2015). Perpetuating online sexism offline: Anonymity, interactivity, and the effects of sexist hashtags on social media. *Computers in Human Behavior, 52*, 436–442.

Gabriel, D. (2016). Blogging while Black, British and female: A critical study on discursive activism. *Information, Communication & Society, 19*(11), 1622–1635.

Jane, E. A. (2014). 'You're an ugly, whorish slut': Understanding e-bile. *Feminist Media Studies, 14*(4), 513–546.

Jane, E. A. (2016). *Misogyny Online: A Short (and Brutish) History*. London: Sage.

Kendall, L. (2000). 'Oh no! I'm a nerd!' Hegemonic masculinity on an online forum. *Gender and Society, 14*(2), 256–274.

Lumsden, K., & Morgan, H. M. (2017). Media framing of trolling and online abuse: Silencing strategies, symbolic violence, and victim blaming. *Feminist Media Studies, 17*(6), 926–940.

Mantilla, K. (2015). *Gendertrolling*. Westport, CT: Praeger.

Massanari, A. (2017). #Gamergate and the Fappening: How Reddit's algorithm, governance, and culture support toxic technocultures. *New Media and Society, 19*(3), 329–346.

Salter, M. (2018). From geek masculinity to Gamergate: The technological rationality of online abuse. *Media, Culture and Crime, 14*(2), 247–264.

5

Online/Offline Continuities: Exploring Misogyny and Hate in Online Abuse of Feminists

Ruth Lewis, Mike Rowe and Clare Wiper

Introduction

Online abuse has received considerable political and media attention in recent years, in the UK and beyond. It has often been presented as a new phenomenon posing new challenges about how criminal justice agencies and social media platforms should respond to it. Debates relating to online abuse have developed in relation to questions of freedom of speech and practices of 'no-platforming'[1] in universities and the espousal of extremist views and hate. Together, these developments can seem like a 'perfect storm' of urgent, troubling, new challenges. However, in this chapter, we argue that online abuse is, in fact, a new manifestation of old problems. Focusing on the technological context of such abuse leads to an emphasis on what is new, distinctive and

R. Lewis (✉) · M. Rowe · C. Wiper
Department of Social Sciences, Northumbria University,
Newcastle upon Tyne, UK

emergent. Our approach has been to concentrate on victim perspectives, which suggest considerable continuity with older forms of 'offline' hate and misogyny. Using data from a national survey of feminists in the UK who engage in online debate, we argue that the online abuse they receive can be conceptualised as a form of the long-established offences of violence against women and as a form of hate crime.

It has long been established that domestic violence and sexual offences comprise a significant proportion of police workloads, even though the majority of incidents are not reported to the police and do not result in convictions (HMIC 2014, 2015). In addition, there are worrying gaps in terms of important concepts such as 'coercive control', outlawed in the UK in 2015 but poorly understood by police (HMIC 2015; Wiener 2017). In 2016, Nottinghamshire Police announced that they had begun recording misogynistic incidents as hate crimes, a classification subsequently discussed in a meeting of the All Party Parliamentary Group on Domestic Abuse. In May 2017, North Yorkshire Police became the second force to recognise misogyny as a hate crime. While this might enable more accurate recording of incidents reported, it is not clear that in itself it will make any significant improvements to the wider practice of criminal justice, particularly since tightened resources reduce police capacity to respond effectively.

Regardless of policing practices, consideration of online abuse as a form of violence against women and as hate crime raises questions about whether existing categories can encompass new manifestations, whether and how they need to adapt to be able to do so, and whether the categories are fit-for-purpose for contemporary experiences of misogyny. Violence against women and girls is now recognised as a criminal matter only as a result of previous and ongoing efforts of feminist scholars, activists and practitioners who have long fought for such offences to be seen as a matter of public, legal, social and political concern rather than as a private matter, as they have traditionally been seen. Categories of criminal offences had to be expanded to encompass this widespread behaviour that had been conceptualised as a private, marital problem; for example, in English law, until 1991, 'rape' was a category that excluded marital rape. Even now, efforts to expand these categories continue; for example, Walby et al.'s work to analyse Crime Survey of England and Wales data 'challenge[s] the focus of serious violent crime policy on violence between men' (2015: 1227) by exposing the significant proportion of such crime that is perpetrated by men against women.

A challenge to the category of hate crimes is that a defining characteristic is that they are 'signal crimes' (Innes and Fielding 2002) intended to communicate to wider communities that they are unwelcome, inferior, at risk (Chakraborti and Garland 2009). This requires that the offence occurs in a public domain, such that it can 'speak' to a wider audience. Our research suggests that considerable abuse was experienced in an online environment where the distinction between public and private space is complex. If the virtual environment continues to become more significant as the domain in which gendered violence occurs then these difficulties will become more salient and, we argue further below, the concept of hate crime itself needs to be refined. In this chapter, we draw on data from a study about online abuse towards feminists to present the rationale for considering such abuse as a form of Violence Against Women (VAWG) and a form of hate crime. We argue that, far from presenting new challenges, this form of abuse presents a new manifestation of a well-established phenomenon for which categorisations and conceptualisation already exist. In the section below, we set out the research from which our data were generated. Then we present, first, the ways in which online abuse towards feminists can be considered as a form of VAWG, followed by the ways in which it can be considered hate crime. Throughout, and in the final section, we discuss the limitations of these categories.

Researching Online Abuse

This chapter draws on data collected for a study about the online abuse of women who engage in feminist debates. The specific experiences of these respondents might not be representative of all experiences of online abuse but their consideration contributes to wider debate about how to interpret and respond to misogynistic crime.

Two data collection strategies were used. An online questionnaire gathered data about the use of social media for feminist debate; experiences of online abuse; the impacts of and responses to abuse, including engagement with formal and informal agencies. To gather rich, detailed information about experiences of abuse, multiple choice and open questions were asked about the nature, frequency, duration and volume of abuse. The open questions generated fulsome responses, creating an extensive qualitative dataset, and enabling analysis of the concept of 'hate' as it emerged in respondents' accounts of their experiences. In total, 227 valid responses were received.

The second data collection method was a set of 17 in-depth interviews with volunteers from the survey. The qualitative survey and interview data were analysed thematically, through collaborative processes of reading and re-reading the data, discussing emerging themes and then coding the data. The study has benefitted from the exceptional richness of data provided by respondents. In the sections that follow, these data are presented unedited in line with Jane's (2014) call for presenting unexpurgated data to break the tyranny of silence around cyber-violence against women.

Online Abuse as a Form of VAWG

Campaigns such as Reclaim the Internet, evoking the traditional feminist campaign to 'reclaim the night', have helped to name online abuse as misogynistic and to draw comparisons with the long history of violence against women and girls. Other political initiatives, such as the Committee on Standards in Public Life's report on Intimidation in Public Life (2017), prompted in part by the abuse of women in politics, have helped frame some forms of online abuse as misogynistic. This links the apparently new form of abuse with many forms of violence against women and girls—sexual violence and harassment, child sexual abuse, intimate partner violence—that have long fought for recognition in social, political and legal arenas. In this section, we trace the similarities between VAWG and online abuse towards feminists, detailing the ways in which, far from being a form of behaviour unique to the cyber environment, online abuse of feminists shares several features of offline VAWG.

Scholarship has demonstrated that violence against women and girls, far from being exceptional, is part of the everyday lived experience for many women (for recent examples, see Bates 2018; Vera-Gray 2016; Walby et al. 2015). Similarly, in our survey, most women who participated experienced more than one kind of online abuse and almost half experienced it as a routine, regular part of their online lives. In this way, it is experienced as a course of behaviour rather than individual acts just as intimate partner violence, sexual abuse and harassment, for example, are often experienced. The justice system, however, has traditionally struggled to recognise this feature of these offences. Intimate partner violence, for example, has high rates of repeat victimisation (Walby et al. 2015), although it is often framed and treated, problematically, as discrete acts (Kelly and Westmarland 2016; Lewis et al. 2001). While the criminal justice system has traditionally focused on individual incidents that fit into existing categories of crime, women have increasingly conceptualised such behaviour as constituting a 'culture' of violence. This is illustrated by both the #MeToo movement in response to the exposure of widespread abuse in the film and other industries, and by attempts to address misogynistic cultures linked to gender-based violence in universities (Anitha and Lewis 2018; Phipps et al. 2018; Phipps and Young 2015; Universities UK 2016).

The similarities between online and offline misogyny extend to attempts to sexually degrade women and girls. Significant features of online abuse are sexual harassment and threats of sexual violence, experienced as degrading violations. Participants in our research gave details of the sexually abusive messages and images they received:

> He told me I was a 'fat ugly cunt who no one would rape' (I have rape survivor in my bio). He then upped the ante and four or five people who seemed connected to him joined in. I was threatened to be raped. I was threatened to be 'boned' and thrown all sorts of insults at. (Respondent 238)

> A man sent me multiple images of his genitals and a video of himself masturbating and when I told him this made me uncomfortable he proceeded to send more and send messages calling me a slut and a whore and telling me to graciously accept his compliment instead of a being bitch. He then went on to tell me all of the sexual acts he would like to perform on me, some of them very violent. (Respondent 154)

> I was sent horrible porn in a direct message. (Respondent 2)

The use of online environments to humiliate and degrade women sexually has been well-documented (see, for example, Hall and Hearn 2017) in relation to 'revenge pornography' or what McGlynn and Rackley (2017) call 'image-based sexual abuse'. This phenomenon is another example of an old, familiar form of men's abuse towards women that, with the help of technological 'advances', manifests in a new form.

There are similarities too in terms of the characteristics of perpetrators of online abuse and offline offences, although relatively little is known about online abusers and there is a need for future research to focus on the motivations, aims and consequences for online perpetrators. We do know, however, that VAWG is committed most often by perpetrators known to victims, demonstrating that risks are in not just public, but also private, familiar and familial spaces. Even in the relatively anonymous online environment, a third of our sample reported that perpetrators were members of their online community. VAWG online and offline is often committed by lone men but harassment—both online and offline can have a public—performative aspect; Phipps and Young (2015) for example, see some forms of 'laddish' harassment as a form of homosocial bonding. Participants reported that some perpetrators collaborated with others to intensify their abuse:

> Too much to say, but harassment from known stalker … saying that I was [a named person] (I'm not) and encouraging others to get me. Also threatened my life and that of my son. Ongoing with little police action. (Respondent 207)

I wrote a blog about sexual consent. Men's rights activists decided I needed to be 'taken down'. A forum section was devoted to me on Reddit. I was told my son would probably kill himself, that I was a man hater, that I deserved to die a slow and painful death (I am seriously ill). Hundreds of comments to the blog accused me of every man-hating crime under the sun. (Respondent 100)

I was targeted initially by one individual as I had been quoted in the media through my work. They misrepresented my views and job, broadening it out to my personal life and my appearance. They got others involved and when I tried to engage with the discussion there was a call out for others in pro sex work lobby to come and join the 'pile-on'. The abuse and insults escalated and my twitter feed was full of verbal abuse and threats. (Respondent 45)

Notions of private and public—which have been deployed in relation to VAWG to render it invisible and yet 'normal'—do not translate so easily to the online world. The online world can be conceived of as an ambivalent space that is simultaneously both private and public. Social media may offer forms of private space so that interaction is only performed in front of those 'followed' or 'befriended' rather than to a wider public. However, it is easily recirculated and might be considered public in the sense that it is shared, even if only amongst invited contacts. In terms of the content, many respondents suggested that perpetrators intended their messages to have communicative action that served to exclude targets from online spaces often conceived as 'creative commons', a place in which cultural, social and political exchanges occur. Similarly, there is a 'performative' aspect of online abuse, as noted above, linked to the identity and status of the communicator. The experience of receiving abuse may be individual, private and solitary, even while the communication of abuse is public, social and performative.

A key feature of VAWG online and offline is the apparent attempt to silence women and limit their engagement in public worlds. It is difficult to ascertain perpetrators' motivations due to the lack of research which engages with perpetrators, and to limited reliability of their accounts (exceptions being, Dobash et al. 1998; Kelly and Westmarland 2016;

Hearn 1998) but victim/survivors' accounts suggest these are motivations of various forms of VAWG. For example, sexual violence and harassment can be experienced and interpreted as a way of communicating to women that they do not 'belong' in certain environments—such as the workplace or the street—and its effects can be to limit women's freedom in these environments. A key feature of intimate partner violence is the attempt by perpetrators to isolate victims, to limit their contact with family and friends, their access to work, and to engage in public activities. Similarly, respondents in our research gave many examples of abuse that seemed to indicate they were attempts to silence women from engaging in public debate:

> General insults and derision for being a woman that talks. (Respondent 27)

> I was discussing a news story (originating from a tweet from a news outlet) concerning male violence against women with several other women on a couple of different threads. This discussion was then interrupted by first one then several men (MRAs [men's rights activists]) and degenerated into them tweeting 'go jump of a bridge whore' and 'kill yourself' tweets and idiotic threatening images. (Respondent 61)

> I posted a link to a petition requesting that SUFC ban Ched Evans from returning to the game after his conviction for Rape and was repeatedly attacked by a number of SUFC fans about it and how they would use various tactics to silence me. (Respondent 185)

Attempts to silence women have a long, ignominious history. Mary Beard (2015: 809) noted that the 'first recorded example of a man telling a woman to "shut up" … [is] immortalised at the start of the Odyssey'. We do not have to look far for recent examples of attempts to silence women in public debate. Anti-suffragette cartoons drew on similar ideas that women, their voices and ideas were 'out of place' in public spheres and often depicted violent images of women's tongues being chained to stocks and their mouths being clamped shut in a head brace. More recently, in the UK Prime Minister Cameron's patronising 'calm down, dear' evoked notions that women's behaviour is unsuitable for the male-dominated world of public debate (see BBC News 2011).

To an extent, attempts to silence women were successful. Participants responded to abuse in various ways, including avoiding encounters with potential abusers, withdrawing from debates, and self-censoring. As noted in the literature on cyber-security and crime prevention in real-world contexts (Garland 2001; Burney 2009), this finding suggests that recipients felt 'responsibilised' to take measures to prevent recurrence. Responses from police about how women might reduce the risk of receiving abuse—such as by changing their online profile, or blocking people—not only indicate their ignorance of the use of social media and its technological features, but also reflect this problematic focus on victims being held responsible for their own victimisation.

Online abuse, like offline VAWG has significant impacts. At the most extreme, both can lead to symptoms of PTSD especially if the recipient has previous experiences of abuse that are 'triggered' (see Pain 2014 for a comparison of intimate partner violence with modern international warfare). Participants reported a range of impacts to their emotional and physical well-being:

> Depression and anxiety, triggering of past experiences of real-life abuse, increased mistrust of people. (Respondent 72)

> Just general distress and caused me to have panic attacks (I have anxiety and depression), sleepless nights thinking they would be at my door in the morning and overall higher level of stress. (Respondent 64)

The frequency of abuse is a feature of its impact. Our data (reported more fully in Lewis et al. 2016) show those who experience high-frequency abuse are more likely to experience it as 'traumatic', suggesting that, far from diluting its effects, frequency exacerbates significance. The routine, everyday nature of online abuse for some women means it accumulates to feel like the 'wallpaper of sexism' (Lewis et al. 2015) adding to its harm, even while coping strategies may lead women to speak of it as insignificant:

> Part of being a woman online for me. Not so different from IRL [in real life] experience as a woman. (Respondent 73)

> Depression and anxiety, continuation of constant harassment. I shrug it off now in a way as I'm so used to it but it still has long term impact on health. (Respondent 85)

These tactics of reluctant 'normalisation' of abuse reflect the wider tendency for both online and offline VAWG to be 'normalised' in ways which support dominant heteronormativity and gender relations (Hlavka 2014) and, arguably, increase the harm by communicating that it is not worthy of significant attention. Another common coping strategy that reflects the 'normalisation' discourse was for participants to downgrade their own experiences in comparison with other women's or to minimise the impacts of the abuse, for example:

> It was a much more minor incident than the sustained harassment (in some cases from users with offline positions of power) that friends of mine have received - relatively speaking it did not matter that much. (Respondent 121)

The evidence presented demonstrates that online abuse experienced by feminists has many similarities with offline violence against women and girls. Far from being a new phenomenon, it is, rather, a new manifestation of the age-old phenomenon of misogyny. While new technologies enable abuse to be communicated in different ways, and in different contexts, and to reach a far wider number of recipients, the abuse itself is strikingly familiar. Similarly, online abuse bears many similarities to hate crime, as discussed in the following section.

Online Abuse as a Form of Hate Crime

Since its development in the USA in the early 1970s and the UK a decade or so later, hate crime scholarship and policies have not recognised VAWG as a form of hate crime. Gill and Mason-Bish (2013) note that this reflects institutional sexism and patriarchal ideology that does not acknowledge gender-based prejudice. VAWG has traditionally been excluded from hate crime categorisations in part because of the definition of hate crime as perpetrated against strangers rather than those known to the victim (see McPhail 2002 on this process in the USA, Gelber 2000, in Australia, and Gill and Mason-Bish 2013, on the British experience). In this section, we argue that there are significant similarities between online abuse and hate crime, by exploring broad themes: (i) the conceptual difficulty of the term 'hate' as applied to complex and contradictory forms of offending; (ii) the ways in which hate crimes have a communicative element in that they have some wider exclusionary intent beyond the harm intended to the primary victim; and (iii) the nature of public and private space in which hate crimes occur.

'Hate' is the defining concept of hate crime, yet its meaning is contested. Can we know that perpetrators are motivated by hate or, might 'hate' exaggerate the motivations of offenders (Bowling 1998; Ray et al. 2004), some of whom might be very young and engaging in activities that they (and others) might regard as relatively minor forms of anti-social behaviour? Can we know that perpetrators of 'ordinary' offences are *not* motivated by hate? In terms of VAWG and other forms of hate crime perpetrated by friends, family members or carers, 'hate' seems a clumsy description of the complex emotional connections. Some scholars suggest alternative terms such as 'bias' or 'prejudice' (Lawrence 1999; McPhail 2002), 'gender hostility' (Walters and Tumath 2014), or 'mate crime' (Thomas 2016) may be more useful ways of conceptualising imputed intentions.

Although not asked directly about hate crime, respondents in our study drew on concepts and terminology from that framework as they reflected on the abuse they had received:

It's scary knowing how many people hate you. (Respondent 31)

One of the comments 'I wish you'd fallen into the path of Peter Sutcliffe' and that, you know, that's grim. That's somebody who really hates women and things like that I would say are really the things that would still touch me now. (Interviewee 16)

> They are little men - I think that's a phrase that has been used over the years isn't it? - Who were probably, I don't know, bullied by their mother or something, and now they seem to hate all women in the world and particularly women who have achieved more than they have. (Interviewee 15)

While 'hate' was seen by many victims to characterise the motivation of abusers it does not necessarily follow that all misogynistic offending can be characterised in such terms. Firstly, the nature of intersectional identity meant that respondents sometimes reflected on their experiences of gendered abuse as a form of hate speech but noted that their racialised identity or perceived sexuality was connoted in the language and terminology used, so the focus was not misogyny alone. Women suggested that they were subject to sexist hate crime but in ways that drew upon other offensive tropes, in particular about sexuality. For example, one survey respondent reported that:

> I was quoted in a press article speaking out about violence against women. The Facebook newspaper page included … comments like 'she needs a good kicking in the cunt' … 'she's a man-hating lesbian and needs a good fucking to sort her out ' … 'someone should shut her up by sticking a cock in her mouth' … 'why doesn't someone kick the shit out of that ugly bitch?' (Respondent 98)

During an interview, a respondent described how the abuse she received online and offline was targeted at her gender and ethnicity and had a significant cumulative impact:

> A lot of these were people starting to become slightly racist in the language they were sending and so I got my husband to look at some of them, he said, 'I want to delete these, I don't ever want you to look at them' and I asked him to leave them because one day I will be strong enough to look at them but because my address is public I started to get these letters and I got an incredible set of letters which were very racially motivated … So then eventually [my employer] suddenly realised what was going on with my post and they then start to filter and take the post away and deal with it and agree to send any stuff which is racist, or sexist, or death threats to the police … I'd got so that I was like beside myself, I wasn't sleeping, I felt really fearful the whole time. (Interviewee 12)

Other women reflected on the complexity of (perceived) power relations between perpetrator and victim/survivor. For example, one interviewee indicated that she was targeted because of her senior professional position:

> I don't have an issue with men. But there seems to be a group of men out there who have an issue with women, and it's women with an opinion who have a position in power. And so they will attack them … because you shouldn't be there … any woman that was seen in a man's job I think got more abuse. (Interviewee 15)

Another interviewee reflected on the intersecting nature of power and abuse and suggested that misogyny alone did not account for the abuse directed at her and other feminists:

> This is maybe a really controversial thing to say but Caroline Criado-Perez, when those people were sent to prison for sending those abusive tweets, I looked at the photos of those people and thought, they do not look like happy people, you know, they look like people who have had a bit of a shit life, you know, they look like people who don't enjoy the same privileges as her, and I'm not saying that makes it right what they did, at all, but I'm saying that maybe our analysis of that needs to be a bit more nuanced. And so similarly with the men who are sending me abuse, I don't know who these men are, you know, they might be teenage boys who are kind of working out their anger issues or they might be men who've been out of work for years and years and years and feel like it's the feminists who are ruining their lives and I think, you know, we have to kind of be conscious of that. We're not saying that it's ok, and I think that you have to have an intersectional analysis of it, you can't just say, 'Misogyny! Misogyny!' you know, you have to think of the relative positions of the people involved. (Interviewee 4)

The intersectionality of prejudice reflected in these extracts suggests that debate about whether misogynistic incidents ought to be considered as hate crimes becomes more complex since the prejudicial motivation of perpetrators is often multidimensional. A victim-focused response needs to recognise that offending is experienced in a wider social, cultural and personal context and can be related to multiple forms of marginalisation. Historically, the law has struggled to respond to this intersectional feature of some forms of hate and abuse, as demonstrated by Crenshaw (1991). Racist, homophobic or disablist hatred is exacerbated by combination with misogyny but in ways that are unpredictable, mediated by context, and cannot be read simply from textual, visual or graphical content.

Furthermore, the misogyny expressed in the online abuse may not have been extended to all women, but directed instead at feminist women, or women who speak out, or women who challenge patriarchal, heteronormative norms. One respondent reflected on the social media profiles of perpetrators which represented them as loving towards the women in their lives:

> … fairly young boys between about 15 and 25 who were the main culprits … in their pictures, that's what shocked me, that they would have arms around their own loved females whilst targeting another female and downgrading other females and calling them slags and whores and they would have their arm around the woman you love and then there are the other types of people that did it were sort of those forty-year-old men with a baby in their arms saying, 'You slag, you need fucking raping, lada-ladala'. (Interviewee 16)

Another respondent reflected on this selective targeting of particular women:

> This is really to qualify the sex/gender aspect: I think it is not simply 'you're a woman', it's 'you're a woman who does not stay within the prescribed parameters of what women are allowed to ask for / say / experience.' It is gender nonconformity which is not generally recognised as such because women who transgress gender norms simply by speaking out about women's experience are seen not as non-conforming, just as 'bad'. (Respondent 72)

The targeting of certain women suggests that 'hate' is expressed selectively towards those women who step outside the expected norms of femininity rather than to all women. This is, of course, a key feature of patriarchal values; that women are valued, admired and praised if they conform to expectations of traditional femininity (e.g. by being loving mothers or wives) but are derided, denigrated and punished if they do not (e.g. by being single mothers, lesbians or powerful women). Nonetheless, this complexity of attitudes towards women makes it difficult to apply the simple term 'hate' to abusive behaviour towards them. Similar points have been made about the problematic application of the concept of hate in relation to racist crimes. Ray et al. (2004), for example, argued that perpetrators they interviewed were motivated by a combination of resentment, shame and grievance rather than 'racial hatred' in a pure form. As a heuristic device, hate does not capture the complex and contradictory gendered construction of appropriate social identities that was foundational to the abuse uncovered in our research. Perpetrators seemed not to hate women in a categorical sense but rather to be motivated by a perception that women engaging in feminist debate were transgressing appropriate gender roles. In terms of considering the online abuse of women as a form of hate crime, our data suggest that this is problematic in ways that are complex and challenging in relation to other offence types that have been categorised as hate crime.

A defining feature of hate crimes is that they communicate prejudice not only to the victim but also more widely. As Gelber (2000: 278) argued, hate crimes are a form of signal crime, since they 'have a ripple effect beyond their individual victims because they contribute to creating conditions in which violent crimes against some groups in society are able to be justified and condoned'. In the context of racist hate crime, authors such as Bowling (1998) and Cohen (1997) have noted that incidents convey messages of white territoriality and exclusionary intent that are aimed at the wider community that the immediate victim is seen to represent. In relation to the symbolic dimension of rape and sexual violence, Walters and Tumath (2014) note that such offences—as with hate crime—constitute a form of terrorism intended to instil fear across the wider community.[2]

As discussed above, research participants very clearly interpreted the abuse that they received as an attempt to deny their participation in online debate. Respondents reflected that the abuse sought to contest not only their expressed views and arguments but their fundamental right to participate. In many ways, this reflects the signalling component of hate crime, a defining element that raises the gravity and impact of such offences. The message communicated is not only to the recipient but to the wider audience of women (and men) who follow feminist debate online.

If perpetrators did intend to exclude or silence women, their aim was not always realised. Although many women reported the abuse had a range of negative impacts, a majority felt 'galvanised' by their experience and, far from being silenced, became more vocal in their political activism. 54% agreed it made them 'more determined in your political views'. A third (33%) agreed it made them feel motivated to continue to engage in debate. Moreover, while negative impacts reduced over time, feelings of being galvanised to act increased in the long term. This suggests that online abuse may silence some women but its affects are multi-directional. It might be that this galvanising effect may be more evident in this sample of feminists than in the wider population of women. It may be that women who are engaged in feminist debate draw on a feminist analysis to understand their experiences, whereas women less or not at all engaged, might have fewer resources to draw on when dealing with online abuse and might feel silenced by it. Even in our sample, the galvanising effect was found alongside reports that women changed their online behaviour, limiting their engagement in selected sites or debates. Clearly, it is not a matter of recipients of abuse being *either* silenced *or* galvanised; both consequences may co-exist.

Our findings suggest there was a clear exclusionary intent behind abuse, intended to debar participation which was deemed to transgress acceptable gender norms. In this respect, it appears that the experiences of victims of online misogyny parallel other forms of hate crime victimisation targeted at those held to be 'out of place' in terms of their physical presence in real-world environments. An important contribution from Chakraborti and Garland's (2004) study was that the 'othering' process aimed at minority ethnic people combined a sense of localism, racism and a concept of authentic belonging in rural communities. Other studies of racist abuse (most notably Bowling 1998; Hesse 1992) have identified the white territorialism that suggests minority communities are not a legitimate presence in certain neighbourhoods. Similarly, our study suggests that the exclusionary intent was context-specific; respondents interpreted the abuse as signalling the perpetrator's view that their participation in online public debate was not legitimate because it transgressed gendered norms.

Attempts to exclude women highlight the issue of where abuse occurs and reveal the fuzzy boundaries between private and public spaces and between online and offline spaces. VAWG has been excluded from hate crime legislation partly on the grounds that it is distinct from hate crime because it tends to occur in a private rather than a public setting, grounds disputed by Gill and Mason-Bish (2013) who cite a body of research suggesting that many incidents of hate crime are perpetrated in private domains by perpetrators who are known to victims, as family members, friends, carers, and so on. However, this private/public dichotomy is considerably more problematic in the context of the online environment where there may also be an overlap between online and offline spaces.

As Awan and Zempi (2016) demonstrated in relation to Islamaphobic hate crime, online and offline space are best considered as a continuum rather than distinct domains. Their argument was based, in part, on the notion that victims do not clearly distinguish their online victimisation from that in the real world; both form part of a whole experience. This point is reinforced by our research data as many of our respondents spoke of threatening experiences such that online 'talk' was directed towards offline real-world assaults of an extreme kind, for example:

> … one evening, I was sat with my partner and I got an email from [name] and the subject of the email was 'please tell me this is not your address'; and I had taken a break from Twitter for an hour … and he had posted my home address in full online immediately after he had sent a tweet saying, 'This is how you rape a witch, you hold her under water and when she comes up for air that's when you enter her'. (Interviewee 3)

Similarly, another respondent's account demonstrates the interconnections between online and offline experiences:

> Knowing that he was so vociferously trying to find out who I was, was really frightening. It's not so much now … because I've moved, so he's got my old address and he put that online, he put a picture of me, my address, [daughter's] name, my ex's name, names of my cats and you know he blogged that and then repeatedly tried to Tweet it as well so that was the point when it was very frightening because I'd lived in that house with my daughter … So if anybody had taken him seriously they could have turned up on the doorstep to do whatever and my specific fear was that it would be [ex-partner] because all he needed was an excuse to come, you know, and [perpetrator] knew this, he knew that he was exposing my identity to an abusive ex-husband who could have done absolutely anything and luckily he hasn't. … But I had a police panic alarm; the police took it very seriously at that point so they came and installed a panic alarm at the old address. (Interviewee 16)

It seems that the police responded in the instance above, and the continuum between online and offline abuse provides a clear imperative for the criminal justice system and other agencies (social media companies for example) to treat online abuse seriously. While many online perpetrators do not continue their perpetration offline, as Jane (2017: 74) notes:

> It is, indeed, impossible to know whether online threats are credible threats. But this is precisely the reason they carry such force. Women cannot divine the inner machinations of online antagonists. As such, they are left wondering, 'what if this is the one time a man *does* do what he is threatening to do?' Given that cyber abuse tends to arrive *en masse*, women know that, even if the vast majority of men threatening rape, mutilation or death have no intention of following through, one non-empty threat is all it would take.

The links between offline world VAWG and social media environments are significant to offences of 'coercive control'. The Crown Prosecution Service guidelines (2016) on communications via social media stipulate that 'online activity is used to humiliate, control and threaten victims, as well as to plan and orchestrate acts of violence' (CPS 2016) but a recent survey suggests the justice system is failing to adequately address this new form of coercive control (Travis 2017).

In terms of this aspect of hate crime as an attempt at exclusion, the place in which our respondents experienced misogynistic abuse was significant, as it is in 'real world' environments. That the abuse was virtual did not lessen its impact because, in many cases reported, there was a clear link between online and offline worlds since both abuse and misogyny in general terms were experienced in both environments. Moreover, the private space of online communication was breached in various ways as abusive content was shared within networks that are an important site of political and social activism for our respondents.

There are, then, similarities between hate crime and online abuse. While the concept of hate is problematic when applied to online abuse, this problem is not unique to this type of offending; parallel complexities apply to forms of hate crime that are broadly recognised in research, policy and legal terms. As with other forms of hate crime, misogynistic online abuse has exclusionary intent, albeit it not in an absolute and categorical sense, but expressed towards women deemed to transgress patriarchal gendered norms. Furthermore, the location of the abuse was significant, as with many forms of hate crime. However, the distinction between private online spaces and public real-world sites is no binary hierarchy. Rather, the two spheres intersect.

Concluding Thoughts

Far from being a new challenge, online abuse is a novel manifestation of familiar forms of behaviour. Taking a victim-centred approach rather than focusing on the technological context reveals that online abuse can be considered as both VAWG and as hate crime. However, as discussed above, these categories are not unproblematic. VAWG has traditionally been defined as private offences which have been categorised as outwith the concern of the justice system. The category 'hate crime' has been problematic because of its assumption that such crimes occur in public and act as 'signal offences', thereby excluding VAWG. Moreover, the term 'hate' is a clumsy description for the complex emotional context when the offender is a friend, relative or carer of the victim. In addition, the category 'hate crime' has not reflected the intersectional nature of some offences, which target victims' identities (such as their ethnicity and their gender). Despite these difficulties with the categories, the justice system *has* developed ways to recognise VAWG and hate crime, largely in response to pressure from activists and scholars. Therefore, although its categorisations and practices regarding these offences are not unproblematic, it does have a foundation from which to respond to the harm they cause.

Notes

1. No-platforming is the practice of not giving a platform to certain speakers. Traditionally used to prevent far-right organisations using speech to promote racism and to incite racist violence, more recently it has been used, particularly in universities, to prevent a range of controversial speakers including those expressing views about transgender issues.
2. McGuire (2014) notes that this point, in relation to sexual violence against Black women, was originally made by US Civil Rights activists such as Ida B. Wells and Rosa Parks.

References

Anitha, S., & Lewis, R. (2018). *Gender Based Violence in University Communities: Policy, Prevention and Educational Initiatives*. Bristol: Policy Press.

Awan, I., & Zempi, I. (2016). The affinity between online and offline anti-Muslim hate crime: Dynamics and impacts. *Aggression and Violent Behavior, 27*, 1–8.

Bates, L. (2018). *Misogynation: The True Scale of Sexism*. London: Simon & Schuster.

BBC News. (2011). David Cameron criticised for 'calm down, dear' jibe. http://www.bbc.co.uk/news/uk-politics-13211577. Accessed April 25, 2018.

Beard, M. (2015). The public voice of women. *Women's History Review, 24*(5), 809–818.

Bowling, B. (1998). *Violent Racism: Victimization, Policing, and Social Context*. Oxford: Clarendon Press.

Burney, E. (2009). *Making People Behave: Anti-social Behaviour, Politics and Policy* (2nd ed.). Cullompton: Willan.
Chakraborti, N., & Garland, J. (2004). *Rural Racism*. Cullompton: Willan.
Chakraborti, N., & Garland, J. (2009). *Hate Crime: Impact, Causes and Responses*. London: Sage.
Cohen, P. (1997). *Rethinking the Youth Question*. London: Macmillan.
Committee on Standards in Public Life. (2017). *Intimidation in Public Life: A Review by the Committee on Standards in Public Life*, Cm 9543. London: Houses of Parliament.
Crenshaw, K. (1991). Mapping the margins: Intersectionality, identity politics, and violence against women of color. *Stanford Law Review, 43*(6), 1241–1299.
Crown Prosecution Service (CPS). (2016). *Guidelines on prosecuting cases involving communications sent via social media*. http://www.cps.gov.uk/legal/a_to_c/communications_sent_via_social_media/#content. Accessed February 17, 2017.
Dobash, R. P., Dobash, R. E., Cavanagh, K., & Lewis, R. (1998). Separate and intersecting realities: A comparison of men's and women's accounts of violence against women. *Violence Against Women, 4*(4), 382–414.
Garland, D. (2001). *The Culture of Control*. Oxford: Oxford University Press.
Gelber, K. (2000). Hate crimes: Public policy implications of the inclusion of gender. *Australian Journal of Political Science, 35*(2), 275–289.
Gill, A. K., & Mason-Bish, H. (2013). Addressing violence against women as a form of hate crime: Limitations and possibilities. *Feminist Review, 105*, 1–20.
Hall, M., & Hearn, J. (2017). *Revenge Pornography: Gender, Sexuality and Motivations*. London: Routledge.
Hearn, J. (1998). *The Violences of Men: How Men Talk About and How Agencies Respond to Men's Violence to Women*. London: Sage.
Hesse, B. (1992). *Beneath the Surface: Racial Harassment*. Aldershot: Avebury.
Hlavka, H. R. (2014). Normalizing sexual violence: Young women account for harassment and abuse. *Gender & Society, 28*(3), 337–358.
HMIC. (2014). *Everyone's Business: Improving the Police Response to Domestic Abuse*. London: HMIC.
HMIC. (2015). *Increasingly Everyone's Business: Improving the Police Response to Domestic Abuse*. London: HMIC.
Innes, M., & Fielding, N. (2002). From community to communicative policing: 'Signal crimes' and the problem of public reassurance. *Sociological Research Online, 7*(2), 1–12.

Jane, E. A. (2014). 'Back to the kitchen, cunt': Speaking the unspeakable about online misogyny. *Continuum: Journal of Media and Cultural Studies, 28*(4), 558–570.

Jane, E. A. (2017). *Misogyny Online: A Short (and Brutish) History*. London: Sage.

Kelly, L., & Westmarland, N. (2016). Naming and defining 'domestic violence': Lessons from research with violent men. *Feminist Review, 112*(1), 113–127.

Lawrence, F. M. (1999). *Punishing Hate: Bias Crimes Under American Law*. Cambridge, MA: Harvard University Press.

Lewis, R., Dobash, R. E., Dobash, R. P., & Cavanagh, K. (2001). Law's progressive potential: The value of engagement with the law for domestic violence. *Social & Legal Studies, 10*(1), 105–130.

Lewis, R., Sharp, E., Remnant, J., & Redpath, R. (2015). 'Safe spaces': Experiences of feminist women-only space. *Sociological Research Online, 20*(4), 1–14.

Lewis, R., Rowe, M., & Wiper, C. (2016). Online abuse of feminists as an emerging form of violence against women and girls. *British Journal of Criminology, 57*(6), 1462–1481.

McGlynn, C., & Rackley, E. (2017). Image-based sexual abuse. *Oxford Journal of Legal Studies, 37*(3), 534–561.

McGuire, K. M., Berhanu, J., Davis, C. H. F., & Harper, S. R. (2014). In search of progressive black masculinities: Critical self-reflections on gender identity development among black undergraduate men. *Men and Masculinities, 17*(3), 253–277.

McPhail, B. A. (2002). Gender-bias hate crimes: A review. *Trauma, Violence, & Abuse, 3*(2), 125–143.

Pain, R. (2014). Everyday terrorism. *Progress in Human Geography, 38*(4), 531–550.

Phipps, A., & Young, I. (2015). Neoliberalisation and 'lad cultures' in higher education. *Sociology, 49*(2), 305–322.

Phipps, A., Ringrose, J., Renold, E., & Jackson, C. (2018). Rape culture, lad culture and everyday sexism: Researching, conceptualizing and politicizing new mediations of gender and sexual violence. *Journal of Gender Studies, 27*(1), 1–8.

Ray, L., Smith, D., & Abrams, D. (2004). Shame, rage and racist violence. *British Journal of Criminology, 44*(3), 350–368.

Thomas, P. (2016). Hate crime or mate crime? Disablist hostility, contempt and ridicule. In A. Roulstone & H. Mason-Bish (Eds.), *Disability, Hate Crime and Violence* (pp. 135–146). London: Routledge.

Travis, A. (2017). Abuse victims failed by police and courts over online harassment. *The Guardian.* https://www.theguardian.com/world/2017/may/08/abuse-victims-failed-by-police-and-courts-over-online-harassment. Accessed October 26, 2018.

Universites UK. (2016). *Changing the Culture: Report of the Universities UK Taskforce Examining Violence Against Women, Harassment and Hate Crime Affecting University Students.* London: Universities UK.

Vera-Gray, F. (2016). *Men's Intrusion, Women's Embodiment: A Critical Analysis of Street Harassment.* London: Routledge.

Walby, S., Towers, J., & Francis, B. (2015). Is violent crime increasing or decreasing? A new methodology to measure repeat attacks making visible the significance of gender and domestic relations. *British Journal of Criminology, 56*(6), 1203–1234.

Walters, M. A., & Tumath, J. (2014). Gender 'hostility', rape, and the hate crime paradigm. *The Modern Law Review, 77*(4), 563–596.

Wiener, C. (2017). Seeing what is 'invisible in plain sight': Policing coercive control. *The Howard Journal of Crime and Justice, 56,* 500–515.

6

'The Price of Admission': On Notions of Risk and Responsibility in Women's Sexting Practices

Rikke Amundsen

Introduction

This chapter draws on interview material collected for a study on adult women's experiences of taking, sharing, and receiving private sexual images (PSIs) in their romantic and/or sexual relationships. As such, my aim with this chapter is twofold. I set out to explore: (1) how women understand and approach the risk of having their PSIs shared without their consent and: (2) what these accounts of risk can reveal about this particular non-consensual act as a form of 'online othering'. In doing so, my focus will be on the role postfeminism plays in influencing these women's accounts. When referring to 'postfeminism', I mean a sensibility centred on the notion that—under the present conditions of reflexive modernity and extensive individualization—the gender equality goals of feminism have already been met. As such, postfeminism is based on the idea that, as women and men are thought to have

R. Amundsen (✉)
Department of Sociology, University of Cambridge,
Cambridge, UK

become equal, society has moved 'beyond' the need for feminism as a social movement (McRobbie 2009; Ringrose et al. 2013). A postfeminist sensibility hence casts feminist goals as largely having been achieved and, on these grounds, dismisses feminist ideas as passé. It is this double-entanglement of feminist and anti-feminist convictions—meaning that feminism is cast as both important and unnecessary—that constitutes the contradictory nature of a postfeminist sensibility (Gill 2007). Furthermore, I take postfeminism to be inherently linked to neo-liberalism, by which I mean the ways in which market principles have come to manifest themselves in all aspects of everyday life, leading to a form of governmentality marked by increased individualization and responsibilization (Elias et al. 2017; Gill 2017; Gill and Scharff 2011). These neo-liberal processes affect some gender groups more than others. It is primarily women who are called on to self-discipline and self-regulate (Gill 2007).

Rosalind Gill (2007) has put forward seven different features characteristic of a postfeminist sensibility, all of which are structured by and coexist with continuing inequalities and exclusions with regard to class, age, 'race', ethnicity, disability, sexuality, and gender. In this chapter, my focus is on one specific element of this postfeminist sensibility—the predominance of individualism, choice, and empowerment—and on how this feature operates in relation to gender. Drawing on work by Joanne Baker (2010), I set out to show how my interviewees made sense of the risk of non-consensual sharing of their PSIs by thinking with and through individual choice and female empowerment frames. Indeed, they cast this risk as essentially negotiable, due to an enhanced perception of women's agency in the domain of speech about sex online. I also find that the women in this study were eager to avoid any association with victimhood, primarily because of its inherent association with a lack of agency (Baker 2010). They were hence eager to stress their ability to avoid such a status by engaging in practices designed to mitigate the risk of their PSIs being shared further without their consent. An unintended consequence of this focus on female agency as a desired character trait, however, was the fact that it effectively operated so as to cast women as *responsible* for managing their own at-risk status.

Consequentially, women were also rendered accountable for their own misfortune if this risk was to materialize. The women's accounts of this risk thus came to exemplify the wider neo-liberal trend whereby risks have come to be individualized, and whereby individuals have come to take on personal responsibility for protecting themselves from victimization (Elias et al. 2017; Stringer 2014). The non-consensual sharing of women's PSIs hence operates as othering on more than one level: the othering is not simply an effect of the actual non-consensual sharing of their PSIs, but also an aspect inherent in the harsh (self-) critique directed at the women who fail to make the 'right' choices in order to protect themselves from it.

This chapter will commence in the following order: First, I am going to explain the phenomenon of non-consensual sharing of PSIs and, second, the methodology applied when conducting the interviews on which this chapter draws. Then, in the following two sections, I examine how the women interviewed for this study addressed the risk of further non-consensual sharing of their PSIs by employing trust as a means of risk mitigation. Crucially, this particular form of risk mitigation was cast as an indicator of their ability to make the right choices in terms of whom they decided to trust with their images. Next, I go on to examine quotes from interviews with two women whose accounts stood out from the rest, because they did *not* draw on notions of individual choice and female empowerment in order to make sense of the risk of non-consensual sharing of women's PSIs. By comparing these two accounts to the other interview material, my aim is to show how the influence of a postfeminist discourse can lead to particular ways of understanding such acts of 'online othering' (Harmer and Lumsden, this volume). In conclusion, therefore, I put forward the argument that women's thinking with and through a postfeminist framework when aiming to make sense of this risk can lead to a form of accountabilization, whereby the responsibility for acts of 'online othering' (Harmer and Lumsden, this volume) is shifted from those actually doing it to those affected by it, who usually are women (Henry and Powell 2016; McGlynn et al. 2017).

PSIs as a Tool for 'Online Othering'

Arguably, the term that is used most frequently in the media and in academic discourse in reference to abusive acts of non-consensual sharing of PSIs is 'revenge porn' (Henry and Powell 2016: 401). Nevertheless, it is a contested term, primarily because of its association with both 'revenge' and 'pornography' (Henry and Powell 2016: 400–401; McGlynn et al. 2017). This association can be incorrect, because the person sharing a PSI without the consent of the person in it need not be motivated by revenge (Henry and Powell 2016). Moreover, PSIs are a much broader genre than pornography, a genre generally defined by its explicitness and by its particular purpose to arouse its audience (McNair 2002; Henry and Powell 2016). This lack of fit between term and concept might also explain why the women contributing to this study were generally reluctant to use the term in reference to their own accounts and experiences. Indeed, I have decided to use the term 'non-consensual sharing of PSIs', rather than 'revenge porn', precisely because the latter is a concept that fails to account for the complexity of meaning inherent in both the consensual and non-consensual sharing of PSIs. Furthermore, when discussing acts of non-consensual sharing in the context of this chapter—as a form of 'online othering'—I do so with a strict focus on acts that are conducted with the intention to distress the person(s) depicted in the image. As such, I am not going to discuss cases in which PSIs are shared non-consensually for example by accident or as a joke. In reference to the practice of consensually sharing PSIs, I use the term 'sexting', a term generally applied with reference to this activity as it occurs within romantic and/or sexual relationships, by my interviewees as well as in the media and in academic discourse (Lenhart 2009).

So far, little statistics and data have been produced to indicate the prevalence of non-consensual sharing of PSIs as it occurs in the UK. The data there is, however, indicate that this is a form of 'online othering' that is persistently on the rise. For example, during the year of its launch in 2015, the Revenge Porn Helpline received 500 reports from British citizens who were concerned about PSIs being shared non-consensually online. In 2017, their number of yearly reports had risen to over 1000 (Baggs 2018). About 80% of the calls received by the

Revenge Porn Helpline in the UK between 2015 and 2016 were from women (Laville and Halliday 2016). Certainly, research from the UK and beyond indicates that this is a form of 'online othering' that primarily affects women and that can have significantly negative consequences for those subjected to it, including feelings of shame and humiliation (Henry and Powell 2016; McGlynn et al. 2017). Indeed, research by Samantha Bates (2017) shows that those subjected to this phenomenon respond to it in much in the same way as those subjected to offline sexual assault.

This chapter is written in order to assist the development of an improved understanding of the ways in which this form of 'online othering' is understood and experienced by those it affects the most, namely women (Henry and Powell 2016; McGlynn et al. 2017). So far, little research has been conducted within this field, and the research that exists, is mainly limited to addressing the experiences of children and adolescents (see, e.g., Albury and Crawford 2012; Burkett 2015; Döring 2014; Ringrose and Harvey 2015; Ringrose et al. 2013; Salter 2016). Few projects have examined how this problem is understood outside of youth culture, with Bates' (2017) research on its psychological effects on adult women being a notable exception. Shifting the focus of this field of research with regard to age is important, because the people affected by this form of 'online othering' belong to a much broader age group than most of the existing research indicates. By way of example, the average age of those who reported such incidents to 31 of the 43 police forces in England and Wales between April and December 2015 was 25 years old, with the youngest being 11 and the oldest over 60 (Sherlock 2016). A strict focus on non-consensual sharing of PSIs in relation to youth culture is also problematic, because it can operate so as to draw attention away from the inherently 'gendered nature' of this phenomenon (Henry and Powell 2015). We need more research that explores what it is about this phenomenon that renders it so 'suited' to operate as an act of othering of especially women. Herein, I explore how women themselves make sense of the non-consensual sharing of their PSIs. In doing so, I focus on one particular dimension of this type of 'online othering', namely that which is brought about by the ways in which women respond to and make sense of it as risk.

Methods

The interview data on which this chapter is based were collected for a project on adult women's accounts and experiences of the impact of new media and digital technology on their romantic and/or sexual relationships, with a particular focus on the digital creating, sharing, and receiving of PSIs. My primary aim in conducting this research was to collect data that enabled the development of in-depth insights into women's individual perceptions of practices like sexting. I hence decided to conduct semi-structured individual interviews. Indeed, this is one of the best methods to achieve my above-stated research aims, precisely because such interviews are based on a relatively open interview guide, something which renders the interviewee free to determine the particular focus and course of the conversation (Ayres 2008). The open-ended interview guide that I operated with was centred on four key questions concerned with the interviewees' direct and/or indirect experiences of the consensual and non-consensual sharing of PSIs. These questions asked: (1) What are your views on the consensual sharing of private sexual images and films? (2) What are your experiences of the consensual sharing or taking of private sexual images and films? (3) What are your views on the non-consensual sharing of private sexual images and films? and (4) What are your experiences of non-consensual sharing of private sexual images and films? During interviews, my main task was to come up with relevant probes in relation to the interviewees' narrative, as it was relayed to me in relation to the four key questions (Ayres 2008).

Having been granted ethical approval by the Cambridge University Sociology Ethics Committee, I started recruiting interviewees in May 2016. In doing so, I was looking for adult women based in a specific county in the east of England, UK. A call for research participants was distributed both online and offline, for example in community centres and through charities. In order to reach out to potential interviewees, I also relied on network and snowball sampling, meaning that I asked members of my various social networks and research participants to pass on my call for participants to other relevant women (Roulston 2010; Seale 2012).

Between June 2016 and February 2017, I conducted 44 interviews. In terms of ethnicity, 35 of the interviewees identified as White British or White Other, four as South Asian, two as East Asian, two as Mixed British/African, and one as Mixed British/Asian. 42 of the women were either studying for a university degree or had already obtained one university degree or more. 22 of the interviewees were single and 22 were in relationships. 30 identified as heterosexual, ten as bisexual, one as lesbian, one as queer, and two as not sure about their sexualities. Whilst 14 of my 44 interviewees did not identify as heterosexual, all of the women predominantly discussed their experiences of taking, sharing, and receiving PSIs in relation to past or current heterosexual relationships. The focus of this chapter is thus restricted to their reflections on such practices when in romantic and/or sexual relationships with men.

Because much of my recruitment occurred via social networks, my primary concern in assigning pseudonyms to the interviewees was to reduce the likelihood of 'deductive disclosure' (Kaiser 2009). That is, I wanted to limit the possibility that any readers of my published research, who had also been involved in the process of recruitment, could recognize some of the interviewees. Rather than providing each interviewee with a pseudonym that matches their social and/or cultural background, I hence operate with pseudonyms that consist of randomly allocated initials. All other identifying characteristics have been removed from the interview material.

I recorded each interview and transcribed them verbatim. I then used coding software Atlas.ti to assist my thematic analysis of the interview material, using it to code each interview and to organize these codes into themes. In the next section of this chapter, I address some of the key themes that I derived from conducting this thematic analysis; namely trust, risk, and responsibility. Drawing on some of my interview material, the aim is to show how the thinking with and through a postfeminist framework informed how my interviewees made sense of sexting in relation to these themes.

Trust Assessment as Risk Mitigation

When asked about their perceptions of risk in relation to their practices of sending PSIs, the majority of the women in this study stressed that the digital nature of their sexting practices rendered their images particularly vulnerable to abuse. That is, because there was no way for them to physically control the further distribution of their PSIs—once they had been shared with their romantic and/or sexual partner—the women considered their images especially exposed to misuse. However, only eight of the interviewees stated that they never had and never would share PSIs because of the risk involved. The remaining 36 of my interviewees argued that, regardless of the risk, they had or would continue to send PSIs, but that they addressed the risks that such practices involve by engaging in a range of risk mitigating practices. These practices included, for instance, the looking for a 'morality maker' in the man's life, hiding features by which they could be identified in the image—like their face, hair, or tattoos—'just in case' it was to end up in public, or sending their images using technology that made it harder to save the image for further distribution (like Snapchat). That being said, the most common act of risk mitigation that these women engaged in was the careful application and reliance on the trust established between themselves and their intended receiver. All of the women who had either engaged in or planned to engage in the sending of PSIs stressed the significance of establishing trust between themselves and their romantic and/or sexual partner, prior to their sending him an image. Indeed, trust was cast as their main means of risk mitigation, as explained in this quote by L1 (early twenties):

> […] I'd go mental at the person that distributed it who I trusted. But um yeah, I'd be really, really angry um cos somebody's betrayed some trust somewhere, or done a really indecent thing, um but hopefully I think what I'd said that I'd do as sort of precautionary measures would limit the damage potential, like my you know, me being really careful about only sending it to people I could fully trust and like I've like judged them as, that they wouldn't do that – even if they hated me – as they've realized how horrible that would be.

L1 presented her level of trust in the receiver as not just implicit or assumed, but as something that was based on her individual assessment of him: she only sent images to men that she had 'judged' as people who 'wouldn't do that'. L1 referred to this act of interpersonal trust assessment as a 'precautionary measure', thus enabling her to develop an idea of how much risk she would be taking if she decided to send a PSI. Trust, that is, was perceived as something that reduced risk: the more trustworthy the receiver (according to L1's assessment), the lesser the experience of risk in sending. This perception of risk as measured in relation to trust was reflected in the majority of my interviews and presented as a way of safeguarding their images into the future. The interviewees generally appeared to be of the perception that this kind of trust assessment was not simply a clever thing to do, but their obligation as 'responsible adult[s]', a notion here explained by C2 (late teens):

> […] I think, because of the way the world works – and it's not ideal – there are always gonna be points where you, where something goes wrong like the, you always have to have a contingency plan, like, you can take precautions, you can be in a loving, trusting relationship, but that doesn't mean it's not going to go wrong. […] But, to think […] ahead and be like: "you need to delete our photos if we break up" and to think ahead from that, the things that you would do, the action plan that you would take if that wasn't the case. It's something that you've just gonna do as a responsible adult, it's something that you just have to take responsibility for.

To C2, risk mitigation by way of assessing the trust between the person sending the image and the intended receiver was perceived as the responsibility of those who wanted to engage in the sending of PSIs. Furthermore, in associating extensive risk mitigation with being a responsible adult, the ability to protect oneself from the risk of non-consensual sharing was cast as a desirable ability. The majority of my interviewees, regardless of their age, associated successful risk mitigation with responsible adulthood. A consequence of making this association was the fact that would-be victims of the non-consensual sharing of PSIs effectively were cast as immature people, less capable of managing their own risk mitigation by making the right choices in terms of who to trust with their PSIs. This understanding became especially clear during my interview with J1 (mid-twenties), where I asked her if she could tell me whom she thought was the most likely to be affected by the non-consensual sharing of PSIs:

J1: Mainly women who aren't as strong. I pride myself on being pretty strong and outspoken and confident. So people who aren't as strong and confident. Um, youth, especially. Teenagers who have […] access to phones now. Um, kids as young as nine and ten I've seen them with cell phones and I think that's terrifying, because they don't really know what they are and what to use it for really. And there's very limited controls a parent can have of a phone these days anyway. So youth, um teenagers who don't know better, don't know the consequences. They get themselves into some pretty hairy situations without really realizing it, the implications of it. […]

Rikke: So it's mainly women and young people?

J1: Yeah, women and young people.

Rikke: Why do you think women?

J1: [Exhales]. Maybe it's because most of my experiences are women who've been pressured into giving images um and it's usually men who are taking the images in that role. […] I guess it's any person who's, um… naïve and trusting, I, eh, I'm biting my words now… People who are most likely to send these images. Yeah, young people or people in a more vulnerable state, so whether they are lonely and wanting somebody, really looking for a relationship, something steady. Um, entering into compromising relationships with people who might not have their best interests etcetera at heart. I suppose, um age doesn't really matter, it's kind of a state of mind. If you're um, will-, if you end up putting yourself in that compromising position with somebody who you shouldn't be trusting, then you're kind of opening yourself up to the dangers of that. I mean, it could be a lot of fun if you trust the person and you know what you're doing, but it's always that risk involved.

Here, J1 described the typical would-be victim of non-consensual sharing of PSIs as someone who is naïve, not strong, and/or vulnerable. Interestingly, J1 appeared to associate such character traits with people who are young—children or adolescents (even though she later claimed that she supposed 'age doesn't matter')—and/or women. With J1 also being female, she operated actively so as to distance herself from her own characterization of would-be victims. By making it clear that she herself was 'strong and outspoken and confident', she also worked so as to emphasize the fact that she was capable of taking responsibility for her own risk mitigation.

J1's account of would-be victims of non-consensual sharing of PSIs is also representative of the general view expressed to me in interviews with regard to issues of trust in sending images: when trust could not be applied strategically as a source of risk mitigation, it was cast in a more negative light. Trust was only viewed positively when it could be used as a means to further enhance one's individual position in relation to the receiver of the image. For instance, the idea that being too trusting was a bad character trait, because it illustrated a person's inability to make the right choices in terms of who to trust, thus placing you at risk, was reflected in my interview with G1 (early twenties). When I asked her who she thought the non-consensual sharing of PSIs could happen to, she answered the following:

> Oh! Somebody with a poor taste in men [short laugh]. No, no, no – I think it could happen to anybody, cos you have no idea. I mean, I'm pretty sure even if I were to cheat on my boyfriend he still wouldn't share the photos, like even if he was really angry he still wouldn't do it. I, I wouldn't blame the person [that it happened to] … I don't know, it's difficult, I wouldn't blame the person sending the photo for then having it shared, but at the same time, it's up to them to judge whether they should send it or not. So it's, if somebody else sends it without their consent then it's obviously that person's fault, um but there is maybe some not lack of judgment but just, yeah.

To G1, a would-be victim of non-consensual sharing was someone who had conducted a bad trust assessment prior to sending her PSI. That is, in not carrying out a sufficiently thorough and strategic judgement of the person for whom the PSI was intended, they had failed to act in a responsible manner. Even though G1 was reluctant to hold victims of non-consensual sharing accountable for what had happened to them, she still appeared to hold women somewhat responsible for having made the abuse of their images possible in the first place by choosing to trust the wrong kind of person with their images.

The Responsibility of Risk Mitigation

In the quotes by J1 and G1 in the section above, we can see how a postfeminist discourse highlighting the significance of exerting one's free choice correctly worked through their accounts of would-be victims. In emphasizing the fact that each woman is free to choose who to trust with her images, they were—purposefully or not—holding women accountable for their own at-risk status: the non-consensual sending of PSIs was seen as a direct consequence of a woman making the wrong choice following a poor trust assessment prior to her act of sending. In other words, a would-be victim of the non-consensual sharing of PSIs was someone who could not take control of her own risk mitigation by ensuring that she had a sufficient level of strategic trust in her intended receiver, before sending him anything. Like J1 and G1, several of the women interviewed for this study discussed women's risk mitigation as a matter of exercising one's free choice. That is, they stressed the significance of not just making *a* choice, but of making the *right choice* in terms of who to trust with one's images. Even though choice was discussed as something that was completely free, the women in this study still operated with the notion that some choices were more socially acceptable than others, thus introducing a regulative dimension to their notion of free choice (Baker 2008; McRobbie 2004). A consequence of their holding this view was the fact that it rendered them less likely to express wholehearted empathy for (would-be) victims of non-consensual sending (Baker 2010; Stringer 2014). This was not just a view imposed on others, but also a perception that many of the women had internalized, meaning that they were likely to take on some of the responsibility for the sexting-related injustices and concerns that affected them (Illouz 2012). Certainly, some of the women in this study came to blame themselves for the difficulties that they faced due to their sending of PSIs. For example, during my interview with M1 (mid-twenties), she told me that she had once been the victim of non-consensual sharing of her PSIs. M1's ex-partner had created a fake online dating profile in her name, including her full contact details and, crucially, the PSIs that she had once sent him, trusting that he would not share them any further. After describing the ordeal that she had gone through in relation to this experience, M1 started telling me about the ways in which this past experience impacted on her present practice of sexting her current partner:

> *M1*: […] I think images like that, they don't go away ever. I completely trust my boyfriend now, but I lost all trust in sending pictures. But when, when you're in, I don't know, when you're in that situation where you're a bit lonely and you've been talking to someone for a while and super horny [short laugh], you just … I don't regret, I don't ever regret, I don't regret anything I've sent, because it's what, I've only done it because I've wanted to, so I don't, I don't cast a judgment on anyone for doing it.
>
> *Rikke*: So is that something – since that happened – something that you've been thinking about when sharing images?
>
> *M1*: No, I trust him [my current partner] massively with the pictures. I don't judge everyone to his [my ex-partner's] standards… I'm quite level headed, so I'm so forgiving, not to him [my ex-partner], but like, to myself a bit. I don't, I won't tell him [my current partner] like 'no more pictures'. But you – I make excuses for myself and forgive myself for doing it and just keep sending them. I think, I don't know, I think it's normal – is it normal?

In the quote above, we can see how notions of individual choice and accountability informed M1's understanding of her past experience to such an extent that she ended up casting herself as partly responsible for the injustice that she faced at the hands of her ex-partner. On the one hand, M1 claimed that she did not 'cast a judgment on anyone' for choosing to send PSIs. On the other hand, she stressed how she felt the need to 'forgive' herself for having once trusted her ex-partner enough to choose to send him images. She also mentioned that she felt the need to 'make excuses' for herself when sending images to her current partner, somehow implying that she should know better. Interestingly, the person whose forgiveness M1 was seeking for making these choices was herself. As it stood, it appeared that M1 was her own worst critic.

M1 seemed to be disappointed in herself for having romantically trusted a man who later turned out not to be worthy of this trust. In explaining her worries by, first and foremost, looking to her individual choice biography as if it occurred in isolation, M1 did not take into consideration the social and/or structural influences that might have rendered her more likely to make these choices in the first place, such as the increasing pressure on women to be 'always up for it' as a means of relationship maintenance (Harvey and Gill 2011: 63) or the sexualization of culture, whereby sexual representations of particularly girls and young women have come to be normalized or even expected due to their proliferation in various media sources (García-Favaro and Gill 2016). As such, M1's account illustrates how the thinking within a postfeminist framework marked by the promotion of notions of individual choice and female empowerment can render women more likely to cast themselves as responsible for the difficulties they face in relation to their sexting practices, such as the othering involved in the non-consensual sharing of their PSIs. Crucially, this postfeminist framework obscured from view any wider social and/or gender inequalities in the domain of speech about sex that, arguably, made this form of othering possible in the first place (Gill and Scharff 2011). Now, I am going to turn to an examination of two interviews that stood out from the rest, primarily because the women giving them did *not* rely on a postfeminist discourse in order to explain their practices of sending PSIs. In looking to these interviews, my aim is to explore how their reluctance to draw on postfeminist notions of individual choice and female empowerment also rendered their accounts of the risk of non-consensual sharing of PSIs different from those of the other women who participated in this study.

Making Choices in a Sexualized Society

During my interview with D1 (late twenties), she recalled her past experience of having sent PSIs to a man whom she now had very little trust in. Upon sharing her story with me, D1 also told me about how 'isolating' the experience of worrying about the potential further distribution of these images could be. According to D1, this was the case for herself as well as for other women in similar situations, as they would ask themselves questions like: 'Why am I so stupid? Why was I so stupid?' However, when I asked D1 whether she did in fact feel like she had been stupid in sending PSIs to her ex-partner, her response was different:

> But no, I don't think back of myself and think that I was unusually stupid, or being unusually stupid is not the reason that it happened. The reason that it happened is that I was desperate to believe that some man one day would find me attractive and this guy […] had expressed interest, and there was no one else around me to make me feel these sorts of feelings that I was getting from him. And part of the price of admission, was being in an open relationship and part of the price of admission was like, sending him these pictures. And I just took that for granted and I wasn't wrong to take it for granted in terms of what I see happening around me in other people's relationships and what I saw happening around me at the time as well. […] Yeah, it's not stupidity. It's a set of desires that could not be satisfied in a safer way.

By not seeing her practice of sending PSIs as an individual choice taken as if in isolation, but as a choice made in response to a set of socially informed expectations, D1 was somewhat able to distance herself from the discourse of responsibility and self-blame (thus stating that 'being unusually stupid is not the reason that it happened'). Rather than perceiving the feelings of uneasiness and worry that she was now going through—knowing that her untrustworthy ex-partner probably still possessed PSIs of her—as if they were due to no fault but her own, she removed herself from such accounts by placing the responsibility for what she was experiencing with the society that had created the set of intimate expectations that she (and possibly her ex-partner) had been responding to in the first place. As such, she presented her decision to send PSIs not so much as a free choice, but more as a form of acquiescence: sending PSIs had been her way to satisfy a set of socially generated desires and to meet what she perceived to be the predominant expectations of her, both in her relationship and as a member of society (Baker 2008).

Following my interview with D1, I have been led to wonder why, unlike D1, most of the self-blaming women in this study generally rejected explanations for their sexting-related worries and concerns that looked beyond their own choice biographies by trying to contextualize them in relation to a broader set of societal expectations. I can only speculate as to why this might be, but one possible answer to this question can be found in my interview with H2 (early twenties). After several 'damaging' experiences related to her sending of PSIs—including experiences of both being threatened with and of having her PSIs shared without her consent—H2 decided to stop engaging in such practices. H2 had reached this decision, as she was no longer seeing the taking and sending of PSIs as an expression of an empowered female sexuality, but as a performance of a specific type of sexuality that had been imposed on her and other women by society. However, taking on this view had not proved to be entirely unproblematic to H2. For example, she found that her rejection of discourses of free choice and female empowerment in relation to the sending of PSIs attracted the scorn of her friends, who consequentially branded her as a 'prude' and not 'a proper feminist':

> […] I think that modesty is actually a, a quite a good move for female empowerment, um whereas a lot of the people I know who identify as feminist think that, um… fully embracing sexuality and making that public, a public display of sexuality is empowering. And because I personally never found publicly displaying my sexuality empowering, that's not an argument I get on board with […] but so I think um, I am often viewed by um – for example I have a friend who's a feminist […]. Um and I think she thinks I'm a massive prude. […] Um and then, and then therefore I couldn't possibly be a proper feminist. Um, but I kind of think it's a broad church.

In H2's account above, we can see how her rejection of the idea that sending PSIs—referred to as 'publicly displaying my sexuality'—can be an empowering choice for women, brought with it a feeling of detachment from her friends. Because H2 did not make sense of such performances through postfeminist frames, casting it as an entirely free choice for which she was individually responsible, she felt that her friends saw her as someone who failed to contribute to her own sexual emancipation by 'fully embracing' her sexuality through the taking and sharing of PSIs. Crucially, this perception of female sexuality as 'fully embraced' when actively performed is a largely postfeminist notion whereby neo-liberal ideas have come to be fused with liberal feminism (Baker 2008: 54). Here, the exercise of choice and agency in the sexual domain has come to work as an example of women's sexual freedom. It is perhaps not all that surprising, then, that many of the women in this study, like H2's friends, stuck to the seemingly more positive rendering of their sending of PSIs as illustrative of their being empowered and able to make free and individually informed choices to act out their sexualities through the sending of PSIs, even if it involved them taking on the responsibility for the injustices they might face because of it. The alternative option of seeing both their perceptions of female sexuality and the ways in which they exercise it as somehow imposed on them from the outside might be too depressing.

Conclusion

Women's engagement in practices of self-sexualization, like the taking and sharing of PSIs, can be both empowering and disempowering and need not be simply the one thing or the other (Harvey and Gill 2011; Ringrose 2011; Thompson and Donaghue 2014). However, as we have seen, the viewing of these acts primarily through a postfeminist lens promoting notions of individual choice and female empowerment is problematic, because it can bestow upon the women involved a feeling of responsibility for the potential and actual abuse of their PSIs as committed by others (Stringer 2014). In reducing questions regarding harmful non-consensual sharing to a matter of women's right or wrong choices, we fail to see how the othering involved in non-consensual sharing of women's PSIs is not just working against their free choices, but through them (Baker 2008, 2010; Gill 2017). I thus want to conclude this chapter by cautioning against any reading of these practices as primarily about decontextualized acts of free choice and female empowerment, precisely because such simplistic accounts render wider gender inequalities in the domain of speech about sex online incredibly hard to address and discuss. They obscure from view the social and cultural pressures that might inform how and why such choices are made, effectively enabling particularly dangerous forms of victim-blaming (Gill 2014; Thompson and Donaghue 2014; Stringer 2014). In cases of non-consensual sharing of PSIs, we too often see that stigma and responsibility are lived by and directed at those subjected to it, rather than those who actually carried out this act. In changing the discourse surrounding women's creation and distribution of PSIs as well as our approaches to the risks surrounding it, we would be taking an important step towards the de-stigmatization of this form of 'online othering'.

References

Albury, K., & Crawford, K. (2012). Sexting, consent and young people's ethics: Beyond Megan's Story. *Continuum, 26*(3), 463–473.

Ayres, L. (2008). Semi-structured interview. In L. M. Given (Ed.), *The SAGE Encyclopedia of Qualitative Research Methods*. Thousand Oaks, CA: Sage.

Baggs, M. (2018). Revenge porn: What to do if you're a victim. *BBC News*. http://www.bbc.co.uk/news/newsbeat-42780602. Accessed January 24, 2018.

Baker, J. (2008). The ideology of choice: Overstating progress and hiding injustice in the lives of young women: Findings from a study in North Queensland, Australia. *Women's Studies International Forum, 31*(1), 53–64.

Baker, J. (2010). Claiming volition and evading victimhood: Post-feminist obligations for young women. *Feminism & Psychology, 20*(2), 186–204.

Bates, S. (2017). Revenge porn and mental health: A qualitative analysis of the mental health effects of revenge porn on female survivors. *Feminist Criminology, 12*(1), 22–42.

Burkett, M. (2015). Sex(t) talk: A qualitative analysis of young adults' negotiations of the pleasures and perils of sexting. *Sexuality and Culture, 19*(4), 835–863.

Döring, N. (2014). Consensual sexting among adolescents: Risk prevention through abstinence education or safer sexting? *Cyberpsychology: Journal of Psychosocial Research on Cyberspace, 8*(1). https://journals.muni.cz/cyberpsychology/article/view/4303.

Elias, A. S., Gill, R., & Scharff, C. (2017). Aesthetic labour: Beauty politics in neoliberalism. In A. Elias, R. Gill, & C. Scharff (Eds.), *Aesthetic Labour: Rethinking Beauty Politics in Neoliberalism* (pp. 3–49). London: Palgrave Macmillan.

García-Favaro, L., & Gill, R. (2016). 'Emasculation nation has arrived': Sexism rearticulated in online responses to Lose the Lads' Mags campaign. *Feminist Media Studies, 16*(3), 379–397.

Gill, R. (2007). Postfeminist media culture: Elements of a sensibility. *European Journal of Cultural Studies, 10*(2), 147–166.

Gill, R. (2014). Unspeakable inequalities: Post feminism, entrepreneurial subjectivity, and the repudiation of sexism among cultural workers. *Social Politics: International Studies in Gender, State & Society, 21*(4), 509–528.

Gill, R. (2017). The affective, cultural and psychic life of postfeminism: A postfeminist sensibility 10 years on. *European Journal of Cultural Studies, 20*(6), 606–626.

Gill, R., & Scharff, C. (2011). Introduction. In R. Gill & C. Scharff (Eds.), *New Femininities: Postfeminism, Neoliberalism and Subjectivity* (pp. 1–17). Basingstoke: Palgrave Macmillan.

Harvey, L., & Gill, R. (2011). Spicing it up: Sexual entrepreneurs and the sex inspectors. In R. Gill & C. Scharff (Eds.), *New Femininities: Postfeminism, Neoliberalism and Subjectivity* (pp. 52–67). Basingstoke: Palgrave Macmillan.

Henry, N., & Powell, A. (2015). Embodied harms: Gender, shame, and technology-facilitated sexual violence. *Violence Against Women, 21*(6), 758–779.

Henry, N., & Powell, A. (2016). Sexual violence in the digital age: The scope and limits of criminal law. *Social & Legal Studies, 25*(4), 397–418.

Illouz, E. (2012). *Why Love Hurts: A Sociological Explanation*. Cambridge: Polity Press.

Kaiser, K. (2009). Protecting respondent confidentiality in qualitative research. *Qualitative Health Research, 19*(11), 1632–1641.

Laville, S., & Halliday, J. (2016). 'They didn't know they were victims': Revenge porn helpline sees alarming rise. *The Guardian*. https://www.theguardian.com/technology/2016/may/08/they-didnt-know-they-were-victims-revenge-porn-helpline-sees-alarming-rise. Accessed November 30, 2016.

Lenhart, A. (2009). *Teens and Sexting: Pew Research Center: Internet, Science & Tech*. http://www.pewinternet.org/2009/12/15/teens-and-sexting/. Accessed December 14, 2016.

McGlynn, C., Rackley, E., & Houghton, R. (2017). Beyond 'revenge porn': The continuum of image-based sexual abuse. *Feminist Legal Studies, 25*(1), 1–22.

McNair, B. (2002). *Striptease Culture: Sex, Media and the Democratization of Desire*. London: Routledge.

McRobbie, A. (2004). Post-feminism and popular culture. *Feminist Media Studies, 4*(3), 255–264.

McRobbie, A. (2009). *The Aftermath of Feminism: Gender, Culture, and Social Change*. London: Sage.

Ringrose, J. (2011). Are you sexy, flirty, or a slut? Exploring 'sexualization' and how teen girls perform/negotiate digital sexual identity on social networking sites. In R. Gill & C. Scharff (Eds.), *New Femininities: Postfeminism, Neoliberalism and Subjectivity* (pp. 99–116). Basingstoke: Palgrave Macmillan.

Ringrose, J., & Harvey, L. (2015). Boobs, back-off, six packs and bits: Mediated body parts, gendered reward, and sexual shame in teens' sexting images. *Continuum, 29*(2), 205–217.

Ringrose, J., Harvey, L., Gill, R., & Livingstone, S. (2013). Teen girls, sexual double standards and 'sexting': Gendered value in digital image exchange. *Feminist Theory, 14*(3), 305–323.

Roulston, K. (2010). *Reflective Interviewing: A Guide to Theory and Practice*. London: Sage.

Salter, M. (2016). Privates in the online public: Sex(ting) and reputation on social media. *New Media & Society, 18*(11), 2723–2739.

Seale, C. (2012). Sampling. In C. Seale (Ed.), *Researching Society and Culture* (3rd ed.). London: Sage.

Sherlock, P. (2016). Revenge pornography victims as young as 11, investigation finds. *BBC News*. http://www.bbc.co.uk/news/uk-england-36054273. Accessed May 7, 2018.

Stringer, R. (2014). *Knowing Victims: Feminism, Agency and Victim Politics in Neoliberal Times*. London: Routledge.

Thompson, L., & Donaghue, N. (2014). The confidence trick: Competing constructions of confidence and self-esteem in young Australian women's discussions of the sexualisation of culture. *Women's Studies International Forum, 47*, 23–35.

7

'There's a Bit of Banter': How Male Teenagers 'Do Boy' on Social Networking Sites

John Whittle, Dave Elder-Vass and Karen Lumsden

Introduction

Young men's experiences with digital technologies are still relatively underexplored despite the acknowledgement that technology is gendered and implicated in gender relations (Light 2013). In this chapter, we add to studies of youth, masculinity and digital media by focusing on the use of banter as a form of gendered talk by male teenagers on social networking sites. Despite previous studies on the use of banter

---

J. Whittle
Further, London, UK

D. Elder-Vass (✉)
School of Social Science, Loughborough University, Loughborough, UK

K. Lumsden
Leicester, UK

by men in work and organisational settings (Hawkins 2013; Plester and Sayers 2007; Sollund 2007; Decapua and Boxer 1999), as part of university 'lad culture' (Phipps and Young 2015), and also its use by women (Lerum 2004; Sanders 2004; Pollert 1981), scarce attention has been paid to banter in youth or teenage interactions in online and offline contexts (with exceptions: Hein and O'Donohoe 2014; Harvey et al. 2013; Kendall 2002; Willis 1977). There has also been a plethora of studies on young people's use of the Internet and social networking sites (i.e. Livingstone 2015; Marwick and boyd 2014; Buckingham 2008); however, the role of banter in framing social interactions in these spaces has not been fully explored.

This chapter argues that banter is a means of performing masculinity, male bonding and creating boundaries to inform in-group acceptance and out-group rejection. Decapua and Boxer (1999: 5) define banter as 'an exchange of light, playful teasing remarks; good-natured raillery', whilst Hein and O'Donohoe (2014: 1303) view the term as 'quite elastic, incorporating insults, teasing, competing, contesting and caring for one another…'. Banter, like humour, can thus be viewed as a means of performing and constructing gender and social identity and as a means of 'disciplining' individuals to 'routinely comply with the customs and habits of their social milieu' (Billig 2005: 2). Banter plays a crucial role in the construction of masculine identity and group identities for young male teenagers in the digital world, which is further mediated, reinforced and regulated via offline relations (Harvey et al. 2013). We explore the deployment of banter by male teenagers on social networking sites such as Facebook and the ways in which it facilitates the performance of hegemonic masculinity (Connell 1995) and male bonding via the creation of in-group and out-group boundaries (Goffman 1963). We argue that banter, in contrast to bullying, is a more ambivalent phenomenon which provides opportunities for both protagonist and target to positively or negatively affect social status.

We begin by reviewing literature on gender and the performance of hegemonic masculinity by teenage boys, including recent work addressing online contexts, and literature on gendered talk and banter. After outlining the methods, we present findings from qualitative interviews and focus groups with teenagers in England, discussing: male teenagers learning to banter; the relationship between banter and bullying; and how banter overflows into other distinct but related practices. We conclude that banter is central to how these young people perform and construct masculinity and that banter operates to establish and create boundaries of acceptability via in-group and out-group norms and expectations (Goffman 1963). Digital interactions which young men engage in on Facebook mediate and reinforce offline hegemonic constructions of masculinity.

Gender and the Performance of Teenage Masculinities

Masculinity is a performance and has an influence on bodily experience, personality and culture. For Connell, 'hegemonic masculinity' is a particular set or style of masculine practices that contributes to institutionalising men's dominance over women (Carrigan et al. 1985). Hegemonic forms of masculinity emphasise, in particular, aggression, competitiveness, invulnerability to emotion and disregard for the emotions of others, and men are judged and classified on the basis of how far they conform to these ideals. However, few men can achieve the full standard of hegemonic masculinity. As Connell (1990) points out, a man attempting to display prowess through sporting achievement, for example, may have to forgo many other hegemonic male activities (like drinking or smoking), which could affect his performance. To some men, despite his athletic achievements, refusing these activities would render him less 'manly'. Given such complexities in the negotiation of gendered identity, male teenagers face significant challenges in learning how best to 'do boy' (Buckingham 2008). Through participating in normatively approved behaviours, individuals seek to place themselves within a group (Goffman 1959). This involves being socialised by others, through negative and positive reprisals, into the correct form of masculine behaviour (Connell 1990).

Butler (1990) and Connell (1990) envisage masculinity as a series of acts which often work to subordinate others. For Butler, the subordinated 'others' are women, whilst Connell (1990) includes women but focuses on the targeting of other men. Hegemonic masculinity, for example, is heterosexual and thus involves the subordination of homosexuality (Carrigan et al. 1985). As Renold (2004: 249) notes: 'boys define hegemonic masculinities in relation to and against an Other through techniques of domination and subordination'. For example, some acts which promote an individual's grasp of masculinity may be performed at the expense of women (through derogatory gender judgements) (Hawkins 2013), or they may utilise apparent weaknesses in other men to display dominance.

Networked Masculinities

Light (2013: 245) suggests that despite influential work on masculinity and digital media over the past two decades, we still need to do more to consider the rise of 'networked masculinities'—'those masculinities (co)produced and reproduced with digitally networked publics'. In an update to her work on masculinity, Connell (2012) argues that masculinity studies need to be cognisant of the institutions in which gender relations are embedded. For young men today, this must include the institutions of digital media.

For example, studies of masculinity and digital media have demonstrated how hegemonic masculinity is not unchanging or universal in form. Siibak's (2010) study of young males' performances on Estonian social networking sites demonstrates how digital platforms provide adolescents with a vehicle to represent current cultural trends and styles that might portray them as popular. In his study, the representation of a male image shifted in line with changes to what was culturally accepted as 'masculine' (Siibak 2010). Some representations were more in keeping with aspects that had previously been defined as feminine.

Harvey et al.'s (2013) work on the use of social networks by young people during the 2011 London riots demonstrates that designer goods and labels which symbolised wealth were used to embody 'cool masculine swagger' and attain popularity 'ratings' in social networks. 'Ratings' were a gendered form of social and cultural capital, commonly conferring safety and movement around the boys' local area. The circulation of images through mobile online technologies enabled the construction of 'particular classed and racialised norms of popular masculinity'

(Harvey et al. 2013: para 1.5). Social networking produces new ways for value to be acquired and circulated (e.g. via 'likes' on Facebook). However, online value must also be verified offline leading Harvey et al. to argue that 'an analysis of symbolic value in digital contexts and in embodied everyday life helps in understanding new regulative formations of gender and masculinity' (2013: para 1).

Kendall's (2000, 2002) participant observation of BlueSky (an online interactive text-based forum) explores participants' understandings of themselves as 'nerds' and the relationship of this identity to hegemonic masculinity and expectations of heterosexuality. The BlueSky participants enacted a form of masculinity related to computer culture. Joking within the BlueSky community, particularly in the form of 'obnoxious bantering' (Kendall 2000: 271) about women as sexual objects, was also important for the construction of group identity and reaffirmed hegemonic masculine values. Kendall (2000: 271) notes that the enactment of a 'white nerd masculine identity' demonstrates its divergence from, and convergence with, hegemonic masculinity.

These studies illustrate how men, within a digital landscape, go about negotiating and creating new masculine values as well as following more traditional roles (Siibak 2010). They also show how complex and intricate the process of compliance with hegemonic masculinity and its evolving standards can be. Finally, studies such as these are sociologically important for demonstrating how social networks have become a valued platform on which young males can explore social norms and produce their own performances in line with, or in conflict with, hegemonic masculinity.

Gendered Talk: Banter and Bonding

Banter is an example of gendered talk which:

> …functions […] to perpetuate and enforce asymmetrical gendered behavior by means of reconstructing social relations between and among females and males in countless ordinary daily conversations over a lifetime. (Sheldon 1990: 6–7)

Billig (2001: 33) reminds us that: 'Teasing can be an inherently ambiguous activity, whose meaning is often contested by the participants. There is evidence that teasers consider their actions to be friendly and more humorous than do the recipients of their teasing'. Previous studies of banter have demonstrated how it helps to forge organisational cultures and have focused on its use by men in workplace settings (Hawkins 2013) such as IT companies (Plester and Sayers 2007), police 'canteen banter' (as sexist and racist) (Sollund 2007) and male bonding in brokerage firms (Decapua and Boxer 1999). In these male-dominated contexts, banter and forms of 'male posturing' involve aggression being '(often playfully) distributed within the group, drawing in all men present to defend themselves against personal sleights' (Tolson 1977).

Although the literature tends to take a critical stance towards banter, Williams (2009) has identified some more positive features of banter in a study of discussions about health care between fathers. For these fathers, 'having a laugh', 'banter' and 'taking the piss' were 'pleasurable and important aspects in which fathers talked about their health experiences' (Williams 2009: 74; Coates 2003: 53). Williams also highlights the humour that characterises many of these experiences (and which is also evident in our study). Williams observed a link between banter and humour, as both framed the interactions between men as an enjoyable pastime, where experiences and ideas could be discussed in a way that displayed masculinity. Thus, humour was vital not only in creating interactions that were enjoyable, but also as a method of performing the role of an 'accepted' man (Williams 2009: 77). However, Williams (2009) found that it could also produce isolation, when it targets individuals through ridicule or uses humour to mask the true feelings of those involved. Rather than expressing important information about how they felt, humour could be used to conceal embarrassment and vulnerability (Coates 2003: 55), thus demonstrating that 'they were "normal" or "proper" hegemonic men' (Williams 2009: 79).

More critically still, banter has been seen as a means of expressing sexual aggression (Eder 1995) and as a form of sexual harassment which targets both men and women (Lerum 2004). In a study of teamwork amongst colleagues in an office, Hawkins (2013) notes that banter (which in her study is dominated by the sexualisation of women) is used to create '…a pecking order amongst consultants. Rankings in teams are informed by the extent to which individuals demonstrate their commitment… by embodying masculinist team values…' (Hawkins 2013: 122). Men attempt to build their social status through the subjugation of women using language which marks them out as 'playthings' and through the subordination of other men. Eder (1995) views banter as an expression of gender tension and sexual aggression manifested through teasing and insults (Willis 1977). Phipps and Young (2015: 311) observed how male university students in England used banter as a means of defending irony or covering up behaviours with humour, which risked 'normalising problematic attitudes and behaviours'. Therefore, in these studies there is a 'link between sexual aggression and bullying behaviour in which boys as well as girls [are] targeted' (Eder and Nenga 2006: 169).

Whilst the literature tends to suggest that for men, banter is a 'form of aggression and dominance', it has also been argued that there are gendered variations in the use of banter and that, like humour, banter can establish intimacy for women (Decapua and Boxer 1999: 5). Pollert (1981) found that women factory workers were equally capable of taking part in sexualised, 'masculine banter' as a means of expressing resistance to managerial staff. Lerum (2004) also notes the function of 'sexual banter' in female-dominated service environments (including strip clubs, diners and a high-end restaurant in the USA), as a means of facilitating camaraderie and empowerment. Powell and Sang (2015) argue that for women in the workplace, 'sexist banter' is difficult to challenge (see also Lumsden 2009). Sanders (2004) highlights the banter that takes place between female sex workers and highlights the banter of protecting personal and emotional well-being.

Banter has been observed to strengthen relationships bonds between men (Williams 2009) by asserting the value of specific norms like heterosexuality, but also as alienating others who do not adhere to these norms, or who do not participate in banter (Decapua and Boxer 1999). As Hein and O'Donohoe (2014: 1308) note: 'Banter among smaller groups of friends seem[s] to reflect, and perhaps produce, a stronger bond'. This is the inclusive side of establishing group boundaries but such bonding may also exclude a marginalised group who lack the ability to take part (Goffman 1963).

The above studies explore how banter facilitates interaction but much of the work that has been conducted on banter has related it to bullying (Eder and Nenga 2006). These accounts often explore banter from an outsider perspective, which focuses on the effects these male interactions may have on victims (intended or otherwise). This study, by contrast, presents the perspectives of the participants themselves, giving them a voice to discuss the role of banter in peer-group interactions on social networking sites such as Facebook.

Methods

The discussion is based on data collected during a study into teenagers' social media use and its relationship to friendship and identity formation in an English town in the East Midlands, over the course of two years. 10 semi-structured interviews and 7 focus groups were conducted by the first author across three secondary schools which taught a range of children (aged 11–16) from varying ethnic and economic backgrounds. This includes individuals who identified as being from Christian, Muslim, Hindu, and Sikh backgrounds, and from working-, middle- and upper-class families. Semi-structured interviews also took place in local homes. The research involved 98 participants in total, of whom 20 were girls and 78 were boys.

Thematic analysis and an iterative-inductive approach were adopted in order to analyse the data, with the intention of 'allowing the data to speak for themselves as far as possible' (O'Reilly 2005: 27). This enabled the identification and analysis of key themes and patterns emerging from the transcripts. Gender, and specifically the role of banter amongst male participants, emerged as a pertinent theme during the data collection phase. Once banter had been identified as a theme, the researcher incorporated specific questions which would prompt further discussion of this in the interviews and focus groups.

The project received institutional ethical approval. The identities of the participants have been fully anonymised, using pseudonyms selected by the participants. Allen and Wiles (2016: 162) note that allowing participants to choose their own pseudonyms gives participants the opportunity to direct how they will feature in an academic study whilst also ensuring that the privacy of those who take part is upheld. It also encourages participation by making the process more informal for teenagers (for instance, some of them elected to choose a comical pseudonym).

'There's a Bit of Banter': Learning and Performing Masculinity

Learning to 'Banter'

For the male teenagers in this study, bantering on social networking sites such as Facebook was an important rite of passage for socialising them into masculine norms and values, and particularly the performance of hegemonic masculinity. For instance, the focus group extract below includes an exchange related to a horror video on Facebook. We can see how David, through his response that the video was 'scary' and his agreement with Anna, prompts derision from the other boys for not adhering to typically masculine traits such as strength and stoicism:

> *Anna*: There are so many videos on Facebook that come up now, like scary things, that I like, don't think other people should click on. But so many people sort of do it anyway.
> *David*: Yeah like also I realized, I saw a video, like it was meant to be an illusionist. And they made you stare right into this little dot.
> [The other boys chuckle]
> *David*: And then it turns into this scary face, screaming at you and…
> *Juan*: And that's funny!
> *David*: Yeah it is…
> *Juan*: What it did to you is like when you take a little kid to do it…
> (Focus group with Anna, David, Paul and Juan, 12–16 years old)

The opening lines between Anna and David were typical of interactions during the session, in that it appeared that David was somewhat in awe of Anna. Often, after she had spoken, he would be quick to agree and show his support. Up until this point, this had little impact on his standing in the conversation, yet on this occasion it placed him into a vulnerable position with his male peers. Through engaging with her sentiments and mirroring the language she used, he incites derision from the other boys. When he expresses his view of this video as 'scary', the others are quick to contradict this and instead define it as 'funny'. This technique of conflicting opinion is used to imply that David, by finding the video shocking in the same manner as a girl, is less masculine than his peers, who found it humorous. This is supported moments afterwards when Juan openly compares David and his reaction to that of a child. During this small focus group, Paul was fairly quiet and hesitant to offer strong views. Yet he was a participant in the banter through his role as a member of the audience. The reactions he expressed, both to Juan's masculine dominance and David's attempt to reclaim his masculine capital, are critical to these interactions. As he was not engaged in either 'confrontation', he was perfectly placed to judge on the success of these exchanges. Although not necessarily an impartial judge, for the boys within that exchange, his reactions (and also those, in part, of Anna) were the deciding factor in who was the banter victor.

This is an example of how social norms create boundaries that can divide groups (Goffman 1963). These boys are performing their own hegemonic masculinity (Connell 1990). As the other boys are older than David, it is also likely that this interaction is evidence of the younger teen being socialised, through a series of negative responses (McGuffey 2011). This is supported by David's attempts later in the conversation (not included in the extract above) to reassert himself and show through his behaviour that he belongs to the same group as his peers through acting in a way that is similar to them. In his justification, he appears to alter his reaction to agree with the humorous response that was reported by the other boys. We observe a moment of gender socialisation, via the 'mocking' of feminised behaviour in a younger male adolescent (Butler 1990; Connell 1990). Part of this socialisation is about 'othering' perceived feminine traits/behaviour. David is being exposed to the influence of the 'norm circles' for banter and for a certain style of masculinity (Elder-Vass 2010). He is coming to learn that certain ways of performing masculinity are more likely to be endorsed by his teenage peers than others, and even within this short conversation, we see evidence that he is responding to this pressure.

This is not a social phenomenon that is confined to a single platform, or encountered solely offline or online. The participants rarely distinguished relationships and interactions as being bounded by a specific digital device or application. Indeed, the excerpt above centres on an online activity which then becomes relevant in face-to-face discussion. Online or offline, however, for many male teenagers, performing their masculinity includes normalised forms of conflict with other boys, through which they are able to manage their social status and group identity. However, the norms of banter also discourage boys from reacting emotionally or honestly if they are upset or angered. To do so would be to act in a feminised manner that conflicts with 'emotional restraint, one of the key values inherent in hegemonic masculinity' (Coates 2003: 47). Being socialised into banter is a step towards the adult masculinity that Williams (2009) observed, in which banter, although useful for facilitating bonding and social ordering, also often prevented his group of fathers from being able to openly express how they felt.

It was also often difficult to establish how boys truly felt about the insults and jibes that they received and traded. Although discussions like the one between David and Juan were framed as humorous and good-natured exchanges, there were often signs that individuals were unhappy. This was displayed through muted responses, pauses in communication as individuals worked to control emotions and reply suitably and defensive or tense body language. David exhibited some of these characteristics as he worked to control his reactions to the comments from Juan.

Unlike the female participants, who had no issue talking about the emotions that similar confrontations had evoked, the boys were always reticent to reveal how they felt, especially when it was related to how banter might affect them. Through claiming that insults are harmless, or by downplaying the emotional impact it might have, these boys are aligning themselves with hegemonic ideas about what it means to be male.

Banter or Bullying?

The teenage boys frequently expressed derisive judgements of their male peers. Although at first glance these jibes resemble bullying, we suggest that they represent a distinct and consciously different process, at least in the eyes of these participants. One of the crucial differences is the manner in which such interactions are publicly framed and how this relates to masculinity. In the excerpt below, we can see how male teenagers reference banter and justify its use in social interactions with peers. They take care to distinguish banter from bullying:

> *Interviewer*: In terms of social networking have you experienced times when there has been conflict?
> *Mark*: There's a bit of banter.
> *Interviewer*: What do you qualify as banter?
> *Mark*: Something that both people find funny.
> *Interviewer*: Ah right, so you've made it clear there that it is not bullying…?
> *Mark*: Yeah.
> *Steven*: Yeah.
> *Interviewer*: So how often do you think, something crosses over from banter to bullying? Or how much is there of either?
> *George*: I don't think I often see bullying. There's not really much of either. There's a bit of banter between friends.
> *George*: Not really bullying.
> (Focus group with Mark, Steven and George, 14–15 years old)

Although Mark identifies banter as a form of conflict, he and his peers—even after prompting by the interviewer—continue to distance this behaviour from an act that might be classified as harassment or as harmful to the recipient. In their study of 'lad culture', Phipps and Young (2015: 311) discovered that male university students used banter as a means of defending irony or covering up behaviours with humour, which risked 'normalising problematic attitudes and behaviours'. By reframing their verbal exchanges, the boys continued to engage in an activity that to an outsider might seem detrimental to their friendships. Their perception of banter is linked to masculine norms such as competition, conflict and strength. This is also perhaps why it was difficult to ascertain whether any teenager had experienced their inclusion in banter as bullying. Maintaining 'face' (Goffman 1955) in these interactions was a vital strategy for ensuring acceptance by the male peer group.

In another focus group, Dash described a typical piece of 'online banter'. This involved tagging male friends in online photos. Tagging is a function on certain social networking sites, which alerts the tagee and friends to the presence of a photo of the tagee. It is used to show who was present in the picture, share events that friends had experienced together and allow peers to witness the photos and the relationships they represent. However, in the cases discussed below it is used to 'tag' a photo of another person with the name of the target of the banter, suggesting that the target shares some feature with the actual individual in the photo. In this instance, the photo used is that of a man considered 'skinny' with the words 'He lifts' typed below:

> *Interviewer*: What do you think boys do on social networking?
> *Dash*: Taking the mick out of each other.
> [The group agrees with a chorus of 'yes'.]
> *Dash*: There are a few pictures with like… We tag a few of our thin friends in, say like, 'He lifts' and stuff.
> [Laughter from the group].
> (Focus group with Dash, Michael and Charlotte, all 15 years old)

By hegemonic standards of masculinity, men who lack muscle or do not engage in physical activities are viewed as inferior (Connell 1990). There is still a strong argument that a powerful physicality is part of the projection of the hegemonic man (Connell 1990). By tagging his friend in the photo of the skinny man, Dash is appealing to this gendered ideal. He aligns his friend with this inferior image whilst positioning himself in opposition to it.

The use of the words 'He lifts' further undermines the 'tagee's' 'masculine capital'. 'Do you even lift?' is a common male insult that alludes to an individual's physical weakness. This is not a positive comment for those boys who are in search of social acceptance, and Dash's choice of phrase—'He lifts'—is arguably as damaging. The phrase implies that the individual has exercised but still failed to develop muscle. This can increase the negativity associated with the image and the 'tagged' recipient as it demonstrates a failure of masculine control and dominance. The recipient of the sleight is represented simultaneously as weak and as unable to affect a change regardless of their efforts.

Amongst these boys, banter is part of the cultural process of defining masculinity through and against derogatory representations of both women and other men by constructing them as 'Other' (Renold 2004), but their motivations for taking part in this process are complex. On the one hand, such insults were seen by male teens as part of a competitive jostling for status in the peer hierarchy, demonstrating that 'men's talk' is competitive (Hein and O'Donohoe 2014). There is a sense of this in the example above where the reputation of the boy is diminished by associating him with feminised characteristics (such as lack of muscle). Such insults both appeal to and reproduce prevailing standards of 'hegemonic masculinity' (Connell 1990).

Overflowing Practices and Failed Banter

Despite the frequency with which banter and humour were reported together, there were also occasions when it was not well received. In the focus groups and interviews, boys seemed loath to bring up accounts where they had experienced, or knew of, occasions where banter had taken a more serious turn. Yet it was clear that there had been occasions where insults had led to more serious provocations. In one focus group, a respondent called Lionheart (aged 14) described an interaction which 'just kicked off' in response to a comment on Facebook, leading to physical violence between the two parties, an outcome that was perceived by onlookers to be 'ridiculous':

> *Interviewer*: Was that offline, like a proper fight?
> *Lionheart*: Yeah.
> *Kesha*: Owen's an idiot.
> *Lionheart*: That's just on Facebook, but this guy Michael is like a complete muppet and Owen said something and it just kicked off from there.

> I was with Owen at the time and we were just laughing loads, because it's just funny… I got started on but I didn't do anything and neither did Owen but then people started saying other stuff and Owen got annoyed. But it's just ridiculous.
> (Interview with Kesha and Lionheart, 14 years old)

These interactions and their interpretations by the individuals involved highlight the complexity of male-versus-male interaction and its navigation. Despite many adolescents appearing to endorse the ideal of male physicality, in examples when a fight does ensue it is perceived negatively as an exchange in which banter failed. Rather than continuing with a witty response, the target steps outside the bounds of banter with an aggressive over-reaction. Part of the culture of banter is that derogation is humorous, and although it is humour at someone's expense, it is not continuous with aggression or violence, which are to be directed at outsiders, whilst banter is directed at insiders (Goffman 1959). Equally, an aggressive or hostile response that is not camouflaged with humour represents unfamiliarity with the tactics of banter. Whether it is the original comment or the response, this shifts the participants out of the banter ritual and into the sphere of bullying. This does not mean that banter is a form of violence or bullying, but rather, that banter may overflow into other interaction practices when it is conducted with insufficient skills or knowledge, or when the participants are ambivalent about their intentions.

Evaluating exchanges as either banter or bullying is challenging for outsiders, partly because ambiguity may be used as a shield for verbal bullying—'it's just banter, innit?'—if the boy is called out for their behaviour. On the one hand, participants may not speak freely about their feelings due to the relationship that such practices have with masculinity and the masking of emotions. 'Display rules' specify appropriate overt expressions of emotion in response to banter. Following these rules involves an element of 'surface acting' as part of the boys' 'emotion management' in relation to gendered expectations (Hochschild 1983). On the other hand, statements that seem cruel and hostile to outsiders may be received more positively as part of an ongoing bonding ritual by the participants.

Banter failures can arise from the unsuccessful deployment of banter. The target of banter must always evaluate whether the intent of the initiator is inclusive or if such comments trespass over acceptable lines. As the literal verbal content takes the form of an insult in both cases, there is always the possibility that the target might not respond verbally, but physically. A statement intended as banter may thus be taken as aggression instead, and not only because the target is unskilled but also if the initiator fails to provide enough contextual clues to show that banter is intended. In a focus group, Colin reported that a member of their peer group would often try to banter with others by correcting their grammar. However, his persistence in doing this and his apparent lack of social mastery of the appropriate clues and interpersonal boundaries had resulted in a number of altercations:

> *Colin*: Oh the one with Jamie Kind, there is always one with Jamie Kind. Because he always corrects people's grammar and they get REALLY angry.
> *Interviewer*: Is this a boy in your year?
> [There is a chorus of 'yes' and angry muttering from the whole group].
> (Focus group with 15-year old boys)

In this example, Jamie had alienated himself from a number of peers because, despite actively engaging in this male pastime, he had failed to meet the humour requirement for successful banter.

A further difficulty with executing banter online is that the contextual clues distinguishing banter from bullying are also more ambiguous. Tone of communication, timing, facial expression and body language clues from both the initiator and the observers are absent. The recipient must decide how to interpret the insult based on how it is embedded in the context of communication and in the history of the relationship between initiator and target. When 'online banter' is executed between people who also have offline relationships, this context and history may be well developed, having benefitted already from the much richer contextual clues available in face-to-face interaction. The social actors, in other words, have had the opportunity to build up a level of trust that informs their interpretations of each other's remarks. Lacking this context, 'online banter' can be more difficult to execute competently and constructively than 'offline banter'.

Conclusion

This chapter focused on male teenagers' use of banter on social networking sites such as Facebook and its role in constructing a form of hegemonic masculinity (Connell 1995). We argued that banter is a more complex practice than has previously been suggested and that it has connections to various aspects of masculinity and social inclusion. It has characteristics which appear to set it apart from bullying. One key difference lies in how the comments are interpreted. Through accepting the banter that is levelled at him/her, and not reacting in an open and aggressive way to what has been said, the individual is able to mitigate the chance of being viewed as a victim, or in the case of a boy, as a weaker male, and thus 'losing face' in online interactions with their peers (Goffman 1955). Banter offers an opportunity to later reclaim both status and image, by deploying similar verbal tactics in the same manner. This is not to suggest that the comments which are exchanged by these teenagers cannot be hurtful and/or received negatively. As many insults in banter exchanges are deliberately styled to irritate, part of their purpose is to offend and provoke a response from an appropriate target. These insults may be similar in content to those employed in cases of bullying, but the response structure is different.

In a bullying interaction, individuals are usually selected that are already excluded from a set in-group, and the derogatory comments further enforce this boundary. By contrast, banter invites a verbal retort which is actively considered by all involved, whilst also including peers in the group and marking off boundaries to distinguish those deemed to be outsiders. Thus, whilst bullying could be compared to a one-sided battle, banter is a contest utilising verbal assaults that are judged by peers. The role of third-party witnesses in banter resonates with the work of Goffman (1959), who argued that our portrayals of self depend on appealing to an audience. The value of the responses and comments that constitute banter will be judged against the groups' beliefs with regard to masculinity, humour, verbal skill, etc., and the mastery of how these aspects are combined.

As it is an interactional style that is bounded by the norms of masculinity, one of the most crucial aspects for those involved is to be able to mask any effect that they feel from the banter. One of the issues that make banter so complex is that each exchange is a constant test of control and verbal dexterity, pitching insults that will offend the target just enough without crossing into territory that might be viewed as too offensive by other males. As we saw above, this can result in a physical confrontation that damages the credibility of all involved through displaying a weakness of self-control and thus 'losing face' (Goffman 1955). Avoiding this outcome is one reason why the presence of humour is so valued during these communications. For the participants in banter to maintain face, they must cooperate to preserve a definition of the situation as humorous and comradely, and it is this cooperation that distinguishes banter most decisively from bullying. It is partly because in learning to banter boys learn to cooperate in preserving such a definition that banter can be a useful tool in promoting bonding amongst group members. This is a form of interaction in which the participants exchange not only insults but also recognition (Coates 2003: 2–3). The frequency with which banter was mentioned by our participants, and the emphatic care that was taken in setting it out as both good-natured and non-threatening on all sides, seemed to place this mechanism as a vital part of being masculine. To 'do boy' (Buckingham 2008; Butler 1990) for many participants (stated by both boys and girls in this study), centred on being able to hold one's own in the swift and brutal exchanges of verbal wordplay.

Attempts to banter online with people who do not share an offline relationship (such as friendship) with the initiator are risky, since it is more likely that insults will be interpreted as hostile, as in cases of 'trolling', for example (cf. Lumsden and Morgan 2017). It seems likely that *some* behaviour that is experienced as 'trolling' by its targets is seen as an attempt at banter by the initiator. This, in turn, seems more likely when the initiator is an inexperienced or unskilled 'banterer'. Some cases of 'trolling' are carried out by those with poor social skills who have difficulty in distinguishing the subtleties of different forms of communication. As we noted earlier, Billig (2001) shows that 'teasing' can be an ambiguous activity, with meanings contested by participants, and in online banter this ambiguity can be amplified.

By exploring the use of banter online by teenage boys, we have seen how it can be used to order both social status and individual identity within peer groups. We have also noted how banter offers an opportunity for all involved to engage in 'online othering' in order to negotiate their place within a male group in a way that is not present in exchanges that can be classed merely as bullying or victim-focused. Through accepting the 'bantering' jibes or insults, rather than responding aggressively or appealing to authority figures that might intervene, the recipient is later able to claim some credibility back if they effectively retort and are judged successful by their peers.

We recognise that we have mainly explored the use of banter within male peer groups in a very specific sociocultural setting and therefore have not drawn attention to its use to subordinate girls and women in certain (online) settings such as via 'sexist banter' (Lerum 2004; Phipps and Young 2015). There is also a need for research on many other intersections of gendered, classed and raced identities, and their performance in the complex negotiations of conflict, gendered identities, status and hierarchies, that are so crucial for teenagers in their everyday lives. The focus of this paper, however, has been to make the case for seeing banter as a complex social practice in its own right, with both positive and negative roles in the socialisation of contemporary male teens.

In this chapter, we contributed to the sociological study of youth, masculinity and digital media. We highlighted the need to explore the construction, enactment and reproduction of masculinities in digital media spaces in order to account for the ways in which gender relations are embedded in social institutions and structures (including digital/social media) and in a global context (Connell 2012). We also add more specifically to sociological studies of 'networked masculinities' (Light 2013) and the study of banter in online settings. An exploration of banter and masculinity reveals how male teenagers feel about its role and the exchanges they share, and how hegemonic masculinity's power is further reinforced via digital media exchanges between young boys, at such an early age. Thus, learning to banter both offline and online plays a crucial role for our male teenagers in socialising them into the norms and values of hegemonic masculinity.

References

Allen, R. E. S., & Wiles, J. L. (2016). A rose by any other name: Participants choosing research pseudonyms. *Qualitative Research in Psychology, 13*(2), 149–165.

Billig, M. (2001). Humour and embarrassment: Limits of 'nice-guy' theories of social life. *Theory, Culture & Society, 18*(5), 23–43.

Billig, M. (2005). *Laughter and Ridicule*. London: Sage.

Buckingham, D. (2008). *Youth, Identity and Digital Media*. Cambridge: MIT Press.

Butler, J. (1990). *Gender Trouble*. London: Routledge.

Carrigan, T., Connell, B., & Lee, J. (1985). Toward a new sociology of masculinity. *Theory and Society, 14*(5), 551–604.

Coates, J. (2003). *Men Talk*. Oxford: Blackwell.

Connell, R. W. (1990). An iron man: The body and some contradictions of hegemonic masculinity. In M. Messner & D. Sabo (Eds.), *Sport, Men and the Gender Order*. Champaign: Human Kinetics Books.

Connell, R. W. (1995). *Masculinities* (2nd ed.). Cambridge: Polity Press.

Connell, R. W. (2012). Masculinity research and global change. *Masculinities and Social Change, 1*(1), 4–18.

Decapua, A., & Boxer, D. (1999). Bragging, boasting and bravado: Male banter in a brokerage house. *Women and Language, 22*(1), 5–22.

Eder, D. (1995). *School Talk*. New Brunswick, NJ: Rutgers University Press.

Eder, D., & Nenga, S. K. (2006). Socialization in adolescence. In J. Delamater (Ed.), *Handbook of Social Psychology* (pp. 157–182). New York: Kluwer Academic.

Elder-Vass, D. (2010). *The Causal Power of Social Structures*. Cambridge: Cambridge University Press.

Goffman, E. (1955). On face-work. *Psychiatry: Journal for the Study of Interpersonal Processes, 18*, 213–231.

Goffman, E. (1959). *The Presentation of Self in Everyday Life*. New York: Random House.

Goffman, E. (1963). *Stigma*. London: Penguin.

Harvey, L., Ringrose, J., & Gill, R. (2013). Swagger, ratings and masculinity. *Sociological Research Online, 18*(4). http://www.socresonline.org.uk/18/4/9.html.

Hawkins, B. (2013). Gendering the eye of the norm. *Gender, Work & Organization, 20*(1), 113–126.

Hein, M., & O'Donohoe, S. (2014). Practising gender: The role of banter in young men's improvisations of masculine consumer identities. *Journal of Marketing Management, 30*(13–14), 1293–1319.

Hochschild, A. R. (1983). *The Managed Heart*. Berkeley: University of California Press.

Kendall, L. (2000). 'Oh no! I'm a nerd!': Hegemonic masculinity on an online forum. *Gender and Society, 14*(2), 256–274.

Kendall, L. (2002). *Hanging Out in the Virtual Pub*. Berkeley: University of California Press.

Lerum, K. (2004). Sexuality, power and camaraderie in service work. *Gender & Society, 18*(6), 756–776.

Light, B. (2013). Networked masculinities and social networking sites. *Masculinities and Social Change, 2*(3), 245–265.

Livingstone, S. (2015). *Digital Technologies in the Lives of Young People*. London: Routledge.

Lumsden, K. (2009). 'Don't ask a woman to do another woman's job': Gendered interactions and the emotional ethnographer. *Sociology, 43*(3), 497–513.

Lumsden, K., & Morgan, H. M. (2017). Media framing of trolling and online abuse: Silencing strategies, symbolic violence and victim blaming. *Feminist Media Studies, 17*(6), 926–940.

Marwick, A., & boyd, D. (2014). 'It's just drama': Teen perspectives on conflict and aggression in a networked era. *Journal of Youth Studies, 17*(9), 1187–1204.

McGuffey, S. (2011). Playing in the gender transgression zone: Race, class, and hegemonic masculinity in middle childhood. In K. Spade & C. Valentine (Eds.), *The Kaleidoscope of Gender*. Thousand Oaks, CA: Pine Forge Press.

O'Reilly, K. (2005). *Ethnographic Methods*. London: Routledge.

Phipps, A., & Young, I. (2015). Neoliberalisation and 'lad cultures' in higher education. *Sociology, 49*(2), 305–322.

Plester, B. A., & Sayers, J. (2007). 'Taking the piss': Functions of banter in the IT industry. *Humor, 20*(2), 157–187.

Pollert, A. (1981). *Girls, Wives, Factory Lives*. London: Macmillan.

Powell, A., & Sang, K. J. C. (2015). Everyday experiences of sexism in male-dominated professions: A Bourdieusian perspective. *Sociology, 49*(5), 919–936.

Renold, E. (2004). 'Other' boys: Negotiating non-hegemonic masculinities in the primary school. *Gender and Education, 16*(2), 247–265.

Sanders, T. (2004). Controllable laughter: Managing sex work through humour. *Sociology, 38*(2), 273–291.

Sheldon, A. (1990). Pickle fights: Gendered talk in preschool disputes. *Discourse Processes, 13*(1), 5–31.

Siibak, A. (2010). Constructing masculinity on a social networking site. *Young: Nordic Journal of Youth Research, 18*(4), 403–425.

Sollund, R. (2007). Canteen banter or racism. *Journal of Scandinavian Studies in Criminology and Crime Prevention, 8*(1), 77–96.

Tolson, A. (1977). *The Limits of Masculinity*. London: Tavistock.

Williams, R. (2009). 'Having a laugh': Masculinities, health and humour. *Nursing Inquiry, 16*(1), 74–81.

Willis, P. (1977). *Learning to Labour*. London: Saxon House.

8

Othering Political Women: Online Misogyny, Racism and Ableism Towards Women in Public Life

Rosalynd Southern and Emily Harmer

Introduction

Formal political institutions have historically been dominated by men. This trend persists despite the legal, social and cultural gains made by women during the twentieth century and into the twenty-first. Women have often struggled to achieve equal levels of participation as political representatives due to a number of barriers such as the domination of political party structures by men, gendered stereotypes, social expectations amongst voters about who should be involved in politics, and material inequalities which leave them disproportionately responsible for domestic labour (Childs 2008). Women who also happen to have a disability and be Black Asian or Minority Ethnic (BAME) or LGBT+ have found it even harder to achieve the levels of political representation than they deserve due to a whole host of structural and material inequalities which intersect with their gendered

R. Southern · E. Harmer (✉)
Department of Communication and Media,
University of Liverpool, Liverpool, UK

identities (Evans 2015; Ward 2016). The role of mainstream media in reproducing inequalities experienced by women in politics generally is well-researched (Ross 2002; O'Neill et al. 2016; Harmer et al. 2017) but there are far fewer studies that adopt an intersectional framework to take into account the extent to which gender is just one layer of inequality for women from under-represented backgrounds (Ward 2016).

In the twenty-first century, women politicians also have to contend with the ways in which digital media can also contribute to their continued marginalisation. There has been a good deal of public discussion and indeed academic research which explores the potential benefits of social media for political discussion and deliberation (Papacharissi 2002; Dahlgren 2005). However as has been experienced by other women in public life, there are also hugely problematic consequences of engaging in social media for women in politics. The abuse suffered online, and particularly on Twitter, by female and Black Members of Parliament (MPs) in the UK has been well-documented in news coverage. Both Labour shadow cabinet minister Diane Abbott (*The Guardian*, 12 July 2018) and Scottish National Party MP Mhairi Black (*The Independent*, 8 March 2018) have spoken publicly and in parliament about the abuse they have suffered online from complete strangers who send offensive and inappropriate messages and images directly to them, with much of the content explicitly denigrating their racial identity and sexuality, as well as being gendered. This chapter analyses all of the tweets directly sent to the 33 women members of the UK Parliament who are BAME, LGBTQ+ or have a disability of some kind, and who have active Twitter accounts. (Their details are explained below.) We focus specifically on these women in order to ascertain whether women from currently under-represented groups are particularly likely to experience online othering behaviours on Twitter, and the particular nature of that othering.

First, the chapter will outline literature on the relationship between women politicians and media and the extent to which online spaces can be considered hostile to women. The methods used in this study will then be explained in detail before we move on to present our findings. We will address four themes which we identified in the data: gendered and racist abuse; silencing and dismissal; questioning intelligence and position; and 'benevolent othering'.

Women, Media, Politics

Media representations are an important means of understanding women's participation in formal politics. Research has shown that mainstream media provide important insight into the ways in which the news media constructs and shapes female politicians and their contribution in specifically gendered ways. The presence of political women in the news is paramount because it allows voters to conceive of politics as other than just a male-dominated arena, remote from their interests. This is seen as being especially important to engage women voters in the political process (Sreberny-Mohammadi and Ross 1996). Numerous studies have demonstrated the extent to which women politicians tend to be marginalised in political news (Ross et al. 2013; O'Neill et al. 2016; Harmer and Southern 2018a), both in terms of the amount of coverage they receive and how much their voices and opinions are heard through direct citation. Women politicians are often also subjected to different media treatment than male colleagues. Women tend to be associated with political change or renewal which positions them as political outsiders; they are often portrayed as breaking through social convention to participate in politics, and their political experience downplayed; or they are represented as agents of change who could alter traditional ways of doing politics (Norris 1997). There are negative consequences to these forms of framing because women are thus required to square an impossible circle where they have to be tough and assertive like men but are also expected make politics a more conciliatory process (Ross 2002). This much-observed trend of presenting women as political outsiders therefore lends female politicians a novelty value that makes them particularly newsworthy at certain times which goes against the trend noted above. The attention paid to women's clothes and other aspects of their appearances and family arrangements are further examples. These phenomena have been observed in a number of different countries (Lawrence and Rose 2010; Garcia-Blanco and Wahl-Jorgensen 2012). Framing serious women politicians in this manner reveals a dangerous tendency to trivialise and undermine them as effective political actors (Ross 2002). Gill (2007) argues that there is nothing innocent about such representations and that they are part of an operation of power which trivialises the perspective of women and serves to keep them in their place. Recent work underpinned by the Black feminist concept of intersectionality (Crenshaw 1989; Hill Collins 1990) also demonstrates the extent to which media depictions can be even more problematic for women who are othered by the intersection of gender and race/ethnicity. Women of colour in politics tend to be marginalised in news coverage and have their identity emphasised in sometimes problematic ways (Gershon 2012; Ward 2016). The advent of digital technologies means that women politicians also have to deal with the demands not only of a digital news environment which appears to reflect mainstream print and broadcast patterns of representation (Harmer and Southern 2018b) but the demands of social media whereby they can be directly contacted by anyone and which offers increased opportunities for them to be discriminated against and othered online.

Violence Against Women in Politics

Despite the fact that women's participation in formal politics has increased globally, this has been accompanied by another trend: the rise of violence *against* women in politics. Mona Lena Krook's (2017) extensive review of this trend suggests that this takes five forms: physical violence, sexual violence, psychological violence, economic violence and symbolic violence. She identifies a number of empirical studies from Sweden, Bolivia, Australia and the UK which suggest that sexist hostility and intimidation have driven female politicians out of politics. Krook demonstrates that the majority of definitions of violence against women highlight three basic elements. First, that it involves aggressive acts aimed largely or solely at women in politics. Secondly, that women are targeted via explicitly gendered means, for example, the use or threat of sexual violence. And finally, that the goal is to deter participation of the targeted group in formal politics. Crucially, for our purposes, the concept of violence is not limited to physical manifestations. 'Harassment', 'intimidation' and 'discrimination' are also important because they draw attention to non-physical acts of aggression or resistance to women's participation in politics. There are clear parallels here with the conceptualisation of online harassment and trolling as a form of symbolic violence (Lumsden and Morgan 2017) whereby these behaviours act as 'silencing strategies' in order to discourage the recipients (and other people like them) from participating. Online harassment is a way of further excluding women and their voices from digital spaces (Megarry 2014). As Banet-Weiser and Miltner (2016) point out the Internet affords many opportunities to direct vitriol and violence towards women in online spaces. Furthermore, women of colour are particularly targeted since these forms of violence are not only misogynistic, but racist as well. Evidence suggests that women are more likely to be targets for online abuse and are less likely to be its authors (Jane 2014). The findings from a number of studies further indicate that online attacks are aimed disproportionately at women, and in particular at women of colour or those advocating explicitly feminist messages (Banet-Weiser and Miltner 2016; Lewis et al. 2017). A plethora of misogynist tactics, such as trolling (Buckels et al. 2014; Shaw 2016), making sexist 'humorous' comments (Jane 2014; Fox et al. 2015), silencing (Garcia-Favaro and Gill 2016; Shaw 2016), and tacit shaming strategies (Abraham 2013), all attempt to silence women's voices online and re-inscribe the Internet as a place where women do not belong.

Whilst the anonymous nature of online interaction, the structures and policies of online platforms, and an insufficient legal framework for policing such behaviour are often seen as contributing factors, it is crucial not to lose sight of the deeply embedded social and cultural factors that legitimate the denigration of women. There is now an emerging body of work that seeks to measure and analyse the nature of online abuse and discrimination online. However much of this research assumes that this sexism is always aggressive or hostile. This is not always the case. As Fox et al. (2015) argue, one defence of online sexism is to dismiss it as merely a joke. They argue that regardless of tone, online sexism is pernicious and reinforces and normalises the idea that people are entitled to belittle and demean women. Regardless of the intentions of the culprit, the othering of women online can be detrimental to their status as equal participants in society. This is an important point for our analysis too, as we see that although few of the messages that women MPs received were abusive or misogynistic, they reinforce women's outsider status in subtler and potentially enduring ways. This 'ambient sexism' can therefore impact on all women in politics, regardless of whether or not they have been individually targeted.

If we consider the realm of formal politics, this becomes increasingly problematic because online violence 'may operate in ways analogous to physical violence in excluding women from political life' (Krook 2017: 79), and as such 'efforts to harm, intimidate and harass women should thus be seen as a serious threat and affront to democracy, rather than dismissed as an unfortunate feature of "politics as usual"' (Krook 2017: 75): or indeed social/digital media as usual, not least when female Members of Parliament have an obligation to communicate with those they represent, which may necessitate their use of social media to some degree. Therefore, efforts to restrict the participation of women online in these ways is deeply problematic and highlights the role that 'online othering' can have in sending a broader and unambiguous message that women as a group do not belong in politics and/or on social media. Therefore, they may be at the very least at a political disadvantage if they do not make use of platforms like Twitter, or they may be perceived as out of touch by voters who have a right to contact their elected representatives.

Online Abuse of MPs: The Evidence So Far

A growing number of recent studies have sought to examine the extent to which women MPs have been subjected to abuse online. In conjunction with *Buzzfeed News*, Greenwood et al. (2017) studied 840,000 tweets which were sent between 8 May 2017 and 8 June 2017 (one month before the last General Election in the UK). Their results suggest in general that the percentage of tweets that were likely to be seen as abusive made up between 2 and 4% of all tweets sent to politicians and that the overwhelming majority of insulting tweets were targeted at a relatively small number of prominent politicians. When the findings are broken down by political party and gender, male Conservative candidates received the highest percentage of abusive tweets. They did however note that women candidates were more likely to receive abuse which was in some way gendered, such as referring to them as a 'witch' for example. Similarly, in their study of 270,000 tweets directed at MPs over a two-and-a-half-month period, Mcloughlin and Ward (2017) also found that the number of abusive tweets was relatively low with just 2.6% of tweets being coded as abusive. Furthermore, they noted that tweets which contained 'hate speech' were even rarer, with only 125 tweets (or 0.42%) being identified as such. They found that 62% of MPs had received at least one abusive tweet whereas only 6.6% of MPs received a tweet containing hate speech. The results indicated that increased name recognition of the MP has a positive relationship with increased levels of abusive tweets. When the results were broken down by gender, they found that men received more abusive tweets than women, however women received a significantly higher proportion of hate speech than men—86% of tweets that contained hate speech were directed at women MPs. Stambolieva (2017) in contrast found that the vast majority of online abuse directed at politicians was aimed at women politicians. The study also revealed that one MP, Diane Abbott (the most prominent Black woman in British public life) received almost half of all the abuse that was featured in the study and that another woman of colour Tasmina Ahmed-Skeikh (a member of the Scottish Parliament) was the second most abused politician. Krook (2017) highlights that women who are younger or who belong to racial or ethnic minorities seem particularly susceptible to being targeted.

Whilst these studies give some indication of the extent to which Members of Parliament receive abusive messages on Twitter, this does not tell us the whole story. As Fox et al. (2015) make clear, sexist and racist content does not necessarily have to be explicitly hostile or abusive. Sexism and racism can be subtler, yet no less pernicious, way of othering women online in order to undermine them and remind others that they do not belong in the political realm. Since the studies discussed above tend to use automated software to perform a basic sentiment analysis, we argue that this means that subtler forms of othering will not be identified with these particular methods. For the purposes of this study, we have employed a qualitative analysis in order to explore the extent to which MPs who are women of colour, identify as LBGT+ and/or have disabilities are othered on Twitter.

Methods

The study focuses on a small sample of political representatives from the UK Parliament. In order to analyse the ways that women politicians are othered and discriminated against on Twitter, we chose to sample the tweets sent directly to women MPs who have two or more characteristics that are traditionally under-represented in parliament such as women BAME, women who are LGBT+ and women who have a known disability. Of the MPs included in the analysis, nine were Lesbian or bisexual women and 23 were Black or other minority ethnic women. There is only one MPs who has three intersecting characteristics—Marsha de Cordova, who is a Black woman who also has a disability. A full list of the women included in the analysis and their characteristics are included in Table 8.1.

These criteria resulted in the identification of 33 currently serving MPs. We collected the tweets over the course of a week between 6 June 2018 and 12 June 2018 inclusive because we were particularly interested in the everyday interactions that MPs have with members of the public rather than messages they might receive during particularly high profile political events such as elections. We used NodeXL software to scrape and download the tweets. This software allows users to scrape seven days of tweets directed at whichever accounts are specified. We then removed any tweets where the MP in question had been included as a result of multiple replies, so that we focused only on tweets which were directly aimed at the MP. This resulted in 12,436 tweets. The MP with the most tweets sent to her was Joanna Cherry—1697 tweets in total. The MP with fewest tweets was Valeria Vaz with 14 tweets. The tweets were then analysed using thematic analysis (Braun and Clarke 2006). We read each tweet and inductively coded them in order to determine if and how these MPs were othered online. We then worked these codes up into themes by analysing which were the most prevalent trends in the data. We have chosen not to anonymise the tweets so that the extent to which women MPs experience online othering is discussed overtly. A number of these women have spoken publicly about their experiences of online abuse and we believe it is desirable to identify these instances clearly so that the extent of the abuse is known.

Table 8.1 List of MPs selected plus their intersecting characteristics and party

Name	Lesbian/Bisexual	BAME	Have a disability	Party
Margot James	1	0	0	Conservative
Justine Greening	1	0	0	Conservative
Helen Grant	0	1	0	Conservative
Priti Patel	0	1	0	Conservative
Kemi Badenoch	0	1	0	Conservative
Nusrat Ghani	0	1	0	Conservative
Suella Fernandes	0	1	0	Conservative
Seema Kennedy	0	1	0	Conservative
Angela Eagle	1	0	0	Labour
Cat Smith	1	0	0	Labour
Nia Griffiths	1	0	0	Labour
Dawn Butler	0	1	0	Labour
Diane Abbott	0	1	0	Labour
Rushashana Ali	0	1	0	Labour
Lisa Nandy	0	1	0	Labour
Chi Onwuhra	0	1	0	Labour
Yasmin Qureshi	0	1	0	Labour
Naz Shah	0	1	0	Labour
Rosena Allin Kahn	0	1	0	Labour
Marsha de Cordova	0	1	1	Labour
Preet Gill	0	1	0	Labour
Valerie Vaz	0	1	0	Labour
Seema Malhotra	0	1	0	Labour
Thangam Debonaire	0	1	0	Labour
Rupa Huq	0	1	0	Labour
Kate Osamore	0	1	0	Labour
Fiona Onasanya	0	1	0	Labour
Eleanor Smith	0	1	0	Labour
Layla Moran	0	1	0	Liberal Democrat
Mhairi Black	1	0	0	SNP
Angela Crawley	1	0	0	SNP
Hannah Bardell	1	0	0	SNP
Joanna Cherry	1	0	0	SNP

Findings

Four themes were identified within the data. Firstly, gendered and racist abuse were the most explicit examples of othering that we observed. The second theme was tweets that were not necessarily abusive but either attempted to silence women MPs or were somehow dismissive of them and their ideas. The third theme includes subtler forms of othering that whilst not overtly gendered, sought to question the intelligence or qualifications and credentials of the recipients in order to suggest that they do not belong in political life. The final, somewhat unexpected theme was what we have called 'benevolent' othering where despite tweeters seeming to heap praise or positive evaluations on women MPs, the tweets themselves still othered the recipients in problematic ways that reinforced their perceived difference from normative ideas of political representatives. In our analysis of each theme, we have kept the original spelling and format of the tweets in question. In places, we have added some notes in brackets to aid clarity.

Gendered and Racist Abuse

The first theme includes examples where tweeters directed gendered and/or racist abuse at the woman concerned. These ranged from sexualised comments or comments about the appearance of the MP to outright insults:

> @lisanandy Do you like rimming?
>
> @lisanandy is sexiest female Member of Parliament.

The first example directly addresses the MP in question and asks her a sexualised question whilst the second tweet is an unsolicited comment about her perceived attractiveness which directly objectifies her. These forms of gendered comments are completely unrelated to the work that women MPs do, and yet they subtly remind the recipient—and indeed anyone else observing the message—that women should be perceived as being women first and MPs second. This phenomenon seems like a continuation of mainstream news coverage which makes women MPs feel uncomfortable for focusing on their appearance rather than their political record (see Ross 2002).

Women MPs also received tweets which chastised them for their appearance:

> @DrRosena Wow… do you ever want attention. Your poor husband.
>
> @patel4witham You've got fat!!

The first example accuses the MP in question of deliberately cultivating her own appearance in order to attract attention from men and implies that she is not fulfilling her traditional role as a wife. The second example overtly criticises the MP for having gained weight. These two examples demonstrate a double bind as far as women MPs are concerned. They are not supposed to be concerned with their appearance yet they receive criticism when they are not. This once again mirrors mainstream media discourses around the appearance of women politicians (Ross 2002).

Abuse was also evident from images that were attached to some tweets. One featured a picture aimed at Diane Abbott with her face photoshopped onto the body of a Black model in a very revealing Wonder Woman outfit. The model was significantly larger in size than Abbott is herself, so we infer this was supposed to be insulting to her appearance. It was emblazoned with the legend 'Blunder Woman' which appears to be a reference to a so-called car crash interview she gave during the 2017 election in which she misquoted some statistics about police funding (Harmer and Southern 2018b). As well as insulting her size, this image also appears to question her intelligence and political efficacy (which we will discuss in detail later).

Given what we already know about the nature of online abuse directed at women MPs, it is unsurprising that the most egregious examples of othering in our research were directed at women of colour (see Stambolieva 2017). A number of these tweets were abusive:

> @RupaHuq So your against the people #thickbitch.
>
> @HackneyAbbott you are fucking trash. Carl Benjamin [a prominent alt-right YouTuber also known as Sargon of Akkad] is NOT far right, you fucking commie whore.

Both tweets contain examples of gendered insults: 'bitch' and 'whore'. They also both seem to be taking issue with the political opinion or perspective of both MPs. The first indicts Rupa Huq as undemocratic whilst the other accuses Diane Abbott of being a communist. Given that Twitter is used by politicians to communicate with constituents and the wider public about their political work this is not surprising, but the uncivil and abusive nature of the criticism demonstrates the extent to which communicating on social media as an elected representative can be very unpleasant. Furthermore, some of the tweets also contained explicitly racist insults:

> @RupaHuq carry on apu [reference to an Indian character from *The Simpson's*].
>
> @HackneyAbbott You fucking niggers are the racist. You fucks have to move to white societies to survive. You fucking walking tuna can.
>
> @NazShahBfd Are you not even a little embarrassed supporting rapists? I know the corann encourages such behaviour but still children?!?!?! Time to adopt a more civilised stance.

Here three different women of colour are subjected to openly racist insults. Rupa Huq is compared to a well-known Indian character from the US television series *The Simpsons* (whose portrayal by a white voice artist has itself become more controversial in recent years). The other two examples feature explicitly racist abuse. The first uses a well-known racial slur which hardly needs explanation, whilst the final example is explicitly Islamophobic and accuses Naz Shah of being 'uncivilised' and supporting child rapists due to her Muslim faith. These somewhat extreme examples taken from a routine week demonstrate the extent to which women of colour who are MPs have to deal with abuse on a regular basis.

An element of the tweets which we found interesting involved mainly white men, as far as could be discerned from their profiles (which have been showed to be accurate to a fair degree, Sloan et al. 2013) calling Black and minority ethnic female MPs racist:

> @HackneyAbbott Diane Abbott is a racist Neo-Nazi.
>
> @NazShahBfd still wondering about that RT of yours "shut up for the sake of diversity" was it??? Are you a racist?

@NazShahBfd No one cares what you think!! Resign Racist!!

@NazShahBfd Your to (sic) racist to say who the culprits are. Think of the paki grooming, thousand of white babies raped by pakistani, animals!

This is a particularly pernicious form of abuse. Both women have spoken of the racism they have encountered in their roles and to have this turned back on them seems particularly cruel. We would also argue that these examples can be seen as a strategy of punishing these women for speaking out against racism and as an attempt to silence them from doing this in the future, by trivialising their experiences and denigrating the seriousness of this form of abuse on social media. Strikingly, the fact that women of colour received far more negative and abusive messages in our sample is yet another trend that is reflected in mainstream news coverage of politics (see Ward 2016, 2017) where minority women are more likely to receive negative coverage which highlights their gender than their white counterparts.

Dismissal and Silencing

Some of the messages that make up this theme contained explicitly gendered language, but there were a distinct group of tweets which were merely dismissive of what the MPs tweeted about. Some of these tweets were in response to serious issues such as Brexit or the Grenfell tragedy, topics which MPs would be expected to comment on as part of their job. The fact that those commenting on such topics are told they are 'boring', to 'calm down' and to 'get a grip' is evidence that women MPs are subjected to attempts to put them in their place or silence them in some way:

@RupaHuq We are leaving sorry so calm down dear.

@angelaeagle Get a grip dear.

These examples demonstrate the way in which women MPs are patronised in some of the tweets. Telling a woman to 'calm down' or 'get a grip' implies that she is being overly emotional and irrational playing into traditional ideas of the hysterical woman who is unfit for public office. Other tweets that can be characterised as dismissive sought to inform the recipients that they are boring or unoriginal:

> @KemiBadenoch you are a joke.
>
> @joannaccherry Stick with the day job love….
>
> @DrRosena You're boring.
>
> @CatSmithMP Who gives a sh*t.
>
> @HackneyAbbott Give it a rest. Boring.

The first example tries to trivialise the MP in question by telling her that she is not to be taken seriously. The second example comes with the same patronising tone as the previous set of examples. Referring to her as 'love' also trivialises her. A similar but more extreme behaviour to the dismissal exhibited in the tweets, was silencing. Tweets that did this explicitly tried to silence the MP in question. Although some of the dismissive tweets verged on silencing, these ones openly called for the women to stop talking:

> @NazShahBfd It's such a shame that you get a voice, especially when you champion silencing the most vulnerable.
>
> @RupaHuq I much prefer your sister tbh keeps her mouth shut.
>
> @HannahB4LiviMP god your boring. Shut up
> $Z_zZ_zZ_zZ_zZ_zZ_zZ_zZ_zZ_zZ_zZ_zZ_zZ_zZ_zZ_zZ_zZ_zZ_z$
> [Z's to represent a snoring sound].
>
> @CatSmithMP You are still harping on about this nonsense, instead of living in the real world.

Much has been written about the ways in which Internet trolls and online abuse try to silence women and prevent them from participating (Jane 2014; Lumsden and Morgan 2017) including in this volume (see for instance Chapters 4 and 5). This is problematic but could be considered even more so when the women who are being silenced are elected representatives in a democratic setting, who have an obligation and right to discuss politics in the public sphere, as it poses questions about how they are supposed to perform their function as representatives in such as hostile setting.

Questioning Intelligence and Position

The place of women in positions of authority is often indirectly undermined in various ways. One is by questioning their suitability to hold office. Several tweets called the women in question stupid or questioned their intelligence. The inference here is that she is not fit to be in charge and furthermore is undeserving of the power she might hold. Some of these were fairly benign or seemed to be more generally aimed at all elected officials:

> @RupaHuq Thought I tweeted some stupid stuff but this is bollox.
>
> @lisanandy The absolute state of your grammar.
>
> @RupaHuq Some proper thick MP's… Remind me again how you were elected.

Here elected politicians were referred to as stupid and therefore not intelligent enough to be an MP and had their typos and grammatical errors pointed out and judged. These attempts to undermine women MPs' intellect and abilities in a public forum are problematic because they rely on sexist stereotypes in order portray them as unqualified for political office. Once again, this is a trope that has been identified in mainstream news discourses about women MPs (Harmer et al. 2017). Other examples verged on or were outright abusive:

> @HackneyAbbott Must be joking who takes clown Abbott seriously.
>
> @HackneyAbbott Your brain is made of mush woman ☹.
>
> @RupaHuq Are you FUCKING stupid?
>
> @lisanandy hammer tongued tard [short for 'retard'].

The final example is particularly problematic given the use of slur 'tard', a shortened version of 'retard' which is an ableist slur. Although Lisa Nandy has not publically disclosed being affected by a disability, the tweet by implication reinforces the notion that people with intellectual disabilities do not belong in public office. There were also several examples of tweets which questioned the numerical skills of Diane Abbott, presumably in the wake of the difficult interviews she had during the election (discussed earlier):

> @HackneyAbbott Think you got the sums wrong again.
>
> @HackneyAbbott More your (sic) dodgy arithmetic.
>
> @HackneyAbbott what's 2X2 ?
>
> @HackneyAbbott But at least they can count.
>
> @HackneyAbbott Learn to count.
>
> @HackneyAbbott Hmm someone check her maths, knowing diane it could be just 6 people.

The tweets direct patronising sums towards her and imply that she is unable to do even basic arithmetic. The fact that Abbott is still being reminded of one single incident from over a year ago where she made a mistake, shows the higher price women pay for making mistakes as politicians. It has been noted by the authors elsewhere that similar interviews by men, whereby they forgot the costing for certain policies were not framed in such a condemnatory manner, including men from the same party as Abbot (Harmer and Southern 2018b).

Linked to these suggestions that the recipients are unqualified and incapable is the idea that these women are not fit for political office or that they were somehow elected for spurious reasons. This demonstrates yet another way in which othering can work to undermine underrepresented groups by questioning their right to be in power. There were several examples or this. Some questioned how the women had been elected or had held onto their position:

@NazShahBfd Are you still an MP, get back under your stone you horrible example of a human for the sake of #diversity.

@HackneyAbbott Abbott how you got where you are is beyond belief you really are not fit to be in parliament.

@HackneyAbbott I'll say it again when r u going to retire please soon.

@HackneyAbbott Neither are you dear [in response to a Tweet where Abbot said social housing was 'not fit for purpose'].

The first example explicitly suggests that Naz Shah was only elected due to politically correct ideas about the importance of a diverse set of representatives to advocate for all members of a multicultural society. In fact, there is no formal quota system in operation to elect British politicians of any level but the tweet simply chooses to argue that this must be the only reason she was elected. This is a clear attempt to undermine her position which not only denigrates the MP who is referred to here but all women MPs, particularly women from under-represented groups. The subsequent examples all accuse Diane Abbott of being unfit for office or ask when she is leaving. These explicit suggestions that these MPs do not belong in politics are not only extremely problematic but also to some extent reflect mainstream news discourses which position women, and women of colour in particular as outsiders (Ward 2016). A number of the tweets also sought to imply these women were not carrying out their duties as MPs sufficiently, or could not do it without additional help from other people:

@FionaOnasanyaMP what have you ever done for us constituents?

@MhairiBlack planning on turning up for work anytime soon?!

@ MhairiBlack maybe if you ever did any work.

@KateOsamor Without help you're a waste of space.

These examples are of interest because they are purporting to be holding MPs to account for their job performance which they of course have a right to do as political constituents however it is unclear from the tweets to what extent such claims are warranted. Mhairi Black has spoken out about a period of illness which has meant she has been unable to attend parliament whereby MPs from another party accused her of being lazy. The tone of the final three tweets is also somewhat uncivil. Remarkably, despite the hostile atmosphere in Diane Abbott's mentions, one user accused her of neglecting her political responsibilities by not responding to the tweets that had been directed towards her:

> @HackneyAbbott she never replies to anyone, her minions Tweet. Too important to talk to the likes of us.

This further shows the difficult position female MPs (and particularly women of colour) are in. It is likely that Abbott does not respond or even look at replies due to sheer volume of messages she must receive as a prominent shadow cabinet minister, let alone when the kind of responses she often gets (which have been documented in this chapter) are taken into account. However, this is portrayed as a dereliction of her duties by some and no doubt perpetuates the idea that she is not a fit representative. Recipients of online abuse are often told not to 'feed the trolls' but this is clearly more difficult for elected officials. Another set of tweets appeared to question whether the MP in question had actually done certain work themselves. A number of tweets aimed at Kate Osamore asked her repeatedly whether she had done certain tasks herself:

> @KateOsamor Which speech are you ripping off?
>
> @KateOsamor Did you write this teeet all by yourself or nick it?

This is likely in response to a political blogpost by right-wing blogger Guido Fawkes which claims Osamore plagiarised her maiden speech in the House of Commons from Wikipedia and from a previous speech by Barack Obama (*Guido Fawkes*, 22 May 2018). In a similar way to the many messages ridiculing Diane Abbot's arithmetic above, it seems that the errors of women of colour MPs are repeatedly brought up time and again in order to remind them that they do not belong in positions of power.

'Benevolent' Othering

The final theme that we identified in the data was somewhat unexpected. Marsha de Cordova MP was included in the sample due to her identity as a woman of colour but also because she is visually impaired. In stark contrast to the other women of colour whose tweets we analysed, de Cordova's were almost all very positive in tone. Several of them called her inspirational:

> @MarshadeCordova Wonderful and very inspiring !
>
> @MarshadeCordova What an inspiration!!
>
> @MarshadeCordova Keep up good work Ms Cordova. You're an inspiration.
>
> @MarshadeCordova We need more people like you spreading inspiration and hope. Thank you for sharing 😊.
>
> @MarshadeCordova Wonderful and very inspiring !

These tweets appeared to be referencing a television appearance, where amongst other topics, she discussed the challenges of being visually impaired in parliament. We have termed this theme 'benevolent' othering because although the tweeters are clearly attempting to compliment de Cordova for overcoming some of these challenges, the tweets still foreground a way she is different, not only to their expectations of MPs, but also in terms of her colleagues. Disability studies scholars call this 'inspiration porn' whereby disability is represented as a desirable but undesired characteristic (Grue 2016: 838). This means impairment is portrayed as a visually or symbolically distinct biophysical deficit in one person that must be overcome through the display of physical prowess'. So, although de Cordova is just going about her usual political duties in the same way as her colleagues, depicting her achievements as inspirational actually implies that people with impairments are perceived as having a smaller scope for achievement than able-bodied colleagues, which may well be just as problematic as some of the more overtly aggressive forms of othering already discussed. The implications are that her visual impairment is an individual problem that needs to be overcome by her efforts rather than yet more evidence that the everyday conduct of politics is exclusionary.

Conclusion

The analysis of a week of replies to 33 women MPs on Twitter revealed a myriad of different ways in which these women were othered. We identified four main themes. Firstly, explicitly gendered and racist abuse which were the most overt examples of othering that we observed. These tweets sexualised women MPs, insulted their appearance and were explicitly racist and Islamophobic, demonstrating the extent to which women in politics are subjected to serious forms of hate speech on an everyday basis. The second theme was tweets that were not necessarily openly abusive but either attempted to silence women MPs or were somehow dismissive of them and their ideas. Such tweets openly called for the MPs in question to shut up. The third theme which is somewhat related includes subtler forms of othering that whilst they were not overtly gendered still sought to question the intelligence or qualifications and credentials of the recipients, in order to suggest that they do not belong in political life. The tweets accused women MPs of being stupid or lacking the experience and intelligence needed for participation in politics. These tweets serve to demonstrate the extent to which women are still seen as lacking the necessary skills and qualifications for political office. The final, somewhat unexpected theme was what we have called 'benevolent' othering where despite tweeters seeming to heap praise or positive evaluations on women MPs, the tweets themselves still othered the recipients in problematic ways that reinforced their perceived difference from normative ideas of political representatives, in this case the tweets sought to frame Marsha de Cordova's ability to be an MP whilst having a visual impairment as 'inspirational'. It is striking that our analysis failed to identify any significant othering which sought to denigrate the sexuality of women MPs despite our sampling strategy. This might be a result of the particular week we analysed since LGBT+ MPs have complained of being victimised with homophobic slurs.

These themes are particularly interesting for two reasons. First, there appears to be a real symmetry between the forms of othering that takes place on Twitter and the ways in which mainstream news coverage has been portraying women MPs in news discourses, demonstrating that there is a good deal of continuity in the relationship between women, media and politics. Secondly, the fact that there was so much over just the course of a week suggests that this is a common problem. Over time, it is likely that even the subtler uncivil othering would become a burdensome experience for these representatives. Some of the women in the sample did not receive any replies which could be considered uncivil or abusive but this does not negate the othering directed at their colleagues and does not mean that they do not receive such messages themselves.

There is evidence from a broad range of countries including Sweden, Bolivia, Australia and the UK that suggest sexist hostility and intimidation have driven some female politicians out of politics. Therefore, if their everyday interactions with constituents and the mainstream media are filled with negative and abusive messages which question their right and ability to participate in formal politics, it seems reasonable to suggest that this could act as yet another barrier that might deter women from seeking election or may drive women who experience it out of politics after being elected. Although these might not always lead to physical attacks, the online othering of women from underrepresented groups in particular is extremely problematic. As Krook (2017) suggests this is not just a problem for social media sites and the police but is in actuality an affront to democracy if democratically elected representatives continue to be undermined in this way during the course of carrying out their jobs.

References

Abraham, B. (2013). Fedora shaming as discursive activism. *Digital Culture and Education, 5*(2), 86–97.

Banet-Weiser, S., & Miltner, K. M. (2016). #MasculinitySoFragile: Culture, structure, and networked misogyny. *Feminist Media Studies, 16*(1), 171–174.

Braun, V., & Clarke, V. (2006). Using thematic analysis in psychology. *Qualitative Research in Psychology, 3*(2), 77–101.

Buckels, E. E., Trapnell, P. D., & Paulhus, D. L. (2014). Trolls just want to have fun. *Personality and Individual Differences, 67,* 97–102.

Childs, S. (2008). *Women and British Party Politics: Descriptive, Substantive and Symbolic Representation.* London: Routledge.

Crenshaw, K. (1989). Demarginalizing the intersection of race and sex: A black feminist critique of antidiscrimination doctrine, feminist theory and antiracist politics. *University of Chicago Legal Forum, 1989*(1), 139–167.

Dahlgren, P. (2005). The internet, public spheres, and political communication: Dispersion and deliberation. *Political Communication, 22*(2), 147–162.

Evans, E. (2015). Diversity matters: Intersectionality and women's representation in the USA and UK. *Parliamentary Affairs, 69*(3), 569–585.

Fox, J., Cruz, C., & Lee, J. Y. (2015). Perpetuating online sexism offline: Anonymity, interactivity, and the effects of sexist hashtags on social media. *Computers in Human Behavior, 52,* 436–442.

Garcia-Blanco, I., & Wahl-Jorgensen, K. (2012). The discursive construction of women politicians in the European press. *Feminist Media Studies, 12*(3), 422–441.

Garcia-Favaro, L., & Gill, R. (2016). 'Emasculation nation has arrived': Sexism rearticulated in online responses to Lose the Lads' Mags Campaign. *Feminist Media Studies, 16*(3), 379–397.

Gershon, S. A. (2012). When race, gender, and the media intersect: Campaign news coverage of minority congresswomen. *Journal of Women, Politics & Policy, 33*(2), 105–125.

Gill, R. (2007). *Gender and the Media.* Cambridge: Polity Press.

Greenwood, M. A., Roberts, I., Rout, D., & Bontchieva, K. (2017, July 23). This is what the Twitter abuse of politicians during the election really looked like. *Buzzfeed.* https://www.buzzfeed.com/tomphillips/twitterabuseofmpsduringtheelectiondoubledafterthe?utm_term=.np9NZwnY9#.yujjwyZ2d. Accessed October 20, 2018.

Grue, J. (2016). The problem with inspiration porn: A tentative definition and a provisional critique. *Disability and Society, 31*(6), 838–849.

Guido Fawkes. (2018). https://order-order.com/2018/05/22/kate-osamor-plagiarised-maiden-speech-wikipedia-local-newsletter-predecessor/. Accessed October 20, 2018.

Harmer, E., & Southern, R. (2018a). More stable than strong: Women's representation, voters and issues. *Parliamentary Affairs, 71,* 237–254.

Harmer, E., & Southern, R. (2018b). Alternative agendas or more of the same? Online news coverage of the 2017 UK election. In D. Wring (Ed.), *Political Communication in Britain.*

Harmer, E., Savigny, H., & Ward, O. (2017). 'Are you tough enough?' Performing gender in the UK leadership debates 2015. *Media, Culture and Society, 39*(7), 960–975.

Hill Collins, P. (1990). *Black Feminist Thought: Knowledge, Consciousness, and the Politics of Empowerment.* Boston: Unwin Hyman.

Jane, E. A. (2014). 'You're a ugly, whorish, slut': Understanding e-bile. *Feminist Media Studies, 14*(4), 531–546.

Krook, M. L. (2017). Violence against women in politics. *Journal of Democracy, 28*(1), 74–88.

Lawrence, R. G., & Rose, M. (2010). *Hillary Clinton's Race for the White House: Gender Politics 7 the Media on the Campaign Trail.* Boulder and London: Lynne Rienner.

Lewis, R., Rowe, M., & Wiper, C. (2017). Online abuse of feminists as an emerging form of violence against women and girls. *British Journal of Criminology, 57*(6), 1462–1481.

Lumsden, K., & Morgan, H. (2017). Media framing of trolling and online abuse: Silencing strategies, symbolic violence, and victim blaming. *Feminist Media Studies, 17*(6), 926–940.

Mcloughlin, L., & Ward, S. (2017, April 25–29). *Turds, traitors and tossers: The abuse of UK MPs via Twitter.* Paper presented at the European Consortium of Political Research Joint Sessions, University of Nottingham, Nottingham, UK.

Megarry, J. (2014). Online incivility or sexual harassment? Conceptualising women's experiences in the digital age. *Women's Studies International Forum, 47,* 46–55.

Norris, P. (1997). Women leaders worldwide: A splash of colour in the photo op. In P. Norris (Ed.), *Women, Media and Politics.* Oxford: Oxford University Press.

O'Neill, D., Savigny, H., & Cann, V. (2016). Women politicians in the UK press: Not seen and not heard? *Feminist Media Studies, 16,* 293–307.

Papacharissi, Z. (2002). The virtual sphere: The internet as a public sphere. *New Media and Society, 4*(1), 9–27.

Ross, K. (2002). *Women, Politics, Media*. Cresskill, NJ: Hampton Press.

Ross, K., Evans, E., Harrison, L., Shears, M., & Wadia, K. (2013). The gender of news and news of gender: A study of sex, politics, and press coverage of the 2010 British General Election. *The International Journal of Press/Politics, 18*(1), 3–20.

Shaw, F. (2016). 'Bitch I said Hi': The Bye Felipe campaign and discursive activism in mobile dating apps. *Social Media and Society*, October–December, 1–10.

Sloan, L., Morgan, J., Housley, W., Williams, M., Edwards, A., Burnap, P., et al. (2013). Knowing the Tweeters: Deriving sociologically relevant demographics from Twitter. *Sociological Research Online, 18*(3), 1–11.

Sreberny-Mohammadi, A., & Ross, K. (1996). Women MPs and the media: Representing the body politic. *Parliamentary Affairs, 49*(1), 103–115.

Stambolieva, E. (2017). *Methodology: Detecting Online Abuse Against Women MPs on Twitter*. Amnesty International.

Ward, O. (2016). Seeing double: Race, gender, and coverage of minority women's campaigns for the U.S House of Representatives. *Politics & Gender, 12*, 317–343.

Ward, O. (2017). Intersectionality and press coverage of political campaigns: Representations of Black, Asian, and minority ethnic female candidates in the UK 2010 General Election. *The International Journal of Press/Politics, 22*(1), 43–66.

Part III

Online Exclusion: Boundaries, Spaces and Intersectionality

Karen Lumsden and Emily Harmer

Editors' Introduction

In public discourses concerning 'online othering' particular forms of abuse or hate crime tend to be privileged while other experiences remain largely hidden or unexplored. Those which tend to be hidden can include, for example, the everyday hate and discrimination experienced by members of the LGBTQ community, disabled groups, Islamophobia, and forms of racism, such as rural racism. Therefore, we adopt an intersectional approach to understanding 'online othering' by further highlighting how different aspects of social identity overlap and intersect to frame and shape the types of 'othering' that are constructed, enacted, performed and perpetrated, and how these are experienced (and often resisted) by various individuals and groups. As Kimberlé Crenshaw (1989, 1991) argues, intersectionality offers a way of mediating the tension between assertions of multiple identity and the ongoing necessity of group politics. This approach also highlights the multidimensionality of lived experiences among people who are engaging in online discourses. In addition, intersectionalities are not a collection of layers that are piled or added on; instead, we possess many distinctive social qualities simultaneously which will interplay in unique ways (Pompper 2014). For example, the process of 'othering' can be classed, raced and gendered (Spivak 1985). Therefore 'othering concerns the consequences of racism, sexism, class (or a combination hereof) in terms of symbolic degradation as well as the processes of identity formation related to this degradation' (Jensen 2011: 65). In this part of the book, chapters focus on the intersectionality involved in aspects of 'online othering'. For example, in Kerrigan's chapter he discusses the relationship between ethnicity, race, class and space in relation to 'rural racism', while Kaur focuses on the intersections between age, disability and sexuality in relation to how physically disabled teenagers use the Internet to learn about and negotiate sexual identity.

In the first chapter in this part, Ben Colliver, Adrian Coyle and Maria Silvestri highlight how transphobic hate crime has recently attracted greater social, legal and political attention. However, the ways in which current hate crime paradigms privilege and isolate, extreme and physically violent acts of hate crime, can mask the prevalence and severity of less public acts of hatred and discrimination, including online incidents. Everyday incidents of hate crime and discrimination that are a routine part of transgender and non-gender-binary people's lives can be viewed as inconsequential. In order to explore this, the authors draw on findings which examine mundane experiences of hate crime and abuse reported by transgender and non-gender-binary people. They focus specifically on the discursive resources which are used to construct and position transgender and non-binary people in contemporary online debate on YouTube about 'gender neutral toilets', and the rhetorical and practical affordances created by these constructions. They highlight how these discussions focus on gender neutral toilets as sites of sexual danger. Moreover, those who respond are accused of 'claiming victimhood' while gender neutral toilets are constructed as undermining the rights of non-trans people. The authors argue that these discourses work to both legitimise and delegitimise trans identities in various ways. These discourses ultimately result in the further 'othering' of transgender and non-binary gender individuals, however resistance to this 'othering' is also discussed.

Harminder Kaur's chapter is concerned with the ways in which young people with physical disabilities seek sexual information online and use digital media to express and explore their sexuality. Digital media is used by young people to gain sexual information, to discuss sexual topics in anonymous online settings, to view online pornography, and to find and develop romantic relationships or sexual encounters on social media platforms. However, young people with disabilities are frequently 'othered': labelled as sexually undesirable or asexual. They also encounter few opportunities for sexual expression and experience. Sexual knowledge and activity is often prevented by parents and carers for young people with disabilities in the name of keeping them safe from being sexually abused, or being deviant when expressing their sexual desires. While they may not have access to sexuality exposure offline, their sexuality education may be facilitated through the use of digital media. Drawing on ethnographic research in a special school, Kaur's chapter provides us with novel insights into the ways in which offline spaces often 'other' and exclude young people with physical disabilities in discussions of sexuality. While digital media is regarded as an alternative for finding sexual information, it is argued their access to digital media is often restricted for sexual exploration by parents in the home. The challenges of seeking sexual information online are illustrated via two case studies.

Nathan Kerrigan's chapter is concerned with rural racism in the digital age. He demonstrates how the Internet has rearticulated the ways in which minority ethnic individuals are victimised in rural spaces. Historically, rural communities have been defined as cohesive communities based on close-knit social relations and bounded by a shared physical space. However, today, people living in even the most remote rural areas can exchange messages from their computers, phones and tablets to other individuals living on the other side of the world. This compression of time-space facilitated by the Internet revolution has created a fear that the digitalisation of rural life has weakened social relations and caused greater hostilities between long-term rural residents who use social media to create community groups, and those who participate online within these digital rural spaces but may not be deemed 'local'. By drawing on a digital ethnography, Kerrigan's chapter contributes to literature on rural racism by exploring the ways in which residents of a rural community in the south of England use the Internet to construct an online rural space. This includes how they give meaning to the forum as 'rural', and the extent to which this excludes and 'others' those with perceived differences who are deemed to be 'outsiders'.

References

Crenshaw, K. W. (1989). *Demarginalizing the intersection of race and sex: A Black feminist critique of antidiscrimination doctrine, feminist theory and antiracist politics*. University of Chicago Legal Forum. Chicago: University of Chicago.

Crenshaw, K. W. (1991). Mapping the margins: Intersectionality, identity politics and violence against women of color. *Stanford Law Review, 43*(6), 1241–1299.

Jensen, S. Q. (2011). Othering, identity formation and agency. *Qualitative Studies, 2*(2), 63–78.

Pompper, D. (2014). Social identities are intersectional. In D. Pompper (Ed.), *Practical and theoretical implications of successfully doing difference in organizations* (International Perspectives on Equality, Diversity and Inclusion, Vol. 1, pp. 45–61). Bingley: Emerald Group.

Spivak G. C. (1985). The Rani of Sirmur: An essay in reading the archives. *History and Theory, 24*(3), 247–272.

9

The 'Online Othering' of Transgender People in Relation to 'Gender Neutral Toilets'

Ben Colliver, Adrian Coyle and Marisa Silvestri

Introduction

An interest in the 'othering' of transgender people in recent years has done much to raise the profile of the everyday and normalised nature of victimisation experienced by transgender people. Chakraborti and Hardy (2015) have emphasised that transgender people regularly experience a range of hate incidents whilst doing everyday things such as shopping, eating out

---

B. Colliver (✉)
School of Social Sciences, Birmingham City University,
Birmingham, UK

A. Coyle
Department of Psychology, Kingston University London,
Kingston, UK

M. Silvestri
School of Social Policy, Sociology & Social Research,
University of Kent, Canterbury, UK

© The Author(s) 2019
K. Lumsden and E. Harmer (eds.), *Online Othering*,
Palgrave Studies in Cybercrime and Cybersecurity,
https://doi.org/10.1007/978-3-030-12633-9_9

and travelling on public transport. The online othering of transgender people has not yet attracted significant attention within academic research on prejudice and discrimination. Instead research has focused on more 'established', socially recognised forms and contexts of prejudice and discrimination such as racism, homophobia and anti-religious hate speech (see, for example, Cmeciu 2016; Goodman and Rowe 2014; Weaver 2013). In this chapter, we provide an exposition and critical analysis of some ways in which transgender people are othered online and attempts at resisting or challenging this. This is achieved through a discourse analysis of online comments made in response to YouTube videos concerning 'gender neutral toilets'. The data that we draw upon are taken from a wider research project that examines 'everyday' experiences of hate crime and discrimination targeting transgender and non-gender binary people.

The findings that we present identify some key discursive resources that are used to construct and position transgender people in contemporary online debate about gender neutral toilets, the implications of these constructions, and how they are challenged. The analysis allows us to consider whether the resources used in othering transgender people online are the same as those that have long characterised negative social attitudes and responses to lesbian, gay, bisexual and queer people—groups that have historically been associated with gender 'non-conformity' in the popular imagination. In other words, we ask whether we are seeing something substantively new in the ways in which the othering of transgender people is done and functions online or whether it is the *context* that is (relatively) new—while bearing in mind that substance and context are necessarily interconnected. First, though, we will explain and contextualise some key terms and the study's concerns, beginning with 'transgender'.

Rather than having a single, stable meaning, the term 'transgender' is often applied in ways that are inclusive of identities, expressions and experiences that fall outside contemporary Western gender binaries (Davidson 2007). As Hines (2010: 1) writes:

> The term 'transgender' denotes a range of gender experiences, subjectivities and presentations that fall across, between or beyond stable categories of 'man' and 'woman.' 'Transgender' includes gender identities that have, more traditionally, been described as 'transsexual,' and a diversity of

genders that call into question an assumed relationship between gender identity and presentation and the 'sexed' body.

Despite this definitional scope, there has been debate about the use of the term within and between communities that it seeks to encompass. For example, it has been suggested that the term's breadth of application has a homogenising effect, covering over the specific features and needs of the groups to which it is applied, and that the term 'gender diversity' may be preferable, given that the explicit reference to diversity warns against homogenisation (Monro 2003). The term 'non-binary' has also been favoured and used by people who feel that their gender identity cannot be defined within the male/female categories afforded by the traditional gender binary (Hegarty et al. 2018). However, 'transgender' *has* been welcomed as connoting a shift away from terms frequently used in the past, such as 'transsexual' and 'transvestite', with their highly medicalised connotations and their associations with a taxonomic endeavour within sexology concerning non-conformity with gender expectations (Pearce et al. 2019).

Public toilets are perhaps the most frequently encountered sex-segregated spaces in daily life in many countries and have been described as spaces of anxiety and challenge for transgender individuals (Faktor 2011). In recent years, the provision of public toilets where access is not gender specific has become a topic of public debate. Providing 'gender neutral toilets' can be (and has been) framed within a discourse of broad inclusivity and rights, given that they allow people who may require assistance, such as people with disabilities and children, to be accompanied to the toilet by a helper of any gender. However, the topic has largely acted as a lens for public discussion and debate about transgender people and communities who are assumed to be the primary group whom the provision of gender neutral toilets (and/or any relaxation of restriction in usage predicated on 'biological sex') is designed to accommodate. The debate has been engaged with from an academic perspective (see, for example, Jeffreys 2014; Nirta 2014) but has been more socially visible in contemporary political and policy discussion and in media and social media. For example, in 2017, President Donald Trump rescinded instructions that had been issued in 2016 by then-President

Barack Obama instructing schools across the USA to allow students to access toilets appropriate to their gender identity.

Studies of public attitudes to transgender people conducted in various countries have found associations between negative attitudes, gender and age, with women and older cohorts expressing more negative attitudes in some studies (see, for example, Hill and Willoughby 2005; King et al. 2009; Nagoshi et al. 2008; Tee and Hegarty 2006) and men in other studies (see, for example, Norton and Herek 2013). Negative attitudes have also been related to lower levels of education (King et al. 2009), greater religiosity and religious fundamentalism (Nagoshi et al. 2008; Tee and Hegarty 2006) and less support for general egalitarian ideals (King et al. 2009). Attitudes towards sexual and gender minorities are highly correlated but significantly more negative attitudes have been found towards transgender people than towards members of sexual minorities (Norton and Herek 2013).

These studies used various attitudinal measures. For example, a questionnaire used by Tee and Hegarty (2006) featured items concerning a biological or environmental basis for gender, the possibility of a person subjectively creating their gender identity rather than it being determined by their bodies, the possibility of changing gender through surgery, and the normality of transgender people. However, attitudes tend to be studied in decontextualised ways outside the natural contexts in which they are called forth and enacted. Moreover, criticisms have long been levelled at the assumption that data on 'attitudes' map onto underlying psychological objects or dispositions that have some stability. Analyses of people's talk or writing on any subject in a natural context show that views vary depending upon the functions that the talk or writing is performing at any given point (Potter and Wetherell 1987). In the study reported in the present chapter, we focus on what is *accomplished* by comments on YouTube videos on gender neutral toilets, that is, the text's 'action orientation' and function-in-context, rather than using text as a way of trying to assess what commenters may or may not have been thinking (for example, their intentions and motivations).

The ways in which negative attitudes—or talk/text that constructs transgender people in a problematizing fashion—play out are being increasingly studied. In this emerging research, transgender people have reported being subjected to pressure to conform to normative, binary views of gender in order to be seen as legitimate (Blumer et al. 2013; Iantaffi and Bockting 2011). Transgender people may well experience erasure and invisibility when those whom they encounter fail to recognise or validate their gender identity (Hegarty et al. 2018). In recent years, some feminists have argued that the unqualified categorisation of self-identified transgender women as women carries serious social and material implications for cisgender (that is, non-transgender) women, including lesbian women (see, for example, Stock 2018). Those who advocate this perspective have been labelled 'trans exclusionary radical feminists' ('terfs') by transgender activists and have been accused of promoting the delegitimisation of transgender women. Delegitimisation and erasure can be seen as an ultimate othering because they result from a refusal even to acknowledge the validity of the transgender person's account of their gendered being. Research has pointed to the serious practical implications of this othering in terms of implicit and explicit prejudice and discrimination, hate crime and compromised psychological well-being (see, for example, Antjoule 2013; Chakraborti and Hardy 2015; Grant et al. 2011; Jamal 2018; Riggs et al. 2015).

Today, problematic talk and text can occur face-to-face but can also readily occur anonymously in social media and online networks. A body of literature is emerging that explores the similarities and differences between offline and online hate speech (Awan and Zempi 2016; Brown 2018) and the ways in which minority and historically othered groups are constructed and positioned in online contexts. Research has also started to explore online representations of transgender people. For example, McInroy and Craig (2015) studied trends in contemporary media representations of transgender people offline and online, focusing on the perspectives of transgender young people. However, social media and material such as YouTube comments on potentially controversial videos were not addressed. The present study adds to this emerging literature through its examination of how gender neutral toilets and transgender people are constructed in YouTube videos on the former topic and pays particular attention to how transgender people are othered in this online setting.

Method

The final data set consisted of 1756 comments posted on ten randomly sampled YouTube videos that were identified using the search term 'gender neutral toilets'. Standard procedures for sampling online data were employed (see, for example, Snee 2013).

Videos were sampled on 1 May 2017, with sampling restricted to material that had been uploaded in the previous 12 months. Out of 431 videos identified through an initial search, 100 met our inclusion criteria concerning relevance to the topic of gender neutral toilets, having elicited at least five comments from viewers and not being duplicates of other videos. An online random number generator was then used to select a manageable sample of ten videos. Three videos (two from the UK and one from the USA) involving discussions about and the sharing of opinions on gender neutral toilets were produced by cisgender people and two (one from the USA and one from the UK) by transgender people. One other video produced in the USA involved a transgender woman asking members of the public if they would be concerned about sharing a toilet with her. One video was a feature from the *Jimmy Kimmel Live* show (a late-night talk show in the USA) asking the American public what they thought about gender neutral toilets. Three videos were produced by US news stations and covered a news story relating to President Obama's guidance to schools allowing students to access toilets according to the gender with which they identified. Comments on these ten videos were excluded from the data set if they did not directly address 'gender neutral toilets' or transgender people or if they were illogical or irrelevant to the study. Using these criteria, the 2328 comments produced in response to the videos were reduced to 1756 comments that were relevant to the study.

These were subjected to a form of discourse analysis referred to as critical discursive psychology (Wetherell 1998; see Coyle 2016 for a contextualisation of this approach). As a social constructionist approach, this accords with the epistemological stance of the study's research questions and has also been used productively in other research on prejudice and discrimination (see, for example, Goodman and Burke 2010, 2011).

Thematic Overview

Three themes were developed from the data. We shall discuss in detail the theme entitled 'The delegitimisation and othering of transgender people' but first we shall contextualise this in relation to the other two themes.

The theme of 'gender neutral toilets as sites of sexual danger' was pervasive in the data and forms a central part of the case that was worked up against the implementation of gender neutral toilets. In this theme, male sexuality was constructed as uncontrollable, with commenters drawing upon notions of sexual violence, child victimisation and distinctions between public and private spaces. The data also constructed transgender people as potential sexual offenders through essentialising sexual trauma and deviance and conflating these with 'transgender' as a category and with transgender people. These recurrently mobilised constructions problematised gender neutral toilets in socially recognisable ways by using child imagery, by constructing women as vulnerable and in need of protection and by pathologising transgender people and (uncontrollable) male sexuality. This serves to maintain the status-quo of sex-segregated toilets and to construct 'gender neutral' toilets as sites of danger to women and children whilst simultaneously reinforcing gendered norms of male dominance. The outcome of these constructions was a categorical division between a constructed 'us', the dominant, normal majority, and 'them', the problematised, othered transgender minority.

The second theme concerned 'claiming victimhood: gender neutral toilets as undermining the rights of cisgender people'. Notions of 'victimhood' and the right to claim a victim position were worked up in the data. A construction of cisgender people as the victims of political forces was identified, with political correctness and a wider political agenda being said to mask the 'real issues' that society faces. This functioned as a means of refusing to acknowledge the legitimacy of claims about transgender people experiencing prejudice, discrimination and victimisation and the need to take action to address this. Cisgender populations were constructed as inclusive and willing to work towards equality but rights-based claims by transgender communities were deemed 'special privileges' that fall outside the category of reasonable requests. Here, the claiming of victim status for cisgender people reinforced a distinction between a gender normative 'in-group' and a transgender 'out-group', again emphasising the otherness of transgender people. We turn now to the central theme yielded by the analysis.

The Delegitimisation and Othering of Transgender People

The central theme focused on the delegitimisation and othering of transgender people, which surfaced in the other themes too, as noted above. It consisted of four subthemes. Due to space constraints, we shall focus on two subthemes that dealt with a fundamental basis of delegitimisation and that elicited some resistance or qualification in the data set. We shall then sketch the remaining two subthemes. In the data excerpts that will be used to illustrate the subthemes, the comments are presented as they appeared on YouTube so any spelling or grammatical errors remain. Where necessary, we have clarified commenters' material within square brackets. The origins of each comment are also noted using the commenter's YouTube identifier.

Transgender People as Challenging the Given Order: Invocations of Nature and Biology

'Nature' and 'biology' (and the allied and broader constructs of 'medicine' and 'science') were routinely invoked in various forms in the delegitimisation of transgender people. Together with 'God' and related religious and moral ideas (which will be examined under the next subtheme), these were key elements in the delegitimisation repertoire within the data. They operated in various combinations but performed the same basic function of establishing a given and in some sense ultimate order of things which should not or could not be breached but which transgender people challenge and (try to) contravene. The status assigned to nature and particularly to biology/science within and outside the data conferred authority on comments that invoked them.

'Nature' has long been used as a discursive resource in the denigration of lesbian, gay, bisexual and queer people who have been positioned as 'unnatural' (for example, see Baker 2004), although nature has also been invoked in defence of sexual minorities (see Hegarty 2010, for a brief overview). It was not surprising therefore to find repeated invocations of nature and 'naturalness' within the data. For example:

1. 'Try to make unnatural behavior mainstream. This will be their downfall.'
   (*Video 9, direct response from 'Anglosax88' to video*)
2. 'Have fun slowly getting even more depressed while you regret mutilating your penis. You'll never seem or look like or act like or BE a NATURAL woman.'
   (*Video 1, direct response from '_Dude' to video*)

The first comment offers a version of a standard claim in the data: that transgender people are engaging in behaviour that is contrary to nature but are seeking to have it seen as something normal and regular and that this (either the unnatural behaviour or the normalisation effort) will carry unspecified negative implications for them. In its focus on behaviour, this comment is more nuanced than other comments that invoked nature and that mostly constructed transgender people as unnatural in essence.

The second comment positions transgender women outside the category of 'natural' but in a different way. It presents transgender women as sharing the aim of becoming or appearing to others as cisgender, 'natural' women and constructs that aim as impossible. The nature and scope of the impossibility are stressed through the use of an extreme case formulation ('you'll never') (Pomerantz 1986), a three or perhaps four-part list ('seem or look like or act like or BE') (Jefferson 1990), and upper case lettering in 'BE' and 'NATURAL' that presents gender in essentialised terms of 'being'. The implications of transgender women engaging in this fruitless pursuit of 'natural woman' status through surgery are presented in terms of impaired mental health but note that mental health problems are constructed as a pre-existing state for transgender women ('even more depressed'). We shall return to the construction of an intrinsic connection between transgenderism and mental health problems later. For now, we note that the positioning of transgender people as unnatural in behaviour or in essence or as falling short of the 'natural' in their claimed or aspired gender serves to delegitimise and other them.

Invocations of biological and scientific discourse mostly functioned within the data to reassert a gender binary and negate the possibility of transgenderism as real or authentic. For example:

1. 'At the current time, science and basic biology tell us that you cannot be born the wrong gender.'
   (*Video 10, response from 'HarryMcKenzie' to other users debating the existence of transgender people*)
2. 'You aren't Transgender because nobody is…since choose or changing your gender is medically and biologically impossible!'
   (*Video 2, response from 'JoeKehoe' to another commenter identifying as transgender*)
3. 'You are either a boy or a girl. There is no "choice" in the matter. There is no gender fluidity or gender binary or whatever other 76 genders that have been invented. If you are a biological man you go to the male bathroom. If you are a biological female you go to the female bathroom. There is no debate.'
   (*Video 10, response from 'HarryMcKenzie' to a commenter stating that transgender people should use whichever toilet they identify with*).
4. 'If u have a dick use the mans room. Its that simple. We don't need a third bathroom. Transgender people are ridiculous and will never be accepted as the sex they want to be.'
   (*Video 2, direct response from 'CHAFFY6six6' to video*)

The first three comments invoke science, biology and medicine to reject a culturally recognisable understanding of transgenderism ('born in the wrong body' or, as the commenter puts it, 'born the wrong gender') and the possibility of legitimately inhabiting a different gender. The case being made here relies on a version of gender as a biological and fixed phenomenon that, in the third comment, allows only two categories—male and female. That comment explicitly denies the legitimacy of any claims that gender can exist outside that binary, with those claims constructed as lacking reality and lampooned through their invocation in exaggerated form ('or whatever other 76 genders that have been invented'). In the third and fourth comment, the implications of the biologically based gender binary for toilet use are spelled out in conditional sentences that orient towards closing down debate, with gender being physiologically determined by genitals in the fourth comment ('If u have a dick use the mans room. Its that simple. We don't need a third bathroom'). That notion of gender as a fixed, biological phenomenon written in or on the body surfaced repeatedly in the data. Within the terms set up by these comments, transgenderism is constructed as a scientific/biological illogicality and a fabrication. People who claim to be transgender are constructed as mistaken, deluded or duped about their very being (the fourth comment labels them as 'ridiculous') and are thereby delegitimised.

However, the specification of biological and physiological conditions for determining which toilet people should use appeared to be qualified elsewhere in the data. Some comments specified conditions based on a transgender person's capacity to fulfil the appearance expectations of their gender identity, that is, to 'pass' successfully as a cisgender man or woman:

1. 'If you look like a man go into the mens room if you look like a women go into the womens room, whats the problem?'
   (*Video 1, direct response from 'HayleyAnne' to video*).
2. 'Trans people who don't pass well should use these bathrooms.'
   (*Video 1, direct response from 'FayAngel' to video, with 'these bathrooms' referring to gender neutral toilets*).

There is an indication of a hierarchy of transgender people in these comments, with people who can pass successfully being valued over those who cannot. The first comment offers a formula for determining which toilet to use that accommodates transgender people within the gender binary based on physiological appearance. This is presented as an obvious, effective response ('whats the problem?') but transgender people whose appearance does not fit within standard gender expectations are erased from consideration, which, as we suggested earlier, is an ultimate form of othering. The second comment constructs gender neutral toilets as suited to this group and as a solution to failures of gender performance ('Trans people who don't pass well'). The construction of a fixed male/female gender binary and its ordering of this aspect of the social world are left unchallenged. For these reasons, what might appear here as qualifications of the biological/physiological conditions for toilet use that were created elsewhere in the data fail as instances of resistance.

Given that 'nature', 'biology' and 'God' function in the same way in the discursive denigration of lesbian, gay, bisexual and queer people, next we shall consider the mobilisation of religious and moral values and norms in the delegitimisation and othering of transgender people in the data set. This extends our discussion above because the construction of transgender people as challenging the fundamental, given order has clear moral tones.

Mobilisation of Religious and Moral Values and Norms

There is a long history of conflict and prejudice between (sectors of) religious communities and sexual and gender minority communities (Herek and McLemore 2013; Miceli 2005), although religion may also be associated with attitudes of acceptance (Horn 2006) including towards transgender people in recent years (for example, Beardsley and O'Brien 2016). In the data, religious and moral values and norms were frequently mobilised to justify querying or denying the legitimacy of transgenderism and transgender people. Notions of a 'higher power' were invoked to determine and legitimate parameters of 'rightness' and 'wrongness'.

1. 'Deuteronomy 23:1-25 KJV [King James Version, a 17th century English translation of the Bible]. A man that has his stones crushed or private cutt off shall not enter into the congregation of God. God isn't no respecter of men I liken women that get their Tubes burned or tied shut sterilization castrating or making themselves into transsexual lesbians would some under his same category as same as crushed stones for a man, sex change operations or vasectomy to tell God their going to have sex, without concern without consequences of making babies.'
(*Video 2, direct response from 'PamelaGoForth' to video*)
2. 'In my opinion, I don't understand why Trans people are trans. God doesn't make mistakes, and even if you don't believe in him, its ungrateful. Be a tomboy, or a boy who is kinda girlish. Geez.'
(*Video 7, direct response from 'JoJo The Keeper' to video*)
3. 'One, its not USA. It's the DEMOCRATS. The LEFTIST immoral garbage who rejected God in Christ and now worship the devil.'
(*Video 3, response from 'Armando7654' to another user claiming the USA is now a global embarrassment*)

In the data excerpts above, God is invoked as the ultimate authority who cannot or should not be defied or disobeyed, at least not without negative consequences. Transgender people are constructed as contradicting the divine will in themselves or as exemplifying a social rejection of the divine will. The first comment conflates gender reassignment surgery with sterilisation and constructs these as defiance of divine will, which is worked up and evidenced through the invocation and rather free-form interpretation of Biblical text. The second comment urges universal compliance with a divine will that is said to be inerrant. The comment orients towards accommodating transgender people though, by permitting displays of limited gender non-conformity ('Be a tomboy, or a boy who is kinda girlish'). The third comment constructs transgenderism as a consequence of a rejection of God and an embrace of the devil by part of the body politic. In all three comments, transgender people are positioned in opposition to God and to a divinely ordained gendered social order. For audiences for whom religion is an important evaluative resource in determining what is and is not legitimate, this constitutes an ultimate othering.

The working up and use of religious norms and values to delegitimise transgender people did not go unchallenged. Many commenters challenged the legitimacy of religion and bluntly denied the existence of a 'higher power':

1. 'A) There is no God and B) Transgender people are literally born with the brain of the opposite gender therefore meaning they are born in the wrong body.'
    (*Video 1, response from 'RegularGirl' to another commenter claiming it is sinful to undergo gender reassignment surgery*)
2. 'I'm not really into fiction books so I'll have to pass, but thank you for the recommendation.'
    (*Video 2, response from 'Isley Reust' to another commenter quoting from the Bible*)
3. 'change their sex? Its not something you choose, it's how your were born, irregardless of what you were assigned at birth, stop using your outdated and oppressing beliefs to restrict others.'
    (*Video 1, response from 'ElleStevenson' to another commenter claiming it is sinful to undergo gender reassignment surgery*)

In the first comment, a rhetoric of factuality is used in denying the existence of God and also in advancing the culturally recognisable biological explanation of transgenderism that we noted earlier ('born in the wrong body'). With an ironic tone, the second comment constructs the Bible as a work of fiction and hence as lacking the ultimate authority as arbiter of right and wrong that another commenter assigned to it. In the third comment, religious values and norms are constructed as tools of oppression that are utilised to restrict others' freedom and are thereby delegitimised. An accusatory tone is also achieved here as the comment positions religious advocates as perpetuating oppression. Here, we see that, although legitimacy was a recurrent concern in the data, this extended beyond transgenderism and transgender people. That was expected as contestations about legitimacy have long been recognised as a standard feature of argumentation (see, for example, Gergen 1989).

The subject of moral values was also discerned in attributions made about difficulties that transgender people experience. These difficulties were acknowledged but were attributed to bad decisions and choices made by transgender people. Responsibility for creating these difficulties was often assigned to transgender people themselves who were constructed as authors of their own misfortune.

1. 'There is no confusion over the transgender issue being pushed down people's throats; the issues of trans people are self created and self imposed.'
   (*Video 4, direct response from 'Vutube379' to video*)
2. 'I say the same to people who are desirous of making themselves freaks! Yes, I do. When you VOLUNTARILY ELECT to undergo such drastic unnatural physical changes, then it is on YOU to fend for yourself. A total nation should not be FORCED TO ACCOMMODATE your self imposed special needs.'
   (*Video 4, response from 'Vutube379' to another commenter challenging this commenter's view that body modification among transgender people is wrong*)

In both comments above, notions of free will are mobilised to construct transgender people as having actively made a decision or choice that does not align with wider societal expectations about gender expression and as experiencing societal censure as a result of their decision. The free will aspect is crucial within this construction. If gender non-conformity were to be essentialised into transgender people's psyches and if transgenderism were not presented as a matter of choice, this could make it more difficult to evaluate transgender people negatively or at least it could call for more complexity in evaluation. The second comment confers on transgender people a responsibility for themselves and perhaps for their own safety by virtue of their having freely chosen to alter their bodies and thereby defy nature ('unnatural physical changes'). As we noted earlier, the positioning of transgender people as unnatural and as having freely chosen to transgress against societal norms about gender delegitimises and others them. Furthermore, it represents them as not entitled to the collective protection that would have come with the decision to adhere to societal expectations about gender expression. In this way, any abuse that transgender people may experience is constructed as having been provoked by transgender people themselves through their infraction of the natural order and as understandable or even morally legitimate. Of course, there is nothing new about victim-blaming rhetoric framed within moral discourse, most notably in cases of sexual assault and domestic violence, even if the framing is not always straightforward (see, for example, Hayes et al. 2013; Valor-Segura et al. 2011). It was not unexpected to see it as a recurrent feature of the online othering of transgender people.

This was mostly challenged in expected ways. Commenters who offered negative evaluations of transgender people were positioned by others as intruding in an unwarranted way into an issue that is not theirs, as being judgemental and as perpetuating hate—in other words, as morally problematic. This can be seen in the first two comments below:

1. 'Call it whatever you like. A lifestyle, a mental disease, a delusion. The fact is that there are people who concern themselves with things that have nothing to do with them. There are many people who just blatantly prey off of those who live this way for absolutely no reason.'
(*Video 1, direct response from 'Rebecca Patch' to video*)
2. 'I remain dumbfounded as to how, after millennia, we have not come to understand that judging others beliefs, life choices, biology, or nature leads to conscious and unconscious hate, and that is going to be our downfall.'
(*Video 6, direct response from 'Sarah Munoz' to video*)

3. 'I'm so disgusted by this comment section. Where are people's hearts??'
    a. 'I identify myself as a heart. Stop offending me!!!!'
    b. 'Excuse me, I identify as a CRUEL HEARTLESS BASTARD. Don't judge me.'
   (*Video 1, direct response from 'Katie Gallivan The Rat' to video followed by (a) response from 'iPhone iPhone' to 'Katie Gallivan The Rat' and (b) response from 'Everyones'sFavoriteCritic' to 'iPhone iPhone' and 'Katie Gallivan The Rat'*)

However, the third comment above sees that mode of challenge queried when it is accompanied by expressions of personal hurt or moral offence. The first commenter expresses 'disgust' at negative responses and calls for empathic understanding of transgender people. Two other commenters respond to this by problematising entitlement claims made on the basis of subjective identification, showing the limits of the logic of this ('I identify as a CRUEL HEARTLESS BASTARD. Don't judge me') and enabling subsequent personally framed challenges to anti-transgender talk to be resisted—which is what then happened in this online interaction. As can be seen from this example, the framing of effective resistance to anti-transgender online talk is not straightforward. A framing within moral discourse is vulnerable to challenge owing to the likelihood of morals and moral values being treated as subjective and therefore lacking authority.

Delegitimisation Through Pathologisation and Construction as a Media Artefact

The remaining two subthemes concerned the delegitimisation of transgenderism and transgender people by constructing them as psychopathological in themselves or as the result of psychopathology, and the construction of transgenderism as a 'modern trend' created by media and social media. We have already seen evidence of a discourse of psychopathology in operation, with transgender people positioned as potential sexual offenders, as deluded and, in the case of transgender women, as having had mental health problems before revising their gender identity. A framing in terms of psychopathology has long been a feature of hegemonic constructions of sexual minorities (see, for example, Gonsiorek 1982; Taylor 2002). It was therefore not surprising to find commenters locating transgender people within a discourse of psychopathology, particularly given that the American Psychiatric Association's (2013) classification of mental disorders includes a category of 'gender dysphoria' that refers to the distress a person experiences as a result of the sex and gender they were assigned at birth. (As can be seen below, this was explicitly invoked in some comments in ways that provided warrant for a pathological framing.) The construction of transgenderism as or in relation to psychopathology carries a powerful potential for social taint and delegitimisation, as indicated by the substantial literature on the stigma associated with mental health problems (see, for example, Rüsch et al. 2005). Commenters also used a construction of transgenderism as psychopathology to advocate that transgender people should be referred for psychiatric or psychological treatment and to represent any other response as a failure of moral responsibility. These features can be seen below:

1. 'No child should have to share the same bathroom with these mentally deranged people who are so frickin deluded that they think they are the opposite gender.'
   (*Video 2, direct response from 'Raven R' to video*)
2. 'A person's belief that he or she is something they are not is, at best, a sign of confused thinking. When an otherwise healthy biological boy believes he is a girl, or an otherwise healthy biological girl believes she is a boy, an objective psychological problem exists that lies in the mind not the body, and it should be treated as such. These children suffer from gender dysphoria. Gender dysphoria (GD), formerly listed as Gender Identity Disorder (GID), is a recognized mental disorder in the most recent edition of the Diagnostic and Statistical Manual of the American Psychiatric Association (DSM-V).'
   (*Video 9, response from 'Thyalwaysseek' to another commenter who stated that transgenderism is not a mental illness*)
3. 'We need to stop treating this crap like its normal and get these folks the mental help they need.'
   (*Video 8, direct response from '4Delta' to video*)

The final subtheme involved the construction of transgenderism as a 'modern trend' created by media and social media and as lacking substance and any requirement for social change. Caitlyn Jenner (an American transgender woman and media personality who, as Bruce Jenner, was an Olympic gold medal-winning decathlete) was referenced repeatedly. The sustained media attention that Jenner's announcement of her transgender status attracted in 2015 was invoked as evidence of transgenderism as a media fad that would pass. For example:

1. 'Who ever saw a transgender person before 2 years ago? It's a fad. Before this sex and gender were synonymous.'
   (*Video 1, response from 'CaseyDia' to another commenter who claimed that people do not understand the difference between sex and gender*)
2. 'If you think about it, couldn't you honestly at any moment just decide you want to be part of this new fun "transgender" trend? You would be like Caitlin Jenner.'
   (*Video 2, direct response from 'First Last' to video*)

Resistance to this took the form of the crafting or invocation of (elements of) histories of transgenderism, constructing it as a trans-historical and trans-cultural phenomenon and imparting an enduring reality to it. In both of these subthemes, the validity of transgender people's experiences and conclusions about their gender were overridden. Transgender people and their reported experiences were constructed as not to be trusted or taken seriously because they have no inherent or enduring authenticity.

Conclusion

What then does our analysis say in relation to the aims of the research that were outlined in the introduction? The themes and subthemes identified the discursive resources that were used to construct and position transgender people in online debate about gender neutral toilets. These were chiefly uncontrollable male sexuality, notions of vulnerable women and children, entitlement to victim status, nature, biology, religious and moral values, psychopathology, and the idea of media fads. The implications of these constructions were charted: the delegitimisation and othering of transgender people through denying the authenticity and validity of their experiences and of their very being and the positioning of transgender people as a problematised and problematic out-group who are responsible for any distress they experience and any negative social responses they encounter.

The resources that were used and the ways they were used in othering transgender people in the data overlap significantly with the resources that have long been used in the offline discursive denigration of sexual minority groups. Several times we expressed a lack of surprise at the resources used in the data and the functions they were performing. For example, the motifs concerning nature and biology and the delegitimisation that we discerned through our analysis echoed Bornstein's (1994) elaboration of Garfinkel's (1967) identification of beliefs about gender that are created, expressed and reinforced through social interaction. Bornstein and Garfinkel pointed to beliefs that there are only two genders and this binary is natural; a person's gender is invariant; genitals are the essential sign of gender; and any exceptions to the two genders are not to be taken seriously. The discursive resources and motifs that we discerned are woven into and indeed constitute the fabric of our social world. Sexual and gender non-conformity—and other forms of difference that pose a potential threat to hegemonic ways of understanding and ordering the social world (see, for example, Rowe and Goodman 2014)—is responded to from a limited pool of tropes that delegitimise and other non-conforming people (from the perspective of the responder) in culturally recognisable ways.

If we want to develop and refine effective ways to challenge and resist the online othering of transgender people and communities, it is important to know in detail how these resources are used and how they function in online interaction. Such challenge and resistance are important because delegitimisation and othering have very practical implications if they (re)gain uncontested political traction and serve to deflect any need to take action to address the problems experienced by many transgender people. Instances of challenge and resistance to the othering discursive repertoire were examined in the analysis. There we noted the difficulties that can occur when challenging and resisting within the same discourse used in text that delegitimises and others transgender people (as in the case of a discourse of morality) or when a challenge rests upon the same basic problematic assumptions as that text (as in the case of a fixed gender binary). To reiterate our earlier observation, the framing of effective resistance to anti-transgender, othering online talk is not straightforward. That is no reason to shy away from the challenge. Rather it calls for creative, evidence-based, contextually informed discursive labour alongside key stakeholders. We hope that our work will contribute to this endeavour.

References

American Psychiatric Association. (2013). *Diagnostic and Statistical Manual of Mental Disorders* (5th ed.). Arlington, VA: American Psychiatric Association.

Antjoule, N. (2013). *The Hate Crime Report: Homophobia, Biphobia and Transphobia in London*. London: Galop.

Awan, I., & Zempi, I. (2016). The affinity between online and offline anti-Muslim hate crime: Dynamics and impacts. *Aggression and Violent Behavior, 27*(March–April), 1–8.

Baker, P. (2004). Unnatural acts: Discourses of homosexuality within the House of Lords debates on gay male law reform. *Journal of Sociolinguistics, 8*(1), 88–106.

Beardsley, C., & O'Brien, M. (Eds.). (2016). *This Is My Body: Hearing the Theology of Transgender Christians*. London: Darton Longman & Todd.

Blumer, M. L. C., Ansara, Y. G., & Watson, C. M. (2013). Cisgenderism in family therapy: How everyday clinical practices can delegitimize people's gender self-designations. *Journal of Family Psychotherapy, 24*(4), 267–285.

Bornstein, K. (1994). *Gender Outlaw: On Men, Women and the Rest of Us*. New York: Routledge.

Brown, A. (2018). What is so special about online (as compared to offline) hate speech? *Ethnicities, 18*(3), 297–326.

Chakraborti, N., & Hardy, S. J. (2015). *LGB&T Hate Crime Reporting: Identifying Barriers and Solutions*. Manchester: Equality and Human Rights Commission.

Cmeciu, C. (2016). Online discursive (de)legitimation of the Roma community. *Journal of Media Research, 9*(1), 80–98.

Coyle, A. (2016). Discourse analysis. In E. Lyons & A. Coyle (Eds.), *Analysing Qualitative Data in Psychology* (2nd ed., pp. 160–181). London: Sage.

Davidson, M. (2007). Seeking refuge under the umbrella: Inclusion, exclusion, and organizing within the category. *Transgender: Sexuality Research & Social Policy, 4*(4), 60–80.

Faktor, A. (2011). Access and exclusion: Public toilets as sites of insecurity for gender and sexual minorities in North America. *Journal of Human Security, 7*(3), 10–22.

Garfinkel, H. (1967). *Studies in Ethnomethodology*. Cambridge: Polity Press.

Gergen, K. (1989). Warranting voice and elaboration of the self. In J. Shotter & K. Gergen (Eds.), *Texts of Identity* (pp. 70–81). London: Sage.

Gonsiorek, J. (Ed.). (1982). *Homosexuality and Psychotherapy: A Practitioner's Handbook of Affirmative Models*. New York: Haworth Press.

Goodman, S., & Burke, S. (2010). 'Oh you don't want asylum seekers, oh you're just racist': A discursive analysis of discussions about whether it's racist to oppose asylum seeking. *Discourse and Society, 21*(3), 325–340.

Goodman, S., & Burke, S. (2011). Discursive deracialization in talk about asylum seeking. *Journal of Community and Applied Social Psychology, 21*(2), 111–123.

Goodman, S., & Rowe, L. (2014). 'Maybe it is prejudice…but it is NOT racism': Negotiating racism in discussion forums about Gypsies. *Discourse & Society, 25*(1), 32–46.

Grant, J. M., Mottet, L.A., Tanis, J., Harrison, L., Herman, J., & Keisling, M. (2011). *National Transgender 467 Discrimination Survey Report on Health and Health Care*. Washington, DC: National Center for 468 Transgender Equality and National Gay and Lesbian Task Force.

Hayes, R. M., Lorenz, K., & Bell, K. A. (2013). Victim blaming others: Rape myth acceptance and the just world belief. *Feminist Criminology, 8*(3), 202–220.

Hegarty, P. (2010). A stone in the soup? Changes in sexual prejudice and essentialist beliefs among British students in a class on LGBT psychology. *Psychology & Sexuality, 1*(1), 3–20.

Hegarty, P., Ansara, G., & Barker, M. J. (2018). Nonbinary gender identities. In N. K. Dess, J. Marecek, & L. C. Bell (Eds.), *Gender, Sex, & Sexualities: Psychological Perspectives* (pp. 53–76). New York: Oxford University Press.

Herek, G. M., & McLemore, K. A. (2013). Sexual prejudice. *Annual Review of Psychology, 64*, 309–333.

Hill, D. B., & Willoughby, B. L. B. (2005). The development and validation of the genderism and transphobia scale. *Sex Roles, 53*(7–8), 531–544.

Hines, S. (2010). Introduction. In S. Hines & T. Sanger (Eds.), *Transgender Identities: Towards a Social Analysis of Gender Diversity* (pp. 1–22). New York: Routledge.

Horn, S. S. (2006). Heterosexual adolescents' and young adults' beliefs and attitudes about homosexuality and gay and lesbian peers. *Cognitive Development, 21*(4), 420–440.

Iantaffi, A., & Bockting, W. O. (2011). Views from both sides of the bridge? Gender, sexual legitimacy and transgender people's experiences of relationships. *Culture, Health & Sexuality, 13*(3), 355–370.

Jamal, J. (2018). *Transphobic Hate Crime*. Basingstoke: Palgrave Macmillan.

Jefferson, G. (1990). List construction as a task and resource. In G. Psathas (Ed.), *Interaction Competence* (pp. 63–92). Lanham, MD: University Press of America.

Jeffreys, S. (2014). The politics of the toilet: A feminist response to the campaign to 'degender' a women's space. *Women's Studies International Forum, 45*(July–August), 42–51.

King, M. E., Winter, S., & Webster, B. (2009). Contact reduces transprejudice: A study on attitudes towards transgenderism and transgender civil rights in Hong Kong. *International Journal of Sexual Health, 21*(1), 17–34.

McInroy, L., & Craig, S. (2015). Transgender representation in offline and online media: LGBTQ youth perspectives. *Journal of Human Behavior in the Social Environment, 25*(6), 606–617.

Miceli, M. (2005). Morality politics vs. identity politics: Framing processes and competition among Christian right and gay social movement organizations. *Sociological Forum, 20*(4), 589–612.

Monro, S. (2003). Transgender politics in the UK. *Critical Social Policy, 23*(4), 433–452.

Nagoshi, J. L., Adams, K. A., Terrell, H. K., Hill, E. D., Brzuzy, S., & Nagoshi, C. T. (2008). Gender differences in correlates of homophobia and transphobia. *Sex Roles, 59*(7–8), 521–531.

Nirta, C. (2014). Trans subjectivity and the spatial monolingualism of public toilets. *Law and Critique, 25*(3), 271–288.

Norton, A. T., & Herek, G. M. (2013). Heterosexuals' attitudes toward transgender people: Findings from a national probability sample of US adults. *Sex Roles, 68*(11–12), 738–753.

Pearce, R., Steinberg, D. L., & Moon, I. (2019). Introduction: The emergence of 'trans'. *Sexualities, 22*(1–2), 3–12.

Pomerantz, A. M. (1986). Extreme case formulations: A new way of legitimating claims. *Human Studies, 9*(2–3), 219–229.

Potter, J., & Wetherell, M. (1987). *Discourse and Social Psychology: Beyond Attitudes and Behaviour.* London: Sage.

Riggs, D. W., Ansara, Y. G., & Treharne, G. J. (2015). An evidence-based model for understanding transgender mental health in Australia. *Australian Psychologist, 50*(1), 32–39.

Rowe, L., & Goodman, S. (2014). 'A stinking filthy race of people inbred with criminality': A discourse analysis of prejudicial talk about gypsies in discussion forums. *Romani Studies, 24*(1), 25–42.

Rüsch, N., Angermeyer, M. C., & Corrigan, P. W. (2005). Mental illness stigma: Concepts, consequences, and initiatives to reduce stigma. *European Psychiatry, 20*(8), 529–539.

Snee, H. (2013). Making ethical decisions in an online context: Reflections on using blogs to explore narratives of experience. *Methodological Innovations Online, 8*(2), 52–67.

Stock, K. (2018, July 6). Changing the concept of 'woman' will cause unintended harms. *The Economist.* https://www.economist.com/open-future/2018/07/06/changing-the-concept-of-woman-will-cause-unintended-harms. Accessed July 18, 2018.

Taylor, G. (2002). Psychopathology and the social and historical construction of gay male identities. In A. Coyle & C. Kitzinger (Eds.), *Lesbian & Gay Psychology: New Perspectives* (pp. 154–174). Oxford: BPS Blackwell.

Tee, N., & Hegarty, P. (2006). Predicting opposition to the civil rights of trans persons in the United Kingdom. *Journal of Community and Applied Social Psychology, 16*(1), 70–80.

Valor-Segura, I., Exposito, F., & Moya, M. (2011). Victim blaming and exoneration of the perpetrator in domestic violence: The role of beliefs in a just world and ambivalent sexism. *Spanish Journal of Psychology, 14*(1), 195–206.

Weaver, S. (2013). A rhetorical discourse analysis of online anti-Muslim and anti-Semitic jokes. *Ethnic and Racial Studies, 36*(3), 483–499.

Wetherell, M. (1998). Positioning and interpretative repertoires: Conversation analysis and post-structuralism in dialogue. *Discourse & Society, 9*(3), 387–412.

10

Young Men with Physical Disabilities Struggle for Digital Sex(uality)

Herminder Kaur

Introduction

It is now well known that young people use digital media to educate themselves about sex and engage in practices to explore their sexuality online (DeHaan et al. 2013; Daneback et al. 2012; Moran et al. 2018). Young people use several online social platforms to find partners for romantic relationships and sexual encounters, to flirt, break up, follow and/or stalk ex-partners, validate their sexual identity, and to obtain sexual health information (Meenagh 2015; Valkenburg et al. 2005; Mowlabocus 2010; Moran et al. 2018). Young people's use of digital media as a means for engaging in digital sexual practices and learning about sex has also been pertinent to the updated Sex and Relationship Education (SRE) curriculum in the United Kingdom. From 2020, pupils will be taught how to keep themselves and their personal information safe and private on online platforms, how to navigate online,

H. Kaur (✉)
Middlesex University London, London, UK

© The Author(s) 2019
K. Lumsden and E. Harmer (eds.), *Online Othering*,
Palgrave Studies in Cybercrime and Cybersecurity,
https://doi.org/10.1007/978-3-030-12633-9_10

how to challenge harmful content, and how to balance their online and offline lives (GOV.UK 2018). This updated national curriculum is designed to address the challenges faced by young people who are growing up in a digital world. However, the body of research which currently exists on how young people use digital media to learn about sex and to engage in sexual practices does not include the experiences of young people with disabilities (for an exception, see Kaur et al. 2018).

Studies which focus on the sexual lives of people with a range of disabilities reveal the struggles they experience to be recognised as sexual beings (Shakespeare et al. 2000; Liddiard 2018). People with disabilities are sexually othered and, viewed as incapable of possessing or exercising a sexual life (Campbell 2017). Young people with disabilities tend to receive inadequate sexual knowledge from formal networks (i.e. parents and schools) in comparison with non-disabled people, and they struggle to resist the values held by parents and teachers concerning how they should express their sexuality (Löfgren-Mårtenson and Ouis 2018). Furthermore, for people with disabilities, sexual education often takes place in a heteronormative context, giving little recognition to people with disabilities identifying with homosexuality and growing up with contradictory cultural norms (Campbell 2017; Löfgren-Mårtenson and Ouis 2018). Despite the sexual othering that people with disabilities experience and the struggles they undergo to acquire sexual knowledge, express their sexuality, or have access to sexual health services, research has thus far failed to focus on how sexual othering is sustained or shaped by their online experiences.

Young people with disabilities are also perceived as being more vulnerable to online sexual risk. Access to digital media means that they can possibly encounter cyber solicitation, pornography, sexting, and other undesirable online behaviours (Normand and Sallafranque-St-Louis 2016; Livingstone and Mason 2015). Parents are key mediators of digital media technologies in the home, and therefore, their role is considered important in order to encourage young people to enjoy the opportunities offered by digital media, whilst preventing them from encountering inappropriate content online (Ólafsson et al. 2013). Parents employ several mediation strategies in order to do so (Livingstone and Helsper 2008). However, we lack an understanding of the role of parents and young people with disabilities in the mediation process.

This chapter addresses these gaps in the literature on young people with physical disabilities use of the Internet by drawing on two case studies of young men with physical disabilities use of the Internet and social media platforms. The case studies reveal how young people avoid parental mediation of digital media in the home to engage in sexual practices and to gather information and knowledge relating to sex(uality). The structure of the chapter is as follows: first, I consider research on the sexual lives of people with disabilities and parental mediation of digital media in the home. Following this, I outline the methods employed in this study which primarily consisted of, ethnographic research in a special school over a two-year period and the use of video diaries to film participants' journeys through and across social media platforms. I draw on two case studies of young men with physical disabilities in order to demonstrate their intersectional experiences of disability with gender and sexual orientation when they engaged with digital media whilst evading parental mediation to learn about sex(uality). This study highlights the importance of future research in understanding the everyday sexual lives of young people with disabilities, focusing on both their online and offline lives.

Sexual Othering, Disability, and Digital Media

Young people with disabilities sexual experiences are an important area of study as they are found to encounter sexual othering via their marginalisation (Campbell 2017; Shakespeare et al. 2000). This can happen when young people with a disability are denied access to knowledge about sexuality or when members of society perceive people with disabilities as lacking sexual desires (Shakespeare et al. 2000). Young people with physical disabilities also experience exclusion when forming relationships offline, often by being disregarded and treated disrespectfully in public by non-disabled people (Cahill and Eggleston 1995), or by having fewer opportunities to meet potential partners or healthcare professionals unsupervised by carers, guardians or parents. Taleporos and

McCabe (2003) argue that being perceived as asexual and unattractive by heteronormative standards limits and, in some cases, stops people with physical disabilities from establishing sexual relationships. Sexual othering also extends to people with disabilities being less likely to participate in formal sex education programs in comparison with non-disabled peers (Lofgren-Martenson 2012). Furthermore, these programs are limited to teaching the anatomy and physiology of sex rather than providing people with disabilities with sexual knowledge that is individualised to their needs. Parent's mediation of their children with disabilities' access to sexual knowledge can also result in sexual othering via withdrawal from sex education initiatives (Berman et al. 1999).

Berman et al. (1999) argue that sex education initiatives should provide people with disabilities with knowledge on sexual functioning which is unique to their disability, their feelings, emotions, worries about attractiveness and aspirations for family planning, and also further information on how they can obtain this knowledge. Academics acknowledge the need for young people with physical disabilities to be taught intersectional experiences of disability with gender, ethnicity, and sexual orientation (Bahner 2018). Not catering to their needs holds people with disabilities back from fully participating in society and realising their sexuality.

Research demonstrates that people with disabilities use digital media for identity exploration in similar ways to non-disabled people. People with disabilities also use digital media to explore and engage in the development of romantic relationships online. Saltes' (2013) participants used online dating sites to strategically disclose their disabled identity online, often having more successful outcomes finding a partner online than offline. Seymour and Lupton (2004: 301) show that digital media has enabled people with disabilities to 'hold off the body' and engage in time spent developing relationships. People with disabilities, who are easily identified as being disabled by their impairments, are said to benefit from going online, as online spaces that offer visual anonymity can reduce the stigma of being visually different, as experienced offline (Chadwick and Wesson 2016). However, others have argued that masking a disability online may do little to reduce stigma (Furr et al. 2016; Bower and Tuffin 2002).

Several studies have found that, developing and maintaining social relationships online can enhance social capital (broadly speaking, a concept used to describe the benefits of being in a social relationship with others, e.g. emotional benefits, increasing self-esteem, etc.) (Ahn 2012; Steinfield et al. 2008; Vitak and Ellison 2012). It is argued that affording people with disabilities Internet access allows them to accrue online social capital (Chadwick and Wesson 2016). Several studies have found that online communication enhances people with disabilities' social interaction with people with similar disabilities (Braithwaite et al. 1999; Finn 1999; Guo et al. 2005; Soutter et al. 2004). People with physical disabilities also report using the Internet for disability-related activities that would help them to find medical assistance, i.e. disability support groups online as found by Obst and Stafurik (2010).

Digital media has provided informal opportunities for people with disabilities to develop relationships, enhance social capital online, and find medical assistance and support forums. Digital media can provide, as demonstrated above, an alternative resource for exercising sexual rights. However, access to digital media for many people with disabilities is not straightforward and remains limited (see Kaur et al. 2018). Digital media technologies remain unaffordable and non-user-friendly, with websites and their content being inaccessible while assistive technologies are merely an afterthought rather than being inbuilt in the design of the technologies (Adam and Kreps 2009; Dobransky and Hargittai 2006).

Mediated Access to Digital Sex(uality)

Alper and Goggin (2017) argue that access to digital media tends to be structured around protection for young people with disabilities. Protection involves managing their exposure to sexual content and practices, preventing their exposure to cyberbullying, pornography, and the possibilities of online sexual abuse and exploitation. There are several reasons why young people with disabilities are particularly regarded as vulnerable and of requiring protection in relation to online spaces. For example, Whittle et al. (2013) argue that young people with disabilities may trust unfamiliar adults online because they develop trusting relationships with many adults who provide care in offline settings. They also argue that young people with disabilities may not be as competent as their able-bodied peers in recognising their exposure to online grooming or be able to manage such an encounter in an online or an offline context. Livingstone et al. (2011) found that parents of children with disabilities perceived their children to be less able to cope with online environments. Similarly, Lathouwers et al. (2009) found that parents of children with physical disabilities were overly protective, warning their children more about online risks and placing more restrictions on their use of the Internet than parents with non-disabled children. Chadwick and Wesson (2016) note that as people with disabilities are more likely to be viewed as being vulnerable online by gatekeepers such as parents, teachers, and carers, it is likely that they will be further excluded from digital access through fewer opportunities to access the Internet, and reduced support and guidance.

The responsibility of regulating young people's access to digital media filters down to parents and young people in the home (Livingstone and Bober 2006). Regulation of digital media in the home has been researched by scholars, mainly using large-scale surveys to look at the different parental strategies and practices they adopt in order to mediate their children's online activities. However, these studies provide little insight into how children respond to these parenting strategies and practices. Livingstone et al. (2015) argue that these strategies include 'active mediation', whereby parents talk to their children about online experiences or sit next to their child as they use the Internet to discuss online content with them. This also includes 'restrictive mediation', whereby parents set rules and limitations to their child's use of the Internet. This can be done by limiting the time spent online, placing restrictions on location of the computer, and restricting access to certain websites and activities. Some parents may also put filters in place to block or restrict access to websites. They may also scroll through the history of online activities their children engage in. These findings are contested when it comes to settling on which parental strategy dominates the mediation of digital media in the home. Some scholars note that parents adopt a relaxed measure, while others are found to be authoritative (Aunola et al. 2000; Ayas and Horzum 2013; Eastin et al. 2006; Özgür 2016). Recently, Livingstone et al. (2017) found that parents often choose both strategies in varying measures. Parents who consider themselves to possess digital skills, use these skills to support their children's online activities, while using active mediation of technical controls and monitoring to lower their risks. In contrast, parents who are less confident in their own and their child's digital skills implement restrictive measures which limit their child's digital inclusion.

Therefore, parental mediation of young people with disabilities use of digital media is deemed to be important. Newman et al. (2016) report that many young people with disabilities require personalised support to be able to use the Internet. Tailored one-to-one support provided to young people with disabilities in their use of social networking sites has proved to be effective (Grace et al. 2014). Kaur et al. (2018) reveal how young people with physical disabilities require their parents to set them up with digital media technologies and to provide support to help them navigate online. These studies highlight how the role of gatekeepers in providing Internet access and in supporting Internet use is vital for young people with disabilities.

Digital media is not the only source through which young people can gain access to information about sexuality (Buckingham and Bragg 2004). However, studies have demonstrated that it is an important tool that is increasing its relevance by offering young people with another way to exercise their sexuality, to view explicit material online, to engage in sexual practices, and to look up sexual content and information (Lykens et al. 2017; Burkett 2015; Scarcelli 2014). These studies show digital and social media are an accessible means through which young people can discover and explore their sexuality without experiencing restrictive sexual standards (Eleuteri et al. 2017). However, this literature overlooks the experiences of people with disabilities, and how they respond to the regulation practices in the home to access digital media for sexual learning and exploration. This study provides us with initial insights on how young men with physical disabilities use digital media to explore sexual information, content, and activities, and how this takes place against their efforts to evade parental mediation in the home.

Methods

The case studies presented in this chapter are from a two-year ethnographic study which was primarily concerned with exploring the ways in which young people with physical disabilities used digital media in their everyday lives. Researching the use of digital media by young people with physical disabilities in its entirety in one context is unfeasible, as previous studies note that young people use digital media differently in a school setting in comparison with the home (boyd 2014; Livingstone and Sefton-Green 2016; Raghavendra et al. 2013). To gather a holistic understanding of young people with physical disabilities' use of digital media in these two settings (home and school), the study utilised three qualitative methods including: participant observation, semi-and unstructured interviews, and video diaries.

The research was conducted at a special school in the UK which educated young people with physical disabilities. Permission to conduct research in the school was negotiated by working voluntarily as a classroom assistant before, during and after the research had been completed. The main method used was overt participant observation, involving:

> …direct and sustained contact with human beings, in the context of their daily lives, over a prolonged period of time; draw on a family of methods, usually including participant observation and conversation; respects the complexity of the social world; and therefore, tells rich, sensitive, and credible stories. (O'Reilly 2012: 4)

To produce 'thick description' (Geertz 1973: 6) of the unfolding events required the researcher to keep a record of social action and conversations taking place in the school that would be of importance to the study. While keeping a notebook during research is advisable (O'Reilly 2012), this was unfeasible, as classroom teachers thought the researcher was making notes on their teaching during the lessons. Both teachers and participants wanted to see the researchers' notes and this became a distraction during class sessions. To be able to jot down quick and short notes, a paper and pen was carried in a pocket to lessons that allowed the researcher to quickly note keywords that would serve as a reminder when writing up notes at the end of the day. Often, lengthy notes were made on a mobile phone in the school toilets, away from the school staff and students; at other times, mental notes of events and conversations would be made.

Over time, trust was developed with the teaching staff and with participants, allowing the researcher to 'follow' (Marcus 1998: 90) participants from one class to another and in places in the school where students spent their free time (including a computer lab at break times). Therefore, the ethnography became 'multi-sited' (Marcus 1998) as participants use of the Internet was studied across different sites (i.e. in school, at home and to mainstream colleges). Ethnography in the school allowed for opportunistic questioning of students and school staff during informal chats. Observation also involved the researcher being invited to conversations taking place in the school amongst friends, as well as in private group conversations online.

After spending six months in the special school, participants were identified for the interview stage and the final sample consisted of 11 participants (four female and seven male students aged 14–19 years old). All participants had physical disabilities which limited their bodily movements, while some were also diagnosed with mild intellectual or developmental disabilities. Participants were recruited on a one-to-one basis, via private face-to-face meetings in the school. During the meeting, the research process was discussed, and students were provided details of the study in booklet form. Written consent was sought from the participants and their parents for home visits, interviews, and for participants to keep video diaries.

Formal semi-structured interviews were also conducted with parents and staff. This included interviewing 7 parents of the 11 participants, 14 members of staff at the special school and two college teachers. The interviews were 'conversations with a purpose' (Burgess 1984: 102). All of the semi-structured interviews (with students, parents, and school/college staff) were recorded and fully transcribed by the researcher.

The research also involved the participants making video diaries of their Internet use at home. Participants were given a hand-held video camera and instructions on the safe and ethical use of video recording as had been advised and requested by the school. The study was tailored to the needs of the participants in terms of their home lives and disabilities. Participants could film their use of the Internet sporadically over a one-year period at home. The video included narration by participants to inform the researcher as to what the participants were doing online, as well as personal reflections. When filming their Internet use, the diaries allowed participants to express their experiences and feelings in the moment. For the participants who recorded their use of the Internet via a video diary, the formal interviews discussed above were also a time in which they could reflect on their recordings and the researcher could probe further their use of the Internet taking place in the home.

The study received full ethical approval from the university's research ethics committee. Participants chose their pseudonyms and the material collected has been anonymised to ensure confidentiality (e.g. names, physical conditions, and other compromising information has been removed or changed).

Data analysis was not a distinct phase of data collection. They were interlinked and, through the process of data collection, key topics that required further attention were identified, i.e. access and use of digital media, social relationships online, disability, and regulating access to digital media. Consequently, data emerged on how young people with physical disabilities accessed digital media in the home and particularly for sex(uality). There is no set procedure for analysing ethnographic data, but the various kinds of data produced from field notes, interview transcripts, observations, and informal conversations with participants across research sites, required the analysis for broad categories, which were future analysed against literature. These categories helped to make sense of the vast ethnographic data (Hammersley and Atkinson 2007). This chapter analyses ethnographic data, data from video diaries and interviews with participants and parents, against literature on digital media, disability and accessibility, regulations on Internet safety, and online risks. The next section presents two case studies which illustrates how young people with physical disabilities evaded parental mediation in order to use digital media for learning and exploring sex(uality).

Steven: Sexual Entertainment

At the time of conducting the study, Steven was 16 years old. Having previously been bullied in his school abroad, he enjoyed his relocation to the UK and particularly his time in the special school. The school provided him with the one-to-one support required when working on educational tasks and when accessing a desktop computer. Seated in his electronic wheelchair, designed with his favourite colours (red and blue), he could independently navigate his way around the school and on digital devices, only requiring support from an adult every now and then in order to set the equipment. In addition to his physical disability, Steven has a visual impairment and requires small features on his digital device to be enlarged to ease its use.

In school, Steven is easily identifiable, one of the well-dressed and well-mannered students wearing his neat clothes and matching accessories. Dressing up and looking good is a trait that defines Steven. He is a sociable teenager who is hardly ever seen to be disruptive. His well-mannered nature and loud laughs set him apart from those in his class. His dislike for peers who disrupt the classroom or say words that Steven considers to be 'rude' or ill-mannered was exemplified by his choice to avoid certain peer groups and instead spend his free play and break time playing games on the school computer.

Apart from being fascinated by his favourite colours and games online, Steven also enjoys watching programmes related to human physiology. During school time, Steven would often call the researcher over in his quiet polite voice and challenge her to an arm wrestle, often to show his strength and at times to tender the hand of the female researcher. It is not rare for young people in the special school to reach out and make physical contact by touching the hands, or arms of adults, or by asking for hugs. Many students in the special school displayed this type of affection towards adults. Steven was frequently seen to make such gestures with adult carers and teachers in the school. He would excitedly talk to, and develop, relations with new female and male carers and volunteers in the classroom.

At home, Steven mainly used his tablet to go online. This was set up by his mother or father in his bedroom, and placed in front of him as he sat in his wheelchair. While Steven can use digital media devices on his own, when he does so, his parents leave his bedroom door partially or completely open. Steven does not like feeling alone, and this allows him to feel part of the domestic atmosphere as well as allow his parents to watch his tablet screen from a distance. As they frequently walk past his bedroom to enter the kitchen or the living room, they mention the odds are very low for him to engage in activities like online pornography without them knowing about it.

His mother explains that she frequently checks the history on his device to keep tabs on his online activities. While Steven is aware of this he has never objected to it. As Steven is now 16, he has fewer restrictions placed on him for using sites like Facebook or YouTube. His parents appreciate that his disability makes it difficult to engage in textual conversations with his friends online, and therefore, his use of digital media is '*more about entertainment*'.

His parents understand that Steven uses digital media to search for information that intrigues him: he'll '*often go and find videos or Google it and find what he can find … that's become a gateway for him to do everything*'. His parents assert that Steven understands what is '*right*' and '*wrong*' online, and while they have seen him look at online content that includes '*some girls, topless girls and things*' they understand that this is related to his medical interest and is not because of its '*sexual nature*'. His father discloses his concerns for having to explain sexual issues to his son when he becomes attracted to the opposite sex in the future.

At school, Steven reveals to the researcher through informal chats outside of class that he has been using digital media to watch '*rude*' things online, and to ensure that he does not land himself in trouble with his parents he watches the rude content by viewing cartoons on YouTube that show women in revealing attire or as being topless. He giggled after the revelation and mentioned that he does not do anything '*wrong*' online but watches medical programmes too (i.e. operations which would reveal parts of a naked body). This was partly due to his interest in medical physiology, but also to learn about the sexual body and to make sense of his curiosity regarding female genitalia.

Gary: Validating Sexuality

Gary had been placed in the special school by his parents since his primary school years. He remained there until he progressed to further education in a mainstream college. While at the special school Gary developed strong friendships with many female peers; his childhood friend went on to become his girlfriend. However, as a couple they did not share a romantic or intimate relationship; rather, they continued to be friends with the status of being in a romantic relationship. While at the special school affectionate displays of love were not permitted. Gary also recalled not being attracted to his girlfriend at the time. This worried Gary and led him to question his sexuality.

At home, Gary had access to a shared desktop computer, which was mainly used for gaming and online searches. He was allocated time restrictions when using the computer, to ensure that his two brothers could also use the device. He remembers using the computer to search for naked female bodies and recalls having no reaction when he saw these. He then searched for images of naked male bodies and remembers being rather amused and attracted. He would delete any trace of such activity from the computer to prevent his siblings and parents finding out what he would '*get up to*' online.

At the age of 12, Gary's best friend Daniella, who he had been dating, set up his Facebook profile. Gary remembers that at that time Facebook had received bad publicity when a girl was murdered by a man she met online. Gary states that he knew Facebook '*wasn't like this but my parents didn't*'. He was questioned by his mother whether he had a Facebook account, and remembers replying with an assertive '*No!*'. Later, when his father set up his brother with a Facebook account, Gary also pretended to create a new one for himself.

As Gary entered his teenage years, he was bestowed with his own laptop, parental restrictions became more relaxed, and this meant Gary could now access digital media in the privacy of his bedroom, with few restrictions in place. '*I was able to go on the internet on my own, without people behind me and without my history, potentially being looked on*'. He remembers that one day he used his laptop to search for '*gay porn*'.

He was shocked by the number of sites that appeared, but most of all how easy it was for him to access them. Gary then went on to explore solo videos of men masturbating. Often these videos would show men '*being whipped, poked with sticks…tied [up]*'. Gary expressed concern regarding why these men would film themselves engaging in such acts for the world to see.

It was not until Gary used his mobile phone that his '*world expanded*'. He mustered the courage to sign up to gay 'hook-up' apps on his mobile phone and downloaded apps when his parents were out of house as he, '*didn't want to be caught using it*'. He used the apps to chat with other men, develop friendships, exchange sexual images, and arranged meet-ups with men he Skyped at night in his bedroom while his parents were asleep. Often this meant typing out messages rather than engaging in verbal conversations online, and not uploading a visual image of himself online in case people found out about his sexuality.

Conclusion

The two case studies outlined above demonstrate how young men with physical disabilities utilise various forms of digital media (such as Internet searches and dating apps) to learn and explore sex(uality). However, their access to digital media is not straightforward. Steven, aged 16, is still not recognised as having sexual desires despite using the Internet to view 'topless girls and things'. Instead, his interest in viewing such content is considered by his parents to be related to his interest in medicine. Steven also uses this to his advantage by continuing to watch cartoons and medical programmes to learn more about specific body parts and to explore his sexual desires. Steven's parents mediate his use of the Internet described by Livingstone et al. (2015) as being restrictive, this entails watching over him as they walk past his room and by scrolling through his online activities and history. As they rarely leave Steven alone for long periods of time, Steven does not engage with strategies of deleting his online activities; as he also requires tailored support to use digital media (Newman et al. 2016; Kaur et al. 2018) he finds alternative subtle ways to view 'rude' content online, by watching medical operations that reveal specific nude body parts or cartoons which portray illustrations of body parts.

In contrast, Gary is older and more physically able than Steven. This is reflected in his independent use of a range of digital media devices to access a broad range of online activities. Like Steven, Gary uses the Internet to search for nude images; however, unlike Steven, he deletes the history of his online activities. Gary can also avoid his parent's detection of his online activities by using digital media devices to chat with other gay men when his parents are out of the house or sleeping. By turning to digital media and downloading 'hook-up' apps, Gary is able to explore and validate his sexual identity in a private manner (see Albury and Bryon 2016).

Crucially, the two case studies demonstrate how both Steven and Gary struggle to explore and learn about their sex(uality) offline, and how by turning to digital media they can explore alternative ways to do this in online spaces and to an extent in ways which caters to their own needs and desires. However, parental mediation strategies, particularly in the case of Steven, still restrict their use of digital media in order to explore and learn about sex(uality). Whereas digital media has been found to provide young people with access to many means to explore sex and sexuality online (Eleuteri et al. 2017; Burkett 2015), young people with disabilities may not be able to take advantage of this in similar ways to their non-disabled peers, adding a further layer to the 'sexual othering' that takes place when digital media technologies are being mediated by parents, the educational establishment and guardians.

References

Adam, A., & Kreps, D. (2009). Disability and discourses of web accessibility. *Information, Communication & Society, 12*(7), 1041–1058.

Ahn, J. (2012). Teenagers experiences with social network sites: Relationships to bridging and bonding social capital. *The Information Society, 28*(2), 99–109.

Albury, K., & Byron, P. (2016). Safe on my phone? Same-sex attracted young people's negotiations of intimacy, visibility, and risk on digital hook-up apps. *Social Media and Society, 2*(4), 1–10.

Alper, M., & Goggin, G. (2017). Digital technology and rights in the lives of children with disabilities. *New Media & Society, 19*(5), 726–740.

Aunola, K., Stattin, H. K., & Nurmi, J. (2000). Parenting styles and adolescents' achievement strategies. *Journal of adolescence, 23*, 205–222.

Ayas, T., & Horzum, M. B. (2013). Internet addiction and internet parental style of primary school students. *Turkish Psychological Counselling and Guidance Journal, 4*(39), 46–57.

Bahner, J. (2018). Cripping sex education: Lessons learned from a programme aimed at young people with mobility impairments. *Sex Education*, ifirst. https://doi.org/10.1080/14681811.2018.1456417.

Berman, H., Harris, D., Enright, R., Gilpin, M., Cathers, T., & Bukovy, G. (1999). Sexuality and the adolescent with a physical disability: Understandings and misunderstandings. *Issues in Comprehensive Paediatric Nursing, 22*(4), 183–196.

Bowker, N., & Tuffin, K. (2002). Disability discourses for online identities. *Disability & Society, 17*(3), 327–344.

boyd, d. (2014). *Its Complicated: The Social Lives of Networked Teens*. London: Yale University Press.

Braithwaite, D. O., Waldron, V. R., & Finn, J. (1999). Communication of social support in computer-mediated groups for people with disabilities. *Health Communication, 11*(2), 123–151.

Buckingham, D., & Bragg, S. (2004). *Young People, Sex and the Media*. Basingstoke: Palgrave Macmillan.

Burgess, R. G. (1984). *In the Field: An Introduction to Field Research*. London: George Allen & Unwin.

Burkett, M. (2015). Sex(t) talk: A qualitative analysis of young adults' negotiations of the pleasures and perils of sexting. *Sexuality and Culture, 19*(4), 835–863.

Cahill, S. E., & Eggleston, R. (1995). Reconsidering the stigma of physical disability: Wheelchair use and public kindness. *The Sociological Quarterly, 36*(4), 681–698.

Campbell, M. (2017). Disabilities and sexual expression: A review of the literature. *Sociology Compass, 11*(9), 1–19.

Chadwick, D. D., & Wesson, C. (2016). Digital inclusion & disability. In A. Attrill & C. Fullwood (Eds.), *Applied Cyberpsychology: Applications of Cyberpsychological Theory and Research*. Basingstoke: Palgrave Macmillan.

DeHaan, S., Kuper, L. E., Magee, J. C., Bigelow, L., & Mustanski, B. S. (2013). The interplay between online and offline explorations of identity, relationships, and sex: A mixed-methods study with LQBT youth. *The Journal of Sex Research, 50*(5), 421–434.

Deneback, K., Månsson, S. A., Ross, M. W., & Markham, C. M. (2012). The internet as a source of information about sexuality. *Sex Education, 12*(5), 583–598.

Dobransky, K., & Hargittai, E. (2006). The disability divide in internet access and use. *Information, Communication & Society, 9*(3), 313–334.

Eastin, M. S., Greenberg, B. S., & Hofschire, L. (2006). Parenting the internet. *Journal of Communication, 56*(3), 486–504.

Eleuteri, S., Saladino, V., & Verrastro, V. (2017). Identity, relationships, sexuality, and risky behaviors of adolescents in the context of social media. *Sexual and Relationship Therapy, 32*(3–4), 354–365.

Finn, J. (1999). An exploration of helping processes in an online self-help group focusing on issues of disability. *Health and Social Work, 24*(3), 220–231.

Furr, J. B., Carreiro, A., & McArthur, J. A. (2016). Strategic approaches to disability disclosure on social media. *Disability & Society, 31*(10), 1353–1368.

Geertz, C. (1973). *The Interpretation of Cultures*. New York: Basic Books.

GOV.UK. (2018). *New relationships and health education in schools*. https://www.gov.uk/government/news/new-relationships-and-health-education-in-schools. Accessed August 1, 2018.

Grace, E., Raghavendra, P., Newman, L., Wood, N., & Connell, T. (2014). Learning to use the internet and online social media: What is the effectiveness of home-based intervention for youth with complex communication needs? *Child Language Teaching & Therapy, 30*(2), 141–157.

Guo, B., Bricout, J. C., & Huang, J. (2005). A common open space or a digital divide? A social model perspective on the online disability community in China. *Disability & Society, 20*(1), 49–66.

Hammersley, M., & Atkinson, P. (Eds.). (2007). *Ethnography: Principles in Practice*. London: Routledge.

Kaur, H., Saukko, P., & Lumsden, K. (2018). Rhythms of moving in and between digital media: A study on video diaries by young people with physical disabilities. *Mobilities, 13*(3), 397–410.

Lathouwers, K., de Moor, J., & Didden, R. (2009). Access to and use of internet by adolescents who have a physical disability: A comparative study. *Research in Developmental Disabilities, 30*(4), 702–711.

Liddiard, K. (2018). *The Intimate Lives of Disabled People*. Abingdon, Oxon: Routledge.

Livingstone, S., & Bober, M. (2006). Regulating the internet at home: Contrasting the perspectives of children and parents. In D. Buckingham & R. Willett (Eds.), *Digital Generations: Children, Young People and New Media*. Mahwah, NJ: Lawrence Erlbaum.

Livingstone, S., & Helpser, E. J. (2008). Parental mediation of children's internet use. *Journal of Broadcasting & Electronic Media, 52*(4), 581–599.

Livingstone, S., & Mason, J. (2015). Sexual rights and sexual risks among youth online: A review of existing knowledge regarding children and young people's developing sexuality in relation to new media environments. eNACSO, *European NGO Alliance for Child Saftey Online*. http://eprints.lse.ac.uk/64567/1/Livingstone_Review_on_Sexual_rights_and_sexual_risks_among_online_youth_Author_2015.pdf. Accessed October 20, 2018.

Livingstone, S., & Sefton-Green, J. (2016). *The Class: Living and Learning in the Digital Age*. New York: New York University Press.

Livingstone, S., Haddon, L., Görzig, A., & Ólafsson, K. (2011). *EU Kids Online: Final Report EU Kids Online*. London, UK: London School of Economics & Political Science.

Livingstone, S., Mascheroni, G., Dreier, M., Chaudron, S., & Lagae, K. (2015). How parents of young children manage digital devices at home: The role of income, education and parental style. *EU Kids Online*. London: London School of Economics.

Livingstone, S., Ólafsson, K., Helsper, E. J., Lupiáñez-Villanueva, F., Veltri, G. A., & Folkvord, F. (2017). Maximizing opportunities and minimising risks for children online: The role of digital skills in emerging strategies of parental mediation. *Journal of Communication, 67*(1): 82–105.

Löfgren-Mårtenson, L. (2012). 'I want to do it right!': A pilot study of Swedish sex education and young people with intellectual disabilities. *Sexuality and Disability, 30*(2), 209–225.

Löfgren-Mårtenson, C., & Ouis, P. (2018). 'We need "culture-bridges"': Professionals' experiences of sex education for pupils with intellectual disabilities in a multicultural society. *Sex Education*. ifirst. https://www.tandfonline.com/doi/full/10.1080/14681811.2018.1478806.

Lykens, J., Pilloton, M., Silva, C., Schlamm, E., & Sheoran, B. (2017). *TECHsex: Youth Sexuality and Health Online*. Oakland, CA: YTH.

Marcus, G. E. (1998). *Ethnography Through Thick and Thin*. Princeton, NJ: Princeton University Press.

Meenagh, J. (2015). Flirting, dating, and breaking up within new media environments. *Sex Education, 15*(5), 458–471.

Moran, J. B., Salerno, K. J., & Wade, T. J. (2018). *Snapchat* as a new tool for sexual access: Are there sex differences? *Personality and Individual Differences, 129*, 12–16.

Mowlabocus, S. (2010). *Gaydar Culture: Gay Men, Technology and Embodiment in the Digital Age*. Surrey: Ashgate.

Newman, L., Browne-Yung, K., Raghavendra, P., Wood, D., & Grace, E. (2016). Applying a critical approach to investigate barriers to digital inclusion and online social networking among young people with disabilities. *Information Systems Journal*, ifirst. http://onlinelibrary.wiley.com/doi/10.1111/isj.12106/abstract.

Normand, C. L., & Sallafranque-St-Louis, F. (2016). Cybervictimization of young people with an intellectual or developmental disability: Risks specific to sexual solicitation. *Journal of Applied Research in Intellectual Disabilities, 29*(2), 99–110.

Obst, P., & Stafurik, J. (2010). Online we are all able bodied: Online psychological sense of community and social support found through membership of disability-specific websites promotes well-being for people living with a physical disability. *Journal of Community & Applied Social Psychology, 20*(6), 525–531.

Ólafsson, K., Livingstone, S., & Haddon, L. (2013). *Children's Use of Online Technologies in Europe: A Review of the European Evidence Base*. London: EU Kids Online.

O'Reilly, K. (2012). *Ethnographic Methods*. London: Routledge.

Özgür, H. (2016). The relationship between internet parenting styles and internet usage of children and adolescents. *Computers in Human Behavior, 60,* 411–424.

Raghavendra, P., Newman, L., Grace, E., & Wood, D. (2013). 'I could never do that before': Effectiveness of a tailored internet support intervention to increase the social participation of youth with disabilities. *Child: Care, Health and Development, 39*(4): 552–561.

Saltes, N. (2013). Disability, identity and disclosure in the online dating environment. *Disability & Society, 28*(1), 96–109.

Scarcelli, C. M. (2014). 'One way or another I need to learn this stuff!' Adolescents, sexual information, and the internet's role between family, school, and peer groups. *Interdisciplinary Journal of Family Studies, 19*(1), 40–59.

Seymour, W., & Lupton, D. (2004). Holding the line online: Exploring wired relationships for people with disabilities. *Disability & Society, 19*(4), 291–305.

Shakespeare, T., Gillespie-Sells, K., & Davies, D. (2000). *The Sexual Politics of Disability: Untold Desires*. London: Cassell.

Soutter, J., Hamilton, N., Russell, P., Russell, C., Bushby, K., Sloper, P., et al. (2004). The golden freeway: A preliminary evaluation of a pilot study advancing information technology as a social intervention for boys with Duchenne muscular dystrophy and their families. *Social and Healthcare in the Community, 12,* 25–33.

Steinfield, C., Ellison, N. B., & Lampe, C. (2008). Social capital, self-esteem, and use of online social network sites: A longitudinal analysis. *Journal of Applied Developmental Psychology, 29*(6), 434–445.

Taleporos, G., & McCabe, M. (2003). Relationships, sexuality and adjustment among people with physical disability. *Sexual and Relationship Therapy, 18*(1), 25–43.

Valkenburg, P. M., Schouten, A. P., & Peter, J. (2005). Adolescents identity experiments on the internet. *New Media & Society, 7*(3), 383–402.

Vitak, J., & Ellison, N. B. (2012). 'There's a network out there you might as well tap': Exploring the benefits of and barriers to exchanging informational and support-based resources on Facebook. *New Media & Society, 15*(2), 243–259.

Whittle, H., Hamilton-Giachritsis, C., Beech, A., & Collings, G. (2013). A review of young people's vulnerabilities to online grooming. *Aggression and Violent Behavior, 18,* 135–146.

11

Rural Racism in the Digital Age

Nathan Kerrigan

Introduction

Drawing upon a netnographic (digital ethnography) approach, the following chapter builds upon and provides a novel contribution to the existing literature on rural racism by exploring the ways residents of a rural community in the south of England used Facebook to construct an online rural space through giving meaning to the forum as 'rural' and the extent to which this excludes and others those with perceived differences (e.g. having a foreign name). The book chapter denotes how processes of re-representing rurality online by some residents (mainly those white long-standing residents of the town) led to experiences of targeted hate and victimisation for those minority ethnic residents online as a way to protect, secure and maintain rurality online from the intrusion of the 'other' and difference.

N. Kerrigan (✉)
Birmingham City University, Birmingham, UK

© The Author(s) 2019
K. Lumsden and E. Harmer (eds.), *Online Othering*,
Palgrave Studies in Cybercrime and Cybersecurity,
https://doi.org/10.1007/978-3-030-12633-9_11

The chapter begins by contextualising contemporary sociological and criminological discourses around race, racism and rurality as well as the role of social media and the Internet in constructing rural community in the digital age before highlighting the methodological approach used for the study. Next, findings of the research will be explored. This will include an examination of the re-representation strategies used by some residents online and the exclusionary and racist discourses that arose as a result of these strategies. Finally, the chapter discusses what these findings mean in relation to wider discourses around the protection and maintenance of rurality in an ever changing and diversifying world.

Race, Racism and Rurality

The sociology of race has experienced significant changes in the past few decades which have led to new and developing areas of research. These developments have evolved mainly in an urban context, with this privileging of the urban frame of reference amongst academics tracing back to the Chicago School and followed by academic researchers in Britain in the 1960s (Solomos 2006). These initial studies focused on demonstrating that a 'racism problem' existed and required policies to challenge it. For example, Daniel's (1966) study sought to demonstrate that the black and Asian people who had arrived in Britain during the 1950s and 1960s did not receive the same treatment as their white counterparts and were systematically disadvantaged in the housing and labour markets by direct and indirect discrimination (Robinson and Valeny 2004). Smith's (1974) and Brown's (1984) second and third national surveys then told us more about the nature and impact of racism and made a convincing case, both for further legislation and for more accurate monitoring of ethnic disadvantage, through the inclusion of an 'ethnicity question' for the first time in the 1991 Census.

Moving into the 1980s, a different strand of research sought to focus not on the structural position of minority ethnic groups in British society, but upon the impact of racism on the individual, particularly through racial harassment and racial violence. The Home Office's (1981) report *Racial Attacks* was the first to recognise these phenomena and found that South Asian people were fifty times more likely to become victims of racially motivated incidents than white people. Following this, attempts were made to monitor the volume of such incidents, through both published police data and the British Crime Survey (BCS). However, it is now widely regarded (see, e.g., Clancy et al. 2001) that both police data and the BCS only record the most extreme cases of racist victimisation and that there is another level of taken-for-granted or 'low level' forms of racial harassment that rarely appears in official data. In the *Fourth National Survey of Ethnic Minorities,* Modood (1997) attempted to provide a fuller picture by asking about all forms of racial harassment, and Virdee (1997) used this data to estimate that over a quarter of million people were subjected to some form of racial harassment in the 12-month period between 1993 and 1994.

The consequence of a lack of academic focus on 'race' in rural areas, and an underemphasis of the relevance of 'race' in rural contexts has allowed the 'urban' to become the implicit spatial norm of racism. This 'place blindness'—the fact that experiences of urban minority ethnic groups are taken as the norm: a norm which is rarely made explicit—at the local level was challenged by two trends from the late-1980s onwards. Ingrid Pollard (1989) was one of the first to describe how minority ethnic groups felt even more 'out of place' in the British countryside than they did in urban areas. She used a visual auto-ethnographic approach to describe how she (as a Black woman) was made to feel as an unwelcomed visitor in the rural idyll, examples of the photographs taken included captions such as 'walks through leafy glades with a baseball bat by my side' and 'the owners of these fields… want me off their green and pleasant land…they want me dead' (Pollard 1989: 42–46). It was not until the publication of Jay's (1992) *Keep Them in Birmingham* report, however, that racism was seen as much of a problem in rural areas as it was in urban areas. Jay (1992) had been commissioned by the Commission for Racial Equality (CRE) to study the extent, nature and impact of racism in the south-west of England. He concluded that minority ethnic groups felt threatened, isolated and vulnerable. He described how they experienced racism daily and how their reaction had either been to leave the area, reduce their visibility or retreat into a compensatory stronger ethnic identity. His survey of service providers produced equally negative results, with institutions claiming either that there was 'no problem here' or that race relations were an issue only for parts of the country with a sizeable minority ethnic population.

Jay's (1992) work was subsequently replicated and confirmed by a series of other CRE-sponsored research projects (see, e.g., Derbyshire 1994 in Norfolk; Nizhar 1996 in Shropshire; and De Lima 2001 in rural Scotland). Nizhar (1996: 35), in particular, found clear evidence both of racist victimisation and of the unresponsiveness of officialdom, with one local government officer arguing that special services and support should not be provided for minority ethnic groups because 'they should give up their identity and image and take on board white culture'.

Academic interest in rural-based racism in the field of sociology fell out of favour during the mid-1990s but saw a resurgence of interest in the field of criminology in the early-2000s. Chakraborti and Garland's (2004) edited collection revealed the everyday experiences of racism of minority ethnic groups living in rural settings. They concluded that the nature and impact of racism in rural contexts can be based on 'low-level' forms of harassment that were inflamed by local perceptions of the British countryside being spaces of 'Britishness'. Chakraborti and Garland's work was followed up by further criminological research (e.g. Neal 2009; Plastow 2011). While Plastow's (2011) research denoted racism was rife in the south-east of Scotland, Neal (2009) highlighted the impact environmental and community processes had upon experiences of racism for minority ethnic groups.

Within the past 25 years an extensive body of mainly small scale, qualitative-oriented research has documented and charted the widespread experiences of racisms within rural areas of Britain and the various policy and rural agencies' uncertainties as to how to respond to incidents of racism. However, since the publication of these studies we have experienced rapid technological social change which has transformed people's everyday lives and rearticulated and reshaped the way we engage socially through the gradual inundation of social media platforms. Platforms, such as Facebook, Twitter and YouTube, amongst many others have enabled individuals to make connections by sharing expressive and communicative content and enjoy online social lives. In fact, the widespread presence of social media platforms has driven people to move many of their social and cultural activities to these online environments.

Social Media, the Internet and Rural Communities in the Digital Age

The digitalisation of social life has had a huge impact on rural areas (Rice 2014). Traditionally, rural areas have been defined as cohesive communities based on close-knit social relations and bounded by a shared physical space (Skerratt and Steiner 2013; Johansen and Chandler 2015). However, as the use of the Internet has increased and more and more rural residents are using social media platforms such as Facebook and Twitter, the use of these platforms has been accompanied by, and contributed to, significant shifts in rural social relations. For example, today, people living in even the most remote rural areas can exchange messages from their computers, tablets and phones to other individuals living on the other side of the world (James 2014).

The rapid growth of the Internet and digital technologies has further perpetuated the distanciation of time-space (Giddens 1984; Harvey 1989), that is as the use of the Internet has increased the social relations which make up a locality are less and less constituted within the physical place itself. Typically, within rural spaces, this has facilitated a fear of the diminution of rural community in which there is a perception that the digitalisation of rural life has weakened social ties (Cumming and Johan 2010) and created atomisation between individuals living in rural areas. Woods (2007) suggests this is because the Internet has the ability to deteriorate human capital through only providing 'bite-sized' interactions, such as posting tweets which are only 280 characters in length, that do not allow for human capital to foster and develop. Moreover, the growth of online connectivity can also blur the boundaries between insiders and outsiders in rural environments. For instance, anyone can join a rural community group on Facebook and Twitter from anywhere around the world, increasing the concerns regarding the arrival of newcomers in rural areas within which long-term residents have little understanding whether an individual or group of individuals are local or not (Dargan and Shucksmith 2008; Shucksmith 2010; Johansen and Chandler 2015).

While the rise of the Internet and social media has changed the dynamics of rural community life the burgeoning of digital media technologies have not rendered the physical geography of rural space obsolete (e.g. Berry et al. 2010; Couldry and McCarthy 2004; Falkheimer and Jansson 2006), in fact, it has aided its continuity. This is because in the context of location-aware media, the interfaces of digital media are becoming 'progressively "spatialised"' (Leszczynski 2015: 732). Thus, the physical geography of place is mediatised and materialised in digital realms through not only GPS coordinates but also interactions in the form of photos and textual descriptions. At the same time, digital services such as Facebook contribute to the production of physical-geographical places by affording certain types of interaction.

Social media platforms such as Facebook and Twitter, therefore, can rearticulate the ways in which rural communities construct their identity. This process involves the public posting of (and response to) various experiences and understanding of, interests and investments in and questions and concerns about rural community, identity and social relations. Take, for example, a picture of a rural landscape. As a picture, it does not necessarily foster a sense of rural community and identity but does more so when posted onto a social media platform, such as Facebook, for individuals to collectively reminisce and construct an identity onto it through the posting of comments.

In this respect, practices of constructing rural identity online are a product of what van Dijck (2013: 402) calls 'the culture of connectivity … where perspectives, expressions, experiences and productions are increasingly mediated by social media'. In other words, constructions of rurality online are informed by residents' discourses and the localised spatial meaning given to specific posts through the way residents comment on and share such posts. And as van Dijck (2013) has stressed, as part of a wider networked techno-culture rural community does not disappear but rather carries on through patterns of interaction that are co-constitutionally enmeshed in technological systems commonly designed to inscribe particular social and cultural interests.

Given the increasingly pervasive character of this culture of connectivity, it has become commonplace for people to use social media to construct virtual versions of physical rural communities. Like physical rural communities, the construction of online rural communities has social implications, such as the production of exclusive and exclusionary boundaries. Despite perceptions that the advent of virtual rural communities has blurred the boundaries of insiders and outsiders, they have continued to facilitate them. For instance, when creating community groups on social media platforms such as Facebook, community membership can be either open or closed, therefore allowing those with greater vested interest in the community to actively deny access to individuals unrecognised by other community members.

Consequentially, this enables digital rural spaces to become the same conflictual social world (Woods 2007) as their physical counterparts, wherein the longer-standing residents compete for hegemony and exclude those who operate outside of the boundary of that particular space. In this sense, online rural community forums (although the argument can be made for other community forums) can be viewed as sites of struggle to protect and maintain the existing norms and practices of the community from the illicit intrusion and contamination of 'outsiders'. In the context of this study, I understand Facebook interactions to be potential practices that may seek to establish a specific configuration of ruralised meaning and, hence, a specific identity. Further, I also argue that these interactions performed online to partake in the ever-ongoing constitution of what rurality and rural areas are and how they are used to protect and maintain rural identity from widening social change (e.g. migration) have the ability to exclude (and victimise) particular members of the community who want to join the community forum (specifically minority ethnic members).

Methods

My primary interest was to explore how rurality was defined and redefined online and how place-making via a social media platform by long-term residents gave rise to constructions of a rural identity that excluded and in some incidents overtly victimised minority ethnic residents from belonging within a specific digitised rural space. To do this, this chapter presents findings that were collected as part of a larger self-funded ethnographic study which was conducted from September 2013 to November 2014 that sought to examine how a rural community resisted processes of social change and the exclusionary and racist consequences this had for minority ethnic residents. As part of the study, I chose to study and observe the interactions of a Facebook community forum from a small rural town in the south of England that I have decided to call Brickington and the ways in which the online community communicated and constructed ruralised meaning to/from the commenting on and posting of certain images and ideas about the town. My decision to focus on the Facebook platform was because of its ability to enable different types of social practices, voices and identities (Kavada 2012). For instance, Facebook, as one of the largest social networking services worldwide, is built around ideologies of sharing information and liking information provided by others (van Dijck 2013). This means Facebook allows users the opportunity of setting up 'groups' to connect with others around specific vested interests. These 'groups' can furnish their own profiles with information and pictures, such as a cover photo placed as a banner on the top of the profile page. They can also be public, closed or secret, and users can apply for membership to take part in the sharing of information within the group. Furthermore, groups allow users to post content as well as like, share or comment on the posts of others. They also have the power to remove posts and block users. In this respect, Facebook groups can be useful platforms to analyse and study racism as they have the ability to become quite exclusive, with the commenting on and posting particular images and issues creating exclusionary and potentially hostile consequences for more diverse voices (Kavada 2012).

Typically, studies of online rural communities have tended to examine how rural residents discuss and debate local political issues impacting their area (see Lundgren and Johansson 2017). I have however primarily viewed the online communication in terms of, what Michael Woods (2003) calls the 'politics of the rural'. In other words, the way in which rurality itself is defined and redefined by people's interactions online. By studying the construction of the rural that emerged as a result of networking within the Brickington community Facebook group, I wish to shed light on how meaning around rurality was constituted in this context. What specific digital practices were used? What discourses were employed? And to what extent does this enable racism and victimisation for minority ethnic residents participating within this particular space?

The Brickington community forum Facebook group was selected for analysis because the town had established their Facebook presence relatively recently—in 2012—as a result of the ongoing changes happening in the area such as population growth and housing developments. The data presented in the sections below were collected using netnography. Netnography is described as 'direct and participant observational research rooted in online fieldwork' (Kozinets 2009: 54). It uses computer-mediated communications as a source of data to arrive at the ethnographic understanding of the cultural and social representations of online communities. Therefore, just like traditional ethnographies that will extend organically from the basis of observation to include other elements such as participation, archival data collection, extended historical case analysis and videography to capture naturalistic data, netnography employs a range of approaches to capture the importance of computer-mediated communications and the symbols and signs of the lives of community members online. From here, I employed a thematic analysis (Braun and Clarke 2006) on the data collected. Coding was done within a social constructionist framework and using standard Microsoft Word document and 'track changes'. This involved highlighting text (e.g. phrases and words) which were considered important to the overarching aims and objectives of the study. Superordinate themes were drawn from abductive theorising where key concepts were taken from the literature (e.g. rural identity, community, social media, online) and naturally drawn from the data (e.g. racism, exclusion, belonging/lack of belonging, securing rurality).

There is an ongoing discussion about research ethics in relation to online materials (Fossheim and Ingierd 2015). In this study, I have studied and observed a community group which was 'public', meaning that their content could be accessed without asking for membership. Data from the group are available via Facebook. Nevertheless, while the content published online is publicly accessible, it can still be perceived as private by some users. For this reason, I have elected to use pseudonyms when referring to the Facebook group and the names of individual users. This is important given quotes of posts were considered to be of a sensitive nature, such as those containing explicit accounts of racism.

Findings

What was evident throughout the data analysed was the emergence of two explicit superordinate themes: (i) the re-representation of rurality online and (ii) accounts of racism experienced by minority ethnic individuals who attempted to engage in digital rural spaces. In relation to the first theme, the posting, commenting and sharing of links and images related to geographical space enabled the Brickington community Facebook group to be charged with a particular type of power relations, a power relation which Doreen Massey (1994) identified as 'spatial power'. That is, the posting and commenting on of images were done primarily by those longer-term residents who saw themselves as 'guardians' of the towns in order to maintain and protect the boundaries around which local rural identity was defined within (and indeed outside) the digital sphere.

However, the spatially invested power relations that were used to re-represent a sense of local rural identity online within the Brickington community Facebook group worked in very exclusive and exclusionary ways. It not only created exclusive communication between those with a vested interest in the area (e.g. long-term residents seeking to maintain sense of rurality of place), but also it meant that those minority ethnic voices who attempted to engage in the community online through the posting and commenting on of images were challenged as not 'authentic'. In some instances, this challenging of difference within the Brickington community Facebook group became overtly hostile and resulted in the use of racist discourse towards minority ethnic individuals. It is the first theme to which I now turn.

Re-representing Rurality Online

The interactions observed within the Brickington community Facebook group were primarily used to represent and display the rurality of the town, which the literature has called a discourse of 're-representation of rurality' (Lundgren and Johansson 2017). Central to this is the way rurality is sought to be maintained and protected against widening patterns of social change such as austerity and cutbacks leading to increased poverty, migration and the ongoing urbanised expansion of rural areas within the UK due to housing developments and service industry: objects of critical concern for long-term rural residents of Britain. Re-representing the rural online therefore can be seen as a partly conscious strategy to counter notions of place and space perceived to be 'under threat'.

Brickington was a town undergoing major developments and changes. Not only had the population grown dramatically from 9,940 to 11,756, between the 2001 and 2011 British censuses, but there were ongoing developments happening throughout the town such as the arrival of service industries along the High Street and 500 homes planned to be built on green space. One practice that I observed in the pursuit of maintaining a sense of rurality within Brickington on the Facebook group was the posting of photos representing the beauty and strengths of the area; this included photos posted by members or the sharing of news articles. For example, one member, Steven, did not post many pictures himself but shared a large number of local articles or news stories of which many were symbolised by photographs of local landscapes (e.g. the winding roads leading out of the town, the 'red brick' architecture of the area, the thatched cottages tucked away behind the local church and the church itself). Another common re-representing practice was exemplified with the photos that Donna posted. These photos were of a street of stoned-walled houses looking down a steep hill with rolling greens in the background at sunset.

Regardless of the reasons for posting re-representing photographs, the display and portrayal of such photos managed to produce very idyllic symbols of the local countryside area; in other words, they were 'problem-free images' of rural life. As such, they did not revolutionise the ways in which the countryside has been represented before. On the contrary, idyllic representations of rural Britain are very common (Short 1992; Bunce 2003). However, while these photos were sometimes posted to rejoice in rural charms, it was also done to counter the perceived negative changes happening within the town. Thus, by saying the Brickington community Facebook group was re-representing the rurality of the place, I am not implying that completely 'new' imageries were being produced; rather, they were constituting new ways in which to represent the rural identity of the area, namely through a lens of the digital. In this sense, a re-representation of rurality was present in all photographs posted and commented on within the group.

The re-representation of rurality within the Brickington community Facebook group also took seriously the notion of 'active citizens' in the promotion and maintenance of local rural identity. Lundgren and Johansson (2017) suggest that the representation and re-representation of rurality is not subject to structural deterministic images of the countryside (e.g. the spatial markers of the place); rather, rurality is constructed by the agential—that is people choose to display images and text to make sense of the British countryside. Therefore, the digital world can provide the platform for individuals with a particular set of vested interests to mobilise and organise activities to demonstrate a sense of rurality.

There was one clear example of how the Brickington community Facebook group was used to promote upcoming activities and events that paid tribute to the rurality of the area. In June 2014, the group shared a post to invite other members to the event 'Party on the Rec'. Generally, the post worked to signify Brickington as a place of rurality and rural identity. In the example below, for instance, Brickington is articulated as 'beautiful' and with 'rural cheer':

> It's that time of year again! The Party at the Rec is happening tonight. Are you in the town and want to bring with you your rural cheer and dance and have fun amongst the beautiful backdrops of Brickington? If so, please come on down to the Rec area and we'll see you there! (14 June 2014)

This particular post gave the impression that Brickington's rural identity is being actively managed and supports Lundgren and Johansson's (2017) argument that rurality is agentically constructed. In fact, most of the content on the Brickington community Facebook group was posted by the group owners, portraying, although unwittingly, themselves as guardians of the community. The fact that the content was mainly produced by a specific group of members rather than by everybody may also explain the almost total investment in facilitating narratives around local rural identity. A consequence of this re-representation of rurality within the Brickington community Facebook group was that specific groups of people (minority ethnic individuals) were evidently 'othered' and positioned as threatening the identity of the place. It is these exclusionary and racist consequences of constructing rurality online that the next section now turns to.

'What You Doing on Here?': Accounts of Racism

The way Brickington's rural identity was re-represented online gave way to three openly overt racist discourses on the community's Facebook group. Such discourse portrayed minority ethnic individuals as 'other', different and 'out of place in the countryside' (Cloke 2004: 33). This discourse was often used to challenge, criticise and heckle minority ethnic individuals' sense of belonging within the digital space. Posts often seemed to be filled with emotion and anger as in the following posts by two community group members when noticing Piotr, a youngish Polish male had posted a message to the group:

> Now things have gone too far!!!!!!!!!!!!! Why the heck can't the group membership be closed!!!!!!!!!
>
> Fuckin' hell, what are you doing on here!!!!!!!!?????????

In posts like these, racism is not only present in the affected wording but also in the excessive use of exclamation and question marks. While there are examples of explicit racialised discourse in the above extracts, what is interesting is the way processes of place-making by community members on the Facebook group meant that anyone with a perceived difference got recognised and challenged as not being authentically Brickington or 'rural'. This challenging of difference works effectively with Goffman's (1963: 86) concept of civil inattention where community members displayed social recognition and acknowledgement of the presence of diverse others within the boundaries of the Facebook group and that this process of challenging difference or non-normative practices and behaviours was an attempt to maintain a specific way of doing rurality online.

Others used inquisition rather than anger to make their point. Nevertheless, they helped constitute a clear 'Other' narrative towards minority ethnic individuals engaging with the Facebook group, as in the below quote directed towards a Black male of Mauritian decent:

> Hey you, yes you. Do you actually live here? Do you even know where Brickington is? I have lived in the town for 25 years and have only ever seen one Black person. And you are not them!

This quote is typical of the type of fantasy that is at the core of the discourse surrounding the 'whitening of rural space' (Neal 2002: 443). Within this imagining, rural space is contrasted sharply with the characteristics of urban life: whereas urbanity is often conceived as openly multicultural and superdiverse (or in other words, the diversity of diversity) rurality is constructed as an exclusive space that collapses into whiteness, in so much that it becomes what Neal (2002: 443) identifies as the 'haven of white safety'. A place of escape from the superdiverse and multicultural realities of the city. This whitening of rurality has had a long appeal for those on the extreme right in British politics. John Cato (cited in Lowles 2001: 150), for instance, a leading white supremacist who moved from London to a Lincolnshire village, writing in the irregular newsletter *Lebensraum* declared, 'home, gone from the scum and slime that is the nigger saturated London, its outreaches and Britain's other major towns and cities. We do not need to concern ourselves with Blacks, Jews and communists. Or anything that they may fancy and do. Leave them to it. We are supposed to be Aryans, we should begin living as Aryans. As free spirits and men. Then we can reclaim our nation'. It is perhaps these (mis)conceptions of the rural as a 'white space' that render invisible the presence of diverse others within rural spaces and indeed enable the misinformed racialised discourses such as those exhibited in the extract above to happen.

Furthermore, othering practices were also directed towards minority ethnic individuals who the community members thought should not be using the Facebook group as they did not have the right to stake belonging. This racialised discourse came out in the form of heckling, specially towards those identified as seasonal migrants due to the transient nature of their employment, whereby their presence and activity on the group was ridiculed for not being authentic:

> You don't have a right to comment on posts on here!!!! You are only here during the summer so you can get money and fuck off back to where your (sic) from!!! This group is for locals!!!!!

Nonetheless, what is most striking about the above extract is not necessarily the community member's ridicule of the migrant's authenticity to belong, but rather his use of the 'local' as a discursive category. What this person is doing here is twofold: he is firstly ridiculing and challenging the migrant's stake of belonging to the local community and therefore their credibility in posting questions and information to the Facebook group, and secondly, he is doing so by making assumption that the group is for 'locals only' and that other members know what 'local' means in this particular context. However, this is an unsubstantiated claim to make on part of the community member as the wider rural studies literature has demonstrated that as rural towns and villages grow as a result of globalisation and people are more readily able to access rural environments, the boundaries of who does and who does not belong become increasingly blurred (Chakraborti and Garland 2004; Neal 2009). The Internet revolution and the increased use of social media has only made this more so as people from anywhere in the world can now join and participate in digital communities from the comfort of their own homes; meaning, determining who is and who is not local is little more than a judgement call on the part of those with greatest claims of belonging and vested interest in that specific community.

In summary, this section has outlined that there were three racialised discourses used by community members of the Brickington Facebook group, all of which sought to constitute the re-representation of rurality of the group and challenge and ridicule claims of belonging for minority ethnic individuals who took part within this specific digital space. In this context, Facebook as a platform allowed for the formation of a collective rural identity and for the production of racialised discourses that drew a wedge between the community. Moreover, while there are ongoing discussions within the rural studies literature (e.g. Woods 2007) about the 'death of rural community' in light of the Internet, the data cited in this chapter has demonstrated that online communities do not operate within a vacuum. Instead, they are digitised forms of the same social relations happening within the physical world. In the following section, therefore, I want to turn to a discussion around the threatened and enduring nature of rural space: a discussion that maintains that while the Internet has changed the way ruralities are constructed and maintained, they and the racial tension that exist within these spaces are still very much alive.

Doing Rurality Online

A common perception of rurality is that it is seemingly being eroded. This idea of a moribund countryside has been a constant narrative within the rural sociological literature, particularly within a British context. Within these narrates, the British countryside has often been romanticised and worked up as providing security against the risks of contemporary society (with technological social change being one of them) and offers the same organic social relations of the past which the twenty-first century is less willing to provide.

However, as the data cited throughout this chapter have maintained, the increased use of social media has not facilitated this 'death of rural community' narrative in Brickington. In fact, use of social media provided a tangential but nevertheless connected narrative, a narrative built around the enduring appeal of rurality. This narrative claims that as social change creeps in and changes the socio-spatial dynamism of rural areas, it also aids its continuity as individuals look for alternative means and resources in which to anchor their sense of identity. In this sense then, the Brickington community Facebook group was itself 'living proof' that rurality and constructions of rural identity continue to exist even when social relations are dislocated from the physical world to the digital world. The Facebook activity therefore—posts, photos, comments and links to news media articles—all contributed to the impression that there was a vivid sense of rurality within the town.

As the data already cited in this chapter denoted, this was achieved through a discourse of the re-representation of rurality. Community members used the Brickington Facebook group to illustrate the rural identity of the area through the posting, commenting on and sharing of photos of local landscapes or community events to create positive images of the rurality of the area that implicitly countered more negative changes happening in the town. However, such re-representation practices had very explicit exclusionary and racist consequences for minority ethnic individuals who attempted to engage on the Brickington Facebook group. In this, there were three types of racialised discourses used to challenge minority ethnic individuals' stake of belonging to the group. The first was through the direct challenge of the person's authenticity to the place (e.g. Charlotte and Kris's posts). The second was through the perpetuation of rurality as 'spaces of whiteness' (Neal 2002: 443) where community members such as Jacob were shocked at the presence of Black minorities using the Facebook group, and the third was through the questioning of the legitimacy of a minority ethnic individual's ability to use the Facebook group because of the precarious and transient nature of their employment.

Conclusion

This chapter highlighted how social media platforms such as Facebook, Twitter and YouTube have the ability to (re)constitute spaces of rurality that, rather than see the diminution of rural identities and communities over time due to technological social change, strengthen the identities of rural communities in which social media platforms become used to anchor community members sense of belonging and exclude those 'others' who do not fit within the boundary of such identity work. While previous studies (e.g. Jay 1992; Derbyshire 1994; Nizhar 1996; De Lima 2001; Chakraborti and Garland 2004; Neal 2009; Plastow 2011) have examined the targeted hostility, violence, hate crimes, victimisation and vulnerability of minority ethnic groups based on their perceived difference in rural areas, the central proposal of this chapter has been to explore whether the same incidences of racism that happened offline also occur online, and how such digital constructs of rurality (although I would argue the same can be said about online urban communities) resembled Massey's (2004) notion of place and space as 'relational entities'.

The chapter also shed light on rural community dynamics (e.g. close-knit social relations, the romanticism of rural space and the conflation of rurality with notions of security, familiarity and cultural sameness) that influenced experiences and perceptions of racist 'othering', fear of racist harassment and accounts of victimisation amongst minority ethnic individuals living in rural areas within previous studies can all be seen happening within the digital sphere also. It can be argued, therefore, that these constructions of rurality that help reinforce romanticised ideas of the British countryside being convivial (Neal 2009) and 'problem-free' (Chakraborti and Garland 2004) and which, in turn, can create exclusive hostile environments for minority ethnic groups can all be mapped digitally in the context of rural community Facebook groups.

While my study has indicated that the experiences of minority ethnic individuals living in rural areas are the same online as it would be offline, there is a key limitation to the research. Because this study was part of a larger ethnographic project, it only provides a snapshot and a rather limited and static account of how racist practices emerged out of digital constructions of rurality. Netnography research on a larger scale across multiple online 'field sites' would benefit not only the transferability and confirmability of this study's findings, but also help in furthering our knowledge on the influence of social media in (re)constituting the boundaries around which rurality is defined and how this further perpetuates the exclusion and racism of particular social groups (e.g. minority ethnic individuals).

References

Berry, C., Kim, S., & Spigel, L. (2010). *Electronic Everywheres: Media, Technology and the Experience of Social Space*. Minneapolis: University of Minnesota Press.

Braun, V., & Clarke, V. (2006). Using thematic analysis in psychology. *Qualitative Research in Psychology, 3*(2), 77–101.

Brown, C. (1984). *Black and White Britain*. London: Policy Studies Institute.

Bunce, M. (2003). Reproducing rural idylls. In P. Cloke (Ed.), *Country Visions*. Harlow: Pearson.

Chakraborti, N., & Garland, J. (2004). *Rural Racism*. London: Willan.

Clancy, A., Hough, M., Aust, R., & Kershaw, C. (2001). *Crime, Policing, Justice and the Experience of Ethnic Minorities: Findings from the 2000 British Crime Survey*. London: Home Office.

Cloke, P. (2004). Rurality and racialised others: Out of place in the countryside. In N. Chakraborti & J. Garland (Eds.), *Rural Racism* (pp. 17–35). London: Willan.

Couldry, N., & McCarthy, A. (2004). *MediaSpace: Place, Scale and Culture in the Media Age*. London: Routledge.

Cumming, D., & Johan, S. (2010). The differential impact of the internet on spurring on regional entrepreneurship. *Entrepreneurship Theory & Practice, 34*(5), 857–883.

Daniel, W. (1966). *Racial Discrimination in England*. Harmondsworth: Penguin.

Dargan, L., & Shucksmith, M. (2008). LEADER and Innovation. *Sociologia Ruralis, 48*(3), 274–291.

De Lima, P. (2001). *Needs Not Numbers: An Exploration of Ethnic Minorities Communities in Scotland*. London: Commission for Racial Equality and Community Development Foundation.

Derbyshire, H. (1994). *Not in Norfolk: Tackling the Invisibility of Racism*. Norfolk: Norwich and Norfolk Racial Equality Council.

Falkheimer, J., & Jansson, A. (2006). *Geographies of Communication: The Spatial Turn in Media Studies*. Nordicom: Goteborg.

Fossheim, H., & Ingierd, H. (2015). *Internet Research Ethics*. Oslo: Cappelen Damm.

Goffman, E. (1963). *Stigma: Notes on the Management of Spoiled Identity*. London: Penguin.

Giddens, A. (1984). *The Constitution of Society: Towards a Theory of Structuration*. Cambridge: Polity.
Harvey, D. (1989). *The Condition of Postmodernity: An Enquiry into the Origins of Cultural Change*. London: Wiley.
Home Office. (1981). *Racial Attacks*. London: Home Office.
James, J. (2014). *The Internet and the Google Age*. Dublin: Research Publishing.
Jay, E. (1992). *Keep them in Birmingham*. London: Commission for Racial Equality.
Johnson, P., & Chandler, T. (2015). Mechanisms of power in rural planning. *Journal of Rural Studies, 40,* 12–20.
Kavada, A. (2012). Engagement, bonding and identity across multiple platforms: Avaaz on Facebook, YouTube and MySpace. *Media & Culture, 52,* 28–48.
Kozinets, R. (2009). *Netnography: Doing Ethnographic Research Online*. London: Sage.
Leszczynski, A. (2015). Spatial media/tion. *Progress in Human Geography, 39*(6), 721–751.
Lowles, N. (2001). *White Riot: The Violent Story of Combat*. Bury: Milo Books.
Lundgren, A., & Johansson, A. (2017). Digital rurality: Producing the countryside in online struggles for rural survival. *Journal of Rural Studies, 51,* 73–82.
Massey, D. (1994). *Space, Place and Gender*. Cambridge: Polity Press.
Massey, D. (2004). Geographies of responsibility. *Series B, Human Geography, 86*(1), 5–18.
Modood, T. (1997). Fourth National Survey of Ethnic Minorities. In T. Modood, R. Berthoud, J. Lakey, J. Nazroo, P. Smith, S. Virdee, & S. Beishon (Eds.), *Ethnic Minorities in Britain: Diversity and Disadvantage* (pp. 1–21). London: Policy Studies Institute.
Neal, S. (2009). *Rural Identities: Ethnicity and Community in the Contemporary English Countryside*. Surrey: Ashgate.
Neal, S. (2002). Rural landscapes, representations and racism: Examining multicultural citizenship and policy-making in the English countryside. *Ethnic & Racial Studies, 25*(3), 442–461.
Nizhar, P. (1996). *No Problem? Race Issues in Shropshire*. Telford: Race Equality Forum for Telford and Shropshire.
Plastow, B. (2011). *Suppressing the Diversity of the 'Other': The Nature, Extent, and Impact of Racism Experienced by Visible Ethnic Minorities in Rural Scotland'* (PhD thesis). Leicester, UK: University of Leicester.

Pollard, I. (1989). Pastoral interludes. *Third Text, 7*, 41–46.

Rice, A. (2014). The gendered search to connect: Females and social media in rural Ireland. In J. J. Dublin (Ed.), *The Internet and the Google Age* (pp. 51–61). Research Publishing.

Robinson, V., & Valeny, R. (2004). Ethnic minorities, employment, self-employment and social mobility in post-war Britain. In S. Teles & T. Moodod (Eds.), *Race, Ethnicity and Public Policy in the UK and US* (pp. 54–76). Cambridge: Cambridge University Press.

Short, B. (1992). *The English Rural Community: Images and Analysis.* Cambridge: Cambridge University Press.

Shucksmith, M. (2010). Disintegrated rural development? Neo-endogenous rural development, planning and place shaping in diffused power contexts. *Sociologia Ruralis, 50*(1), 1–14.

Skerratt, S., & Steiner, A. (2013). Working with communities-of-place: Complexities of empowerment. *Land Economy, 28*(3), 320–338.

Smith, D. P. (1974). *Racial Disadvantage in Britain.* Harmondsworth: Penguin.

Solomos, J. (2006). Foreword. In J. Solomos & S. Neal (Eds.), *The New Countryside?* (viii–x). Bristol: Polity Press.

van Dijck, J. (2013). *The Culture of Connectivity: A Critical History of Social Media.* Oxford: University of Oxford Press.

Virdee, S. (1997). Racial harassment. In T. Modood, R. Berthoud, J. Lakey, J. Nazroo, P. Smith, S. Virdee, & S. Beishon (Eds.), *Ethnic Minorities in Britain: Diversity and Disadvantage* (pp. 21–56). London: Policy Studies Institute.

Woods, M. (2003). Deconstructing rural protest: Emergence of a new social movement. *Journal of Rural Studies, 19,* 309–325.

Woods, M. (2007). Engaging the global countryside. *Progress in Human Geography, 31*(4), 495–507.

Part IV

Responding to, Regulating and Policing Online Hate

Karen Lumsden and Emily Harmer

Editors' Introduction

This final part of the book focuses on the questions of how we should respond to, regulate, and police online spaces, and investigate and prosecute in relation to instances of online hate and abuse. Social media corporations have typically been slow to act and respond to user concern regarding toxic online cultures, hate speech and abuse, while police agencies are faced with an ever-changing socio-technical landscape in terms of emerging social media technologies and apps. Questions also abound about how to respond to reports of technologically facilitated crime and abuse. The emergence and expansion of cybercrime has generated numerous debates and tensions over how it can be defined, what the scale of the problem is and who should be responsible for dealing with it (Wall 2008). Researchers have argued that there is little consistency in the policing of criminal activities which involve digital technology (Holt et al. 2015; Brenner 2008). Moreover, police have not adapted to deal with the complexity and volume of interpersonal cybercrime such as online abuse, revenge pornography and domestic incidents (Laville 2016). The police response to victims of technologically mediated interpersonal cybercrime (i.e. in relation to domestic abuse and stalking) has also been criticised for victim-blaming (see Black, Lumsden and Hadlington, this volume).

Therefore, the chapters in this final part focus on the societal response to 'online othering'; for example, through police responses, the role of social media corporations and Internet businesses, and also the development of policies, laws and legislation. The chapter by Jo Smith also provides an important insight into the ways in which women who have experienced or witnessed online misogyny respond to and resist this form of online abuse. We see how understandings and analyses of 'online othering' must also account for the agency of social actors who may be at the receiving end of these behaviours and online interactions. The concept of 'online othering' does not deny agency to individuals but acknowledges that agency can be oppositional. Sameness and difference should not be seen as essentialist categories; rather, 'difference is always a product of history, culture, power, and ideology. Differences occur between and among groups and must be understood in terms of the specificity of their production' (McLaren 1994: 126). Resistance to 'online othering' takes various forms and 'the margin' can also be a site of resistance (Jensen 2011). Examples of resistance (discussed in the Introduction to this book) include Twitter hashtags, campaigns and feminist activism online. Notable examples include the viral #MeToo Movement of 2017, a movement against sexual harassment and sexual assault, and the #EverydaySexism Project which includes a website (set up by Laura Bates in 2012) and Twitter page, both of which catalogue instances of sexism experienced on an everyday basis across the globe.

For example, Jo Smith's chapter in this part focuses on the various ways in which women have responded to instances of online misogyny, including reporting these and/or resisting them via fight responses and 'digilante' actions. She argues that the policing and prosecution of online misogyny is further complicated by the nature of online space, calls to respect freedom of speech, limited legislative provisions, and ambiguity over whether these behaviours are indeed 'criminal'. By providing a detailed overview of the legislative provisions and prosecution guidance for online communications offences in England and Wales,

Smith offers an insight into the ways in which online misogyny might be formally policed by the authorities and social media corporations. She then draws on findings from her research with women who have experienced or witnessed instances of online misogyny. While there is much to be said about online misogyny as behaviour which disempowers and silences women, Smith's chapter gives us an important insight into how women have confronted these acts of abuse and found ways to empower themselves and other women online. In this sense, 'othering' is agential and we see how spaces are available through which to resist and respond to experiences of 'online othering' such as online misogyny.

Philippa Hall's chapter analyses the 'online othering' of disabled people via hate speech on social media platforms. In this chapter, online disability hate speech is analysed through an examination of the Internet's political economy, and also via an analysis of the online/offline distinction. Hall argues that social and legal initiatives to confront online disability hate speech must address and contend with Internet companies' business imperatives including the quest for profit. She argues that the tendency to conceptualise online and offline as distinct 'space' further legitimises calls for the continued deregulation of online space/s in relation to disability hate speech. The chapter also examines the ways in which social and legal reform, such as the UK Crown Prosecution Service's definition of online platforms as public spaces, can reimagine the online/offline distinction and offer avenues through which we can address disability hate speech.

O'Shea, Julian, Prichard and Kelty's chapter draws on two bodies of literature from psychology and information technology to examine how cyberstalking is investigated by the police in Australia. In particular, they consider whether risk assessments for offline stalking, such as the Stalking Risk Profile, are suitable in an online context. The authors argue that for police investigators and prosecutors to be proactive in the policing of cyberstalking, risk assessments must constantly adapt to changing technologies and their implications for interpersonal relationships. By demonstrating a distinction between digital natives and digital immigrants (Prensky 2001), they explore the way in which the police understanding of Internet development and technological advancements impacts on the investigation and prosecution of cyberstalking. Their discussion draws on findings from interviews with police investigators and prosecutors on the challenges for policing cyberstalking, including legislation and risk assessment.

The final chapter of this volume by Alex Black, Karen Lumsden and Lee Hadlington discusses police officer and civilian staff views of reports of interpersonal cybercrime in England. The authors demonstrate how police officers construct notions of the 'ideal victim' (Christie 1986) of online crime, and how this frames their response to public reports of online harassment and cybercrime. The police response results in victim-blaming of online users who are viewed as making themselves vulnerable to cybercrime and hate via their occupation of particular virtual spaces, and their refusal to withdraw from these social spaces (i.e. via police advice to victims to 'just block them'). The authors argue that a substantial reframing of police support for victims of online crime is urgently required in order to acknowledge the serious ramifications of online hate, and to go beyond common-sense assumptions that victimisation in 'the virtual world' is less serious or consequential than it is in relation to what are deemed to be 'traditional' offline crimes. In a similar vein to the other chapters in this part, Lumsden, Black and Hadlington suggest that this online/offline dichotomy must be challenged so that police and agencies can effectively support victims of (interpersonal) cybercrime.

In sum, the chapters in this final part of the book propose that a substantial reframing of state and police support for victims of online crime is urgently required, in order to recognise the serious ramifications of online hate, and to go beyond common-sense assumptions that victimisation in 'the virtual world' is less serious or impactful than it is in relation to traditional offline crimes. This online/offline dichotomy must be challenged so that police and agencies can effectively support victims of cybercrime.

References

Brenner, S. W. (2008). *Cyberthreats: The Emerging Fault Lines of the Nation State.* New York: Oxford University Press.

Christie, N. (1986). The ideal victim. In E. A. Fattah (Ed.), *From Crime Policy to Victim Policy* (pp. 17–30). Basingstoke: Palgrave Macmillan.

Holt, T., Bossler, A., & Seigfried-Spellar, K. (2015). *Cybercrime and Digital Forensics: An Introduction.* Abingdon, Oxon: Routledge.

Jensen, S. Q. (2011). Othering, identity formation and agency. *Qualitative Studies, 2*(2), 63–78.

Laville, S. (2016). Online abuse: 'Existing laws too fragmented and don't serve victims'. *The Guardian.* Accessed April 16, 2018. https://www.theguardian.com/uk-news/2016/mar/04/online-abuse-existing-laws-too-fragmented-and-dont-serve-victims-says-police-chief.

McLaren, P. (1994). White terror and oppositional agency. In D. T. Goldberg (Ed.), *Multiculturalism: A Critical Reader.* Oxford: Blackwell.

Prensky, M. (2001, October). Digital natives, digital immigrants. *On the Horizon, 9*(5), 1–6. NCB University Press.

Wall, D. S. (2008). Cybercrime, media and insecurity: The shaping of public perceptions of cybercrime. *International Review of Law, Computers & Technology, 22*(1–2), 45–63.

12

'When I Saw Women Being Attacked … It Made Me Want to Stand Up and Fight': Reporting, Responding to, and Resisting Online Misogyny

Jo Smith

Introduction

With the interweaving of our on and offline lives, the Internet has increasingly become a site in which we can engage in discussion and debate with others. Whilst usually remaining civil, there are occasions when the conversations and comments become abusive: aggressive, threatening, offensive, and often sexually and physically violent in content. For women—and particularly feminist women—on the receiving end of this 'online gendered hate', participation in virtual spaces and online conversations is made risky by these abusive missives. Policing and prosecuting these behaviours are made more challenging by anonymity online, arguments that free speech should prevail, limited legislative provisions, and ambiguity over the extent to which these behaviours are or should be criminalised.

J. Smith (✉)
Department of Sociology, University of Surrey,
Guildford, UK

A body of research is beginning to explore online gendered hate, drawing on hate crime studies (Citron 2014; Lewis et al. 2016) and feminist works examining power and control, public space, and violence against women (Jane 2014a, b; Megarry 2014; Mantilla 2015; Lumsden and Morgan 2017). Central to most of this research is the idea that online gendered hate is a means by which women and their behaviour can be controlled and 'kept in check'. This occurs through the creation of fear, shame, and distress, by making online spaces intolerable to occupy and by having offline consequences in women's lives. Women have reported experiencing adverse effects on their mental health, cancelling work engagements, and feeling fearful for the safety of themselves and their families (Lewis 2011; Sierra 2014; Mantilla 2015).

Jane's recent examination of responses to cyberhate has allowed her to propose a taxonomy of ways in which women respond to receiving this abuse: metaphorical 'flight or fight' responses. Under 'flight' responses are four actions: distancing oneself from the abuse, rationalising the abuse to make it less personal, restricting Internet use, and engaging in 'technological hygiene' by setting boundaries around technology use (2017b: 50). These responses are noted throughout academic works in this field (Citron 2014; Jane 2014a; Mantilla 2015; Lewis et al. 2016). 'Fight' responses, on the other hand, include confronting the abusers, traditional activism (such as signing petitions and supporting other targets), performance activism (creatively subverting the cyberhate), and digital vigilante ('digilante') activism (Jane 2017b: 51). In addition, reporting to the police and to social media sites can be seen as fight responses. As Jane notes, the deployment of different responses may be contextual, with some proving more effective, appropriate, or safe depending on the particular situation (Jane 2017b: 53). Furthermore, women may adopt several different responses or may vary how they respond at different times.

The data presented in this chapter draws on findings from a larger research project exploring different facets of feminist women's experiences of online gendered hate. Data have been collected using online focus groups and online interviews with 26 self-identifying feminist women in the UK. These participants have either experienced online gendered hate directly (e.g. having received abuse themselves) or have encountered this indirectly, seeing or reading about it happening to other women online. The research seeks to provide a space for the voices of this second group of women, usually overlooked in the popular and academic discourse around online gendered hate, and in doing so has found that the impact of online gendered hate goes beyond those immediately targeted.

In the accounts gathered, most participants in both groups described the flight responses that they had engaged in. The 'message' of hate had been conveyed directly to women who were the targets of the abuse and had subsequently spread from these initial targets to other women occupying the virtual spaces around them. However, it was not only these controlling and constraining flight responses which were evident; participants from across the study also described various fight actions that they had taken.

This chapter will begin with a brief summary of the data collection upon which the findings are based, including reflection on some of the ethical decisions taken during this research. Moving on, the chapter will examine how participants discussed their engagement four forms of fight responses. The first two, reporting to the police and reporting to with social media sites were seen as unlikely to result in action being taken. The second two approaches considered one-on-one engagement with the perpetrators of online gendered hate, and digilante action was seen as having both potential and pitfalls.

Methods

Adopting a feminist methodological approach, in which women's voices are centred and emphasis is placed on seeking to transform women's lives (Oakley 1981; Cook and Fanow 1990; Burgess-Proctor 2015) this research sought to gather the experiences of women who had encountered online gendered hate directly or indirectly. Twenty-six participants were recruited via purposive and snowball sampling techniques; direct contact with women who might be interested in participating, recruiting further participants from those who had become involved in the research, and through advertising in a number of women-only communities on Facebook. Each of the participants identified as a woman, and a feminist, or feminist-sympathising,[1] was aged over 18 years old and lived in the UK. The decisions around recruitment were made with careful consideration given to the safety of participants and to me as a researcher. Approaches made to women to ask if they would participate were undertaken cautiously through the use of careful language, having in mind the risk of 'triggering' memories of the abuse that the women had experienced. The research was advertised in private spaces to avoid the risk of the perpetrators of online gendered hate discovering the project and trying to disrupt or infiltrate the data collection, and to minimise the risk of becoming a target myself. However, the restrictive approach to recruitment meant that inevitably some women could not be accessed; particularly those women who had removed themselves completely from online spaces as a result of experiencing online gendered hate.

Reporting to the Police

> … if someone threatens to rape me I would want that taken as just as seriously regardless of whether than was emailed to me, said to me face to face, written to me in a letter, said to me on Twitter, said to me on Facebook. (Cleo T.)

Despite some high profile successes in policing online abuse (*Guardian* 2014, 2015; Rawlinson 2017), only a few of the participants in this research had attempted to use the criminal justice system as a means of responding to online gendered hate. Where such attempts had been made, the experience had been disheartening and had discouraged them from adopting this form of response in the future, reflecting findings from other research (Mantilla 2015; Eckert 2017).

Kate S. had had the most extensive experience of reporting to the police, having made many reports of the abuse she had received. Her account set out the dismissal and lack of interest she experienced from the police on all but two occasions. Her specific experiences of reporting serious abusive content and then being told that nothing would be done had directly shaped her disillusionment with the effectiveness of reporting to the police, and her willingness to report further. She said there had been 'about 40 or 50 other ones that I've reported that they've done nothing about or that they've just said "oh that Twitter account is closed now"'. Other participants who received abuse echoed this sense that nothing would be done:

> *Charlotte B.*: There is so much abuse that goes on online I guess I just sort of thought to myself 'is anything going to be done about this, probably not, probably not' and I think the only way it would have been done is if it did escalate to offline.

This perception that the police would not take online gendered hate seriously was accounted for in different ways by the participants: a belief that the legislation available to prosecute offenders of online gendered hate was limited, that the challenges posed to police online hate restricted police capacity to properly respond, and because the police did not properly understand the nature of online gendered hate. Having experience of the failures of policing provided participants with support to warrant such beliefs, but even those women who lacked the direct experience held these perceptions; it is understandable why, in such circumstances, women might turn to other fight responses to contend with online gendered hate.

Whilst legislation exists in England and Wales to criminalise abusive online behaviours (see Bakalis 2018), guidance from the Crown Prosecution Service cautions that obscene, indecent and offensive communications will be 'subject to a high evidential threshold and in many cases a prosecution is unlikely to be in the public interest' (CPS 2016). Participants were concerned about the limitations of the legislative provisions and the impact that this had on whether the police are likely to investigate online gendered hate. Legislation was viewed as not fit for purpose, outdated, and incapable of taking into account the extent to which the Internet formed an important part of people's everyday lives. Although improvements to laws were not seen as the only way of improving policing responses to gendered online abuse, the symbolic value of legislating against this behaviour was noted. This mirrors broader academic discourse around the importance of laws in making clear the lines between acceptable and unacceptable behaviours (Dixon and Gadd 2006; Mason-Bish 2011).

Participants also attributed the failure to police online gendered hate to the challenges of policing the Internet. For some, the issues highlighted were more 'structural', with an acknowledgement that the police are under-resourced, understaffed, and lacking in the appropriate knowledge needed to investigate online offences. Participants believed that the police struggle both in not knowing how to investigate online gendered hate, and in not being able to keep up with the fast-paced nature of technological change:

> *Jacqui C*: [My child] is being given lessons in how to stay safe online and he's bringing that home and telling me about it. And he's picking holes in the things they are telling him because he knows that doesn't work … I mean the police, when they came and talked to them last time about not sending dick pics, because teenagers do that kind of thing now, they didn't mention Snapchat because they didn't know about it …

Technological change is linked to a further challenge to policing the Internet: the nature of online space. Some participants noted how the prevalence of online offending, the difficulties establishing which jurisdiction is responsible for undertaking the investigation, and the difficulties added by anonymity made it harder for police to deal with online offending. Others were concerned by the ways in which attitudes towards online gendered hate may result in this not being taken and policed seriously. Sylvia P. situated policing within wider cultural contexts which served to shape attitudes towards online gendered hate:

> *Sylvia P*: So, I think we need a change of attitude on the police, I think we need a change of attitude on how we look at this stuff as a culture, as I said you know people dismiss abuse online in a way that they would never dismiss it if it happened to them in the street.

Policing has been notoriously problematic when attempting to deal with violence against women, treating this as a 'private' matter

(Russell and Light 2006) rather than 'proper' police work (Loftus 2010: 5). Together with hate crimes, crimes of violence against women are seen as low-status crimes, lacking the excitement and action of 'proper' police work (Bowling 1998; Loftus 2010). Negative attitudes and a lack of interest in these offences can undermine women's willingness to engage with policing and despite attempts to improve the way that police deal with vulnerable victims of crime, this remains a problem in a number of areas of the UK (HMIC 2017).

The final explanation given by participants as to why police do not take online gendered hate seriously is centred on the perception that police do not properly understand the nature and seriousness of these behaviours. When Sylvia P. talked about the police, she stated:

> *Sylvia P.*: Ungenerously they don't give a shit because it happens all the time because it's normal, because women receiving death threats online for talking about feminism is the normality. In a way that somebody pulling a knife on somebody in club is not.

Sylvia P.'s perception was that the police see online gendered hate as normal and as such not as problematic or as 'real' a crime as other behaviours. This situation may be exacerbated where women—perceiving that police will not understand the seriousness or harm of their experiences of online abuse—choose not to report to the police unless the matter is very serious, thus reaffirming the conceptualisation that online gendered hate consists only of the most serious threats. The reality, from participants' experience, is that the abuse they have received or encountered is much broader; a continuum including 'high-level' acts of threatening sexual and physical violence, doxing[2] and 'swatting,'[3] as well as "lower-level" behaviours such as mocking, name calling, time-wasting, and belittling 'brushed off as playful banter' (Claire H.).

As several participants noted, the police and the justice system do not understand the significance of the lower-level abusive behaviours. They underestimate the harm that can come from the cumulative impact of repeated exposure to the 'less serious' forms of online gendered hate. Women's experiences make visible these harms and provide insight into this phenomenon which the police are perceived to lack.

This is aggravated when approaches to policing treat individual events as discrete and thus overlook the cumulative effects of low-level offending, something noted in other studies of online gendered hate and in hate crime work (Chakraborti and Garland 2015; Lewis et al. 2016).

The policing of online gendered hate is complex, made more so because at the 'milder' end of the online gendered hate continuum the behaviours may not amount to criminal offences, being more comparable with 'hate incidents' than 'hate crimes'. Whilst participants were not necessarily suggesting that all forms of online abusive behaviour be categorised as criminal, this does not negate the concerning perceptions that the police would not take seriously any matters that were reported to them. Furthermore, by failing to take seriously the lower-level behaviour because they *may* not amount to a criminal offence the police overlook the cumulative nature of repeated lower-level incidents.

Engaging with Social Media Sites

> You do not see the results [of reporting offensive content to social media sites] sometimes and then you question is this having an effect, is this actually just trying to eat soup with a fork or is it making a difference? (Julia A.)

Most social media sites have user agreements which incorporate rules, codes of conduct, terms of service and community standards: in joining the site, users are agreeing to abide by these and can be subject to sanction if the rules are broken (Facebook 2018a, b; Twitter 2018). In addition, many sites now have information on how to report offensive conduct, and how to take measures to protect oneself (e.g. Instagram 2018a, b; Tumblr 2018).

Unlike the limited attempts made by participants to engage the police when they encountered online abuse, many of them had experience of reporting to the websites on which the behaviour occurred. Whilst a few had been successful in getting abusive content removed (although this was not necessarily in relation to *gendered* hate), many more of the participants reported otherwise: they were either encouraged to take action themselves (by blocking the offensive user or content) or told that the content 'did not violate community standards' (Sophia C.). Participants went on to discuss how social media sites—lacking in accountability, failing to communicate with women about their complaints, having unclear or ambiguous policies around harassment, and being driven by corporate interests—are not merely failing to address online gendered hate, but are providing a fertile ground for its persistence.

Criticisms of the policies and practices regarding harassment and hate abounded during the interviews and focus groups, particularly around the lack of clarity and absence of consistent application. This was pertinently expressed during one focus group[4]:

> *Cath B.*: Facebook is just so … inconsistent. It will delete pictures of breastfeeding as obscene, but allow really nasty stuff
> *Elle B.*: OH NOES A WOMAN'S NIPPLE NUKE EVERYTHING
> *Jill H.*: Knowing there is likely to be an automated dismissal is very off-putting - especially if you are reporting something personal, particularly if it is vile or threatening
> *Cath B.*: I report to Facebook all the time
> *Elle B.*: Have reported to FB and Twitter
> *Cath B.*: And I receive "this didn't violate our standards" all the time
> *Elle B.*: yes, that
> *Jill H.*: yes

Accessing information about the policies and how they are applied is difficult and even when such information has been leaked into the public domain—of note, the training manuals for Facebook to the *Guardian* in 2017 (*Guardian* 2017)—this does not provide clarity. Women reporting online gendered hate, therefore, lack even very straightforward information as to how their complaint will (or will not) be dealt with. Those seeking to make reports are denied sufficient information to assess the value of reporting, and after making the report lack any role within that complaints process.

Although clearly frustrated by the inconstancies and automated dismissals, participants persisted in reporting abusive content. This contrasts dramatically with the disinclination to make reports to the police, and might be understood in the context of the ease in which reports can be made to social media sites, particular as compared to reporting to the police. Social media sites have made reporting easier, in response to criticisms of their handling of abuse within their spaces (see, e.g. Twitter Support 2014, 2015a, b), and reporting to social media sites requires little time or engagement, unlike making a report to the police, which can require one to meet with a police officer, provide a statement, and seek updates on any subsequent investigation.

Participants also discussed the advice often given on social media sites; to block abusive content, a form of flight responses (Jane 2017b). Whilst this could be read as empowering users to take control of the situation they find themselves in, and providing them with the power and a mechanism by which to exert that control, it can also be understood as shifting responsibility for dealing with online gendered hate onto the users and—significantly—away from the social media sites. Whilst blocking offensive content can immediately remove abusive content or users from a person's online space, participants noted some significant issues with this approach.

Blocking a user or offensive content does not stop the abuse, it merely makes it invisible to the target. It does not prevent the perpetrator creating a new account and sending the target further abusive missives. Even when blocked, the perpetrator of the offensive material can continue to post hateful messages, albeit not directly targeted at the recipient of the messages, and others may be able to see it. For some users, having the abusive material 'out of sight, out of mind' may work. However, for others such as Claire H., whose work and reputation is related to her social media profile, there is a need to know what is being said in order to try to limit the damage being caused:

> *Claire H.*: All my friends and family were saying 'stop looking' you know, 'stop reading stuff' and I was just 'I can't, I actually can't because I want to know what is being said about me – this is my reputation, my career'.

Considering online gendered hate more broadly—in its effects on more than simply the specific target of the abuse—blocking is also an ineffective approach to dealing with this behaviour. It does not stop other women encountering the perpetrators of abuse or their messages, because it does nothing to sanction or even engage with those writing the missives. It is an approach which then forces other women seeing the abuse to take steps to protect their own safety by also engaging in these flight responses. Requiring women to 'protect themselves' online emphasises that the responsibility is on women to prevent, stop or avoid violence against them, rather than on the perpetrator to stop acting violently (Maher et al. 2017: 22). By placing responsibility on women to avoid online gendered hate, there is the risk that women will be blamed when they are targeted, if they fail to adopt the flight responses, for failing to take steps to avoid the abuse and (if they engage in fight responses) for bringing the abuse on themselves for acting provocatively.

Overall, participants felt that social media site responses to online gendered hate were generally inadequate and that the sites had a responsibility to the users in a way that they were currently not taking seriously. In one particularly apt quote, Sylvia P. said:

> *Sylvia P.*: If I was in a nightclub and somebody came up and threatened me with a knife and a bouncer saw them, then they would be out of that club on their arse really quickly. Because the nightclub doesn't want to get a reputation of allowing that sort of violence on their premises. And if they do allow that violence on their premises and they don't do anything about it, then they could be held liable, particularly if it was an employee for failing to protect those people because they have a duty of care to them in their space. I do not understand why that does not get applied online …

This is reflected in the approach taken by Pavan, who highlights the ways in which Internet intermediaries, including 'participative networking platforms' (2017: 63) play a role in gender-based violence online. In arguing that these sites can act to try to prevent online gendered hate from happening, Pavan emphasises the need to assign some responsibility to the websites themselves. In her analysis, websites are 'free agents', lacking any obligation to disavow or try to prevent online gendered hate beyond the limited legal obligations that they are subject to.

This immunity turns into impunity argues Pavan (2017: 71), mirroring Sylvia P.'s comments above. Whilst engaging with social media sites was at this time seen as a relatively futile approach to dealing with online gendered hate, many of the participants still saw a role for social media as part of a multi-faceted approach to addressing online gendered hate. However, to properly engage with that role would require improvements to the strategies employed by social media sites.

One-on-One Engagement

> Someone's got to, someone has got to be the people countering these stupid misogynists. (Cath B.)

Jane notes that one-on-one engagement with the perpetrators of online gendered hate can be undertaken publicly or privately, and can involve confrontation by way of argument, counter-abuse, comedy, or appeals to the good nature of the attacker (2017b: 51). Within this study engagement with the perpetrators of abuse was discussed in terms of public engagement with perpetrators and was affected by two main factors: an assessment of the potential benefits of intervention (to themselves or to another actor within the situation), and an assessment of the risks.

For those participants who had been the recipients of abuse, the value of engagement was potentially high. This was apparent in Claire H.'s comments about her response to receiving abuse:

> *Claire H.*: I wanted to set the record straight again and again and again, to clarify my position and what I stand for, to explain when my words had been twisted. I wanted to respond from a place of compassion, to educate and inform people.

In Claire H.'s case, the benefits were clear: engaging with the perpetrators of the abuse was a way of trying to restore her reputation, to correct misinformation about her views and opinions, to 'clear my name'. However, this public response from Claire H. was not merely an attempt to make sure that the online world could see the true version of her views, but to try to educate the specific individuals who had been targeting her. She, therefore, went beyond simply treating one-on-one engagement as something to improve her situation, but as an opportunity to try to improve those who had been the very reason for the abuse she had received. This positions Claire H.'s response as similar to the process of restorative justice (see also Walters 2014 for a discussion on how this works in cases of racist and homophobic hate crime).

It was not only those who had been the target of abuse who saw the value of engaging with those who sent abusive missives: those seeing this going on would, on occasion, intervene. These participants were in an interesting situation. They acknowledged the importance of the role that they might be able to play in engaging with those acting abusively, particularly as a means of support for the recipients of the abuse. However, they themselves had little to gain from becoming involved, save for the sense of having done the right thing, the possibility of being able to help another woman feel supported or (potentially) halting the abuse. The priority was often expressed to be the needs of the target: Juliet K. expressed this when she discussed whether she might intervene:

> *Juliet K.*: If someone's already being abusive then it's about looking after the person being abused, which may or may not mean calling the abuser out.

For those (like Juliet K.) who encountered the abuse indirectly, intervention and engagement with the perpetrator can be a symbolic act: stepping into challenge someone acting abusively provides an explicit show of support for the target and disapproval of the perpetrator and their behaviour. However, we might also consider the broader effects of one-on-one engagement, particular by people who are not the direct target of the abuse. Whilst such engagement can appear as merely a response to the perpetrator of the hate, by pushing back and challenging those individuals, participants were also making a visible stand and saying 'this is unacceptable' to wider Internet society. This in turn may provide strength and support for other women who also choose to resist online gendered hate with these fight responses.

Positive resistance by way of increasing engagement with both direct and indirect victims may, therefore, have a snowballing effect, encouraging other women to speak up, a further potential benefit to engaging with the perpetrators of online gendered hate. However, there are risks associated with this behaviour, and these were also part of participants' considerations when they were deciding whether to intervene or engage. For Claire H., the process of engaging had been extremely stressful and emotionally difficult, and in addition, she had found that when attempting to appeal to the good nature of those abusing her, her comments generated further abuse:

> *Claire H.*: I tweeted back saying 'I'm absolutely reeling under the sexist misogynistic abuse that I've been receiving', at which point I then got a lot of tweets saying 'where's the sexism, where's the misogyny, you're sore because you lost the debate, you can't take friendly banter, you can't take criticism, you shouldn't be a public figure if you can't take criticism, this is about your arguments, this it's nothing to do with feminism, you're crying wolf. You are giving women a bad name, who do you think you are'.

She went on to comment that she had stayed up that night 'literally manning my twitter feed constantly, just reading all this stuff going "what do I do, what do I do, do I respond to them?" ... I was in the sort of complete trauma state of just red alert, fight or flight, didn't sleep all night, for many nights'.

Claire H.'s reflections highlight the conflict she felt between wanting to engage to set the record straight and not being sure whether this was the right thing to do—whether to fight or flee. It also draws attention to the risks of engaging: the emotional harm that she felt as a result of trying to decide how to respond, and the perpetration of more abuse in response to her attempts to engage with those targeting her. For those women who had encountered the online gendered hate indirectly, similar fears were expressed. These women did not necessarily benefit directly from one-on-one engagement, in that they were not attempting to correct wrongs done against them, but in engaging opened themselves up to the risk of becoming the target of abuse themselves. Sasha T. talked about how she wanted to engage but was afraid to:

> *Sasha T.*: I'd like to think that I would but I don't know if I would to be honest, if I'm being honest. I'd be too scared of being targeted myself.

According to Perry (2001), an important feature of hate crimes is that they send a message to the target's wider group. In terms of online gendered hate, this online abuse is an attempt to silence women, particularly when they are challenging dominant patriarchal discourses, behaviours, and ideas. Sasha T.'s comments suggest that the message to 'know thy place' is also being received, by some women, as a warning not to intervene to help and support others; this takes the 'message' element of the online gendered hate beyond simply 'do not speak out' to 'do not join in'.

Digilantism

> I like those stories where you know, they find out their girlfriends' phone number or something and talk to them, it feels like a mini victory. (Sasha T.)

Digital vigilante action has been well explored in the Jane's recent works (Jane 2016, 2017a, b), as a form of extra-judicial punishment set within the context of a wider 'vengeance culture' (Hai-Jew 2014: 64; Jane 2016). Citing behaviours such as naming and shaming, publically confronting the perpetrators, and alerting family and employers of the behaviours (see, e.g., Gensler 2018; True 2014; Jane 2017a; Vitis and Gilmour 2017; Tweten 2018), Jane acknowledges the appeal of responses that bypasses more 'legitimate' approaches to online gendered hate: the consciousness-raising, humanisation of the parties involved, empowerment, and catharsis that digilantism can engender (Jane 2017a, b). Furthermore, where formal justice responses have failed to acknowledge the seriousness and harms of abusive online behaviours there is an understandable attraction to alternative approaches which highlight these harms and allow women to regain a sense of control.

Although few of the participants talked about engaging in the kinds of digilante action Jane discusses, there were some examples of this. One participant talked about how International Women's Day was her 'favourite day for Twitter' because she enjoyed 'trolling MRAs[5] on twitter'. Others talked about their experiences of engaging in 'dogpiling'.[6]

For the women engaging in these digilante behaviours, the actions taken were seen as positive responses to abuse; justifiable and reasonable in the circumstances, serving as a form of self-defence and turning the behaviours of the attackers back on themselves. Furthermore, the participants were actively involved in constructing these actions—considered abusive when used by those perpetrating online gendered hate—as a form of positive feminist activism distinct from abusive behaviour. This feminist-focused construction was clear in the discussion that a group of participants had about dogpiling; they acknowledged that the behaviours, from a superficial perspective, could be seen as the same as that of the perpetrators of the abuse, but because of the defensive nature of their response and the power imbalance, the digilante versions of the act were conceived as feminist acts of resistance rather than aggressive acts of abuse:

> *Cath B.*: I guess the men doing the dogpiling see it as the same thing
> *Elle B.*: I don't think so, because the power balance isn't the same
> *Jill H.*: It often gets called the same - but as Elle said the power balance is very different
> *Elle B.*: Plus its usually debate/rebuttal coming from us, but men pile on with threats/insults
> *Jill H.*: Yes
> *Cath B.*: I think, when women wade in, we're supporting each other, showing that we're not lone voices. That the woman isn't alone, that we want our voices to be heard
> […]
> *Elle B.*: We're always trying to get them to understand. They're trying to get us to be quiet.

For the participants framing the behaviours in this way, digilantism held some of those positive characteristics highlighted by Jane (2017a, b). However, there was also some acknowledgement that digilante activism can be problematic in terms of how the action is undertaken and the consequences of this. As Jane's research highlights, it is easy to overlook the dangers of digilantism. Such actions can draw in those whose intentions are more malicious, rather than acting from a place of making a political statement or as a form of defence. Successful digilante campaigns can create a culture of celebrating these actions as *the* way of responding to online abuse: undermining formal judicial approaches, and encumbering women with the expectation that they can and should engage in such responses, regardless of the time and emotional burdens that this can place on women (Jane 2017b). This returns us to the idea of responsibility resting on women, and the ways in which this can shift attention and obligation from the perpetrators to the targets, and from the public to the private sphere (Jane 2017b: 57; Maher et al. 2017).

Talking further in her interview about digilante actions, Cath B. reflected some of these ideas. She noted that digilante action can backfire and create further abuse, referring to a woman who had reported someone harassing her to his employer and had come under fire for the subsequent termination of his employment. She also noted the ways in which responsibility can be placed on women during digilante actions:

> *Cath B.*: You send a picture to their mum and go 'look what your son is doing' which I also have a problem with because why is it the mum, why are we now putting it on the mums or the sisters or the girlfriends, why … how are they responsible for this man's behaviour?

Digilante actions may be somewhat controversial in terms of the acts themselves and consequences of these. Whilst there have been some notable successes, celebrating these needs tempering with an awareness of the risks. Participants had engaged in some digilante actions and to an extent minimised some of the potential problems through their framing of these actions as justifiable responses to (perceived male) aggression, but a few were aware of how such acts might also present a more complex and conflicting picture.

Conclusion

A number of scholars have argued that abusive behaviour online is a means of silencing and exerting control over individuals (Jane 2014a; Mantilla 2015). This is particularly pertinent for feminists who, by the very nature of the political position adopted, are challenging the status quo and attempting to break down some of the controls and constraints placed on women's lives. The flight responses are understandable given the potential consequences of online gendered hate (see Smith 2011; Dryden 2014 for specific examples and Mantilla 2015 for numerous examples of these harms). However, for some women, receiving or seeing this online gendered hate has had the opposite effect, and has made them want to fight back, to respond to and to try to resist the online gendered hate. As Heidi C. commented and set out in the title of this chapter: 'When I saw women being attacked … it has made me want to stand up and fight'.

Within my research participants saw the value of engaging in fight responses, even if some of those were not always successful. They were also aware of the potential consequences of engaging in these: the emotional toll of reporting to the police or social media companies and having the experiences dismissed, the drawing attention to oneself and risking becoming a targeted for abuse. Fight responses can be a powerful tool in the armoury of resisting and fighting back against online hate—be that gendered, or otherwise—particularly when fighting individual instances of abuse. However, stepping back to see the bigger picture, we need to look to longer term solutions for combating online gendered hate, and ultimately to challenge the broader society structures that perpetuate misogyny throughout the on and offline worlds: as Jane so succinctly says 'any discussion of these matters should keep sight of the fact that all the praiseworthy feminist resistance would be unnecessary if it were not for all the lamentable patriarchal oppression' (Jane 2017b: 58).

Notes

1. The term 'feminist-sympathising' was used in the recruitment information to allow for the inclusion of women whose political position would be considered feminist, but who do not want to apply this label to themselves.
2. The publication of private or identifying information on the Internet.
3. Making a hoax call to the police to cause attendance at a victim's address. In 2017, Andrew Finch was fatally shot by police who had responded to a hoax call about a murder and hostage situation at his address (Queally 2018).

4. The focus groups in this research were conducted as a typed chat room, from which a precise transcript was downloaded. Accordingly, the quotes here are exactly what was typed.
5. Men's Rights Activist.
6. The term 'dogpile' describes the process of a group of people joining into a conversation criticise or abuse a specific target. This can also be used as noun to describe the situation where this action has happened (Oxford Dictionaries 2018). See for example, the experiences of the Sexual Violence Won't Be Silenced (SVWBS) group formed to support a friend who had had abusive messages posted about her online, and engaged in actions such as encouraging others to send the perpetrators of the abuse messages, and naming and shaming the perpetrators of further abuse received. A full account of this is found in Jane (2017a).

References

Bakalis, C. (2018). Rethinking cyberhate laws. *Information & Communications Technology Law, 27*(1), 86–110.

Bowling, B. (1998). *Violent Racism: Victimisation, Policing, and Social Context.* Oxford: Oxford University Press.

Burgess-Proctor, A. (2015). Methodological and ethical issues in feminist research with abused women: Reflections on particpants' vulnerability and empowerment. *Women's Studies International Forum, 48,* 124–134.

Chakraborti, N., & Garland, J. (2015). *Hate Crime: Impact, Causes and Responses* (2nd ed.). London: Sage.

Citron, D. K. (2014). *Hate Crimes in Cyberspace.* Cambridge, MA: Harvard University Press.

Cook, J. A., & Fanow, M. M. (1990). Knowledge and women's interests: Issues of epistemology and methodology in feminist sociological research. In J. M. Nieban (Ed.), *Feminist Research Methods: Exemplary Readings in the Social Sciences* (pp. 69–93). Boulder: Westview Press.

CPS. (2016). *Social media: Guidelines on prosecuting cases involving communications sent via social media.* Crown Prosecution Service. http://www.cps.gov.uk/legal/a_to_c/communications_sent_via_social_media/. Accessed October 17, 2017.

Dixon, B., & Gadd, D. (2006). Getting the message? 'new' labour and the criminalization of 'hate'. *Criminology & Criminal Justice, 6*(3), 309–328.

Dryden, A. (2014). Last night you shared a police report I filed against a man who threatened to rape and murder me. *Ashe Dryden*. https://www.ashedryden.com/blog/when-wellmeaning-people-harm-those-they-supposedly-protect. Accessed April 4, 2018.

Eckert, S. (2017). Fighting for recognition: Online abuse of women bloggers in Germany, Switzerland, the United Kingdom, and the United States. *New Media & Society, 20*(4), 1282–1302.

Facebook. (2018a). Community standards. *Facebook*. https://en-gb.facebook.com/communitystandards. Accessed March 5, 2018.

Facebook. (2018b). Statement of rights and responsibilities. *Facebook*. https://www.facebook.com/terms.php. Accessed March 5, 2018.

Gensler, A. (2018). Granniepants. *annagensler.com*. https://www.annagensler.com/granniepants.html. Accessed April 3, 2018.

Guardian. (2014). Man found guilty of sending menacing tweets to Labour MP Stella Creasy. *The Guardian*. http://www.theguardian.com/politics/2014/sep/02/stella-creasy-rape-threats-a-joke. Accessed July 1, 2015.

Guardian. (2015). Two jailed for Twitter abuse of feminist campaigner. *The Guardian*. https://www.theguardian.com/uk-news/2014/jan/24/two-jailed-twitter-abuse-feminist-campaigner. Accessed October 17, 2017.

Guardian. (2017). Facebook files. *The Guardian*. http://www.theguardian.com/news/series/facebook-files. Accessed March 8, 2018.

Hai-Jew, S. (2014). Vengeance culture online: A qualitative meta-analysis and position paper. In C. M. Akrivopoulou & N. Garipidis (Eds.), *Human Rights and the Impact of ICT in the Public Sphere: Participation, Democracy, and Political Autonomy* (pp. 64–93). Hershey, PA: Information Science Reference.

HMIC. (2017). *PEEL: Police Effectiveness 2016*. London: HMIC.

Instagram. (2018a). *Learn how to address abuse, instagram help centre*. https://help.instagram.com/527320407282978. Accessed April 19, 2018.

Instagram. (2018b). *Reporting harassment or bullying on instagram, instagram help centre*. https://help.instagram.com/547601325292351. Accessed April 19, 2018.

Jane, E. A. (2014a). 'Back to the kitchen, cunt': Speaking the unspeakable about online misogyny. *Continuum, 28*(4), 558–570.

Jane, E. A. (2014b). Your a ugly, whorish, slut. *Feminist Media Studies, 14*(4), 531–546.

Jane, E. A. (2016). Online misogyny and feminist digilantism. *Continuum, 30*(3), 284–297.

Jane, E. A. (2017a). Feminist digilante responses to a slut-shaming on Facebook. *Social Media+Society, 3*(2), 1–10.

Jane, E. A. (2017b). Feminist flight and fight responses to gendered cyberhate. In L. Vitis & M. Segrave (Eds.), *Gender, Technology and Violence* (pp. 45–61). Abingdon and Oxon: Routledge.

Lewis, H. (2011, November 3). 'You should have your tongue ripped out': The reality of sexist online abuse. *New Statesman*. http://www.newstatesman.com/blogs/helen-lewis-hasteley/2011/11/comments-rape-abuse-women. Accessed July 24, 2015.

Lewis, R., Rowe, M., & Wiper, C. (2016). Online abuse of feminists as an emerging form of violence against women and girls. *British Journal of Criminology, 57*(6), 1462–1481.

Loftus, B. (2010). Police occupational culture: Classic themes, altered times. *Policing and Society, 20*(1), 1–20.

Lumsden, K., & Morgan, H. (2017). Media framing of trolling and online abuse: Silencing strategies, symbolic violence, and victim blaming. *Feminist Media Studies, 17*(6), 926–940.

Maher, J., McCulloch, J., & Fitz-Gibbon, K. (2017). New forms of gendered surveillance? Intersections of technology and family violence. In L. Vitis & M. Segrave (Eds.), *Gender, Technology and Violence* (pp. 14–27). Abingdon and Oxon: Routledge.

Mantilla, K. (2015). *Gendertrolling: How Misogyny Went Viral*. Santa Barbara, CA: Praeger.

Mason-Bish, H. (2011). Examining the boundaries of hate crime policy: Considering age and gender. *Criminal Justice Policy Review, 24*(3), 297–316.

Megarry, J. (2014). Online incivility or sexual harassment? Conceptualising women's experiences in the digital age. *Women's Studies International Forum, 47,* 46–55.

Oakley, A. (1981). Interviewing women: A contradiction in terms. In H. Roberts (Ed.), *Doing Feminist Research* (pp. 30–61). London: Routledge.

Oxford Dictionaries. (2018). Dogpile. *Oxford Dictionaries*. Oxford: Oxford University Press. https://en.oxforddictionaries.com/definition/dogpile. Accessed October 20, 2018.

Pavan, E. (2017). Internet intermediaries and gender-based violence. In L. Vitas & M. Segrave (Eds.), *Gender, Technology and Violence* (pp. 62–78). Abingdon and Oxon: Routledge.

Perry, B. (2001). *In the Name of Hate: Understanding Hate Crimes*. New York, NY.: Routledge.

Queally, J. (2018, January 26). Fictitious shooting in video game sparked real-life shooting in Kansas swatting case, records show. *LATimes.com*. http://www.latimes.com/local/lanow/la-me-ln-kansas-swatting-records-20180126-story.html. Accessed February 14, 2018.

Rawlinson, K. (2017). Viscount jailed for offering money for killing of Gina Miller. *The Guardian.* https://www.theguardian.com/uk-news/2017/jul/13/viscount-jailed-for-offering-money-for-killing-of-gina-miller. Accessed October 17, 2017.

Russell, M., & Light, L. (2006). Police and victim perspectives on empowerment of domestic violence victims. *Police Quarterly, 9*(4), 375–396.

Sierra, K. (2014, October 8). Why the trolls will always win. *Wired.* http://www.wired.com/2014/10/trolls-will-always-win/. Accessed July 20, 2015.

Smith, S. E. (2011, October 11). Blogging, threats, and silence. *Tiger Beatdown.* http://tigerbeatdown.com/2011/10/11/on-blogging-threats-and-silence/. Accessed April 4, 2018.

True, E. (2014). The gaming journalist who tells on her internet trolls—To their mothers. *The Guardian.* http://www.theguardian.com/culture/australia-culture-blog/2014/nov/28/alanah-pearce-tells-on-her-internet-trolls-to-their-mothers. Accessed April 3, 2018.

Tumblr. (2018). *Malicious speech, Tumblr community guidelines.* https://www.tumblr.com/abuse/maliciousspeech. Accessed April 19, 2018.

Tweten, A. (2018). Bye Felipe. *Instagram.* https://www.instagram.com/byefelipe/. Accessed April 3, 2018.

Twitter. (2018). The Twitter rules. *Twitter.* https://help.twitter.com/en/rules-and-policies/twitter-rules. Accessed April 19, 2018.

Twitter Support. (2014, December 2). Starting today we're rolling out an improved way to flag abusive Tweets: See how it works. *Twitter Support.* https://twitter.com/TwitterSupport/status/539826848641724416. Accessed March 8, 2018.

Twitter Support. (2015a, March 17). Making it easier to report threats to law enforcement. *Twitter Blog.* https://blog.twitter.com/official/en_us/a/2015/making-it-easier-to-report-threats-to-law-enforcement.html. Accessed March 8, 2018.

Twitter Support. (2015b, February 27). We're making it easier to report impersonation and posted private information in Tweets. *Twitter Support.* https://twitter.com/twittersupport/status/571389915851698176. Accessed March 8, 2018.

Vitis, L., & Gilmour, F. (2017). Dick pics on blast: A woman's resistance to online sexual harassment using humour, art and instagram. *Crime, Media, Culture, 13*(3), 335–355.

Walters, M. A. (2014). *Hate Crime and Restorative Justice.* Oxford: Oxford University Press.

13

Disability Hate Speech: Interrogating the Online/Offline Distinction

Philippa Hall

Introduction

Disabled people experience hate speech and hate crime in offline and online settings.[1] The rate of anti-disability hate crime, including speech incidents, is rising exponentially in the UK (Mortimer 2015; Agerholm 2017; Kiteley and Robinson 2017; Pring 2017) along with the rate of hate speech incidents against other marginalized social groups (Dodd 2016, 2017). In the UK, public awareness of the prevalence of disability hate remains limited (Walker 2009), despite a series of high-profile hate crime cases that highlighted the severity of hate speech and hate crime.[2] A 2016 Report for the Equality and Human Rights Commission (EHRC) in the UK noted an overall reduction in reported UK hate crime since 2013, but judged no such firm conclusions on levels of disability hate crime reduction could be reached (Colman and Sykes 2016: v). The EHRC report also indicated that disability hate crime might have distinctive elements that were not shared across hate crime more generally (Coleman and Sykes 2016: viii).

P. Hall (✉)
Independent Researcher, Edinburgh, UK

A 2017 UK Home Office report (O'Neill 2017) also found that rates of disability hate crime differed compared to other protected groups. Disability hate crimes had a greater rate of increase than other types of hate crime. There was a 53% increase in recorded disability hate crime (O'Neill 2017: 4) and the survey found that disability hate crimes more frequently occurred in online contexts (O'Neill 2017: 19).

This chapter explores the rise in online disablist hate speech between 2000 and 2010 (EHRC 2013; Coleman and Sykes 2016; Walters et al. 2016) and UK Home Office (O'Neill 2017) in relation to two main themes: first the extent to which disabled people experience online hate speech differently to other marginalized social groups and second the political and economic context of the Web 2.0 network technology that produced the interactive social media platforms (Mason 2016) that are now key sites for social communication, political debate and hate speech (BBC News 2017). An analysis of the distinct dynamics of online disability hate speech can counter the 'internet-centrism' defined by Morozov (2013: 31) that often frames debates about online communication. Internet-centrism, the perspective that 'the internet' is an autonomous entity existing outside the global economic and political transformations of capital that produced network technology, often implicitly bolsters claims by global technology companies and national governments that online communication is beyond the scope of state regulation.

The chapter has four sections. The first section examines disability hate speech within the context of disabled people's experiences of networked communication set within the context of the network society that began in the 1990s (Castells 1996, 1997, 1998; Mason 2016). I suggest that online communication in the 1990s and early 2000s brought benefits to disabled people's lives that exceeded those enjoyed by much of the wider population, a difference that has heightened the negative impact of the proliferation of online hate speech in the later 2000s. In the second section, I review current disability hate speech legislation within national and international jurisdictions and assess the contribution of international law to the regulation of global technology companies.

In section three, I locate the network technology and the idea of online and offline realms within neoliberal global capitalism that produced the institutional networks, business models and practices that comprise 'the internet' (Morozov 2013). I suggest that the rise in hate speech in the 2010s reflects the consolidation of the globalized, network economy based upon economic opportunism, advertising and big data accumulation that privileges, or at least facilitates, the dissemination and proliferation of hate speech and fake news (Riotta 2018; Bolano and Vieira 2014). I consider the extent to which the predominance of the social media platform company (Srnicek 2017) impedes the regulation of online hate speech. In section four, I draw on the social model of disability (Oliver 1983, 1990; Shakespeare 2006) as a critical perspective to analyse how disabled people secure rights to access and equality of participation in online contexts as public spaces (Stein 2008; Cammaerts 2009; Tierney 2013; Aubin 2014) and public spheres (Habermas 1989; Arato and Cohen 1992; Papacharissi 2002; Dahlgren 2005; Aubin 2014; Murphy 2016; Valtysson 2012, 2017). As online communication offers a public space of equal, and indeed enhanced, access for disabled people, my emphasis is upon the extent to which disabled people experience equality of participation in the public sphere of online communication. I suggest that disablist hate speech diminishes people's opportunities for equal participation in the online public sphere and that the application of the rights to participation foregrounded by the social model of disability to online 'communicative spaces' (Valtysson 2017: 671) can inform the regulation required to counter the disablist hate speech that currently prevents equality of participation in online communication.

Online and Offline Worlds: The Distinct Contexts and Experiences of Disability Hate Speech

Like other marginalized groups, disabled people receive an increasing amount of hate speech online (UK Law Commission 2013). However, online hate speech also appears to be experienced in distinctive ways by many disabled people. I suggest the distinct significance of online communication in many disabled people's lives is in part shaped by the initial positive effects that online communication provided for disabled people in the early years of network technology. The positive transformative effects of early online technologies for many disabled people mean that online hate speech has a disproportionately greater impact upon disabled people than upon other protected groups. The utopian promises of the 1990s network technology to transform people's lives were perhaps most fully realized and encompassed amongst disabled people; technological solutions to physical and social barriers; and creating a new online forum for the formation of new social groups and activism (Trevisan 2013; Pearson and Trevisan 2015). From the information based Web 1.0 to the interactive Web 2.0, network technology provided relatively simple, affordable solutions to geographical and physical barriers (Amichai-Hamburger and Hayat 2013). Physical and psychological barriers to communication caused by impairments of movement, speech, sound and sight, social phobia and agoraphobia could be overcome. Online communication also offered new forms of social interaction of particular significance for disabled users. Anonymity, the control of physical appearance, greater control over the location of communication and finding similar others and accessibility in time and place (Amichai-Hamburger and Hayat 2013) were all distinctive features of online communication that promised to free participants from the discriminatory social interactions based on physical and social characteristics that disabled people often encountered offline. Computer games like Second Life allowed users to create alternative physical identities, and conversely, people with visible or invisible physical and mental disabilities could join online groups based upon a stigmatized identity that was not openly shared offline (Amichai-Hamburger and Hayat 2013).

Online Communication from Web 2.0 Interactivity to Web 3.0 Data Accumulation

Online communication in the early years of the interactive Web 2.0 also offered users a greater sense of control over social interactions. Many disabled users located the online world as a new, accessible communication space in which all users could relate stories from their own perspective and develop fuller lives by joining online groups which expanded different areas of their personality (Amichai-Hamburger and Hayat 2013). In addition, the internet permitted new types of medical care and support (Nilsson et al. 2010). The network technology of the 1990s and early 2000s also emerged in tandem with the resurgent disability rights activism (Goggin and Newell 2003) that built upon the 'social model' of disability (Oliver 1983, 1990). The social model's emphasis upon disability as socially constructed opened up new debates about disabled people's access to public spaces and the new era of online communication promised to facilitate the emergence of a democratized alternative media that could counter disablist marginalization in the mass media (Couldry 2000; Downing 2001; Atton 2004). The early Web 2.0 online network was a transformative forum for online social groups extended public spheres (Fraser 1993), and as a site for disability activism (Oliver 1990). However, the rise in disablist hate speech in the late 2000s and into the 2010s is a stark example of the shortcomings of utopian visions of an egalitarian network society and the demise of free, open and democratic online debate.

The transformative power of the internet for disabled people's lives is what gives online hate speech a distinct significance for disabled people that differs from the experience of online hate speech by other marginalized social groups. The greater practical reliance of some physically and mentally disabled people on online communication increased their vulnerability as hate speech targets. Online medical services reduced health care's social element, whilst unregulated online groups seen as potentially detrimental to users' mental and physical health emerged, such as pro 'ana' anorexic sites (Sproull et al. 2013). Disabled people's greater reliance on online services increased vulnerability to cybercrime, and online anonymity facilitated the hate speech which can precede disability hate crime (Clark 2011). Whilst disability activists used social media to offset limited mainstream media coverage of disability issues (Butler 2012; Trevisan 2013; Pearson and Trevisan 2015), intensified online hate can also limit the opportunities for social media disability activists to communicate with the wider disabled community. In contrast to many in the wider population whose social media use is integrated into their broader offline leisure, the gap between online and offline contexts can remain greater for those disabled people with fewer alternatives to online communication (Amichai-Hamburger and Hayat 2013). Whilst 'netification' has closed the gap between online and offline worlds in the network society more broadly (Kalman et al. 2013), the gulf between online and offline experience can remain far greater for many disabled people than people in the wider population, a discrepancy that underlines the heightened significance of legislation and social policies to regulate online disablist hate speech.

Online Disablist Hate Speech and International Legislation

Legal measures and social policies to counter hate speech must be mindful of the different ways in which disabled people experience online and offline communication. Given network communication is now embedded within social and economic life, advising people to 'turn off the internet' in response to online hate speech is an insufficient remedy for most. Recent studies have shown online hate speech has a direct effect upon outbreaks of offline hate speech and hate crime (*The Economist* 2017), adding urgency to the demands for the regulation of online platforms. International law already provides a legal resource for national governments to counter hate speech as well as question the global technology companies' assertion that hate speech regulation is too unwieldy to implement.

International law passed in the United Nations (UN) and the European Union (EU) has, so far, perhaps made the greatest contribution to the development of UK laws to tackle disability hate speech online. Hate speech was first outlawed in terms of race hate by Article 4, 1965 UN, International Convention on Elimination of Racial Discrimination (ICERD). The UN 1966 International Convention of Civil and Political Rights (ICCPR) s. 20 extended categories to outlaw hate speech based on race, religion or nationality adding in s. 19 (2) clarification rights to freedom of expression were compatible with anti-discrimination law. The European Convention on Human Rights (ECHR) also qualifies the Article 10 right to freedom of expression with the Article 14 freedom from discrimination. The qualification of the right to freedom of expression in discrimination cases has shaped the development of hate speech law in England and Wales. The Public Order Act (POA) 1986, part 3, that introduced measures against hate speech into UK law by outlawing the 'stirring up' of race hate, was deemed not to infringe excluded ECHR Article 10 rights.[3] Since the POA 1986, hate speech legislation has developed in England, Wales and Scotland through the gradual expansion of protected categories,[4] bolstered by the positive rights established in the 1995 Disability Discrimination Act. Under the Convention of the Rights of Persons with Disabilities (CRPD), Article 1, UN law also contributes a definition of 'disability' according to the 'social model', which examines how impairment might impact social participation. In England and Wales, as in Scotland, hate crime legislation eschews the social model and defines disability as impairment.[5] The tests differ; in English and Welsh law (2016/2017), a subjective test of hate crime has existed since the publication of the 1999 McPherson Report, whilst Scots law retains an objective test, a distinction crystallized by the 2018 Offensive Behaviour at Football and Threatening Communication Act 2012 (Repeal) (Scotland) Act.

The Regulation of the Platform Company: European Union Legislation and Guidelines

Much current hate speech law in national jurisdictions draws upon the legal resources provided by the UN international law that produced legal definitions of 'hate speech' as a form of discrimination that did not contradict rights to freedom of expression. European Union (EU) law has also proven innovative in the regulation of global technology companies. Since 2000, the E-Commerce Directive was the legislation that defined the scope of the 'platform' company (2017: 34), in the era before social media became mainstream (UK Parliament 2017). The European Commission showed a willingness to regulate global network companies. The 2015 European Commission against Racism and Intolerance (ECRI), General Policy Recommendation No. 15 on Combating Hate Speech, recommended member states in accord with the Additional Protocol on Cybercrime and are alert to 'conditions conducive to the use of hate speech' (Council of Europe 2016). In 2016, the European Commission and Facebook, Twitter, Microsoft and YouTube agreed on the 'Code of Conduct on Countering Illegal Hate Speech Online', producing a legal resource for member states that required online companies to contribute to platform regulation. The Digital Content Directive 2018 will extend regulation on the supply of online communications services.

UN and EU law detail the ways social policy and legislation can counter hate speech in digital content on network platforms and go against the pervasive 'internet-centrism' (Morozov 2013) that paralyses online hate speech policy. For Morozov, the internet has acquired the status of 'ultimate technology and ultimate network' as 'Silicon Valley's own version of the end of history' which defies critical analysis and regulation as it evolves according to its own imperatives (2013: 23). Morozov's analysis reinserts the internet into the wider economic and political context that produced its technologies, business models, work practices and institutional structures. The internet is the product of its political and economic environment, and the disembodied idea of 'internet freedom' overlooks the power relations encapsulated in its constitutive technologies and companies (Morozov 2013). In short, international law shows how online disability hate speech can be regulated. The effective regulation of online hate speech must be informed by an awareness that the internet's institutions and practices reflect, rather than remake, the society and politics within which online communication occurs.

The Global Internet Economy: Hate Speech and Platform Capitalism

Since 2000, the interactivity of Web 2.0 and the data accumulation of Web 3.0 have further intensified network society (Castells 1996, 1997, 1998). Current legislation against disability hate speech online places the onus on individual hate targets to report hate speech rather than requiring platforms to regulate against it. This means the experience of disability hate speech occurs in an internet-centric context in which hate speech perpetrators claiming 'internet freedom' reiterate wider claims of rights to freedom from state regulation. Such assertions of unlimited online freedom can be interrogated through an analysis of how platform capitalism's business models facilitate hate speech. In short, the role of the internet within the changing configuration of the state, the market and the economy under neoliberalism shows how hate speech can be conceptualized as a by-product of the current privatized form of internet technology developed to serve the requirements of globalized capital.

State-funded science and military research centres created the first network technology. This early publicly funded history meant early online communications were open-ended enough in purpose to be deemed a potential source of open, democratic communication, a sense perhaps reflected in the sharing of open-source software (Mason 2016). Utopian visions of cyberspace were encapsulated in Barlow's (1996) 'declaration of independence' (Marzi 2016: 29) which asserted that the emergence of cyberspace was an 'act of nature … that grows itself through our collective actions' (Marzi 2016: 30), quite a contrast to Zuckerberg's 2017 Facebook mission statement, which aims to produce a top-down 'social infrastructure', to build a 'global community' because in some parts of the world people are opting out of globalization (Solon 2017). Such internet utopianism tended to define online space as a 'new democratic space', a 'digital commons' (Atton 2004: x) that could be destroyed by state regulation. However, during the 2010s, the expansion of the economic interests of platform capitalism and, most recently, the repressive use of online communication by states to undermine democratic politics have problematized online communication as a place of social and political freedoms.

In retrospect, the triumph of economic opportunity online should be no surprise given network technology's role as an infrastructure within global finance capitalism. Neoliberalism rested upon the globalization of production and consumption, a process which restructured the world's economies through the extension of capital across the globe in search of new resources and markets (Harvey 2005). The internet consists of a set of business models, institutions and practices that were crucial to the very emergence of globalization. Online technology facilitated the outsourcing required for global systems of production and consumption through real-time communications, whilst instant online financial transactions allowed finance capital to leverage profit margins through rapid currency flows and facilitated the global consumption of goods and services by online purchasers (Harvey 2005).

Platform Companies and the Regulation of Online Content

The revenue opportunities generated from advertising by Web 2.0 and the data accumulation by Web 3.0 have facilitated the formation of the global technology company (Marzi 2016). The platform model of organization has become the fundamental and pervasive business model of online commerce and social media companies (Srnicek 2017), and consequently, people now often encounter disability hate speech online in the context of services provided by platform companies. Platform companies are driven by the imperatives of finance capitalism's surplus capital supplies (Srnicek 2017) and rely almost wholly upon advertising revenues; for example, advertising makes up 96.9% of Facebook revenues and 89% of Google's revenue (Srnicek 2017). Platform companies tend to move towards dominant market positions, because the success of a social media site is built from the connections made possible when a large number of people use the site. As a result, social media businesses tend to result in monopoly forms which then battle to maintain market share and exclude competitors through securing access to advertising revenue. The Web 3.0 platform model increasingly also rests upon another revenue source, the sale of the large scale data accumulation that is acquired via high usage rates generated by the e-commerce market imperative to be 'constantly and desperately looking for only one thing: information' (Marzi 2016: 11).

Platform capitalism reliance on advertising facilitates the dissemination of both hate speech and fake news as by-products and resists calls for regulation. The economic priorities of the platform company shape the content produced. When a business model rests upon the whims of algorithms that serve advertising and increased market share, such 'leveraging of misinformation…' exaggerates content and creates 'bias towards polarized views whose proponents are self-selected through the volume they project on online space' (Bossier and Holt 2009: 83). Not only does the corporate control exerted by platform business model facilitate disability hate speech and fake news, reliance upon advertising and data mining raises questions about the extent to which that the internet has ever been a space of free expression (Holm 2016). Whilst state censorship can impose repressive measures to restrict the freedom of online communication, the scope of democratic participation online can also be restricted by the platform company's dependence upon advertising revenues and data accumulation.

An analysis of the way that internet technology developed as the infrastructure of globalization highlights the oversights that exist in claims that the regulation of internet communication in order to counter disablist hate speech infringes a space of 'free speech' (Waldron 2012). To date, platform companies have resisted regulation by claiming not to produce content. However, the distinction between platform and content provision appears to be sustainable once the extent to which platform companies already constrain online freedom of content through advertising and data mining. Google's integration of advertising into the location of results by the Google search engine, AdWords, shapes the content viewed by users. Social media applications also increase the control of the platform over the user. Mahlouly notes that platforms 'modify the founding characteristics of social interactions' (2013: 5) and indeed a company's promotional emphasis upon 'connecting people' might obscure the extent to which online communication is managed (Van Dijck 2013; Mahlouly 2013). Furthermore, reliance on advertising revenue facilitates the dissemination of hate speech and fake news by prioritizing the popularity of the message over the reliability and quality of the message content. In short, the platform business model's economic imperatives of advertising and data accumulation mean that profit derives from the amount of times a site is used, and as a result, hate speech and fake news then become likely by-products of platform capitalism.

The economic imperatives of the platform company facilitate the dissemination of hate speech as a by-product and hamper the regulation of disability hate speech in two ways. First, global internet companies claim to operate beyond the regulatory reach of individual nation states and the institutions of international law. Second, the advertising and data accumulation revenues that underpin the platform business model restrict the free flow of information and knowledge by privileging advertisers' interests. However, an analysis of the platform model that is set within the economic and political context of global production and consumption systems can question the perception that the internet is beyond regulation (Morozov 2011, 2013) and, on this basis, assert that platform companies cannot outsource their contribution to the regulation of disablist online hate speech.

Virtual Public Spaces and Plural Public Spheres: Beyond the Online/Offline Distinction

Once the regulation of online communication to counter disablist hate speech is established to be both necessary and possible, I suggest that the social model of disability (Oliver 1983, 1990; Shakespeare 2006) can be applied to inform policies to regulate hate speech. The social model of disability asserts that impairments only became disabilities where socially constructed barriers restrict access and participation in public space (Oliver 1990). If online spaces and spheres are conceptualized as public spaces and public spheres, then the objective of regulation can be the upholding of the disabled people's rights to access and participate in online communication. Access is at the core of the legal definition of the public space[6] and, to a great extent, online communication does meet accessibility requirements for many disabled people. However, the social model of disability (Oliver 1983, 1990; Shakespeare 2006) also identifies participation as a crucial element of access and, at the moment, online disablist hate speech impedes equal participation in the online communication for many disabled users. Whilst access to online public space exists for disabled users, equality of participation online requires the existence of a virtual public sphere of 'reasoned debate' (Aubin 2014: 90) which perhaps only regulation can ensure.

Whilst not all online spaces are—or should facilitate—public spheres, the application of the social model (Oliver 1983, 1990) does suggest that disablist hate speech can be best countered where online communication occurs within public sphere of reasoned debate that can provide both equality of access and participation. The concept of public sphere therefore can be used to interrogate how the economic and political structures in which online communication currently takes place can obstruct disabled users' rights to exercise the freedom of equality of participation. Media reliance on advertising revenues can restrict the scope of the rational public sphere (Habermas 1989), whilst subsequently more expansive and plural definitions of the public sphere (Arato and Cohen 1992; Fraser 1993; Downing 2001) also indicate the media's economic and political institutions can shape the quality and extent of participation of online communication for different social groups. For Valtysson (2012, 2017), social media conversations are shaped by the economic imperatives of the platform company, because such communication occurs in virtual spaces that prioritize advertisers' interests. Whilst online communication offers an accessible space for disabled users, the commercial context of online communication limits the equality of participation required for the development of plural public spheres online.

Rational Spheres of Communication and Unregulated Platform Companies

The proliferation of hate speech and fake news online raises questions about the extent to which it is possible for current network communication platforms to sustain a public sphere as defined in Habermas' terms—that is a 'sphere of rational communication, the realm of social life in which public opinion formed' (Swingewood 2000: 206). The centrality of advertising in the platform business model erodes the scope of rational communication essential to the functioning of a public sphere (Habermas 1989), and furthermore, as Valtysson (2012) suggests, the marketization of users' data by social media platform companies perhaps exemplifies the process Habermas (1981) described as the 'colonization of the lifeworld'. The technology of Web 2.0 in early network technology was deemed to offer a 'new socio-technical paradigm' (Atton 2004: 13) in which the potential for a decentralized, participatory space to extend the public sphere and enhance democratic freedom was the focus of the debate (Kellner 2014; Preston 2001). However, the emergence of large technology companies has produced a tendency towards centralization in the online economy (Preston 2001), reflected in the predominance of the social media platform company (Srnicek 2017). In this 'globalization from above' (Falk 1993: 93), the emergence of a commercialized, global network economy erodes potential for online communication to sustain a public sphere. Public service broadcasting can sustain the rational participatory communication necessary to the public sphere (Preston 2001), but wholly privatized communication companies herald the weak public sphere that accompanies the 'end of public-funded broadcasting, the erosion of citizenship, the dominance of technological rationality, and an entrenched fear of more creative forms of politics and aesthetics' (Stevenson 2002: 224). Public ownership sustains the public sphere and permits the regulation required to protect the rights of disabled people to equal participation in public life.

The demand for 'internet freedom' by platform companies that is outside the reach of national and international law often boils down to the technology companies' preference for the use of unregulated technology rather than a regard for the protection of equal rights of participation in rational public debate. Whilst the emergence of platform capitalism in the twenty-first century differs to the nineteenth-century rise of private press advertising (Mahlouly 2013), Habermas' critique of the impact of economic and political power upon the ways in which media forms can sustain the reasoned debate crucial to democratic processes remains relevant in three crucial ways. First, democracy requires reasoned debate. Second the maintenance of the public sphere in which rational debate occurs requires a particular economic and political configuration to flourish. Third there 'exists conflict between the public sphere and capitalism' (Swingewood 2000: 206). If the public sphere is defined in terms of Habermas' 'ideal of public communication' … which can facilitate people's participation in democracy if 'unfettered by institutional control' (Livingstone and Lunt 1994: 10), then perhaps the public sphere concept remains applicable to the analysis of more recent virtual contexts of communication (Dahlgren 2005).

Through examining the different ways in which disabled people experience online/offline discrimination and by examining rights to access and participate in online communication through the social model of disability, the concepts of online public space and public sphere can be used to gauge the significance and impact of disablist hate speech online. Disabled users can often access the space of online communication easily. However, disablist hate speech works against disabled people's rights to equality of participation in online communication spheres.

The concept of the ideal public sphere can guide the development of social policy and legislation to counter online disablist hate speech. This analytical perspective suggests that publicly owned communication companies, independent from advertisers' interests and with powers to regulate disablist hate speech, can ensure disabled users have equality of participation in online communication. Platform companies have often proven reluctant to regulate counter online hate speech that can marginalize disabled users online, exposing users to far-right narratives that simultaneously invade and seek to exclude people from public spaces and spheres, whilst also citing rights to 'free speech' in order to silence opposing voices (Cammaerts 2009). Recent European Union legislation has shown that regulation can indeed challenge the domination of the global internet companies and the establishment of a publicly owned internet infrastructure would both end the platform company's monopoly of online communication and locate the internet as a space within the reach of national and international regulation.

Conclusion

An analysis of the distinct significance of online communication for many disabled people can provide insights that can inform the creation and implementation of social policies and legislation to counter disablist hate speech online. The technological and social transformations brought in by the internet and network society (Castells 1996, 1997, 1998) have transformed the lives of many people with mental and physical disabilities through the capacity of online technology to overcome physical and social barriers to communication and social interaction. The distinct way in which many disabled people experience the distinction between the online and the offline realms means that that access to, and participation within, the online space has a heightened, practical significance in many disabled people's lives precisely because online communication is so transformative and enabling.

By situating the analysis of disablist hate speech online within the wider context of neoliberalism, I argue that disability hate speech and the unregulated internet are issues that stem from the barriers neoliberalism presents to the regulation of online communication, regulation that is required to sustain disabled users' rights to equality of participation online. Network technology has developed as the infrastructure that serves neoliberal globalization (Harvey 2005) and the business model of the platform company reflects finance capitalism's search for new resources, markets and profits (Srnicek 2017). By analysing the ways in which disability hate speech is facilitated by the current predominance of the economic model of the platform company, future directions for social policy and legislation to counter hate speech can be ascertained. The application of the social model of disability to the analysis and re-imagining of online communication provides a useful tool to evaluate the extent to which disabled people's rights to equality of access and participation can be exercised in online contexts. Policies to counter disability hate speech online can draw upon the ideal concepts of public space and public sphere in order to highlight the extent to which marketed media can encroach upon democratic media freedoms as much as government censorship. The analysis of the ways in which the platform company business models reflect advertiser interests and resist the content regulation disabled users required for equality of participation online. The regulation required to counter disablist hate speech online requires a frame of analysis that goes beyond the online/offline distinction and towards an understanding of the ways private and public media ownership impacts upon disabled people's rights to equality of participation and freedom of expression online.

Notes

1. The term 'disability' is defined according to the social model of disability: a socially constructed state that occurs when people with impairments do not receive adequate support for participation in social life (Oliver 1983, 1990).
2. Reports on the 2007 deaths of Fiona and Francesca Pilkington (Capewell et al. 2015) and Brent Martin (Holt 2008) and the 2010 deaths of David Askew (Disability News Service 2011) and Gemma Hayter (BBC News 2011) raised public awareness of disablist hate crime incidents.
3. In England and Wales, the Racial and Religious Hatred Act 2006, s. 4A inserted Part 3A to the Public Order Act 1986 (POA1986), to outlaw 'stirring up' hate speech based upon racial and religious identities. The Criminal Justice and Immigration Act 2008 amended Part 3A POA1986 to extend 'stirring up' hate speech law to sexual orientation. UK Legislation. https://www.legislation.gov.uk, accessed February 4, 2019.
4. Disability hate crime constitutes an aggravated offence in England and Wales under s. 146 (2) Criminal Justice Act 2003 and under s. 1 Offences (Aggravated by Prejudice) (Scotland) Act 2009 in Scotland. UK and Scotland Legislation. https://www.legislation.gov.uk, accessed February 4, 2019.
5. Criminal Justice Act 2003, s. 146 (5) defined 'disability' as 'any physical or mental impairment'. UK Legislation. https://www.legislation.gov.uk, accessed February 4, 2019.
6. Criminal Justice Act 1972, s. 33, 'any place to which … the public have, or are permitted to have access'. UK Legislation. https://www.legislation.gov.uk, accessed 4 February 2019.

References

Agerholm, H. (2017, October 16). Hate crimes against disabled children rise 150% in two years. *The Independent*. Accessed July 26, 2018. http://www.theindependent.co.uk.

Amichai-Hamburger, Y., & Hayat, Z. (2013). Internet and personality. In Y. Amachai-Hamburger (Ed.), *The Social Net: Understanding Our Online Behavior*. Oxford: Oxford University Press.

Arato, A., & Cohen, J. (1992). *Civil Society and Political Theory*. Cambridge: MIT Press.

Atton, C. (2004). *An Alternative Internet: Radical Media, Politics and Certainty*. Edinburgh: Edinburgh University Press.

Aubin, F. (2014). Between public space and public sphere: An assessment of Francophone contributions. *Canadian Journal of Communication, 39*(1), 89–110.

Barlow, J. P. (1996, February 8). A declaration of the independence of cyberspace. *Electronic Frontier Foundation*. Accessed August 30, 2018. https://www.eff.org.

BBC News. (2011, September 12). Gemma Hayter murder: Three jailed for life. *BBC News*. Accessed February 4, 2019. https://www.bbc.uk.

BBC News. (2017, August 21). Hate crime: Online abuse as serious as face-to-face. *BBC News*. Accessed March 5, 2018. https://www.bbc.uk.

Bolano, C. R. S., & Vieira, E. S. (2014). The political economy of the internet: Social networking sites and a reply to Fuchs. *Television and News Media, 16*(1), 61–62.

Bossier, A. M., & Holt, T. J. (2009). Online activities, guardianship and malware infection: An examination of routine activities theory. *The International Journal of Cyber Criminology, 3*(1), 400–420.

Butler, P. (2012, August 20). Disability activists use social media to put care cuts on the political agenda. *The Guardian*. Accessed July 26, 2018. https://www.theguardian.com.

Cammarets, B. (2009). Radical pluralism and free speech in online public spaces: The case of North Belgian extreme right discourses. *International Journal of Cultural Studies, 12*(6), 555–575.

Capewell, C., Ralph, S., & Bonnett, L. (2015). The continuing violence towards disabled people. *Journal of Research in Special Educational Needs, 15*(3).

Castells, M. (1996). *The Rise of the Network Society; The Information Age: Economy, Society and Culture* (Vol. 1). Oxford: Blackwell.

Castells, M. (1997). *The Power of Identity; The Information Age: Economy, Society and Culture* (Vol. 2). Oxford: Blackwell.

Castells, M. (1998). *End of Millennium; The Information Age: Economy, Society and Culture* (Vol. 3). Oxford: Blackwell.

Clark, N. (2011, September 13). Disability hate crime begins with verbal abuse. *The Guardian*. Accessed July 26, 2018. https://www.theguardian.com.

Colman, N., & Sykes, W. (2016). *Crime and Disabled People: Measures of Disability Related Harassment. Research Report 103.* Manchester: Equality and Human Rights Commission. Accessed July 26, 2018. https://www.equalityhumanrights.com.

Couldry, N. (2000). *The Place of Media Power: Pilgrims and Witnesses of the Media Age.* London: Routledge.

Dahlgren, P. (2005). The internet, public spheres and political communication: Dispersion and deliberation. *Political Communication, 22*(2), 147–162.

Disability News Service. (2011, March 4). The death of David Askew: Hate crime ordeal lasted 40 years. *Disability News Service.* Accessed February 4, 2019. https://www.disabilitynewsservice.com.

Dodd, V. (2016, July 11). Police blame worst rise in recorded hate crime on EU Referendum. *The Guardian.* Accessed July 26, 2018. https://www.theguardian.com.

Dodd, V. (2017, August 21). CPS to crack down on social media hate crime, says Alison Saunders. *The Guardian.* Accessed July 26. https://www.theguardian.com.

Downing, J. (2001). *Radical Media: Rebellious Communication and Social Movements.* Thousand Oaks, CA: Sage.

Equality and Human Rights Commission (EHRC). (2013). *Manifesto for Change: Progress Report 2013.* Manchester: Equality and Human Rights Commission. Accessed February 4, 2019. https://www.equalityhumanrights.com.

European Commission Against Racism and Intolerance (ECRI). (2016). *General policy recommendation no 15: On combating hate speech.* Accessed July 26, 2018. https://www.coe.int/t/dghl/monitoring/ecri/activities/GPR/EN/RecommedationN15/REC-15-2016-015-ENG.pdf.

Falk, R. A. (1993). The making of global citizenship. In J. Brecher, J. B. Childs, & J. Cutler (Eds.), *Global Visions: Beyond the New World Order.* Boston: South End Press.

Fraser, N. (1993). Rethinking the public sphere: A contribution to the critique of actually existing democracy. In C. Calhoun (Ed.), *Habermas and the Public Sphere* (pp. 109–142). Cambridge: MIT Press.

Goggin, G., & Newell, C. (2003). *Digital Disability: The Social Construction of Disability in New Media.* London: Rowman & Letterfield.

Habermas, J. (1962 [1989]). *The Structural Transformation of the Public Sphere.* Cambridge: Polity Press.

Habermas, J. (1981). *The Theory of Communicative Action Volume Two: Lifeworld and System: A Critique of Functionalist Reason*. Boston: Beacon Press.
Harvey, D. (2005). *A Brief History of Neoliberalism*. Oxford: Oxford University Press.
Holm, N. (2016). *Advertising and Consumer Society*. Basingstoke: Palgrave Macmillan.
Holt, A. (2008, January 22). Fears over disability hate crime. *BBC News*. Accessed February 4, 2019. https://www.bbb.co.uk.
Home Office. (2017, October 17). Hate crime in England and Wales: 2016 to 2017. *Statistical Bulletin, 17, 17*. Accessed July 26, 2018. https://www.assets.publishing.service.gov.uk.
Kalman, Y. M., Raban, D. R., & Rafaeli, S. (2013). Netified: Social cognition in crowds and clouds. In Y. Amichai-Hamburger (Ed.), *The Social Net: Understanding Our Online Behavior*. Oxford: Oxford University Press.
Kellner, D. (2014). Habermas, the public sphere and democracy. In D. Boros & J. M. Glass (Eds.), *Re-imaging Public Space: The Frankfurt School in the 21st Century*. London: Palgrave.
Kiteley, P., & Robinson, B. (2017, October 15). Disabled children hate crime reports increase. *BBC News*. Accessed March 5, 2018. https://www.bbc.co.uk.
Law Commission. (2013). *Hate Crime: The Case for Extending the Existing Offences*: *A Consultation Paper*. United Kingdom Law Commission Consultation Paper Number 213. London: UK Law Commission. Accessed July 26, 2018. https://www.lawcom.gov.uk.
Livingstone, S., & Lunt, P. (1994). The mass media, democracy and the public sphere. In S. Livingstone & P. Lunt (Eds.), *Talk on Television Audience Participation and Public Debate*. London: Routledge.
Mahlouly, D. (2013). Rethinking the public sphere in a digital environment: Similarities between eighteenth and twenty first century. *New Horizons, 20*(Spring 2013). Accessed July 26, 2018. https://www.gla.ac.uk.
Marzi, A. (Ed.). (2016). *Psychoanalysis, Identity and the Internet: Explorations into Cyberspace*. London: Karnac.
Mason, P. (2016). *Post Capitalism: A Guide to Our Future*. London: Penguin.
Morozov, E. (2011). *The Net Delusion: The Dark Side of Internet Freedom*. London: Penguin.
Morozov, E. (2013). *To Save Everything, Click Here: The Folly of Technological Solutionism*. London: Penguin.

Mortimer, C. (2015, November 8). Hate crime against disabled people rises to 41% in a year. *The Independent*. Accessed July 26, 2018. https://www.theindependent.co.uk.

Murphy, M. (Ed.). (2016). *Habermas and Social Research: Between Theory and Method*. London: Routledge.

Nilsson, C., Skar, L., & Soderbergh, S. (2010). Swedish district nurses' experience on the use of information and communication technology for supporting people with serious chronic illness living at home: A case study. *Scandinavian Journal of Caring Services: Empirical Studies, 24*, 259–265.

Oliver, M. (1983). *Social Work with Disabled People*. Basingstoke: Palgrave Macmillan.

Oliver, M. (1990). *The Politics of Disablement*. London: Palgrave Macmillan.

O'Neill, A. (2017, October 17). Hate crime, England and Wales, 2016–2017. *Statistical Bulletin, 17/17*. London: UK Home Office. Accessed February 8, 2019. https://www.assests.publishing.service.gov.uk.

Papachrissi, Z. (2002). The virtual sphere: The internet as a public sphere. *New Media and Society, 4*(1), 9–27.

Pearson, C., & Trevisan, F. (2015). Disability activism in the new media ecology: Campaigning strategies in the digital era. *Disability and Society, 30*(6), 924–950.

Preston, P. (2001). *Reshaping Communication: Technology, Information and Social Change*. London: Sage.

Pring, J. (2017, November 30). Major law reform would help close 'huge justice gap' in disability hate crime. *Disability News Service*. Accessed July 26, 2018. https://www.disabilitynewsserive.com.

Riotta, G. (2018, March 13). Una bussola per fermare le fake news. *La Stampa*. Accessed July 26, 2018. https://www.lastampa.it.

Shakespeare, T. (2006). The social model of disability. In L. Davis (Ed.), *The Disability Studies Reader*. London: Routledge.

Solon, O. (2017, February 17). Mark Zuckerberg pens major Facebook manifesto on how to burst the bubble. *The Guardian*. Accessed July 26, 2018. https://www.theguardian.com.

Sproull, L., Conley, C., & Moon, J. Y. (2013). The kindness of strangers: Prosocial behavior on the internet. In Y. Amichai-Hamburger (Ed.), *The Social Net: Understanding Our Online Behaviour*. Oxford: Oxford University Press.

Srnicek, N. (2017). *Platform Capitalism*. Cambridge: Polity Press.

Stein, L. (2008). Speech without rights: The status of public space on the internet. *The Communication Review, 11*(1), 1–23.

Stevenson, N. (2002). *Understanding Media Cultures*. London: Sage.
Swingewood, A. (2000). *A Short History of Sociological Thought*. London: Palgrave Macmillan.
The Economist. (2017, November 4). *Editorial: Does social media threaten democracy?* Accessed July 26, 2018. https://www.economist.com.
Tierney, T. (2013). *The Public Space of Social Media: Connected Cultures of the Network Society*. London: Routledge.
Trevisan, F. (2013). *Connected Citizens or Digital Isolation? Online Disability Activism in Times of Crisis* (PhD thesis). University of Glasgow, UK.
United Kingdom Parliament. (2017). *Intimidation in public life: A review by the committee on standards in public life. cm 9543.* Accessed July 26. https://www.assets.publishing.services.gov.uk.
Valtysson, B. (2012). Facebook as a digital public sphere: Processes of colonization and emancipation. *TripleC: Cognition, Communication, Co-operation, 10*(1), 77–91.
Valtysson, B. (2017). Digitizing Habermas: Digital public spheres and networked politics. In M. Murphy (Ed.), *Habermas and Social Research*. London: Routledge.
Van Dijck, J. (2013). *The Culture of Connectivity: A Critical History of Social Media*. Oxford: Oxford University Press.
Waldron, J. (2012). *The Harm in Hate Speech*. Cambridge, MA: Harvard University Press.
Walker, P. (2009, September 24). Incident diary reveals ordeal of mother who killed herself and daughter. *The Guardian*. Accessed July 26, 2018. https://www.theguardian.com.
Walters, A., Brown, R., & Wiedlitska, S. (2016). *Causes and Motivations of Hate Crime. Research Report 102*. Manchester: Equality and Human Rights Commission. Accessed February 4, 2019. https://www.equalityhumanrights.com.

14

Challenges in Policing Cyberstalking: A Critique of the Stalking Risk Profile in the Context of Online Relationships

Brianna O'Shea, Roberta Julian, Jeremy Prichard and Sally Kelty

Introduction

Cyberstalking has been defined as a repeated pattern of behaviour that utilises technology to harass or demand intimacy from another person (Lyndon et al. 2011). Cases of cyberstalking are becoming more visible in the media and in police investigations—for example, the media report of Dr. Angela Jay who was stalked in Australia by her Tinder

---

B. O'Shea (✉) · R. Julian
Tasmanian Institute of Law Enforcement Studies (TILES),
University of Tasmania, Hobart, TAS, Australia

J. Prichard
University of Tasmania, Hobart, TAS, Australia

S. Kelty
University of Canberra, Bruce, ACT, Australia

© The Author(s) 2019
K. Lumsden and E. Harmer (eds.), *Online Othering*,
Palgrave Studies in Cybercrime and Cybersecurity,
https://doi.org/10.1007/978-3-030-12633-9_14

date, stabbed 11 times and doused in petrol with the intent to rape her and burn her alive (Doyle 2017). Dr. Jay had recently ended the relationship and took out a family violence order due to receiving hundreds of calls threatening self-harm if she did not take him back (Proudman and Olding 2016). Some media reports focus upon cases in which cyberstalking is overshadowed by coinciding offline stalking that results in extreme physical violence. Such coverage may understate the role of technology in facilitating abuse. This raises questions about how police understand and investigate cyberstalking. Are its characteristics similar to or different from 'traditional' offline stalking? What impact does this have on how police investigate and prosecute cyberstalking? This chapter addresses these questions by presenting the challenges police themselves have identified in an Australian jurisdiction. The chapter begins by discussing cyberstalking as a form of technology-facilitated abuse in the context of family violence. This highlights two areas that are problematic for investigating and prosecuting cyberstalking: legislation and risk assessment. This chapter critically discusses these two areas of concern and, in doing so, identifies some of the key challenges for police in investigating and prosecuting cyberstalking.

Defining and Policing Stalking and Cyberstalking

Stalking is broadly defined as 'wilful, malicious, and repeated following or harassment of another person' (Tjaden and Thoennes 1998: 1). It occurs among a wide variety of relationships including between ex-intimates, family/friends, professional relationships, workplace contacts, casual acquaintances, identified strangers or unidentified strangers (Mullen et al. 2006). However, stalking is most commonly associated with family violence. Past research has consistently shown that most commonly stalking is perpetrated against females by ex-intimate male partners (Mullen et al. 2009). Stalking is often a means by which family violence continues following separation (Victorian Royal Commission into Family Violence 2016). Risk assessments have determined that ex-intimates are the most at-risk group for stalking and this is reflected in Australian laws that criminalise stalking under family violence legislation (Mullen et al. 2006; Scott et al. 2010). Stalking is illegal in all states and territories of Australia, although definitions of stalking differ.[1]

One of the key approaches to policing family violence incidents such as stalking is that police officers assess and respond to risk in terms of a risk paradigm, typically by following risk assessment tools (McCulloch et al. 2016). A study conducted by Perez Trujillo and Ross (2008) examined a sample of 501 risk assessments on family violence completed by police officers in Victoria, Australia. Importantly, police officers were required to estimate the likelihood of future violence on a 5-point scale: *rare, unlikely, possible, likely or almost certain*. It was found that 76% of incidents involved current or ex-intimate partners. The most common response by police officers was applying for an intervention order, and in 44% of incidents, police gave advice or referrals but did not take any action. Police officers perceived the risk of future violence as *likely or almost certain* when the incident was one of a sequence that was escalating.

Stalking is a course of conduct, whereby the behaviour must occur on more than one occasion creating a sequence of repeated actions (Banyard et al. 2017; Mullen et al. 2009). Therefore, it would be reasonable to suggest that stalking could be regarded as family violence that police perceive as having a high risk of future escalating violence (Rosenfeld 2004; Thompson et al. 2013). In relation to police decision-making, the location of the incident has very rarely been a focus of examination and past research has primarily focused on urban incidents (Avakame and Fyfe 2001). Therefore, the effect of the incidents occurring in cyberspace and the challenge this poses for police decision-making remains largely unknown.

Technology-facilitated abuse such as cyberstalking has been given very little attention in initiatives aimed at addressing family violence (Al-Alosi 2017). The 2016 Victorian Royal Commission into Family Violence identified that technology is becoming increasingly important in the area of family violence. It outlines that 'we need swift solutions to combat the ways perpetrators use mobile phones, social media platforms and surveillance devices to stalk and harass their victims' (Victorian Royal Commission into Family Violence 2016: 13). It was found that the most commonly used technology and online platforms, as perceived by family violence workers, were smartphones (82%), mobile phones (82%), social media (82%), email (52%) and GPS tracking (29%) (Woodlock 2013). Given this increased use of technology in family violence incidents, we argue that risk assessments targeted towards family violence-related offences such as stalking need to accommodate the use of electronic or Internet-capable devices.

Currently, there are no adequate risk assessment tools that police in Australia can use to assess the risk of cyberstalking. There are significant difficulties in developing a risk assessment tool for cyberstalking partly because there is no universally accepted definition of what constitutes cyberstalking. 'Cyber-obsessional pursuit' is a term used to describe 'using technology-based stalking behaviours to harass or demand intimacy from another person' (Lyndon et al. 2011: 711). Cyberstalking may result from cyber-obsessional pursuit if the behaviours are repeated and form a pattern of behaviour that would cause a reasonable person fear (Lyndon et al. 2011). Identifying risk of cyberstalking is further complicated by the fact that stalking and cyberstalking are inter-related. Cyberstalking is claimed to be one of the most common ways that a pattern of stalking begins (Mishra and Mishra 2013). Furthermore, cyberstalking should not be considered in isolation as the majority of cyberstalkers also engage in offline stalking behaviour (Cavezza and McEwan 2014). All these factors create a challenge for understanding and identifying risk of cyberstalking and this contributes to the difficulties experienced by police in the investigation and prosecution of cyberstalking.

Challenges for the Police

It is important to note that police are confronted with a number of challenges when investigating and prosecuting cyberstalking. There are two broad sets of challenges: (1) new/changing technology and (2) the relevance of existing understandings of stalking risk:

1. *Technology* is becoming increasingly prevalent in facilitating family violence offences such as stalking. Ongoing changes in Web development, in particular the increased prevalence of Internet-capable devices is identified as an emerging area of concern for police.
2. *The Stalking Risk Profile* (MacKenzie et al. 2011) represents the existing understanding of stalking risk in Australia. The challenge for police is whether this risk assessment tool is sensitive to changes in the nature of relationships in an online context. Therefore, the way in which police understand both technology and its associated risks in cases of cyberstalking will be explored.

Prevalence

There has been very little research on the prevalence of cyberstalking in Australia and internationally. Nevertheless, crude estimates of cyberstalking provided in a few studies can provide an indication of the extent of the problem (Bocij 2004; Cavezza and McEwan 2014). For example, Mishra and Mishra (2013: 40) state that:

> Out of the estimated 79 million population worldwide on the Internet at any given time, we could find 63,000 Internet stalkers travelling the information superhighway, stalking approximately 474,000 victims.

Generally, women are at greater risk of cyberstalking than men (Casey 2011). In addition, new Internet users are at greater risk of cyberstalking than experienced Internet users (Casey 2011). The Australian Cybercrime Online Reporting Network (ACORN) found that cyberbullying and stalking comprised more than 6% of incidents reported to them (Piovesan 2016). Overall, some Australian states have reported up to a 20.5% increase in stalking over the past two years; however, the prevalence of cyber technology in this increase remains largely unknown (Crime Statistics Agency 2017).

As technology advances, stalkers are discovering new ways of acquiring victims, gathering information, monitoring victims, hiding their identities and avoiding capture (Casey 2011). Primarily, cyberstalkers use electronic or Internet-capable devices to monitor or communicate with victims. Monitoring devices include mobile phones, listening devices, computer programs and global positioning systems (Reyns 2010; Reyns et al. 2012). Communication methods involve the use of email, blogs, social networking sites, message boards and forums, online dating sites, IM messages, text messages, video messages and chat rooms (Reyns 2010). A 2010 study found that cyberstalking victims are active users in social networking mediums such as Facebook, online forums and instant messaging (Haron and Yusof 2010). Most recently, phone apps have been identified as a way that stalkers monitor their victims (Victorian Royal Commission into Family Violence 2016).

Changing Stages of Web Development and Understandings of Risk

The normalisation of technology and its continuous development have facilitated abuse on the Internet. It has been noted that the Internet can significantly increase a victim's risk in traditional criminal investigations of stalking (Casey 2011). Barassi and Treré (2012) highlight the dynamic relationship between technological structures and social use. Stalkers are inventing innovative ways of using Internet-capable devices to cyberstalk their victims. This is a cyber threat for victims of stalking who are at risk of further victimisation experienced online. In Australia, there were reported to be approximately 13.5 million Internet subscribers at the end of December 2016 (Australian Bureau of Statistics 2017). The Victorian Royal Commission into Family Violence (2016: 30) suggests that 'technology-facilitated abuse has been normalised as a result of the increasing use of technology in relationships'.

Changes in the development of the Web raise a challenge for police because it is difficult to maintain expertise. The Web refers to an integrated techno-social system that enhances human cognition, communication and cooperation (Barassi and Treré 2012; Fuchs et al. 2010). The first stage, Web 1.0 (The Web), was created in 1996 and allowed millions of users to search for information and read it (Naik and Shivalingaiah 2008). The second stage, Web 2.0 (The Social Web), in 2006 connected billions of users in the Web of social participation (Naik and Shivalingaiah 2008). Web 2.0 introduced two-way communication through social networking, email, chats, blogging and tagging (Naik and Shivalingaiah 2008). Social networking technology 'provides the openness and transparency to the contents of The Social Web, along the way the technology also exposes users to cyber threat' (Haron and Yusof 2010: 237). The third stage, Web 3.0 (The Semantic Web), was introduced in 2016 and enables trillions of users to immerse themselves in the Internet through multi-user virtual environments and avatar representation (Naik and Shivalingaiah 2008). In addition, Web 3.0 has seen the introduction of Internet-capable devices which have exacerbated stalking as a crime due to the misuse of this technology (Victorian Royal Commission into Family Violence 2016).

There is a clear distinction in the understanding of Web development between digital natives and digital immigrants. According to Prensky (2001), digital natives refer to native speakers of the digital language which incorporates the Internet, email, instant messaging, mobile phones, video cameras and computer games as integral components of their lives. Digital language encompasses a knowledge of how people commonly behave and interact across Web stages 1.0–3.0. In contrast, digital immigrants are defined as being in the process of learning the digital language and who speak an outdated language of the pre-digital age (Prensky 2001).

Technological advancements may pose challenges for police who are viewing stalking in a traditional sense and this may create complexities when police are deciding whether to investigate, progressing through an investigation or examining the outcomes of an investigation. It seems feasible that difficulties may be greater for police who are digital immigrants. We argue that it is essential to the investigation of cyberstalking cases that police have knowledge of constantly developing technology.

The Changing Nature of Online Relationships and Risk

The risk assessments currently used in Australia include measures of static and dynamic risk factors that may predict further violence between current or ex-intimate partners (Perez Trujillo and Ross 2008). Static risk factors are unchangeable based on past behaviour and personal characteristics (McEwan et al. 2011). For example, the Stalking Risk Profile outlines victim–offender relationship types as ex-intimate, family/friend, professional relationship, workplace contact, casual acquaintance, identified stranger or unidentified (Mullen et al. 2006: 443). Dynamic refers to 'changeable risk factors that can be modified through intervention to reduce risk' (McEwan et al. 2011: 182). As individuals change over time, so to do the changes to risk in stalking incidents and assessment tools need to be sensitive to these changes (McEwan et al. 2011). These tools also need to be sensitive to broader changes in the nature of stalking over time—such as in the increased prevalence of cyberstalking. The authors of the Stalking Risk Profile themselves have said that 'the term cyberstalking now has a life of its own' (Mullen et al. 2009: 152). We argue that the changing nature of relationships has become increasingly dynamic as a result of Web development and technological advancements which need to be considered in terms of risk assessment. While the Stalking Risk Profile has been considered useful for assessing risk of offline stalking, its suitability in the context of assessing risk of cyberstalking can be questioned.

The Stalking Risk Profile

Police rely heavily on risk assessment when investigating and prosecuting family violence offences such as stalking (Perez Trujillo and Ross 2008). However, typologies in risk profiles are not developed in the light of police investigations, rather are primarily for clinicians to administer appropriate treatments for any underlying mental health problems (Casey 2011). The Stalking Risk Profile is the most commonly used professional tool in Australia to assess and manage risk in stalking cases for psychological assessment (MacKenzie et al. 2011). This risk profile therefore informs police understandings of stalking as police are often the first point of contact for victims, and the ones to ultimately confront the stalker.

The authors of the Stalking Risk Profile, MacKenzie et al. (2011), have contributed a large body of research to the stalking literature. Schwartz-Watts (2006) argues that the Stalking Risk Profile is not an actuarial scale, but rather an assessment to be used on a case-by-case basis. The Stalking Risk Profile enables the clinician to determine the risk of violence, persistence, recurrence and psychosocial damage according to the stalker's motivation (MacKenzie et al. 2011). The Stalking Risk Profile incorporates five domains:

1. The nature of the relationship between the stalker and the victim;
2. The stalker's motivations;
3. The psychological, psychopathological and social realities of the stalker;
4. The psychological and social vulnerabilities of the victim;
5. The legal and mental health context in which the stalking is occurring (Mullen et al. 2006: 442).

These five domains outline the risk factors that are used to inform the stalker types in the Stalking Risk Profile.

Five stalker types have been proposed by MacKenzie et al. (2011). These stalker types can be used as a frame of reference for clinicians to assess risk although they are not mutually exclusive (Mullen et al. 2006). First, the rejected stalker arises from the breakdown of a close relationship and involves the stalker attempting to reconcile the relationship or seeking revenge for a perceived rejection (MacKenzie et al. 2011). Second, the resentful stalker feels as though they have been mistreated or that they are the victim of some form of injustice or humiliation and victims are strangers or acquaintances (MacKenzie et al. 2011). Third, the intimacy-seeking stalker arises out of a context of loneliness and victims are usually strangers or acquaintances who become the target of the stalker's desire for a loving relationship (MacKenzie et al. 2011). Fourth, the incompetent suitor is motivated by wanting to establish a short-term sexual relationship in a context of loneliness or lust and targets strangers or acquaintances (MacKenzie et al. 2011). Fifth, the predatory stalker is usually male and targets an unsuspecting female stranger for deviant sexual practices, interests and a sense of power and control (MacKenzie et al. 2011).

The first part of the paper outlined the increased prevalence of stalking overall and the critical role of technology in facilitating this abuse.

New technology, technological advancements and Web development were identified as creating increased risk for stalking victims. Risk assessment tools were not designed specifically for police use or technology-facilitated stalking which are likely to become problematic in an already emerging area of concern for police. These all create significant challenges to police in the investigation and prosecution of cyberstalking. The rationale for this preliminary study is to determine current police knowledge and understanding of technology used by stalkers, cyberstalking behaviour, legislation and victim safety protocol which are challenges in the investigative process. This is to ensure that police investigators and prosecutors have an adequate understanding of technology and its role in facilitating stalking to be proactive in policing cyberstalking in their respective jurisdictions.

Method

Participants

A preliminary study was undertaken to explore how investigations and prosecutions of cyberstalking are influenced by police knowledge and understanding of cyber technology. This was the first exploratory study of its kind to interview police with high levels of experience in policing cyberstalking. It is part of a larger study that is examining the investigation and prosecution of cyberstalking in Australia. The larger study involves the analysis of 38 reported stalking cases and judges sentencing remarks from two Australian jurisdictions as well as follow-up interviews with police investigators and prosecutors in multiple police jurisdictions. A total of five key investigators and prosecutors from an Australian police jurisdiction participated in the study. The sample comprised three females and two males who were key informants on investigating and prosecuting cyberstalking cases in an Australian jurisdiction. This preliminary study used the intense, personal experiences of these highly qualified police investigators and specialised police prosecutors. Intensity sampling enabled participants to be chosen on the basis of their extensive knowledge and experience in policing information-rich cyberstalking cases (Hansen 2006). This sampling strategy was considered appropriate as it is often the case that the same one or two police officers are assigned to stalking cases as they are confronted with a complex sequence of behaviours across months or even years (Mullen et al. 2009). The study was conducted in accordance with the ethical requirements of the Social Sciences Human Research Ethics Committee at the University of Tasmania.

Materials

Data were collected through qualitative interviews that were semi-structured using an interview schedule. A number of topics were able to be covered using the conversational style of semi-structured interviews. This allowed for flexibility in individual participant's responses based on their in-depth knowledge of cyberstalking investigations and prosecutions (Edwards and Holland 2013). The semi-structured interviews enabled lines of discussion to open up in the conversation which suited the exploratory nature of the study (Edwards and Holland 2013). Participants were asked about their knowledge and understanding of cyberstalking behaviour and the technology used by stalkers. Two initial questions were used in the opening stages of the interview:

1. In your professional opinion, what is cyberstalking?
2. What types of activities are classed as cyberstalking in your jurisdiction?

Further questions were designed to initiate a discussion of the investigative process:

1. Can you walk me through the stages of the investigation when a report of cyberstalking is made?
2. Who is involved in the investigation of a case of cyberstalking?

Finally, towards the end of the interview questions explored police investigators' and prosecutors' knowledge of current legislation and victim safety protocol:

1. What measures are put in place to ensure the safety of victims of cyberstalking?
2. In your experience, how well are the needs of cyberstalking victims dealt with under current laws?

Throughout the interview, participants were encouraged to reflect on and discuss any differences in the way in which police investigate offline stalking compared to cyberstalking.

Procedure

Participants were recruited by their superiors who invited them to participate in the study. Superiors were chosen because they offered an effective means of accessing highly experienced police investigators and prosecutors who were directly involved in policing cyberstalking in an Australian police jurisdiction. After agreeing to participate in the interview, participants read the information sheet and signed the consent form before being asked the questions in a semi-structured interview schedule. One researcher interviewed the participants individually at the police stations where they were located. Each of the interviews was conducted in 2015 in individual sessions that lasted one hour on average. All interviews were recorded and transcribed. No rewards were offered for participation in this study and no participants withdrew from the study. To ensure confidentiality, names of participants have been replaced with codes such as A1. The codes are used in presenting the key findings below.

Findings

The findings are divided into four sections which aim to: define cyberstalking and its associated behaviours; discuss police familiarity with the technology; determine the key stakeholders and investigative process; and detail victim safety protocols under the current legislative framework. The data presented are excerpts from interviews with police investigators and prosecutors in an Australian police jurisdiction.

Defining Cyberstalking

The interview data demonstrated that there was a lack of consistency across responses when identifying what technology could be used for a behaviour to be classed as cyberstalking. According to various definitions, cyberstalking can involve the use of smartphones, mobile phones, social media, email and GPS tracking just to name a few (Reyns 2010; Reyns et al. 2012; Woodlock 2013). However, D4 did not consider phones to be Internet-capable devices which can be used to cyberstalk a victim. When asked to define cyberstalking, they referred to it as:

> Unwanted contact that's continuous contact that's not wanted by the other party over the Internet or some type of other medium other than the telephone. (D4)

This perception that continuous unwanted contact via the telephone does not constitute cyberstalking is also evident when this participant discussed different types of technology involved in a case. D4 describes a case where the offender:

> Had also been in contact with them on Facebook, I don't know on the phone a lot too, which probably wouldn't fall into the cyberstalking but when he wasn't on the phone he would use his computer. (D4)

In contrast, B2 acknowledged that in cases of cyberstalking the technology is not limited to the computer:

> You can access things like Facebook on your mobile phone so it doesn't necessarily have to be the computer. (B2)

Police investigators and prosecutors were found to be concerned by their own technological expertise stating that the problem was:

> The technology, it's catching up with it basically. (E5)

A1 explains that police often have limited working knowledge of technology as they are:

> Not particularly tech savvy … often it is the victim telling us what's happened or where it's happened and sometimes they're new things to us so it may be a new website, it may be a new chat program and on their phones or computers. (A1)

Stages of Web development and technological advancements had significant implications for the way in which cyberstalking is investigated. C3 while laughing explained that:

> In the past what we'd do is photograph or film the [computer] screen as its happening. (C3)

Police Familiarity with Technology: Digital Immigrants and Digital Natives

It was found that different participants had different levels of familiarity with the technology. The interviews revealed that predominantly participants could be described as digital immigrants. Digital immigrants refer to police investigators and prosecutors in the process of learning about new/changing technology (Prensky 2001). A digital immigrant noted the difficulty in policing cyberstalking by comparing it to a 'traditional' offence rather than seeing it as a new form of behaviour in an online context:

> It's not like watching an assault or something in the bus mall. (E5)

This not only had implications for how police progressed through the investigation, the prosecution also was hindered by immigration to a digital world. According to Prensky (2001: 2), a key example of the behaviour of a digital immigrant is 'printing out your email'. This was evident in interviews with police prosecutors who explained a lack of technology available in courts. E5 explains that police prosecutors are:

> Printing off as much as we can from the device that it's retrieved from and it's really difficult because you don't get the same picture than what you do on the computer but we don't have the facilities in the [Magistrates] court room. (E5)

In comparison, digital natives understood cyberstalking in different ways; they included more types of technology capable of facilitating stalking in their definitions. Police investigators who were digital natives also investigated cyberstalking differently as they were more likely to utilise technological advancements when conducting their investigations. A1 explains the process where victims are gathering their own evidence or investigators are engaging more with the victims' social media profiles:

> Someone could copy it or screenshot it or we can sit on their Facebook and watch those messages come through. (A1)

Cyberstalking Investigative Process and Its Stakeholders

Interviews with police investigators and prosecutors identified a number of challenges in the investigative process of cyberstalking cases. Police were asked about the stages of the investigation when a report of cyberstalking is made and who is involved. Their responses generally showed an undocumented process involving multiple law enforcement personnel sometimes with cross-jurisdictional involvement. This is inconsistent with initial thoughts by Mullen et al. (2009) who stated that the complex sequence of behaviours involved in stalking across months or even years resulted in the same one or two police officers being assigned to a case. However, the findings from the preliminary study suggest that this is not necessarily the case for cyberstalking as the use of technology to harass or demand intimacy from another person can occur across multiple police jurisdictions.

A challenge identified by the police was that the key stakeholders in the future for this type of offending will be young people. Youth are post-digital ('digital natives') and are native speakers of the digital language which incorporates new/changing technology (Prensky 2001). Police investigators interviewed held particular concerns for youth as technologies such as Internet-capable devices are integral components of their lives. C3 considers the future challenges for the investigative process of cyberstalking when:

> Kids are becoming more tech savvy with things like the Tor network and whatnot and if they start using it the proper way it's just going to be almost impossible for us to deal with. (C3)

A problem that was identified by all of the police prosecutors interviewed was anonymity. This is a challenge for police as explained by E5 who discusses the complexities of establishing that the accused was the author of the repeated and unwanted communication in an online context:

> So we have to establish in our case that this particular accused was the author. We get around it sometimes if the information is so personal that only the accused could have known so we've gotten around it a couple of times on that basis but otherwise we run into a lot of hurdles there. (E5)

Additionally, police are challenged by the techniques used by cyberstalkers such as involving family members as a third party to obtain information to authorise password protection. A1 discusses an example where an offender:

> Made numerous different emails under her personal email and emailed her mum saying 'Oh hey mum, what was our first dog's name?' because some email account passwords will ask for that. Her mum was like 'Why are you asking that? But then gave it because [she assumed] that was her daughter. (A1)

Overall, police are challenged by the anonymity facilitated by new technologies as well as the techniques stalkers are utilising to overcome protections put in place to ensure privacy and safety online.

Current Legislation and Safety Protocols for Cyberstalking Victims

Police responded to questions which asked what measures were put in place to ensure the safety of victims and if they felt that current laws adequately dealt with cyberstalking behaviour. The interviews showed that not all cyberstalking could be clearly covered under a legislative framework of family violence in Australia. For example, in cases involving strangers:

> It was more meeting them and then 'convincing' them to be in a relationship with him but never got past, never got far enough to be an intimate relationship. (D4)

This is a problem because the Commonwealth Criminal Code in Australia does not have a stalking offence; rather, stalking constitutes a type of family violence and strangers do not fit the definition of the family in the 'traditional' sense. This shows that the relationship between the offender and primary victim in cyberstalking cases is not as static as the Stalking Risk Profile suggests. A police investigator details a dynamic relationship where the victim and the offender:

> Had never met, they met online and actually … started controlling the person from interstate over the computer, then [the offender] went over and met [the victim] and came back and it continued online for a long time … once they then met, the [offender] knew where [the victim] lived and then the threats became even more real. (D4)

There was also found to be additional offences which were overlapping with cyberstalking, in particular image-based sexual abuse. A1 discusses a case involving acquaintances where:

> It was quite clear that he was smitten with her and he went a roundabout way of things like … sending apparent nude photographs of her to other people which wasn't her, he put her head on pictures. (A1)

These findings outlined some of the challenges for policing cyberstalking involving strangers or acquaintances under current legislation designed to address stalking as a type of family violence.

Conclusion

This study aimed to identify some of the key challenges for police investigating and prosecuting cyberstalking. A police officer's engagement with the technology and willingness to learn were factors in determining their overall understanding of cyberstalking. This is consistent with the work of Prensky (2001) who suggests that digital immigrants may learn to use new technologies. In order for policing of cyberstalking to be proactive rather than reactive, ways that emerging technologies can be utilised by investigators and prosecutors need to be identified. This will require police to have a good working knowledge of technological advancements and Web development to ensure that adequate solutions are provided to cyberstalking victims to minimise their potential risk. This supports the findings from the Victorian Royal Commission into Family Violence (2016) that there needs to be an emphasis placed on the development and use of technological solutions in the area of family violence.

The findings of this preliminary study demonstrate some concerns around the suitability of the Stalking Risk Profile in the context of assessing risk of cyberstalking. As a result of these technological advancements and Web developments, the nature of interpersonal relationships is adapting to these changes. As technology changes, so to do the potential risks posed to victims of cyberstalking in an online environment.

Surprisingly, only one of five of the types in the Stalking Risk Profile refers to the motivation of an ex-intimate partner, the rejected stalker. It would be reasonable to suggest that ex-intimates could be motivated by additional factors other than 'attempting to reconcile the relationship, or exacting revenge for a perceived rejection' (MacKenzie et al. 2011: 1). Our critique is twofold: (1) only one of the types in the Stalking Risk Profile falls under the current legislative framework in Australia which criminalises stalking under family violence legislation, and (2) although ex-intimate partners are the most at-risk group, they need to have a stronger presence on the Stalking Risk Profile. This twofold critique finds a parallel in the current legislation and risk assessment for stalking and its suitability for policing cyberstalking.

Changes in technology and risk assessment are two key areas of concern for police in the investigation and prosecution of cyberstalking. Furthermore, this preliminary study contributes an understanding of the crucial role police play in identifying risk of cyberstalking. Police investigators' and prosecutors' understandings of cyberstalking varied in that digital natives observed cyberstalking differently when compared to digital immigrants. Digital immigrants were challenged in cyberstalking investigations and prosecutions by their limited working knowledge of Web development and technological advancement. The Victorian Royal Commission into Family Violence (2016) recommended that the development and use of technological solutions are needed, although this preliminary study has shown that some police officers—the digital immigrants—may experience challenges in implementing these solutions.

This chapter has also demonstrated that the Stalking Risk Profile is problematic for cyberstalking. Firstly, the Stalking Risk Profile was developed for assessing risk of offline stalking and did not specifically address the context of assessing risk of cyberstalking. In particular, the changing nature of online relationships between offenders and victims in cyberstalking cases is not as static as the Stalking Risk Profile suggests. Police investigators and prosecutors described online relationships in cyberstalking cases as dynamic risk factors that often transcended cyberspace into real-world stalking. Secondly, the typologies were developed by clinicians for clinicians, rather than police who are crucial in identifying risk of cyberstalking and are heavily reliant on risk assessments (Casey 2011; Perez et al. 2008). Overall, the Stalking Risk Profile was not suitable in adequately covering the varied motivations for cyberstalking by ex-partners who are the most high-risk group and only comprise one type in the existing profile.

Importantly, one of the recommendations of the Victorian Royal Commission into Family Violence (2016) is to identify ways that emerging technologies and resources can be used to streamline and standardise risk assessment processes. However, they did not identify the need for ensuring that the risk assessments themselves are equipped to deal with the changing nature of online relationships in cases of cyberstalking. This preliminary study provides strong evidence for this recommendation to be acted on. In order for police investigators and prosecutors to be proactive in policing cyberstalking, risk assessments need to adapt to technological advancements and their implications for social use. Using risk assessments is not a choice but required by police, and is significant in and for policing cyberstalking.

Finally, a significant problem identified in this study is that many police investigators and prosecutors are digital immigrants while the techniques cyberstalkers are using are often that of digital natives. Maintaining expertise in new/changing technology and having stalking risk assessment tools specifically designed for police use in the light of these changes are crucial to the outcome of the investigation. Further research is needed to explore the implications for policing cyberstalking in the context where othering may be facilitated by the misuse of new/changing technology. Challenges for police investigators and prosecutors were compounded by the fact that the ideal response is to develop technological solutions. However, police will need to have an adequate understanding of technological change in order to implement this response to cyberstalking behaviours.

Note

1. ACT *Crimes Act 1900*, s. 35 (Stalking); NSW *Crimes (Domestic and Personal Violence) Act 2007*, s. 13 (Stalking or intimidation with intent to cause fear of physical or mental harm); NT *Criminal Code*, s. 189 (Unlawful stalking); QLD *Criminal Code Act 1899*, Chapter 33A (Unlawful stalking), ss. 359A–359F; SA *Criminal Law Consolidation Act 1935*, s. 19AA (Unlawful stalking); TAS *Criminal Code Act 1924*, s. 192 (Stalking); VIC Crimes Act 1958, s. 21A (Stalking); WA *Criminal Code Act Compilation Act 1913*, s. 338D and s. 338E (Stalking).

References

Al-Alosi, H. (2017, March 27). Technology-facilitated abuse: The new breed of domestic violence. *The Conversation.* https://theconversation.com/technology-facilitated-abuse-the-new-breed-of-domestic-violence-74683. Accessed October 20, 2018.

Australian Bureau of Statistics. (2017). *8153.0—Internet Activity, Australia.* December 2016. http://www.abs.gov.au/ausstats/abs@.nsf/mf/8153.0. Accessed January 12, 2018.

Avakame, E. F., & Fyfe, J. J. (2001). Differential police treatment of male-on-female spousal violence: Additional evidence on the leniency thesis. *Violence Against Women, 7*(1), 22–45.

Banyard, V. L., Demers, J. M., Cohn, E. S., Edwards, K. M., Moynihan, M. M., Walsh, W. A., et al. (2017). Academic correlates of unwanted sexual contact, intercourse, stalking, and intimate partner violence: An understudied but important consequence for college students. *Journal of Interpersonal Violence*, ifirst. https://doi.org/10.1177/0886260517715022.

Barassi, V., & Treré, E. (2012). Does Web 3.0 come after Web 2.0? Deconstructing theoretical assumptions through practice. *New Media & Society, 14*(8): 1269–1285.

Bocij, P. (2004). *Cyberstalking: Harassment in the Internet Age and How to Protect Your Family*. Westport, CT: Greenwood Publishing Group.

Casey, E. (2011). *Digital Evidence and Computer Crime: Forensic Science, Computers, and the Internet*. London: Elsevier Academic Press.

Cavezza, C., & McEwan, T. E. (2014). Cyberstalking versus off-line stalking in a forensic sample. *Psychology, Crime & Law, 20*(10), 955–970.

Crime Statistics Agency. (2017). *Recorded offences*. https://www.crimestatistics.vic.gov.au/crime-statistics/latest-crime-data/recorded-offences-. Accessed January 19, 2018.

Doyle, M. (2017). *Angela's horror: Stalked, stabbed, doused in petrol by Tinder date*. https://www.news.com.au/entertainment/tv/current-affairs/angelas-horror-stalked-stabbed-doused-in-petrol-by-tinder-date/news-story/a6ccf9175f835ddf34bfa0384bb0912c. Accessed March 30, 2018.

Edwards, R., & Holland, J. (2013). *What Is Qualitative Interviewing?* London: Bloomsbury Academic.

Fuchs, C., Hofkirchner, W., Schafranek, M., Raffl, C., Sandoval, M., & Bichler, R. (2010). Theoretical foundations of the web: Cognition, communication, and co-operation—Towards an understanding of Web 1.0, 2.0, 3.0. *Future Internet, 2*(1): 41–59.

Hansen, E. C. (2006). *Successful Qualitative Health Research: A Practical Introduction*. London: Allen & Unwin.

Haron, H., & Yusof, F. B. M. (2010). Cyber stalking: The social impact of social networking technology. In *International Conference on Education and Management Technology (ICEMT)* (pp. 237–241).

Lyndon, A., Bonds-Raacke, J., & Cratty, A. D. (2011). College students' Facebook stalking of ex-partners. *Cyberpsychology, Behavior, and Social Networking, 14*(12), 711–716.

MacKenzie, R., McEwan, T., Pathé, M., James, D., Ogloff, J., & Mullen, P. (2011). *Types of stalking*. https://www.stalkingriskprofile.com/what-is-stalking/types-of-stalking. Accessed November 16, 2017.

McCulloch, J., Maher, J., Fitz-Gibbon, K., Segrave, M., & Roffee, J. (2016). *Review of the Family Violence Risk Assessment and Risk Management Framework (CRAF)*. Melbourne, Australia: Monash University.

McEwan, T., Pathé, M., & Ogloff, J. (2011). Advancing stalking risk assessment. *Behavioral Sciences & the Law, 29*(2), 180–201.

Mishra, A., & Mishra, D. (2013). Cyber stalking: A challenge for web security. In J. Bishop (Ed.), *Examining the Concepts, Issues, and Implications of Internet Trolling*. Hershey, PA: Information Science Reference.

Mullen, P. E., Pathé, M., & Purcell, R. (2009). *Stalkers and Their Victims* (2nd ed.). Cambridge: Cambridge University Press.

Mullen, P. E., Mackenzie, R., Ogloff, J. R., Pathé, M., McEwan, T., & Purcell, R. (2006). Assessing and managing the risks in the stalking situation. *Journal of the American Academy of Psychiatry and the Law Online, 34*(4), 439–450.

Naik, U., & Shivalingaiah, D. (2008). *Comparative study of Web 1.0, Web 2.0 and Web 3.0*. Paper presented to 6th International Convention on Automation of Libraries in Education and Research.

Perez Trujillo, M., & Ross, S. (2008). Police response to domestic violence: Making decisions about risk and risk management. *Journal of Interpersonal Violence, 23*(4), 454–473.

Piovesan, A. (2016). *New study looks at stalking amid rise in reported cases*. http://www.sbs.com.au/news/article/2016/06/06/new-study-looks-stalking-amid-rise-reported-cases-0. Accessed December 21, 2017.

Prensky, M. (2001, October). Digital natives, digital immigrants. *On the Horizon, 9*(5), 1–6. NCB University Press.

Proudman, D., & Olding, R. (2016). *Man shot by police stalked, stabbed ex-girlfriend after she ended relationship*. https://www.smh.com.au/national/nsw/man-shot-by-police-stalked-stabbed-exgirlfriend-after-she-ended-relationship-20161104-gshwq2.html. Accessed June 9, 2018.

Reyns, B. W. (2010). A situational crime prevention approach to cyberstalking victimization: Preventive tactics for internet users and online place managers. *Crime Prevention and Community Safety, 12*(2), 99–118.

Reyns, B. W., Henson, B., & Fisher, B. S. (2012). Stalking in the twilight zone: Extent of cyberstalking victimization and offending among college students. *Deviant Behavior, 33*(1), 1–25.

Rosenfeld, B. (2004). Violence risk Factors in stalking and obsessional harassment: A review and preliminary meta-analysis. *Criminal Justice and Behavior, 31*(1), 9–36.

Schwartz-Watts, D. M. (2006). Commentary: Stalking risk profile. *Journal of the American Academy of Psychiatry and the Law Online, 34*(4), 455–457.

Scott, A. J., Lloyd, R., & Gavin, J. (2010). The influence of prior relationship on perceptions of stalking in the United Kingdom and Australia. *Criminal Justice and Behavior, 37*(11), 1185–1194.

Thompson, C. M., Dennison, S. M., & Stewart, A. L. (2013). Are different risk factors associated with moderate and severe stalking violence? Examining factors from the integrated theoretical model of stalking violence. *Criminal Justice and Behavior, 40*(8), 850–880.

Tjaden, P. G., & Thoennes, N. (1998). *Stalking in America: Findings from the National Violence Against Women Survey*. Washington, DC: U.S. Department of Justice.

Victorian Royal Commission into Family Violence. (2016). *Summary and recommendations*. http://www.rcfv.com.au/MediaLibraries/RCFamilyViolence/Reports/RCFV_Full_Report_Interactive.pfd. Accessed October 3, 2017.

Woodlock, D. (2013). *Technology-Facilitated Stalking: Findings and Recommendations from the SmartSafe Project*. Carlton, Australia: Domestic Violence Resource Centre Victoria.

15

'Why Don't You Block Them?' Police Officers' Constructions of the Ideal Victim When Responding to Reports of Interpersonal Cybercrime

Alex Black, Karen Lumsden and Lee Hadlington

Introduction

This chapter focuses on the responses to interpersonal cybercrime victims by police forces in England, drawing on data from focus groups and interviews with police officers, and an ethnography of a police force control room (FCR). The discussion centres on how police officers construct notions of the 'ideal victim' (Christie 1986) of online crime, how

---

A. Black (✉)
Department of Law and Criminology, Sheffield Hallam University, Sheffield, UK

K. Lumsden
Leicester, UK

L. Hadlington
De Montfort University, Leicester, UK

© The Author(s) 2019
K. Lumsden and E. Harmer (eds.), *Online Othering*,
Palgrave Studies in Cybercrime and Cybersecurity,
https://doi.org/10.1007/978-3-030-12633-9_15

these inform their attitudes towards victims, and how they respond to reports. Importantly, this chapter demonstrates the ways in which the police response at present could be seen to involve victim-blaming by framing online users as making themselves vulnerable to cybercrime through their occupation (and use) of particular virtual spaces. Police officers' suggestions to withdraw from these social spaces (i.e. via police advice to victims to 'just block them' on Facebook) often meet resistance from victims and risks isolating and excluding victims from everyday forms of online interaction (Hadley 2017).

The emergence and expansion of cybercrime have generated numerous debates and tensions over how it can be defined, what the scale of the problem is, and who should be responsible for dealing with it (Caneppele and Aebi 2017; Wall 2008a). Distinctions in the definitions of cybercrime are made between property cybercrime (committed for financial gain) and interpersonal cybercrime (those behaviours aimed at a particular victim) which can blur the boundaries between offline and online victimisation (Burns and Roberts 2013). For example, online forms of interpersonal abuse are often an extension of, and addition to, offline forms of abuse such as violence and coercive and controlling behaviours (Hadley 2017). Police services in the UK have not yet adapted to deal with the complexity and volume of interpersonal cybercrime such as online abuse, revenge pornography and domestic incidents (Laville 2016). The police response to victims of certain forms of interpersonal cybercrime has also been questioned due to their potential for what may be seen as victim-blaming (Jane 2017a).

This chapter explores police responses and the way in which they draw upon notions of the 'ideal victim' and perceived seriousness of the offence. It then considers how these responses are situated in the sociocultural context of austerity policing. Policing in the UK is currently undergoing substantial changes as a result of the neoliberal context of austerity ushered in post-2008 recession. The government's 2010 spending review enforced a 20% funding reduction to police forces between 2011 and 2015, which amounted to £2.53 billion pounds worth of savings across forces (HMIC 2014). Police officer and staff reductions accounted for a large proportion of these savings, directly impacting on routine and frontline police work, and fostering low morale amongst staff (Lumsden and Black 2018). We argue that the increasing volume of cybercrime within an environment of depleted resources leaves officers negotiating with victims over who should primarily take responsibility for dealing with these offences. These negotiations can be seen as part of a broader opportunity to re-define and narrow what 'post-austerity policing' will look like (Millie 2014). Certain forms of interpersonal cybercrime did not elicit 'ideal victim' status from officers, for example, domestic incidents taking place on social media in which the victim did not remove themselves from the online environment. This was distinct from 'ideal victims' who were more easily considered as blameless victims of an anonymous cyber-criminal. The absence of 'ideal victim' status for certain interpersonal forms of cybercrime contributes to officers' debates over whether to include these offences as a priority in a renegotiated policing landscape. The chapter proposes that a substantial reframing of police support for victims of online crime is urgently required, in order to recognise the serious ramifications of online hate, cyber-stalking, and technologically-mediated domestic abuse, and to go beyond commonsensical assumptions that victimisation in 'the virtual world' is less serious or impactful than it is in relation to traditional offline crimes. It further argues that this online/offline dichotomy must be challenged so that police and agencies can effectively support victims of cybercrime.

The chapter begins with an overview of the definitions and emergence of cybercrime and the policing response to it. It then discusses key terms and ideas within the field of victimology; in particular Christie's (1986) concepts of the 'ideal victim' and the deserving and undeserving victim, and how these apply in the cybercrime context. After outlining methods, the chapter presents findings including: police constructions of the ideal victim; police responses to interpersonal cybercrime and advice for managing victimisation; and police negotiations over responsibilising individuals for managing online risk.

Review of the Literature: Cybercrime, Victimisation and the Police Response

Defining and Policing Cybercrime

The topic of cybercrime has become a critical focus for many, including researchers, law enforcement, and those developing government policies. However, despite the overwhelming interest in the area of cybercrime, it lacks a universally accepted definition (Gordon and Ford 2006; McQuade 2007). This lack of agreement regarding the definition of cybercrime has in turn been linked to widespread confusion about the actions and behaviours that fall into the category (Wall 2008a, b). The term is often used to describe crimes involving computers (McQuade 2007), but can be used to refer to a much broader set of crimes. Researchers have moved away from the use of cybercrime as a term that just refers to the use of the Internet to commit crime, in favour of viewing it in terms of a continuum (Gordon and Ford 2006). This can range from aspects of 'technological crime' (also referred to as cyber-dependent crime) that can only exist within a system such as the Internet, or hardware and software. At the other end of the spectrum is 'people crime' (or cyber-enabled crime), in which technology or the use of the Internet is only a minor part of the crime (National Crime Agency 2016).

Holt et al. (2015) note that the use of the term 'cybercrime' has evolved to describe most criminal activity in the online digital environment. There is a subtle distinction between the two concepts of 'abuse' and 'misuse' in the context of cyber-related activities. Therefore, they use the term 'cyberdeviance' to conceptualise those activities which are not necessarily illegal but can be seen to contravene societal norms and values. This could, for example, include the use of a smartphone in a cinema or theatre during the production. While there is no illegal activity being engaged in (unless the individual is contravening potential copyright laws), they are generally frowned upon by the wider society. Further examples include the viewing of online pornographic images, or sending explicit sex messages (sexting). Neither of these activities is illegal as long as the parties involved are over the age of consent for the particular country (Mitchell et al. 2012). Accordingly, Holt et al. (2015) suggest that the point at which a deviant cyber-related activity becomes 'criminal' is the point at which it transgresses what is 'legal' for that particular country. This also relates to the geopolitical landscape for law enforcement of cybercrime.

Researchers have noted that there is little consistency in the policing of criminal activities which involve digital technology (Holt et al. 2015; Wall 2001; Brenner 2008). Wall (2001) notes that this issue is related to the concept of *nullen crimen sine lege* (or no crime without law). If a particular country does not have laws in place to tackle a specific aspect of cyber-deviant activity, the legality of such cannot be assessed. Where countries engage in the facilitation of information sharing in the context of multi-national agencies tasked with tackling cybercrimes, these are only effective if the activities under investigation are given the same weight by each of the member states (Wall 2001). New forms of online criminality also require amendments to, or additional forms of legislation for police officers to be able to deal with them. This includes, for example, the introduction of a new law in the UK in 2014 to enable prosecution of 'revenge porn' (an offence where people maliciously share sexually explicit pictures of former partners). This problem is in addition to the sheer volume of cybercrime offences that police officers are expected to respond to on a daily basis. As one Chief Constable commented in relation to online abuse: 'The levels of abuse that now take place within the internet are on a level we never really expected. If we did try to deal with all of it we would clearly be swamped' (cited in Laville 2016).

Defining and Policing Interpersonal Cybercrime

As noted above, cybercrime is generally split into two broad categories of 'interpersonal cybercrime' which involves a personal attack on a victim and 'property cybercrime' which primarily involves financial gain (Burns and Roberts 2013). The advancements of the Internet and communication technologies have allowed interpersonal forms of criminality to 'go viral' and for certain individuals to exploit the online environment to commit acts such as cyber-bullying, cyber-intimate partner abuse, cyber-stalking and cyber-harassment (Navarro and Clevenger 2017). The quality of the police response to such forms of interpersonal cyber criminality have been called into question, not only due to of a lack of resources and expertise to deal with these crime reports, but also due to the police-victim interaction that takes place and the level of support provided to victims. Jane (2017b) highlights how police officers can often fail to act in response to interpersonal online victimisation and instead put pressure on victims to withdraw from these online spaces by deleting accounts and changing their phone number. In these instances, it is the victim who is responsibilised to deal with and resolve the cyber threat by closing down their accounts. However, this request by the police that individual victims should remove themselves from cyber spaces fails to acknowledge how integral the online environment is to people's modern-day lives and is a response which places blame and responsibility with the victim. The use of the Internet, especially for younger generations, is an 'established fact' and withdrawal from these spaces has become an unrealistic expectation (Hadley 2017: 9). The requirement to withdraw can also be seen as a victim 'punishment' in that the victim themselves become the excluded party (Jane 2017a).

There is also reliance on the victim, rather than police investigators, to prove the intent and credibility of the interpersonal offences being reported. This form of victim treatment can often be the result of a lack of legislative knowledge on behalf of the police over what constitutes interpersonal cybercrime (Wall 2001; Jane 2017b). There is also evidence to suggest that lower level forms of interpersonal cybercrime are taken less seriously by the police (Bossler and Holt 2012). Yar (2013) details how our social and cultural judgements around risk, harm and seriousness determine where in a 'hierarchy of standing' a particular crime will be placed by police. These judgements are based on the supposed vulnerability of the victim involved, the dangerousness of the offender in question, the immediacy of the police response, and the physical and/or emotional harm caused to the victim.

In this sociocultural context, Yar argues, Internet offences such as child pornography are placed at the top of this hierarchy of standing. They are then responded to with the full weight of traditional forms of state-centred public policing. This is in contrast to other forms of cyber criminality where the victim is seen as less vulnerable and less in danger of harm, for example, Internet 'piracy'. These forms of criminality, that are lower down the hierarchy of standing, are policed less by state-centred agencies and more so by non-state actors such as members of the public, private organisations (such as Internet providers) and volunteers. Responsibility for crime control and self-protection is then shared amongst this network of crime control governance (ibid.).

Research also suggests that police officers do not necessarily feel best placed to take responsibility for responding to cybercrime. A survey of response officers in the USA conducted by Bossler and Holt (2012: 174) found that officers' main suggestion for how best to respond to the increasing issue of cybercrime was for users to 'be more careful while on line', followed by calls for greater education for users in online safety. This could be seen as a negotiation point in 'responsibilising' individuals in the 'privatisation of risk-management' (Duggan and Heap 2014: 26) within the context of this emerging crime type. However, the responsibilising of victims may overlook the blurred boundaries and intersections between online and offline offending that occur in many forms of interpersonal cybercrime. Online abuse can be an extension of offline abuse, especially in domestic abuse situations. For a victim to self-police and restrict their online presence, may further exclude and isolate them (Hadley 2017). Arguments have also been made that the trend towards misogynistic forms of interpersonal cybercrime (including 'revenge pornography', rape threats, and death threats) have a strong silencing effect on women specifically in online spaces and communities, pushing them to withdraw from these spaces (Lumsden and Morgan 2017; Hadley 2017; Jane 2017a). With these complexities in mind, it is pertinent to understand how police officers respond to reports of interpersonal cybercrime, how victims are advised and supported, and to consider which forms of cyber criminality generate full 'victim status' from responding officers.

Victimology and the 'Ideal Victim'

The notion of placing partial responsibility for victimisation on the victim themselves developed in early work in the field of victimology. This work saw the emergence of victim typologies, most notably in the work of Mendelsohn and the notion of victim culpability and Von Hentig's typology of victim proneness (McGarry and Walklate 2015). Both typologies focused on the role of the victim within offending behaviour and, as McGarry and Walklate argue, also focus on the extent to which the victim had made choices that led to their ultimate victimisation. Mendelsohn and Von Hentig sought to distinguish between victim identity (personal characteristics and vulnerability) and the situational context of an offence (provocation, engaging in criminality, relationship with the offender, etc.) which when combined together establish how culpable or blameworthy a victim could be seen to be and thus how deserving they were of victim status. Understanding the 'deservedness' of this victim status highlights how certain victims are viewed and responded to differently in certain situations and the uneven application of the victim identity (Duggan and Heap 2014). Analysing victimisation through the frame of culpability and proneness placed undue blame on the victim and removed the responsibility for offending away from the offender, ushering in a culture of victim-blaming that still persists today (Cross et al. 2018).

The notion of the deserving and conversely the undeserving victim has been highlighted most clearly in Nils Christie's (1986) notion of the 'ideal victim', a set of characteristics that personify society's expectations over victimhood. Christie sought to emphasise how and in what circumstances some victims were legitimated as deserving of sympathy and others were not. In Christie's typology, an 'ideal victim' is physically weaker than the offender, is unknown to the offender, is unambiguously blameless and is engaged in legitimate activities wherein they were targeted by a 'big and bad' offender. Any individual who meets these criteria is afforded the full weight of victim status and the corresponding support of responding agencies and the public. Any transgression of these characteristics challenges the application of this status.

Christie's concept of the 'ideal victim' has been widely utilised in studies of victims and victimology since its publication and has been applied to our understanding of critical issues including victims of international crimes (van Wijk 2013), victims of child sexual abuse (McAlinden 2014) and most recently victims of hacking and data breach (Cross et al. 2018). Christie's work has also been used to understand the construction of the 'ideal victim' in the media (Greer 2007) and how crime victims self-present their status (Jagervi 2014). However, thus far there is scarce work exploring how it relates to cybercrime (although see Jane 2017a; Hadley 2017), including interpersonal cybercrime or how police responses to cybercrime involve notions of the ideal victim.

Methods

The data presented below are drawn from two qualitative studies of the police response to victims and perceptions of cybercrime. The studies were conducted within one year of each other at two police forces in England.

The first project (Study 1) was an ethnographic study of a police FCR in England (see Lumsden and Black 2018).[1] The study was more broadly concerned with the police response to domestic violence calls at the frontline, which included call handling, dispatch and response officers. 66 hours of observation were conducted between November 2016 and February 2017. This involved a combination of day (7) and early evening shifts (6). Author 1 conducted 11 hours of observation while Author 2 conducted the majority of the observations totalling 55 hours. Ethnography allows for detailed investigation of human behaviour and the factors that influence such behaviour (Brewer 2000). We participated in the setting by listening to the calls and observing call handler and dispatch behaviours. We also conducted four focus groups with frontline officers (26 in total) in order to explore their response to domestic abuse calls, and the relationship and interactions between dispatchers in the FCR and frontline officers. The focus groups were audio recorded and transcribed by an independent transcription company.

Access to the FCR was granted via the manager who acted as gatekeeper and made decisions as to which individuals or teams we would sit with. We were given a headset in order to listen to the call handlers and the dispatchers' conversations with response officers and other parties. Short-hand notes of observations and conversations with staff were made in the FCR, either in a notebook or in a mobile phone notes function. This helped to highlight items that we did not want to forget without being intrusive. Field notes were then written up after each observation and described the setting, calls, conversations and incidents.

The second study (Study 2) focused more specifically on front-line police officers' views and perceptions of cybercrime. In total, 16 police officers were recruited by a senior police officer based at a Force Headquarters to take part in four focus groups conducted by Author 1 and Author 3. Each officer had a minimum of 18 months service and they were recruited from a variety of operational backgrounds. The breakdown of the focus groups according to operational background is presented in Table 15.1. 4 people were present in each focus group, and these were conducted in gender homogenous fashion with each focus group lasting for approximately one hour. The focus groups were all audio recorded and fully transcribed by an independent transcription company.

In both studies we adopted an inductive approach to analysis where theory is developed out of analysis, and then additional data collection is guided by the emergent theory. Thematic analysis (Braun and Clarke 2006)

Table 15.1 Focus group break down according to operational background

Focus group	Participants' operational background
Focus group 1 (Female)	Control Room Operations (x2), Incident Response, Investigations Management Unit
Focus group 2 (Male)	Control Room Operations (x2), Investigations Management Unit, Control Room Organisation Team
Focus group 3 (Female)	Investigations Management Unit, Call Management Team, Managed Appointment Unit (x2)
Focus group 4 (Male)	Managed Appointment Unit,[a] Patrol and Resolution Officer, Investigation Management Unit (x2)

[a]Managed Appointment Unit—members of the public can arrange to meet a police officer within a specific time period for non-emergency matters

was utilised to analyse data collected in both studies and adopting an iterative-inductive approach in the first study meant that unanticipated themes, such as those discussed here relating to interpersonal cybercrime, the response to victims of these crimes, and the relationship between social media abuse and domestic abuse offences, were identified through our analysis. All three authors were involved in the process of data analysis for Study 2, while Authors 1 and 2 analysed the data from Study 1.

Both studies received ethical clearance from the respective universities. Participant numbers and/or pseudonyms have been used to disguise the identities of police officers, staff and callers. The police forces and geographical areas have also been anonymised and any identifying factors omitted from field notes so that they do not result in the identification of the forces or employees.

Results: Police Officer Support for Victims of Cybercrime

The 'Genuine' Victim of Cybercrime

In focus groups, police officers across all departments (including frontline officers and call handlers) constructed notions of what they believed to be the 'ideal victim' or 'genuine victim' of cybercrime, in contrast to those individuals who they felt had not taken preventative measures to address cybercrime particularly at the interpersonal level (we explore this theme—of 'block them' further below). The police officer below outlines the genuine victim as someone who is already 'vulnerable' in society and who is therefore an easy target for cyber-criminals:

> *Respondent 1*: You have … the really vulnerable people in society that get taken advantage of, especially by social media and on some of these faceless crimes as well and get encouraged to do things that they really shouldn't be doing. So even though I said my empathy levels are low when you start talking to some of these people it goes up quite rapidly. Because you think, crikey, they are really being taken advantage of. (Focus group 3, Study 2)

The idea of the 'faceless' criminal operating across the Internet fits the popular characterisation in academic and popular literature of cybercrime as anonymously enacted in a distant and unknown cyberspace (Lusthaus and Varese 2017). This type of criminality allows officers to consider the victim as unambiguously blameless as the offender is unknown and the victim would have been unable to prevent it occurring. These notions of the genuine victim should be seen in the context of what officers understand 'proper' cybercrime to be, which mostly characterises property cybercrime, even though many of the cybercrimes reportedly dealt with by officers were interpersonal:

> *Respondent 1*: I always just think of internet and I think of faceless people. You know, you've got that computer screen but – and I think that's one of the frightening things, that you don't know who you're dealing with half the time. I know the other things we've mentioned about Facebook harassment are cyber, but to me it's more the faceless side of the internet, when they target people. That's what springs to my mind first of all. (Focus group 3, Study 2)

Those online offences that are more interpersonal in nature are more likely to imply that the victim and the offender are known to each other, and thus it is viewed that there are more opportunities for the victim to disassociate from the offender, as can be seen in the quote below:

> *Respondent 4*: Yeah, there's a perception from the public that it's cybercrime, definitely, not from the police, I wouldn't have said. It's an open forum where, you know, if you leave yourself open to that sort of thing, and quite often they have their friends on Facebook as opposed to some anonymous person, then, you know, they're allowing that person – you know what I mean, in the first place, they're allowing them to be able to do that because they've friended them and said – then they slag them off, you know. (Focus group 6, Study 2)

As can be seen above, distinctions are made between the 'anonymous' offender and the Facebook 'friend'. Facebook in particular was seen as a domain in which the victim has autonomy over limiting their potential for victimisation by their ability to remove themselves from the platform, even in the context of domestic abuse situations:

> Dispatcher 17 said that they get a lot of Facebook message related domestic abuse incidents. She said: 'Facebook domestics make us want to shoot ourselves'. I asked why and she intimated that it was trivial. She said that people can block exs or that they can come off Facebook. She said that when she was a call handler before she became a dispatcher she would get a large number of people complaining about messages from people over Facebook or about people posting messages or photos of them on Facebook. She said that this was a typical DA incident … She described herself as losing patience with the callers in her manner with them. (Fieldnotes, 8 December 2016, Study 1)

As can be seen above, to not disengage is viewed by this call handler as leaving victims 'open' to abusive situations. This view is echoed by the below police officer, who refers to genuine victims as those individuals who have been exploited. Lower level cybercrime is seen as occurring because individuals have not taken preventative measures to protect themselves from harm online:

> *Respondent 2*: Yeah, we have genuine victims who just didn't see it coming or who have been blatantly exploited, but then we also have the lower-level stuff which is just down to social irresponsibility and people not taking responsibility for their own actions online. And we have everything from, 'Oh, she called me a bitch,' and whenever we get a crime report through for that, from – right through to the old dears who've just been sending money to people, massively exploited to high value as well. We are constantly fighting against the companies to try and get them on board and help us out with these enquiries. It's extremely difficult. (Focus group 4, Study 2)

We can see in the quote above how the respondent constructs these two types of victims as on opposing ends of a scale of victimisation, from irresponsible users to exploited 'old dears'. The construction of the ideal victim here strongly echoes Christie's (1986) example of the defenceless elderly woman and the unknown offender. However, it also raises questions of how serious police officers take the offences which they deem to be at the lower end of victimisation. For this next respondent, lower level cybercrime is seen as a lower police priority. Here we can see the sociocultural context of austerity and reduced resources impacting on where in the 'hierarchy of standing' (Yar 2013) the offences are placed:

> *Respondent 4*: As a force, I don't know, as a police service, I think that we pander too much to that low-level cyber aspect of it and something needs to be done otherwise it's just going to be – obviously with the way things are going, our diaries are made up with these…
> *Respondent 3*: We're struggling.
> *Respondent 4*: And … actually the jobs that require more attention, we're not dealing with them because we're dealing with the he said, she said kind of aspects of these kind of things that people have an option to pull out of or to just block or to – and nobody seems to be taking those reasonable steps. And they just – there's the expectation that police will come in and arrest them and sort it out, but we just haven't got that ability and the resources like we probably – well, a few years ago it wasn't like this, was it? But, you know, it's – I think there's that expectation that we're going to be doing something about it. (Focus group 5, Study 2)

In the above quote, we see the officers navigate the interrelationship of victim culpability, the perceived seriousness of the offence, and the current context of austerity. In particular, interpersonal types of offences ('the he said, she said') where people can 'pull out' of the situation are seen as diverting resources from more serious and warranted offences. What can be seen here are negotiations over the responsibility for dealing with these new forms of criminality within this reduced resource context. The seriousness of the offence and the 'ideal type' of victim act as anchor points to shape this discussion.

'Have You Blocked Them Yet?' Preventing Cybercrime

Police officers demonstrated an acute awareness of the centrality of social media in people's daily lives. They also recognised that their typical advice to victims of removing themselves from these platforms was not necessarily victim centred:

Respondent 4: That, about not taking it seriously, sort of until really the [particular incident] thing if kids said, 'I'm being harassed on Facebook, blah, blah, blah,' we just said, 'Oh well, come off Facebook then.' We didn't take that seriously, did we…? (Focus group 3, Study 2)

However, officers still demonstrated that what they perceived as elements of victim culpability in these interpersonal cybercrime offences shaped their attitudes about the victims and their victim status:

Respondent 4: There's a sense of, well, they shouldn't be talking to me like that. No, they shouldn't be, however, you're not taking the bull by the horns and you're not doing anything to stop it yourself. 'Why should I?' is the classic. 'Why should I?' because – but—
Respondent 1: And whenever you do suggest it that they come up with a reason why they shouldn't. 'Well, I need to get in touch with so and so, so and so's sister,' and you just think, 'Well, privacy settings are there for a reason, set them,' and they don't. People don't do it. (Focus group 5, Study 2)

This description of officers' attitudes towards the victims is not to assert that their response or behaviour towards them was affected, however we do see that the police advice remains the same, even in the face of resistance from the victim. The victim may see the advice from the officers as unjust or victim 'punishment' (Jane 2017a). This then creates an impasse in the dialogue between the officer and the victim, which impacts the officer's empathy for the victim. As can be seen in the quote below, this same frustration emerges even within domestic abuse situations:

Respondent 3: It's hard to safeguard someone … I had a domestic harassment and I said to her like, 'Why not just stop using Facebook or block him?'
Respondent 2: Block them.
Respondent 3: And people are so reluctant to do that.
Respondent 4: Change their number.
Respondent 3: Like they can't see their life past Facebook. And the longer, like eventually she blocked him and we stopped the harassment, so because the harassment stopped, she unblocked him.

> *Respondent 4*: People say, 'Well I keep it open, I haven't blocked his number because then I won't have evidence that he's harassing me.' And it's like, 'Well, you won't be harassed if you…'
> *Respondent 5*: Yeah.
> *Respondent 3*: Can be a little bit frustrating with social media. (Focus group 1, Study 1)

This above discussion between response officers is characteristic of Hadley's (2017) assertion that in the context of domestic abuse situations, telling victims to exclude themselves is an inadequate and potentially 'victim-blaming' response. Online abuse can be an extension of offline abuse which, if encouraged to withdraw from these spaces, can further the isolation of victims as a means of coercion and control. Making the victim responsible for blocking the offender to end the harassment may fail to address the actual behaviours of the offender. As the discussion above continued, the officers acknowledged the role of the offender in these situations, but the victim is still seen as responsible for playing a particular role in reducing these forms of criminality themselves:

> *Respondent 2*: We give them like safety advice and words of advice in terms of what they need to do and stuff like that, but it's whether people choose to – you know. We've all – I think everybody's had some victim that said, 'I don't want to block them because…' and it's like you're saying to them, you know, you can help yourself as well, you know. We can obviously – we definitely go and speak with this person and potentially prosecute them for harassment, but at the same time they're like, 'Oh, I don't want to block them because I don't want to lose my amount of friends on – my Facebook friend numbers,' and, you know, it's an interesting mind set.
> *Respondent 4*: Or I want evidence there or I shouldn't have to.
> *Respondent 1*: Or it's … 'Change your phone number.' 'Why should I? I haven't done anything.' (Focus group 1, Study 1)

These same narratives concerning their negotiations with individuals about taking responsibility appear again here. The resistance of members of the public to the police advice that they should block other users on social media, adds to the officer's frustrations and potentially undermines their acknowledgement of the centrality of social media and information and communication technologies in people's lives.

Negotiating Responsibility for Cybercrime

As previously noted, the expansion of cybercrime has increased the workload for police officers (Laville 2016). Millie (2014) has noted that the post-austerity policing landscape has created uncertainty regarding what the police role should look like. This is due to their reduced resources and amplified democratic accountability over an increasingly wider policing remit. Austerity offers the opportunity for police officers to 'narrow' the focus of policing (Millie 2014). In the discussion of interpersonal cybercrime, police officers demonstrate engaging in this narrowing of roles by negotiating where the responsibility should fall for managing these cyber offences, specifically those that do not easily elicit victim status and those they deem to be of a less serious nature.

As can be seen below, the police do not see themselves as primary responders to interpersonal cybercrime. The victim and then the social media company are placed in positions of responsibility before the police:

> *Interviewer*: Are they difficult to respond to then, the online-based kind of incidents?
> *Respondent 14*: Well you just give the same advice, block them, delete it, you know, etc., and whether they do or not, you have to go on their say-so on that, but—
> *Respondent 20*: I think as well its like, yes, we can be called, however, people – people just don't take a little bit of self-responsibility with stuff. You know, Facebook as an organisation have their processes. They, you know, but no-one – the amount of people I say, 'Have you reported it to Facebook you know, so they can look into it, block it, deal with it?' 'No.' 'But you've called the police straight away? Doesn't that seem like you've jumped a few steps there potentially?' And they're like, 'No.'
> *Respondent 14*: I think as well you find with victims that they need to take a little bit more responsibility of themselves. (Focus group 3, Study 1)

Other organisations were seen as having pushed responsibility on to the police for dealing with cybercrimes:

> *Respondent 3*: When you were at school, when I was at school, if somebody was bullied, school would deal with it, parents were probably brought in, three parties, between them probably resolve it. Now the schools have washed their hands of anything that's cyber-related or social media-related, they'll go, 'Oh, we'll speak to the police.' So the schools are not then taking – it might be going on in the school, it's two kids in the same class, but they don't – they wash their hands of it and say, 'Contact the police'. (Focus group 4, Study 2)

As can be seen above, the officers viewed themselves as filling a gap that schools have left open by refusing to respond to offences such as cyber-bullying. For police officers, these offences are an addition to the existing and increasing workload of police teams. Where children are concerned, this then adds to the amount of time taken to deal with these offences:

> *Respondent 4*: These tiny little jobs actually are – I'm sorry to say, quite meaningless in the grand scheme of things, just have so much ramifications to everything else because when they involve kids you've got the vulnerable person report, that then the vulnerable person's team then get clogged up with all these crap, you know, because—
> *Respondent 3*: Social media.
> *Respondent 4*: Because of social media, and everybody does it and the parents often don't know what's – sometimes no fault for the parents, but they don't know what they're up to, and it's just – it's an absolute minefield that I think that somebody's got to draw the line somewhere…. (Focus group 5, Study 2)

The above quote highlights how the officers are trying to re-establish the boundaries of their work. Parents are viewed as being in a position to manage some of what officers perceive to be less serious offences. There is a need to 'draw the line' over what is considered within the police remit and what is not, with a view to a 'narrowing of focus' for police work (Millie 2014). This negotiation, in combination with the 'hierarchy of standing' for less serious offences was seen to add to the frustration and stresses that police officers faced in an austerity climate. The police officers interviewed are in a position where they feel as though they have to prioritise certain offences over others. This pressure positions offences against one another on this hierarchy, potentially adding to the resistance of officers to particular interpersonal cyber-related offences:

> *Respondent 1*: That's occurring more and more because certainly as time goes on and resources for policing becomes less and less, which it is going to continue getting more and more restricted, we are going to get to a point where we're going to have to turn around and say, 'As the police, we no longer deal with this, this and this.' And if it's a choice between we'll either deal with your Facebook squabbles or we'll deal with the actual physical assaults, which would you prefer? And that's what's happening. You know, we are getting to a point where officers are sent on grade one responses to turn up to be nasty threats online, yet somebody's had their house burgled and having to wait two days for us to attend, and I kind of think, 'Well, I know which one I should be going to.' (Focus group 6, Study 2)

In the above quote, we see the officer position online abuse in opposition to offline offences and in direct competition for resources. Framing offline and online interpersonal crime as a zero-sum game creates tensions within policing and adds to the understanding of who is and is not an 'ideal' victim. This practice allows officers to engage in the 'othering' of victims who they perceive as not having achieved true victim status.

Conclusion

This chapter has demonstrated the ways in which officers understand and respond to interpersonal cybercrime. Officers make a distinction between deserving and undeserving victims of cybercrime depending on the level of victim culpability, in particular, their ability to remove themselves from the risk of initial and ongoing victimisation. Drawing on the work of Christie (1986) and the notion of the 'ideal' victim, it can be seen how officers construct their understanding of who is an 'ideal' victim. These notions are informed by popular characterisations of cybercrime as anonymous and faceless and occurring in an unknown cyberspace (Lusthaus and Varese 2017). These forms of cybercrime, which are mostly property related, allow the offender to be 'big and bad' and position the victim as unknowing and blameless, giving them unquestioning victim status. On the other hand, interpersonal forms of cybercrime generally imply a relationship of some sort between the victim and the offender, for example, in the case of domestic abuse or 'revenge pornography' which then complicates this status. This was especially the case when coupled with what officers denoted as lower level forms of offending which were placed at the lower end of the 'hierarchy of standing' (Yar 2013). These offences were most often deemed as avoidable by officers and raised questions of personal responsibility and ownership of behaviours that may be seen as leaving a person 'open' to victimisation.

Officers engaged in negotiations with victims regarding where responsibility should lie for managing these cyber offences. They would often express their wish for the police response to be the last point of contact for victims after contacting social media platforms, other responsible adults (like parents and schools) and personal behaviours such as deleting social media accounts and changing phone numbers. Officers engaged in boundary work whereby they were renegotiating which offences in this new remit of cybercrime they should have responsibility over, especially in an austerity climate where resources are constrained but police practice is expanding (Millie 2014). The discussion of drawing a line between included and excluded offences within the police remit anchors around considerations of the seriousness of an offence and legitimate victim status. This negotiation creates tensions not only for police officers and the conceptualisation of their own role and function but also between officers and victims.

Advising victims to 'block' offenders and 'delete Facebook' generates resistance from victims who may perceive this as victim punishment

(Jane 2017a) which could result in the further exclusion of people from online spaces. It also fails to understand the centrality of online spaces in people's daily lives. Self-policing through withdrawal from online environments serves to restrict access for particular victims. This is especially problematic for victim groups who may already be experiencing forms of online othering and discrimination, for example, gendered abuse aiming to silence women in online communities (Lumsden and Morgan 2017). It may also overlook the blurring between online and offline offences such as domestic abuse, in which the withdrawal from online environments may isolate victims and further coercive and controlling behaviour (Hadley 2017). Police officers demonstrated awareness that their advice to victims to block people or come off social media platforms was limited and often met with resistance. There was also an acknowledgement that officers needed to take online interpersonal violence seriously and direct their response at the offender. However, their responses continued to be framed in a way that suggests some responsibility is still to be borne by the victim and officers expressed frustration at a lack of self-policing on the victim's part. This was especially the case for those offences where victim culpability was implied.

This chapter has demonstrated how officers seek to define out particular types of offences within the widening scope of cybercrime. Their attempts to 'narrow the focus' of policing (Millie 2014) utilises perceived victim status and the seriousness of the offence as barometers of inclusion criteria. This highlights the uncertain nature of policing in relation to cybercrime as an emerging form of criminality especially within the sociocultural context of austerity. This has implication for victims of interpersonal cybercrime. The police response draws on victim-blaming and victim punishment narratives which may serve to alienate victims and compound othering and discriminatory online practices. Police forces must ensure that they move beyond this approach to one which recognises the centrality of social media and online spaces in individuals' lives and seek ways to provide support for victims that acknowledges the dominance of these spaces for conducting social and political life.

Note

1. Study 1 was funded via a College of Policing/HEFCE Policing Knowledge Fund (Grant No. J04).

References

Bossler, A., & Holt, T. (2012). Patrol officers' perceived role in responding to cybercrime. *Policing: An International Journal of Police Strategies & Management, 35*(1), 165–181.

Braun, V., & Clarke, C. (2006). Using thematic analysis in psychology. *Qualitative Research in Psychology, 3*(2), 77–101.

Brenner, S. W. (2008). *Cyberthreats: The Emeging Fault Lines of the Nation State*. New York: Oxford University Press.

Brewer, J. D. (2000). *Ethnography*. Buckingham: Open University Press.

Burns, S., & Roberts, L. (2013). Applying the theory of planned behaviour to predicting online safety behaviour. *Crime Prevention and Community Safety, 15*(1), 48–64.

Caneppele, S., & Aebi, M. F. (2017). Crime drop or police recording flop? On the relationship between the decrease of offline crime and the increase of online and hybrid crimes. *Policing: A Journal of Policy and Practice*, ifirst. https://doi.org/10.1093/police/pax055.

Christie, N. (1986). The ideal victim. In E. A. Fattah (Ed.), *From Crime Policy to Victim Policy* (pp. 17–30). London: Palgrave Macmillan.

Cross, C., Parker, M., & Sansom, D. (2018). Media discourses surrounding 'non-ideal' victims: The case of the Ashley Madison data breach. *International Review of Victimology*, ifirst. https://doi.org/10.1177/0269758017752410.

Duggan, M., & Heap, V. (2014). *Administrating Victimization: The Politics of Anti-Social Behaviour and Hate Crime Policy*. Hampshire: Palgrave Macmillan.

Gordon, S., & Ford, R. (2006). On the definition and classification of cybercrime. *Journal in Computer Virology, 2*(1), 13–20.

Greer, C. (2007). News media, victims and crime. In P. Davies, P. Francis, & C. Greer (Eds.), *Victims, Crime and Society* (pp. 20–49). London: Sage.

Hadley, L. (2017). *Tackling Domestic Abuse in a Digital Age: A Recommendations Report on Online Abuse by the All-Party Parliamentary Group on Domestic Violence*. Bristol: Women's Aid Federation of England.

Her Majesty's Inspectorate of Constabulary. (HMIC). (2014). *State of Policing*. London: HMIC.

Holt, T., Bossler, A., & Seigfried-Spellar, K. (2015). *Cybercrime and Digital Forensics: An Introduction*. Oxon: Routledge.

Jagervi, L. (2014). 'Who wants to be an ideal victim? A narrative analysis of crime victims' self-presentation. *Journal of Scandinavian Studies in Criminology and Crime Prevention, 15*(1), 73–88.

Jane, E. A. (2017a). *Misogyny Online: A Short (and Brutish) History*. London: Sage.

Jane, E. A. (2017b). Gendered cyberhate, victim-blaming, and why the internet is more like driving a car on the road than being naked in the snow. In E. Martellozzo & E. A. Jane (Eds.), *Cybercrime and Its Victims*. Oxford: Routledge.

Laville, S. (2016). Online abuse: 'Existing laws too fragmented and don't serve victims'. *The Guardian*. https://www.theguardian.com/uk-news/2016/mar/04/online-abuse-existing-laws-too-fragmented-and-dont-serve-victims-says-police-chief. Accessed April 16, 2018.

Lumsden, K., & Black, A. (2018). Austerity policing, emotional labour and the boundaries of police work: An ethnography of a police force control room in England. *British Journal of Criminology, 58*(3), 606–623.

Lumsden, K., & Morgan, H. M. (2017). Media framing of trolling and online abuse: Silencing strategies, symbolic violence, and victim blaming. *Feminist Media Studies, 17*(6), 926–940.

Lusthaus, J., & Varese, F. (2017). Offline and local: The hidden face of cybercrime. *Policing: A Journal of Policy and Practice*, ifirst. https://doi.org/10.1093/police/pax042.

McAlinden, A. M. (2014). Deconstructing victim and offender identities in discourses on child sexual abuse: Hierarchies, blame and the good/evil dialectic. *The British Journal of Criminology, 54*(2), 180–198.

McGarry, R., & Walklate, S. (2015). *Victims: Trauma, Testimony and Justice*. London: Routledge.

McQuade III, S. C. (2007). We must educate young people about cybercrime before they start college. *Chronicle of Higher Education, 53*(14), B29. http://ra.ocls.ca/ra/login.aspx?inst=conestoga&url=http://search.ebscohost.com/login.aspx?direct=true&db=eric&AN=EJ756806&site=eds-live&scope=site%5Cnhttp://chronicle.com/. Accessed April 2018.

Millie, A. (2014). What are the police for? Re-thinking policing post-austerity. In J. M. Brown (Ed.), *The Future of Policing*. Oxford: Routledge.

Mitchell, K. J., Finkelhor, D., Jones, L. M., & Wolak, J. (2012). Prevalence and characteristics of youth sexting: A national study. *Pediatrics, 129*(1), 13–20.

National Crime Agency. (2016, July). *NCA Strategic Cyber Industry Group Cyber Crime Assessment 2016*, 1–16.

Navarro, J. N., & Clevenger, S. (2017). Why me? Understanding cybercrime victimization. In C. Roberson (Ed.), *Routledge Handbook on Victims' Issues in Criminal Justice*. Oxford: Routledge.

van Wijk, J. (2013). Who is the 'little old lady' of international crimes? Nils Christie's concept of the ideal victim reinterpreted. *International Review of Victimology, 19*(2), 159–179.

Wall, D. S. (Ed.). (2001). *Crime and the Internet*. London: Routledge.

Wall, D. S. (2008a). Cybercrime, media and insecurity: The shaping of public perceptions of cybercrime. *International Review of Law, Computers & Technology, 22*(1–2), 45–63.

Wall, D. S. (2008b). Cybercrime and the culture of fear: Social science fiction(s) and the production of knowledge about cybercrime. *Information, Communication & Society, 11*, 861–884.

Yar, M. (2013). The policing of internet sex offences: Pluralised governance versus hierarchies of standing. *Policing and Society, 23*(4), 482–497.

16

Conclusion: Researching 'Online Othering'—Future Agendas and Lines of Inquiry

Emily Harmer and Karen Lumsden

Introduction

This concluding chapter will be used as an opportunity for us to bring together the key themes and areas of crossover brought out by the individual chapters. This will also be a chance for us to reflect on what lines of inquiry need to be followed in order to give us a better understanding of 'online othering' and ultimately what measures might be taken to challenge the potential negative effects that these forms of communication might have on specific groups and societies. This chapter will first recap the concept of 'online othering' and explain why it offers a novel

---

E. Harmer
Department of Communication and Media, University of Liverpool, Liverpool, UK

K. Lumsden (✉)
Leicester, UK

© The Author(s) 2019
K. Lumsden and E. Harmer (eds.), *Online Othering*,
Palgrave Studies in Cybercrime and Cybersecurity,
https://doi.org/10.1007/978-3-030-12633-9_16

and useful way of thinking about the myriad power contestations and abusive behaviours which are manifested on and through online spaces, such as racism, Islamophobia, sexism, misogyny, homophobia, ableism and so forth. Next, we will bring together and synthesise the main issues which resulted from the analyses offered by our contributors in order to discuss what the main challenges are in contesting and countering 'online othering'. First, we will emphasise that 'online othering' and perceptions of it reflect existing patriarchal power relations in society. 'Online othering' is intersectional and therefore this needs to be taken into account when researching online abuse and discrimination and when trying to challenge these behaviours. We will then highlight how 'online othering' is extremely difficult to regulate and protect against due to its multifaceted nature and due to the all-encompassing impact of digital technologies on people's everyday lives and the extended global reach of the online sphere. The third theme we address is the role of online and social media platforms and companies in contributing to and challenging 'online othering' practices both through their unwillingness to regulate and police their users' behaviour, but also through the ways in which the design of their platforms is key to certain toxic behaviours associated with othering. Finally, our concluding remarks will address the limitations of the research into this burgeoning area of scholarship and suggest potential avenues for future research going forward.

'Online Othering': A Conceptual Tool

In the introduction to this volume, we argued that the terms which have previously been used to discuss the ways in which disadvantaged or marginalised groups experience discrimination and abuse online (i.e. abuse, trolling, e-bile, etc.) do not adequately address the ways in which digital technologies reinforce and perpetuate social inequalities. We argued that the concept of 'online othering' better encapsulates the different power contestations and abusive behaviours which are manifested on and through online spaces, and which are variously resisted and challenged by social actors and groups. Furthermore, as the chapters in this volume have demonstrated, 'online othering' is a broader concept that includes abusive or hateful speech, whilst permitting for the inclusion of inadvertent forms of othering. It also allows us to consider benevolent forms of othering where participants might be well meaning but still discriminate against people. Important examples from this volume include: Kaur's chapter which highlights how young people with disabilities are disadvantaged by their parents' attempts to curtail the exploration of their sexuality online. Benevolent othering is also evident in the chapter by Southern and Harmer. The findings from their chapter included Twitter users describing a woman MP with a disability as 'inspirational'. 'Online othering' then is an attempt to move beyond the inflexible ways of categorising examples of harmful behaviours online referred to in varying contexts as 'abuse', 'hate', 'hate speech' or 'trolling'. As we have already argued, 'online othering' offers a conceptual tool through which to analyse and make sense of the myriad toxic and harmful behaviours which are being created through, or perpetuated by, information and communication technologies including the spaces of the Internet, social media platforms, smartphone apps and other interconnected technologies (i.e. the 'internet of things').

The concept of 'online othering' also offers a means of analysing and making sense of online behaviours which seek to (re)draw boundaries in, around and between virtual spaces and shape the rules and norms concerning which individuals and groups are endowed with status and legitimacy when it comes to participation, and those who are not. It is also crucial to recognise that making distinctions between offline (real) / online (virtual) spaces is problematic. Although we use the term 'online', we believe it is important to acknowledge that these behaviours do not occur in a 'virtual vacuum'—they are part and parcel of everyday life and have real consequences in what some have chosen to call the 'real' (versus the 'virtual' world). We argue that it is important to dispense with the well-worn dichotomies of 'online versus offline', and 'virtual world' versus 'real world', and instead acknowledge the interconnected and fluid nature of our use of ICTs.

'Online Othering' is Political

The relationship between online and offline political cultures has been observed in various instances, in both Anglophone and non-Anglophone contexts. The rise of the Alt-Right (and Alt-Light)[1] in politics in various global contexts signifies a concerning drift towards dark times for democracy. As Mondon and Winter (2018) note, whilst the far right remained at first on the margins, its ideas began to seep into the 'mainstream' as they perfected their strategy and gained increased impact in the media and on public discourse in the 1990s and 2000s. They further note that the second half of the 2010s seems to have heralded a new stage in this 'mainstreaming' whereby the far right's ideas have become so normalised that their presence in government is becoming increasingly common. This turn towards authoritarianism has been witnessed across the globe. In Brazil, the election of Jair Bolsonaro as President in October 2018, who has been referred to as a 'far-right, pro-gun, pro-torture populist' (Phillips and Phillips 2018), followed a deeply divisive election campaign. In Hungary in 2018, universities have recently faced state infringement of academic freedom, particularly over research into migration and gender studies (Wilson 2018). The role that the Alt-Right played in the support and Presidential election of Donald Trump in the USA, and the alleged foreign interference in his 2016 campaign, has been well-documented, as have the allegations of sexual harassment and misogyny levelled at the President and other influential male politicians and Hollywood celebrities, partly unveiled and challenged via the global #MeToo movement online. Trump's attempt to confirm Judge Brett Kavanagh as a Supreme Court Justice was also controversial after Dr. Christine Blasey Ford testified to the US Senate Judiciary Committee about an allegation of sexual assault she had made against Kavanagh. She was subsequently subjected to doxing (the Internet-based practice of researching and broadcasting private or identifiable information about an individual or organisation), harassed, received death threats and was impersonated online (Durkin 2018).

In the UK, false promises abounded in the 2016 'leave' campaign's messages to voters in relation to the UK's referendum on leaving the

European Union ('Brexit'), including the ex-leader of UKIP, Nigel Farage's, promotion of anti-immigrant sentiments which were shared online. The normalisation and routinisation of incidents of hate crime in the wake of the 'Brexit vote' have been noted by various charities and organisations. For instance, a report by Tell MAMA in 2018 highlighted the issue of Muslims managing their Muslim identity online and offline with the aim of reducing future abuse: 'the reality of anti-Muslim hate crime creates "invisible" boundaries, across which members of the Muslim community are not "welcome" to step'. Similar findings have been reported in relation to Eastern European migrants in England in the wake of the Brexit vote (see Lumsden et al. 2018). Some writers have drawn attention to what they call the 'radicalisation' of individuals (particularly young men) via the right-wing discourses of politicians and online communities, the Alt-Right and the Alt-Light (i.e. see Marwick and Lewis 2018). However, we argue that the situation is more complex and instead we understand these trends as reflecting the wider normalisation and routinisation of hateful attitudes and discourses and their expressions in mainstream politics, the media and also everyday life including for example prejudices such as: misogyny, sexism, racism, Islamophobia, homophobia and transphobia.

In his chapter in this volume, Aaron Winter observes how the Alt-Right have harnessed the technologies of Internet and social media to access new groups and spaces. The links between offline and online violence are also becoming evident. For example, Robert Bowers, the gunman responsible for the Pittsburgh shooting massacre was reported as having been 'a fringe figure in online world of white supremacist rage' (Beckett 2018). The gunman who murdered 11 people at a Pittsburgh synagogue told a law enforcement officer his motive which was that he believed Jews 'were committing a genocide to his people'. The law enforcement account and his social media profile suggest that Bowers was familiar with the current conversations within white nationalist groups. This volume demonstrates that whilst previous research has focused on online discrimination as uncivil and at times criminal behaviour, 'online othering' is also political via these various attempts to assert the domination of some groups and individuals, whilst actively excluding others.

'Online Othering' is Patriarchal

'Online othering' is a reflection of patriarchal power in two important and interconnected ways. Firstly, online violence and discrimination are organised along traditional power relations where those responsible for othering behaviours tend to be those who are have disproportionate amounts of privilege compared to their targets, mirroring the gendered nature of society whereby men dominate public life. Secondly, scholars have noted that the Internet, and technology in general, has long been conflated with masculinity in Western culture so that technological power accrues disproportionately to men and boys (Wajcman 1991). Therefore, 'online othering' is an extension of traditional patriarchal power relations. This is demonstrated in the chapters by Lumsden and Green on Men's Rights Activists and the Alt-Right respectively, both of which highlight the role of white hegemonic masculinities in the othering of 'outsiders' via social media and Internet forums. Michael Salter argues that 'the widespread stereotype that men have a greater skill and affinity with technology than women is so pervasive' that it translates into everyday experiences of gender, employment, education and even the design of new technologies (2018: 248). This ethos has come to shape the working conditions of technology industries in ways that reinforce the conflation of masculinity with technical competence and innovation, which have served to limit women's professional opportunities, and crucially also informed the ways in which technology is conceptualised and designed (Ranga and Etzkowitz 2010; Massanari 2015). This stands in contrast to the early days of computer programming, which were dominated by women, largely because it was seen as an extension of traditional secretarial work. As it became more professionalised, and actively associated with engineering, women began to be pushed out of the industry (Salter 2018). The abuse received by women journalists and game developers/players in the aforementioned Gamergate also highlights the extent to which these spheres are viewed by (some) men as 'men's domain', and how women who dare to infringe on this space and technoculture find themselves the target of online abuse and vitriol which spills into offline spaces via acts such as doxing and hate mail and vice versa.

The chapters that make up this volume clearly demonstrate that 'online othering' behaviours reflect and reinforce existing disparities in social equality. Many of our contributors focus on the experiences of women online, detailing the forms of othering that women have experienced and how they responded to the provocations of trolls and abusers. For example, Chapter 5 by Lewis, Rowe and Wiper draws on survey data of feminist activists' experiences of online abuse, whilst Smith's chapter examines how such women resist and challenge the othering and harassment they have received in online spaces. Smith outlines in detail how women both experienced and challenge the abuse and harassment they received online and on social media, whilst Amundsen also provides an insight into women's experiences of the sharing of private images online. Colliver, Coyle and Silvestri explore how commenters on YouTube videos construct trans women in particular as posing a danger to cis women and children in public spaces. The patriarchal nature of 'online othering' is also evidenced in the chapters which look specifically at the ways in which men engage in, and indeed experience, forms of 'othering online'. Green's chapter demonstrates that users of Alt-Right forums who dissent from the political consensus are subjected to a form of othering which focuses on attacking their masculinity. Gendered power relations are clearly central to the ways in which 'online othering' operates, demonstrating the extent to which patriarchal status quo is protected and reinforced in the online and offline environment.

'Online Othering' is Intersectional

As well as 'online othering' reinforcing patriarchal power relations, the studies included in this volume also highlight that 'online othering' often manifests in intersectional ways, with social characteristics and locations such as class, gender, age, race, ethnicity, religion, nationality, disability and sexuality becoming increasingly entangled in various forms of online harassment and symbolic violence. Black feminist scholars have highlighted the intersectional aspects of 'othering' in relation to the oppression of women of colour (Hill Collins 1990). It is therefore important to recognise that 'representations of women which "imply" a homogenous category of Otherness render invisible the different experiences of women of varied ethnic, sexual and class locations' (Kitzinger and Wilkinson 1996: 5). For Collins, intersectionality is key as diversity of experiences will be reflected in and shaped by other aspects of identity including class, religion, age and sexuality. Therefore, acknowledging that intersectionality is part of 'online othering' further permits us to account for how social categories are positioned in such a way as to distinguish who 'belongs' and who does not. Patricia Hill Collins (1990) argues that 'othering' is incorporated as part of a 'matrix of domination', a paradigm which explains the organisation of power within society, whereby power is constituted through intersecting systems of oppression which are organised via four interrelated domains of power: structural, disciplinary, hegemonic and interpersonal. The evidence in this volume lends support to Collins' 'matrix of domination' by showing that 'online othering' results from the structural affordances and constraints of online spaces, as well as interpersonal domination. Previous research has shown how the technological aspects of online platforms impact on who can participate and the nature of that participation (see Massanari 2015; Easter 2018; Noble 2018).

The empirical chapters in this volume reflect the intersectional nature of 'online othering'. Not only do our contributors highlight the sheer variety of ways in which 'online othering' can manifest itself; they have also demonstrated that not only is 'online othering' extremely diverse, it also experienced by people in a multitude of ways, based on their gender and sexual identities, race, ethnicity, class, disability and so on. In many cases, othering occurs at the intersection of these different identity categories. As Kimberlé Crenshaw (1989) argues, intersectionality offers a way of mediating the tension between assertions of multiple identity and the ongoing necessity of group politics. This approach also highlights the multidimensionality of lived experiences amongst people who are engaging in online discourses. For example, in Chapter 8, Southern and Harmer's analysis of Tweets sent to UK women politicians demonstrates that members of the UK parliament are frequently othered on the basis of their gender and racial backgrounds, with women of colour receiving the most abusive and unpleasant forms of othering including racial abuse and name-calling. Herminder Kaur's chapter also demonstrates the intersectional nature of othering when discussing the extent to which disability and sexuality can also be combined in experiences of othering, whilst Phillipa Hall outlines the impact of legislation and the role of Internet companies in relation to the hate crime experienced by disabled Internet users. The intersectional nature of 'online othering' means that it is important for researchers in this area to think across these multiple sites of oppression in order to highlight the complexity of these forms of othering but also crucially in order to address and tackle them in a meaningful way.

'Online Othering' is Difficult to Regulate and Police

Researchers have argued that there is little consistency in the policing of criminal activities which involve digital technology, and the authorities have struggled to adapt to deal with the complexity and volume of interpersonal cybercrime that people experience, such as online abuse and revenge pornography. The police response to victims of interpersonal cybercrime has also been criticised for blaming the victim and placing onus on the victim who should protect themselves from online abuse (Black et al., this volume). It can be difficult to determine when uncivil online speech tips over into incivility (Papacharissi 2004), let alone when the abuse crosses the line to become criminal. In some contexts, the nature of online spaces that appear to be uncivil or abusive might not necessarily be harassment, but rather an important form of social or political expression. For example, not all hostile Tweets sent to elected representatives in Southern and Harmer's chapter were personally abusive, but instead some were expressions of political anger directed at a public official in order to hold them to account. Moreover, Whittle et al.'s chapter shows that 'banter' amongst young men, which might appear abusive can also be viewed as an important part of male friendship groups, despite the harm that it might otherwise result in. There are also debates over how the policing of 'online othering' conflicts with ideas about freedom of speech and the appropriate limits of that speech. The global reach of the Internet further complicates how its platforms might be regulated, since it is difficult to regulate companies which are not based in a particular domestic territory, and policing becomes almost impossible across national borders.

As the chapters in Part IV of this volume demonstrate, regulating and policing 'online othering' in its diverse forms can be extremely difficult for a number of reasons: police officers sometimes lack an adequate understanding of specific technologies that are used in interpersonal cybercrime; there is inadequate training available to them; and the police response tends to assume that abuse and harassment in the virtual sphere is somehow different, or not as serious, as that which happens in the offline world. Drawing on interviews with police officers in Australia, O'Shea et al. demonstrate these limitations clearly in relation to cyberstalking, highlighting that these problems are further complicated by the tendency for the perpetrators of cyberstalking to have been previously intimately connected with those who they go on to harass. Another factor which makes policing such online behaviour difficult is the potentially enormous amount of time and resources needed to tackle it. Black et al. discuss in detail the experiences of police officers in the UK who are attempting to tackle cybercrime in a difficult economic environment characterised by the incumbent government's continued austerity agenda, in which police budgets are constantly squeezed. Black et al. argue that a lack of resources means that police struggle to respond adequately to the realities of interpersonal cybercrime.

'Online Othering' is Enabled by Internet Platforms

Online platforms such as Facebook and Twitter showed very little interest in content moderation until their hands were forced by user dissatisfaction. It is also clear that these platforms would prefer not to take responsibility for the material that is published on their sites. The proliferation of 'online othering' demonstrates how critical it is to addressing the role of power and privilege concerning the design of information and communication technologies. As we have already seen, these technologies are largely developed by those in privileged positions, such as white, middle-class men, and without consideration of the potentially harmful consequences which result from these technologies being used to 'other' individuals and groups. The political economy of the Internet is an important consideration in this respect. Christian Fuchs (2009) suggests that the Internet's economic model is built on the commodification of its users, whereby free to access platforms essentially deliver users as targets for advertisers. He also argues that the digital affordances of online platforms impact on the quality of participation (Fuchs 2017). The Internet's status as a capitalist enterprise therefore means that these platforms exist to accumulate profits rather than to enable equal participation, which might go some way to explain the reticence of online platforms to invest vast amounts of resources into moderating the content of their platforms.

Scholars have argued that various social media platforms in particular have been highly conducive to the proliferation of 'online othering' behaviours due to the affordances of these platforms (Salter 2018). The cultural and technological dimensions of these platforms contribute to the development of 'toxic technocultures' which actively exclude various users (Massanari 2015). The culture of Twitter, for example, is orientated towards a more public, broadcasting style of social media debate between strangers. This culture is underpinned by the platform design of Twitter, where the default setting of 'tweets' is accessible to anyone (Van Dijck 2013). This means it can easily be harnessed for spreading abusive messages and encouraging 'pile ons', where multiple followers are directed to the target of abuse (Salter 2018). The chapter by Southern and Harmer demonstrates the public nature of Twitter by revealing how elected representatives in the UK are subjected to 'online othering' in the everyday context of their work. YouTube works in a similar, public, way whereby the most viewed videos are promoted to all its users meaning that problematic content can be easily accessed, even by those who do not go looking for it (Fuchs 2017). In contrast, other large platforms like Facebook are more inwardly focused on networks of family, friends and acquaintances that users are more likely to know offline (Van Dijck 2013). This culture provides its own problems; for example that it can be very difficult for platform moderators to remove problematic content from closed, private groups. Nathan Kerrigan's chapter shows how Facebook groups can be used for the purposes of demarcated boundaries between those who are deemed to 'belong', and those who do not, in his analysis of racism on Facebook groups used by rural communities in the UK.

'Online Othering' Can Be Challenged and Resisted

It is also critical to consider the extent to which the chapters in the volume show that digital media also offer opportunities to resist 'online othering'. Such resistance takes various forms including Twitter hashtags, campaigns and feminist activism online. Examples include the viral #Blacklivesmatter campaign designed to resist police violence against the African American community, the #MeToo movement of 2017–2018, raising awareness and fighting against sexual harassment and sexual assault, and the #EverydaySexism Project which includes a website (set up by Laura Bates in 2012) and Twitter page, both of which catalogue instances of sexism experienced on an everyday basis across the globe. These hashtags are important because they can help to expose the transnational pervasiveness of digital violence and create space/s for marginalised groups and communities to share their own experiences and challenge common-sense understandings of these abuses (Berridge and Portwood-Stacer 2015).

As we noted in the Introduction, an emerging body of literature demonstrates the ways that women and other disadvantaged groups make use of digital media platforms to challenge the sexism, misogyny and racism that they experience in everyday life (Keller et al. 2015; Williams 2015; Khoja-Moolji 2015; Salter 2013). This volume also contributes to this scholarship in important ways. Jo Smith's contribution, for example, focuses on feminist women's responses to encountering harassment in an online context and highlights that women use a variety of means to challenge and contest such behaviour such as reporting incidents and engaging in online activism to counter the actions of perpetrators. Crucially, she argues that the evidence suggests that challenging 'online othering' needs to draw on a variety of approaches in order to be successful. Herminder Kaur also demonstrates that young people with disabilities are able to circumvent the restrictions imposed on them unwittingly by concerned parents in order to explore their sexuality using digital technologies. Similarly, Colliver et al. also demonstrate that whilst YouTube comments on videos about gender-neutral toilets were full of transphobic rhetoric, these forms of 'online othering' were by no means uncontested by other users. Their analysis shows that the comments also contained efforts to resist and challenge these discourses.

'Online Othering' Requires Further Research

This emerging area of study has resulted in some important empirical and theoretical contributions which examine the abuse and discrimination experienced by individuals and specific groups online (Noble 2018; Lumsden and Morgan 2017). This volume has also contributed to our understanding of 'online othering' by demonstrating the diverse experiences of harassment and discrimination across a wide variety of interactive platforms such as discussion fora and social media. It is clear, however, that there is still a lot that we do not know about 'online othering' or aspects of it which we might be able to understand better by engaging in further research.

Although our volume highlights the many different social identity categories which are subject to 'online othering', and we argue strongly for an intersectional approach to analysing 'online othering', more research is needed in this area in order to understand more comprehensively the consequences of the many overlapping ways that already disadvantaged groups continue to be marginalised in online spaces. There are also a number of forms of 'online othering' which are not represented in this collection, which are pervasive, and therefore it is important for researchers to make these public, extending work already in progress. This includes the extent to which Islamophobia and anti-Semitism manifest in the online environment and can have real material consequences for those who are victimised. Another important social stratification which could be the focus of empirical enquiry is the treatment of working-class individuals or groups online, especially given that we know mainstream media has marginalised and demonised working-class communities in a variety of different settings (see Tyler 2008; Wood and Skeggs 2011). Moreover, although Colliver, Coyle and Silvestri (in Chapter 9) address the othering of trans and non-binary people online, more research is needed to understand the ways in which other LGBTQ individuals experience 'online othering', given that they may face very different forms of discrimination.

More research into the global consequences of 'online othering' is also needed. This volume is focused on 'online othering' in largely English speaking cultures. It is important to understand how other languages and national contexts shape 'online othering' behaviours, as well as the experiences of indigenous peoples. Focusing on other countries and languages is also important since it opens up research to online platforms which have huge user bases but have not been analysed in the scholarship so far, including platforms and apps such as WeChat and Sina Weibo which have vast numbers of users in China. Research into these digital spaces would enable a better understanding of these behaviours and how to combat them. To this end, our understanding of online othering would also be enhanced by more comparative research across platforms. Whilst Chapter 3 by Alex Green does incorporate more than one platform within its analysis, much more research which takes this approach is necessary to see if trends can be traced across platforms.

Further research that addresses the phenomenon of 'online othering' from the perspective of social media companies and their moderators would also be extremely valuable in garnering further insight into how best to address such behaviour and to try to prevent it being so easily transferred to new technologies and applications as they are developed. This volume has incorporated research from a wide variety of disciplinary perspectives, and it is our belief that more interdisciplinary studies are needed in order to tackle such a pervasive problem which has very real social, political and legal ramifications.

Note

1. In contrast to the Alt-Right, the Alt-Light are referred to as a loosely defined political movement consisting of various politically motivated groups, activists and commentators with right-wing views who oppose mainstream conservatism.

References

Beckett, S. (2018, October 30). Pittsburgh synagogue shooter was fringe figure in online world of white supremacist rage. *The Guardian*. https://www.theguardian.com/us-news/2018/oct/30/pittsburgh-synagogue-shooter-was-fringe-figure-in-online-world-of-white-supremacist-rage. Accessed October 30, 2018.

Berridge, S., & Portwood-Stacer, L. (2015). Introduction: Feminism, hashtags and violence against women and girls. *Feminist Media Studies, 15*(2), 341.

Crenshaw, K. W. (1989). Demarginalizing the intersection of race and sex: A black feminist critique of antidiscrimination doctrine, feminist theory and antiracist politics. *University of Chicago Legal Forum, 140,* 139–167.

Durkin, E. (2018, September 19). Christine Blasey Ford's life 'turned upside down' after accusing Kavanaugh. *The Guardian*. https://www.theguardian.com/us-news/2018/sep/19/christine-blasey-ford-brett-kavanaugh-sexual-assault-accuser-threats. Accessed October 30, 2018.

Easter, B. (2018). 'Feminist_Brevity_in_light_of_masculine_long-windedness:' Code, space, and online misogyny. *Feminist Media Studies, 18*(4), 675–685.

Fuchs, C. (2009). Information and communication technologies and society: A contribution to the critique of the political economy of the internet. *European Journal of Communication, 24*(1), 69–87.

Fuchs, C. (2017). *Social Media: A Critical Introduction* (2nd ed.). London: Sage.

Hill Collins, P. (1990). *Black Feminist Thought: Knowledge, Consciousness, and the Politics of Empowerment*. New York: Routledge.

Keller, J. M., Mendes, K. D., & Ringrose, J. (2015). Speaking 'unthinkable things': Documenting digital feminist responses to rape culture. *Journal of Gender Studies* (pre-print version).

Khoja-Moolji, S. (2015). Becoming an 'intimate publics': Exploring the affective intensities of hashtag feminism. *Feminist Media Studies, 15*(2), 347–350.

Kitzinger, C., & Wilkinson, S. (1996). Theorizing representing the other. In S. Wilkinson & C. Kitzinger (Eds.), *Representing the Other* (pp. 1–32). London: Sage.

Lumsden, K., & Morgan, H. M. (2017). Media framing of trolling and online abuse: Silencing strategies, symbolic violence, and victim blaming. *Feminist Media Studies, 17*(6), 926–940.

Lumsden, K., Goode, J., & Black, A. (2018). 'I will not be thrown out of the country because I'm an immigrant': Eastern European migrants' responses to hate crime, rural racism and Brexit. *Sociological Research Online*.

Marwick, A., & Lewis, R. (2018). Media manipulation and disinformation online. *Data & Society*. https://datasociety.net/output/media-manipulation-and-disinfo-online/. Accessed October 31, 2018.

Massanari, A. (2015). #Gamergate and The Fappening: How Reddit's algorithm, governance, and culture support toxic technocultures. *New Media & Society, 19*(3), 329–346.

Mondon, A., & Winter, A. (2018). *Understanding the mainstreaming of the far right*. Open Democracy. https://www.opendemocracy.net/can-europe-make-it/aurelien-mondon-aaron-winter/understanding-mainstreaming-of-far-right. Accessed October 30, 2018.

Noble, S. U. (2018). *Algorithms of Oppression: How Search Engines Reinforce Racism*. New York: New York University Press.

Papacharissi, Z. (2004). Democracy online: Civility, politeness, and the democratic potential of online political discussion. *New Media and Society, 6*(2), 259–283.

Phillips, T., & Phillips, D. (2018, October 29). Jair Bolsonaro declared Brazil's next president. *The Guardian*. https://www.theguardian.com/world/2018/oct/28/jair-bolsonaro-wins-brazil-presidential-election. Accessed October 30, 2018.

Ranga, M., & Etzkowitz, H. (2010). Athena in the world of techne: The gender dimension of technology, innovation and entrepreneurship. *Journal of Technology Management & Innovation, 5*(1), 1–12.

Salter, M. (2013). Justice and revenge in online counter-publics: Emerging responses to sexual violence in the age of social media. *Crime Media Culture, 9*(3), 225–242.

Salter, M. (2018). From geek masculinity to Gamergate: The technological rationality of online abuse. *Culture Media Crime, 14*(2), 247–264.

Tell MAMA. (2018). *Report: 'We fear for our lives': Offline and online experiences of anti-Muslim hostility*. https://tellmamauk.org/fear-lives-offline-online-experiences-anti-muslim-hostility/. Accessed October 31, 2018.

Tyler, I. (2008). Chav Mum Chav Scum. *Feminist Media Studies, 8*(1), 17–34.

Van Dijck, J. (2013). *The Culture of Connectivity: A Critical History of Social Media*. Oxford: Oxford University Press.

Wajcman, J. (1991). *Feminism Confronts Technology*. Cambridge: Polity Press.

Williams, S. (2015). Digital defense: Black feminists resist violence with hashtag activism. *Feminist Media Studies, 15*(2), 341–344.

Wilson, L. (2018, September 6). State control over academic freedom in Hungary threatens all universities. *The Guardian*. https://www.theguardian.com/higher-education-network/2018/sep/06/state-control-over-academic-freedom-in-hungary-threatens-all-universities. Accessed October 30, 2018.

Wood, H., & Skeggs, B. (Eds.). (2011). *Reality Television and Class*. Basingstoke: Palgrave.

Index

0-9

4chan 8, 50, 52, 53, 56, 66–73, 76, 78, 83, 85, 86

A

Ableism 2, 187, 380
Abuse 4–14, 20–25, 37, 66, 67, 70, 72, 73, 76, 79, 84, 91, 92, 101–103, 105, 107, 110, 118, 119, 121–139, 152, 155, 161, 188, 191–200, 204, 206, 211, 212, 229, 243, 281–283, 288–294, 296–305, 332, 333, 336, 339, 347, 356–361, 363, 365, 367, 369, 370, 373–375, 380, 381, 383–385, 387–389, 391

Activism 10, 11, 13, 20, 46, 55, 58, 136, 139, 288, 302, 312, 313, 391
Age 17, 21, 93, 146, 149, 153, 154, 183, 212, 213, 218, 251, 260, 263, 337, 359, 385, 386. *See also* Generation
Agency 13, 18, 19, 72, 76, 83, 146, 161, 282, 335, 358
  oppositional agency 19
Alt-Lite 51–53, 55
Alt-Right 1, 8, 13, 23, 35–37, 40, 47, 49–55, 57, 65, 94, 100, 197, 382–385, 393
America 40, 42, 55, 76, 80, 87
Anonymity 4, 5, 51, 75, 92, 95, 242, 287, 292, 312, 313, 346
Anti-Semitism 4, 48, 51, 392
Apps 5, 21, 25, 252, 253, 281, 336, 381, 392

Architecture 78, 79, 269
  of the internet 4
Austerity 269, 368, 373–375, 388
  post-austerity 357, 371
Australia 26, 44, 131, 190, 207, 283, 331, 333–338, 340, 346–348, 388
Authoritarian 35–37, 84

B

Banter 24, 119, 165–167, 170–172, 174–183, 293, 300, 387. *See also* Bullying
Blacklivesmatter 11, 20, 390
Blog 49–51, 93, 111, 127
  blogging 3, 337
Brexit 1, 4, 199, 383
Bullying 5, 119, 166, 167, 171, 172, 176, 177, 179–183, 243. *See also* Banter; Cyber, cyber-bullying

C

Celebrity 92, 95, 102–104
Cis 385. *See also* Femininity; Gender; Masculinity; Trans
  gender 25, 219–221, 223, 225
  identity 25, 219, 225
  men 225
  women 219, 223, 225, 385
Class 17, 19, 21, 76, 146, 172, 212, 246, 247, 249, 250, 372, 385, 386, 389, 392
Coercion 21, 84, 370
Coercive 356, 375. *See also* Domestic abuse
  coercive control 122, 138

Colonialism 18
Community 10, 25, 43–45, 47, 49, 57, 66, 71, 73, 76, 78, 85, 92–94, 96, 102, 126, 135, 150, 169, 211, 213, 214, 259, 260, 262–276, 294, 295, 313, 317, 383, 390
Conspiracy theorist 8, 51, 68
Crime 4, 9, 14, 24, 26, 118, 122–125, 127, 129–131, 135, 137, 139, 212, 261, 281, 284, 293, 309, 313, 315, 325, 335, 337, 355, 357–361, 363, 367, 373
Criminal 26, 122, 281, 282, 294, 325, 336, 347, 350, 357–359, 366, 383, 387
  justice 9, 121, 122, 125, 138, 290
Culture war 35, 37, 92, 101, 109
Cyber 7, 12, 14, 44, 72, 102, 106, 110, 124, 125, 129, 138, 240, 334–337, 340, 357–361, 365, 366, 368, 371–374
  cyber-bullying 5, 360, 372
  cyber-crime 365
    investigation of 337
    legislation 359
    prosecution of 13, 359
  cyber-hate 12
  cyber-stalking 13, 357, 360

D

Death threat 6, 106, 132, 293, 361, 382. *See also* Violence
Democracy 8, 192, 207, 322, 382
Digilante 26, 282, 288, 289, 301, 302

Digital 3, 4, 6–8, 10–12, 23, 25, 26, 36, 37, 57, 58, 73, 75, 92, 93, 100–102, 109, 118, 150, 151, 165–169, 175, 183, 188, 190–192, 213, 239–246, 248–253, 259, 260, 263–265, 267, 268, 270, 271, 273–276, 281, 283, 288, 301, 316, 317, 337, 344, 345, 348–350, 358, 359, 380, 387, 389–392
  digital code 4
  digital images 5
  digital tools of domestic abuse 5. *See also* Domestic abuse; Technology
Disability 9, 22, 23, 26, 146, 187, 188, 194, 202, 205, 212, 241–243, 248–250, 283, 309–311, 313–316, 318–320, 323–325, 381, 385–387
Discrimination 1, 4, 5, 9, 12, 13, 18, 22, 94, 103, 190, 191, 211, 212, 216, 219–221, 260, 314, 315, 323, 375, 380, 383, 384, 391, 392
Domestic abuse 5, 12, 122, 282, 357, 361, 363, 365, 367, 369, 370, 374, 375. *See also* Technology, technology-facilitated sexual abuse

E-bile 91, 380
Email 5, 73, 137, 334, 336, 337, 343, 344, 346

Empower 22, 72, 283
  empowerment 160
England 25, 26, 123, 149, 150, 166, 171, 214, 259, 261, 266, 282, 284, 291, 315, 355, 363, 383
Equality 105, 107, 110, 145, 221, 261, 309, 311, 320, 321, 323, 324, 385
Ethnicity 18, 22, 23, 132, 140, 146, 150, 190, 212, 242, 260, 385, 386
Everyday sexism 10. *See also* Sexism
Exclude 15, 25, 36, 122, 127, 131, 136, 137, 172, 181, 213, 214, 220, 244, 259, 265, 276, 315, 318, 323, 360, 361, 370, 374, 389
Exclusion 10, 14, 119, 139, 146, 241, 267, 276, 375

Facebook 8–10, 13, 48–51, 56, 57, 66, 74, 119, 132, 166, 167, 169, 172, 173, 178, 181, 250, 251, 259, 262–276, 290, 295, 316–318, 336, 343, 345, 356, 366, 367, 369–371, 373, 374, 388–390
Fake news 6, 8, 68, 311, 318, 319, 321. *See also* Media
Far right 35, 36, 197, 382
  far right conservatives 8, 36
Femininity 134, 135
Feminism 54, 55, 94, 96–99, 101, 105, 107, 110, 111, 161, 293, 300
  post-feminism 145, 146

Feminist 1, 2, 10–12, 17, 20, 24, 36, 37, 51, 53, 76, 91, 92, 94, 95, 97, 99, 100, 102–107, 109, 110, 118, 122–125, 130, 133–136, 146, 160, 190, 191, 219, 287–290, 303, 304, 385, 390
   feminist activism 11, 12, 101, 282, 302, 390. *See also* Activism

Flaming 1, 6

Fraud 5

Freedom 4, 8, 11, 36, 118, 128, 161, 228, 314, 315, 317, 319, 321, 322, 324, 382
   of speech 9, 26, 96, 121, 282, 388

G

Gamergate 4, 8, 53, 54, 92, 95, 99, 100

Gender 11, 18, 21, 23, 36, 37, 65, 132, 136, 146, 166, 169, 172, 188, 190, 192, 199, 219, 386. *See also* Cis; Femininity; Masculinity; Trans
   cis gender 25, 219–221, 223, 225
   gender neutral 106, 110, 111
   gender neutral toilets 25, 212, 216–221, 225, 232, 391
   gendertrolling 6, 117. *See also* Trolling

Generation 18, 103, 360. *See also* Age

Government 41, 57, 262, 310, 314, 324, 356, 358, 382, 388

H

Harassment 1, 4–6, 8–11, 13, 14, 20, 21, 26, 36, 41, 53, 72, 73, 99, 100, 103–106, 108, 110, 111, 117, 124–126, 128, 130, 170, 176, 190, 191, 260–262, 276, 282, 284, 295, 332, 366, 369, 370, 382, 385, 387, 388, 390, 391

Hashtag 10, 11, 20, 53, 79, 282, 390

Hate 1, 4, 7, 13, 23–26, 37, 39, 41, 45, 48, 56, 58, 92, 97, 98, 121, 122, 124, 130–132, 134, 135, 137, 139, 206, 212, 229, 259, 276, 283, 284, 287–302, 304, 309, 315, 318, 384
   hate crime 13, 14, 21, 24, 55, 118, 122, 123, 130–133, 135–137, 139, 140, 211, 212, 216, 219, 288, 293, 294, 299, 301, 309, 313–315, 325, 383, 387
   hate speech 4, 8–10, 12, 14, 21, 25, 26, 40, 49, 56, 57, 110, 132, 193, 216, 281, 283, 309–321, 323–325, 381
   online hate 4, 13, 14, 20, 23, 55, 58, 91, 219, 281, 284, 287–289, 291, 292, 296–298, 301, 304, 310–314, 316, 320, 323, 324, 357

Homophobia 2, 24, 37, 48, 84, 216, 380, 383

Hybridity 19

Ideal victim 26, 284, 356, 357, 363, 367. See also Victim
Identity 2, 5, 15, 17, 19, 22, 25, 40, 41, 49, 55, 70, 71, 73, 78–80, 92, 95, 96, 98, 100, 118, 127, 132, 138, 166, 167, 169, 172, 175, 183, 188, 205, 211, 212, 217–219, 225, 231, 239, 242, 253, 261, 262, 264, 265, 267, 268, 270, 271, 274–276, 312, 362, 383, 386, 391
Ideology 20, 36, 50, 94, 105, 130, 282. See also Power
Inclusion 14, 119, 177, 181, 220, 245, 260, 304, 375, 381
Individualism 24, 118, 146
Inequality 98, 117, 188
Information and communication technology 12, 14, 21, 22, 371, 381, 389. See also Technology
In-group 14, 78, 119, 166, 167, 181, 222. See also Out-group
Inspiration 205
Instagram 13, 294
Internet 2–6, 9, 11, 13, 14, 20–23, 25, 26, 36, 39–41, 44–47, 49–51, 53, 55, 65, 93, 95, 98, 100, 107, 117, 118, 124, 166, 191, 200, 212–214, 241, 243–245, 247, 248, 252, 260, 263, 264, 273, 274, 282, 283, 287, 288, 291, 292, 297, 299, 310, 311, 313, 314, 316, 317, 319, 320, 322–324, 335–337, 343, 358–361, 366, 383, 384, 387–389. See also Technology
internet of things 21, 381
Intersection 40, 190
   intersectional 4, 17, 23–25, 37, 65, 118, 132–134, 139, 188, 241, 242, 385–387, 391
   intersectionality 17, 19, 21, 133, 190, 211, 212, 386
Islamophobia 1, 2, 4, 8, 211, 380, 383, 391

K

Knowledge 15, 16, 19, 79, 179, 213, 240–242, 276, 292, 320, 337, 340, 341, 343, 348, 349, 360, 376

L

Law 14, 42, 43, 45–47, 49, 50, 53, 55, 56, 107, 108, 110, 122, 134, 282, 291, 310, 311, 314–316, 320, 322, 325, 333, 345, 346, 358, 359, 383. See also Legislation
Legislation 14, 137, 260, 282, 284, 291, 310, 314–316, 323, 324, 332, 333, 340, 341, 347, 348, 387. See also Law
LGBTQ 9, 188, 211, 392
Liminality 19, 22

M

Manosphere 8, 53, 92, 98, 99, 109

Marginal
  marginalisation 11, 241
Masculinity 23, 67, 75, 81, 82, 96, 97, 99, 118, 165, 166, 168, 170, 177, 179, 181–183, 384, 385
  hegemonic masculinity 24, 25, 36, 37, 83, 84, 98, 119, 166–169, 173–175, 178, 181, 183
Matrix of domination 17, 386
Media 5–8, 10–13, 20, 22, 23, 36, 39, 40, 43, 45, 47–50, 52–55, 57, 68, 70–74, 76, 81, 82, 86, 95, 99, 100, 102, 104, 111, 121, 124, 127, 129, 134, 138, 148, 150, 158, 165, 168, 172, 183, 188–190, 192, 197–199, 207, 213, 217, 219, 230, 232, 233, 239–246, 248, 250–253, 260, 262–265, 267, 273–276, 283, 288, 289, 294–298, 304, 310, 311, 313, 315, 318, 319, 321, 322, 324, 331, 332, 334, 343, 345, 357, 363, 365, 368, 370–372, 374, 375, 380–385, 389–392
  mass media 313
  media corporation 3, 9, 21, 25, 281–283
  transnational media 3
Meme 37, 49–51, 66, 68, 71–73, 85, 86, 100
Men's Rights 76, 92, 94, 96, 97, 106, 110, 111

Men's Rights Activist (MRAs) 13, 23, 24, 36, 37, 51, 92, 97, 99, 111, 128, 305, 384
Metoo 10, 20, 125, 282, 382, 390
Micro-blogging 3
Misogyny 1, 2, 4, 8, 11, 12, 14, 16, 23, 25, 26, 36, 37, 40, 52, 53, 91, 92, 95, 98–101, 111, 117, 119, 122, 125, 130, 132–134, 136, 139, 282, 283, 300, 304, 380, 382, 383, 390

N

National identity 15
Normalisation 130, 223, 336
  of hate 383

O

Offender. *See* Perpetrator
Online othering 2, 7–10, 12, 13, 20–26, 35, 37, 40, 58, 84, 92, 101, 111, 117, 119, 145, 147–149, 162, 183, 188, 192, 194, 207, 211, 212, 216, 229, 233, 282, 283, 375, 379–381, 383–392
Oppression 16, 17, 19, 110, 228, 304, 385–387
Orient 17, 224
  orientalism 17
Other 2, 15–19, 178, 213, 259, 271, 272

Othering 2, 5, 12–20, 22, 37, 100, 101, 110, 136, 174, 211, 212, 215, 276, 373, 385
  benevolent othering 188, 381
Out-group 13, 14, 119, 166, 222. *See also* In-group
Outsider 13–15, 17, 24, 37, 67, 74, 79, 81–84, 172, 176, 179, 181, 189, 192, 203, 214, 263, 265, 384. *See also* Othering; Out-group
  Marginal outsider 17

Parent 93, 154, 253
Participation 3–5, 11, 72, 76, 118, 135–137, 173, 187, 189–192, 206, 267, 287, 311, 315, 319–325, 336, 342, 381, 386, 389
Patriarchy
  Patriarchal 107, 130, 134, 135, 139, 301, 304, 380, 384, 385
Perpetrator 5, 23, 24, 91, 118, 126–128, 131, 133–138, 296–299, 301, 303, 317, 334, 388, 391
Police 9, 12, 13, 23, 25, 26, 67, 76, 111, 122, 126, 129, 132, 138, 170, 197, 207, 261, 281–284, 288–294, 296, 304, 331–338, 340–350, 355–357, 360, 361, 363–366, 368–375, 387, 388, 390
  officer 26, 284, 296, 333, 341, 345, 347, 355–357, 359–361, 364, 365, 367, 368, 371, 373–375, 388
Policing 13, 23, 24, 26, 37, 82, 84, 100, 109, 110, 122, 191, 281–284, 287, 290–294, 333, 340, 342, 344, 347–350, 356, 357, 359, 361, 371, 373, 375, 376, 387, 388
  of cybercrime 281, 357, 371, 375
Political economy 2, 3, 389
Political movement 8, 35, 393
Politician 25, 36, 119, 188–190, 192–194, 197, 198, 201–203, 207, 382, 383, 386
Pornography 82, 85, 95, 126, 148, 213, 240, 243, 250, 281, 356, 361, 374, 387. *See also* Private sexual images (PSIs); Revenge porn
  Deepfake 5
Power 2, 15–21, 36, 57, 66, 78, 81, 97, 98, 100, 104, 106, 107, 110, 130, 133, 190, 201, 202, 204, 266, 268, 282, 288, 296, 302, 313, 316, 322, 339, 380, 384–386, 389
Prejudice 4, 13, 21, 23, 130, 131, 133, 135, 216, 219–221, 226, 325, 383. *See also* Discrimination; Othering; Stereotype
Prevention 129
Private sexual images (PSIs) 24, 118, 145, 148, 150, 155. *See also* Pornography; Revenge porn
Public space 11, 137, 283, 288, 311, 313, 320, 323, 324, 385. *See also* Rural

Public sphere 2, 3, 128, 201, 311, 313, 320–324

R

Race 11, 15, 18, 21, 23, 42, 52, 53, 117, 146, 190, 212, 260–262, 314, 385, 386
Racism 1, 2, 4, 8, 11, 13, 15, 18, 19, 23, 25, 36, 40, 51–53, 58, 96, 119, 136, 140, 193, 199, 211, 212, 216, 260–262, 266–268, 271, 276, 315, 380, 383, 390
  rural racism 212–214, 259
Racist 4, 8, 17, 25, 36, 39, 40, 42, 47, 50, 54, 55, 57, 65, 81, 84, 95, 96, 117, 119, 132, 134–136, 140, 170, 188, 191, 193, 195, 196, 198, 199, 206, 260–262, 266, 268, 271, 275, 276, 299
Rape threat 6, 108, 361. *See also* Violence
Reddit 4, 13, 24, 37, 50, 52, 53, 66, 67, 70–73, 76–78, 82, 83, 85–87, 91–96, 100–102, 127
Reflexive 22, 101, 145
Regulation 12, 13, 23, 39, 40, 244, 245, 248, 310, 311, 314–324
Resistance 10, 22, 42, 44, 79, 82, 96, 171, 191, 212, 222, 225, 230, 232–234, 282, 300, 302, 304, 356, 369, 370, 373–375, 390
Revenge porn 5, 13, 148, 149, 359

Right-wing 36, 40, 51, 55, 57, 65, 66, 71–73, 81, 84, 85, 204, 383, 393
Risk 11, 12, 24, 78, 118, 123, 126, 129, 145–147, 149, 151–156, 158, 162, 240, 244, 245, 248, 274, 283, 290, 297, 298, 300, 303, 333–340, 347–349, 356, 357, 360, 361, 374. *See also* Stalking
  risk assessment 26, 283, 284, 332–335, 337, 338, 340, 348–350
Routinisation 383
  of hate 383
Rural racism. *See* Racism

S

Sex 9, 16, 23, 35, 82, 85, 94, 96, 97, 103, 104, 111, 127, 134, 146, 158, 162, 171, 217, 221, 224, 226, 227, 231, 232, 239, 240, 242, 250
Sexism 2, 4, 7, 10–12, 19, 25, 53, 58, 100, 117, 119, 129, 130, 191–193, 212, 282, 300, 380, 383, 390
Sexting 13, 24, 148, 150, 151, 156–158, 160, 240
Sexuality 6, 17, 22, 23, 25, 82, 132, 146, 160, 161, 188, 206, 212, 213, 221, 232, 239–242, 245, 251–253, 381, 385–387, 391
  sexual identity 25, 96, 212, 239, 253

Sexual violence. *See* Violence
Silencing 7, 25, 119, 188, 191, 200, 303, 361
Sina Weibo 392
Smart home technology. *See* Technology
Smart phone. *See* Technology
Snap Chat 152, 292
Social class. *See* Class
Social justice 49, 55, 66, 92, 94, 95, 100, 101
  social justice warriors (SJWs) 55, 66, 92, 100
Social media 3, 5, 6, 8–13, 20–23, 25, 26, 36, 47–50, 52, 53, 57, 70, 82, 86, 100, 102, 104, 111, 119, 121, 124, 129, 134, 138, 172, 188, 190, 192, 198, 199, 207, 213, 217, 219, 230, 232, 241, 245, 260, 262–265, 267, 273–276, 281–283, 288, 289, 294–298, 304, 310, 313, 315, 318, 319, 321, 322, 334, 343, 345, 357, 365, 368, 370–372, 374, 375, 380, 381, 383–385, 389, 391, 392
Stalking 5, 12, 21, 282, 283, 332–342, 345, 347–350. *See also* Coercion; Cyber, cyber-stalking; Domestic abuse
  Stalking Risk Profile 335, 338
Status 2, 3, 11, 13, 17, 23, 37, 41, 58, 71, 101–103, 105, 110, 119, 127, 146, 156, 166, 171, 175, 178, 181, 183, 191, 192, 221–223, 232, 251, 304, 316, 357, 361–363, 369, 371, 373–375, 381, 385
Stereotype 4, 18, 21, 187, 201, 384
Survivor 14, 125, 128, 133. *See also* Victim
Symbolic violence 7, 190, 191, 385. *See also* Violence

Technology
  smart home technology 5
  smart phone 5
  technological affordances 53
  technology-facilitated domestic abuse 5, 332, 333, 336
  women and technology 4, 384
Teenager 119, 154, 165–167, 172, 173, 175–177, 181, 183, 212, 249, 292. *See also* Youth
Terrorist 46, 56
  terrorism 40
Thirdspace 18, 22
Time-space 213, 263
  compression 213
Toilet 25, 212, 216–218, 220, 221, 224, 225, 247
  gender-neutral toilets 25, 212, 216–221, 225, 232, 391
Toxic 1, 4, 8, 21, 25, 53, 92, 96, 111, 281, 380, 381, 389
  behaviour 1, 4, 21, 92, 381
  culture 25, 96, 281, 389

Trans 9, 54, 212, 219, 225, 226, 228, 232, 385, 392. *See also* Cis; Femininity; Gender; Masculinity; Sexuality
   gender 212, 225, 232
   identity 54
   phobia 312
   sexual 212
Transphobia. *See* Trans
Transport 11, 216
Troll 6–8, 20, 50, 67, 72, 73, 75, 76, 101
Trolling 1, 4–10, 13, 14, 21, 24, 49, 54, 67, 73–76, 84, 91, 92, 96, 100–102, 105, 106, 108, 110, 117, 182, 191, 302, 380, 381
   gendertrolling 6, 117
Trump, Donald 36, 46, 52, 66, 67, 69, 76, 92, 217, 382
Tweet 3, 5, 9, 25, 86, 105, 119, 128, 133, 137, 138, 188, 192–206, 263, 300, 386, 387, 389
Twitter 3–5, 8–10, 13, 25, 48–51, 53, 54, 56, 57, 66, 69, 102, 108, 111, 119, 127, 137, 188, 192–194, 198, 206, 207, 262–264, 275, 282, 290, 291, 295, 300, 302, 316, 381, 388–390

U

United Kingdom (UK) 1, 4, 8, 10, 14, 122, 128, 130, 148, 149, 188, 190, 192, 207, 220, 239, 246, 269, 288, 290, 309, 315, 356, 359, 382, 386
United States of America (USA) 6, 42, 45, 67, 99, 171, 218, 220, 226, 382
Upskirting 14

V

Victim 5, 7, 14, 24, 387. *See also* Survivor
   ideal victim 26, 284, 355–357, 362, 363, 365, 367
   victim-blaming 26, 162, 229, 282, 284, 356, 362, 370
   victim status 101, 103, 105, 110, 221, 232, 361, 362, 369, 371, 373–375
Victimhood 25, 36, 99, 103, 107, 146, 212, 221, 362
Victimisation 24, 25, 118, 125, 129, 136, 137, 215, 221, 259, 261, 262, 267, 276, 336, 356, 357, 360, 362, 367, 368, 374
Violence 5, 7, 9–11, 24, 37, 41, 48, 54–56, 66, 67, 73, 92, 98, 100–111, 122–125, 128, 129, 135, 138, 140, 178, 179, 190–192, 221, 229, 260, 276, 288, 292, 293, 297, 305, 332–339, 346–350, 356, 363, 375, 383–385, 390
   Violence against women and girls (VAWG) 24, 118, 122–131, 137–140

Virtual
  crime 14, 26, 284, 337
  criminal 121
  space 2, 3, 12, 13, 26, 123, 139, 284, 287, 289, 321, 356, 381
  vacuum 14, 22, 381

W
WeChat 392

Y
Youth 47–50, 112, 149, 154, 165, 166, 183, 345. *See also* Teenager
YouTube 3, 9, 13, 25, 48, 50–54, 56, 57, 68–72, 212, 216, 218–220, 222, 250, 262, 275, 316, 385, 389, 391

Printed by Printforce, the Netherlands